# Live Longer with AI

How artificial intelligence is helping us extend
our healthspan and live better too

**Tina Woods**

with Melissa Ream

BIRMINGHAM - MUMBAI

# Live Longer with AI

**Producers:** Andrew Waldron and Jon Malysiak
**Acquisition Editor – Peer Reviews:** Suresh Jain
**Content Development Editor:** Alex Patterson
**Project Editor:** Janice Gonsalves
**Technical Editor:** Karan Sonawane
**Copy Editor**: Safis Editing
**Proofreader:** Safis Editing
**Indexer:** Priyanka Dhadke
**Presentation Designer:** Sandip Tadge

First published: September 2020

Production reference: 1300920

Published by Packt Publishing Ltd.
Livery Place
35 Livery Street
Birmingham B3 2PB, UK.

ISBN 978-1-83864-615-8

www.packt.com

`packt.com`

Subscribe to our online digital library for full access to over 7,000 books and videos, as well as industry leading tools to help you plan your personal development and advance your career. For more information, please visit our website.

## Why subscribe?

- Spend less time learning and more time coding with practical eBooks and Videos from over 4,000 industry professionals
- Learn better with Skill Plans built especially for you
- Get a free eBook or video every month
- Fully searchable for easy access to vital information
- Copy and paste, print, and bookmark content

Did you know that Packt offers eBook versions of every book published, with PDF and ePub files available? You can upgrade to the eBook version at `www.Packt.com` and as a print book customer, you are entitled to a discount on the eBook copy. Get in touch with us at `customercare@packtpub.com` for more details.

At `www.Packt.com`, you can also read a collection of free technical articles, sign up for a range of free newsletters, and receive exclusive discounts and offers on Packt books and eBooks.

*To my dear husband, Nick, and my wonderful sons, James, Gabriel, and Noah. Really, I will always love you more than my work.*

# Foreword

How we see growing older and living longer has been evolving over the last 100 years, as life expectancy has increased and more people live into old age. After reading this tour d'horizon by Tina you will realize that it may be about to change even more.

Just as advances in anatomy, anesthetics, and antiseptics left the barber-surgeon confined to the past, the new tools of genomics, epigenetics, and artificial intelligence will leave parts of our current approach to healthcare behind. That has exciting possibilities for making life longer and healthier.

The potential scope for AI to support this through taking charge of our health, work, and finances is astonishing, albeit at times possessing aspects of science fiction.

That's urgently needed because as more people live into old age and the disease burden shifts to age-related illnesses, the value of aging better increases. Further, the better we get at aging the more valuable further improvements will become. If we can empower ourselves with knowledge and work towards sharing the benefits of longevity, we can move away from negative views of an "aging society" and think about a "longevity dividend."

As each chapter in this book reveals more instances of breath-taking new possibilities, you will get a sense of the potential magnitude for change—for you and society.

You will also be aware of the challenges these developments bring, not just to medicine but to fundamental issues about our identity and how we live our lives. However, you will also be aware of something else—a thread that weaves its way throughout the book. That is a sense of optimism.

It's easy to (rightly) fear a world where doctors are replaced by robots, or our genetic secrets and bodily condition is no longer hidden but out in the open for us and even others to see. When we're sick we're frightened, and we want something comforting that we can cling to—something personal and human to connect to. An AI process that treats our bodies' biological secrets as just a decoded algorithm is far from that.

The famous medic Sir William Osler once remarked, "The good physician treats the disease, the great physician treats the patient who has the disease." While written over a 100 years ago, Osler's insight runs through these pages. The focus of the developments Tina outlines is on improving the life of the individual—each and every one of us. As AI makes machines ever smarter at being machines, we need to make sure that we utilize that as an opportunity to make us smarter at being humans.

That's why it's so refreshing to read in these pages not just about brilliant people pushing back scientific frontiers but also a focus on what is needed to make this work for us as humans. In other words, truly goal-driven AI. And what a goal! The goal of all these committed researchers is to give you more healthy years to your life. Not in a magic bullet, or a single treatment, and certainly not without your help and your contribution, but that's the aim—to get older, better; to live longer with AI.

With this book, Tina's ready to show you how.

**Andrew Scott**

Professor of Economics, London Business School

Co-Author, *The 100-Year Life* and *The New Long Life*

# Testimonials

*"The COVID-19 pandemic has exposed the fault lines in society, including the inequalities that divide us. The message is clear – we must do what we can to keep everyone healthy and well through a much bigger focus on prevention to cope with this pandemic and manage future ones too. Tina's book provides the knowledge and ammunition to persuade people to treat health as their greatest asset—to protect themselves while doing their part in rebuilding global well-being and economic resilience."*

—**Professor Baron Peter Piot KCMG, World Expert in Virology & Global Health; Director of the London School of Hygiene & Tropical Medicine; Handa Professor of Global Health**

*"At a time of maximum anxiety about public health, we need a guide about how we can take control of our own lives and live in good health for longer. Tina Woods' book not only does that but also explains how the development of AI and other technologies can contribute to better aging. Quite literally, people's lives and happiness will depend on individuals and societies following some of the conclusions drawn in this book. It is a hugely important contribution to public debate. An "aging society" should be a matter for celebration, not apprehension. This book explains how we can make that shift."*

—**Right Honourable Damian Green MP, Chair, All-Party Parliamentary Group for Longevity, Former Deputy Prime Minister, UK Government**

"Live Longer with AI *describes how we went from the hope to the promise that aging can be targeted and healthspan can be increased. This book specifically offers horizons to realizing this. Such a future depends on three things. Firstly, we need sophisticated data (omics) from large populations, and basic resources and data to be available to scientists. Secondly, we need the ability to look at this data from different angles utilizing AI. Thirdly, and most importantly, we need a team of experts who know how to lead with the correct questions, without which we will not make significant discoveries. In this book, Tina talks with such experts about how we can move rapidly towards better healthspan."*

**—Nir Barzilai, Professor of Medicine and Genetics, Director, Institute for Aging Research, Albert Einstein College of Medicine**

*"Tina Woods has woven together a masterful combination of interviews and insights in this book. Now that we have finally reached the point in the crusade against aging where the wider world is actually taking it seriously as a medical problem, the foremost requirement is for people to come forward who have the talent to communicate the specifics of how we can hasten the remaining steps towards a post-aging world. Woods is undoubtedly one of those people, and many lives will be saved through the efforts of those who are inspired by this book."*

**—Aubrey de Grey, Chief Science Officer, SENS Research Foundation**

*"Tina Woods is one of the most active advocates and drivers of the longevity biotechnology industry and related policy in the UK. As a credible super-connector, she managed to forge new initiatives and consortiums that will have a lasting impact. In this new book, she provides an overview of the current state of the emerging longevity biotechnology industry and a sense of the direction that advances in aging research and AI are going to take us in the next few years and the next few decades. Both aging research and AI are advancing and converging at an unprecedented pace. A new generation of experts is required in both these fields. This book should be read by anyone wishing to seize the opportunity to enter into this exciting and impactful area and make this world a much better place."*

**—Alex Zhavoronkov, Founder and CEO of Insilico Medicine and Deep Longevity**

*"Understanding aging, and what we might do about it, is one of the most intriguing and important scientific challenges of our time. Tina Woods has mobilized her great energy and insight to give us a book that simply fizzes with the excitement of this quest."*

—**Professor Thomas Kirkwood CBE, FMedSci, FRCP Edin; Emeritus Professor in Ageing, Newcastle University, and Affiliate Professor, University of Copenhagen Center for Healthy Aging**

*"This book sets out to share and explore some of the practical applications and implications of the use of AI in helping humanity to live longer with improved health. The topic is vast, with so much going on across the scene internationally, but Tina carefully links the various areas and initiatives up through the chapters and helps the reader to see the true opportunity and potential inherent in the bold pursuit of exploring the use of advanced, borderless, open data sets, deep learning, and a greater understanding of the coding of life. A must-read for anyone seriously considering developing a longer-term view on population health, the ethical usage of health data, and the potential to make the next transformational leap in human aging and reduction in mortality."*

—**Alan Davies, Innovative Programmes & Partnerships Director, Health Education England**

*"From the time that our ancestors became aware of their own mortality, humans have strived to live longer and better—today we continue this quest by employing advanced technologies. Tina provides us with a heart-felt reflection on the societal and economic consequences of aging populations and guides us through the potential of harnessing AI to unlock the secrets of personalized longevity and resilience. Live Longer with AI will enlighten consumers, health care professionals and policy makers on the importance of technological advances, not only to better tackle the current global health crisis but also to find answers to the age-old question of how we can maintain mental, physical and financial well-being as we grow older."*

—**Dr Richard Siow, Director, Ageing Research at Kings College London (ARK)**

*"Recent generations have achieved the goal of living longer, but with more chronic health conditions than ever before. In order to achieve true healthy aging, we have to translate scientific findings into real-life interventions.* Live Longer with AI *describes how we can achieve true increases in healthy life expectancy for both the individual and populations, by harnessing modern technologies. This book describes the potential of a scientific and technological approach to healthy aging, and lays out what needs to be done in order to achieve it.*

*"This book is a must-read for anybody interested in health, wellness, and the future of true healthcare."*

**—Michael Sagner, MD, Director Sarena Clinic, Director of the Board, European Society of Preventive Medicine, Editor-in-Chief, Progress in Preventive Medicine**

*"Dialoguing with Tina is one of the most satisfying exercises for the mind that can be done. Tina has an extraordinary ability to make you sail far ahead of the challenges of our society while pushing you to explore the hidden folds of opportunity when aging and longevity are associated with emerging technologies. Tina is like a modern-day Virgil: she leads the way, but she does it by leaving you in charge. This book is tangible proof of this."*

**—Professor Nic Palmarini, Director, National Innovation Centre for Ageing**

*"As our society ages, and as more diseases that carry age as a risk factor are uncovered, we are becoming acutely aware of the consequences of prior misunderstandings, our lack of knowledge in specific areas, and our ignorance of the impact of societal influences on living healthily and, importantly, aging healthily. It is critical that we now start to open our eyes and address this, and Tina's book provides one of the tools to enable us to do just that. In her book, Tina uncovers and expands the role of AI and data in improving our health and well-being, something critically important considering the current impact of the pandemic. We all need to take responsibility if we want, hope, to live a long and healthy life – this book underpins how we can do that."*

**—Dr. Carol Routledge, Chief Medical Officer and Chief Scientific Officer, Small Pharma; Former Research Director, Alzheimer's Research UK and Managing Director, Early Detection of Neurodegenerative Diseases (EDoN) Global Initiative**

"COVID-19 has underlined the importance of deploying every tool at our disposal to help address major health challenges for public benefit. The beneficial use of AI is arguably one such tool, as Woods demonstrates. The use of AI with and for people and society has transformative potential. This is a valuable contribution to the emerging literature."

—Reema Patel, Head of Public Engagement, Ada Lovelace Institute

"Like never before, the world is awake to health and wellness being key to both combatting infection and living life without the crippling diseases that have blighted the second half of life for too many. Tina has blended a remarkable mix of expert interviews, science, and personal reflections and created the most comprehensive yet readable book I've seen on maximizing our healthy lifespan. Healthcare AI is advancing fast, but this book is also suffused with Tina's own brand of very human intelligence."

—Professor Richard Barker, Author of *2030 – The Future of Medicine*

"We are living in the third healthcare revolution. The first was the public health revolution, the second the high-tech revolution based in hospitals and health centers, and the third is driven by citizens – the people we used to call patients – knowledge, the Internet, and all that has developed from this technology. This is a handbook for the revolution!"

—Sir Muir Gray, Director, Optimal Ageing

"You can live longer and be happier if you make some changes – that is the theme of this book, which reviews recent learning about our aging societies and looks at how even simple technologies can make some big changes. Well-written and compelling."

—Ben Page, CEO, Ipsos Mori

*"Every reader, regardless of age, will gain access to an extraordinary depth of knowledge on how to have longer, healthier, and more prosperous lives. Tina makes every reader a geoscientist, an economist, and a world futurist, without commercializing or dumbing her material down. There is no need to be an expert or even acquainted with Artificial Intelligence to enjoy this book. Tina presents us with "page-turner" interviews and personal stories from famous scientists, thinkers, and entrepreneurs.*

*Her elegance and concern are evident, as she explores the challenges of COVID-19 to assert that a life worth living is worth preserving through prevention, treatment, and mutual caring for all."*

**—Adriane Berg, Host Generation Bold Podcast, Director of The Kitalys Institute for the Delay and Prevention of Age-Related Diseases**

*"*Live Longer with AI *is a masterpiece about the new advances in life extension and longevity thanks to emerging exponential technologies, from AI all the way to nanotechnology. Tina covers such varied fields with great expertise, including fascinating interviews, new health possibilities, and her own work. In the post-COVID-19 era, it is important to have a fresh look at all the coming opportunities; Tina's book is a must-read for those who want to discover the future of health."*

**—José Luis Cordeiro, Fellow, World Academy of Art & Science; Director, The Millennium Project; Vice Chair, Humanity Plus; Co-Author of *The Death of Death***

*"This book is a life-affirming achievement. Tina's thought-provoking conversations with a wide range of stakeholders (and when it comes to health each and every one of us is stakeholder) made me both concerned and exhilarated. Concerned at the sheer scale and complexity of the challenge ahead and at the likely capacity of some of the incumbent power structures to rise to the challenge, and exhilarated at just how much original and radical thinking is both needed and already being done. We are all now data citizens. Citizenship implies obligations as well as rights—nowhere is this clearer than in the field of health and this book will encourage you to think deeply about what it might be like to inhabit our bodies and our own health data space with compassion for both self and other in the 21$^{st}$ century."*

**—Robbie Stamp, CEO, Bioss International, AI Governance Expert**

*"We're all living longer but those extra years of life are increasingly being spent in poorer health with an ever-widening and unacceptable health gap between wealthy and deprived areas. AI could be part of the solution to meeting this societal challenge and this is something that Tina expertly explores in* Living Longer with AI. *Unlike other books on this topic, you don't need to be a technophile to understand and enjoy it, and it's so important that this book reaches a wide audience.*

*For while the potential of AI is huge, it comes with limitations and significant ethical considerations. These are all sensitively and thoroughly considered by Tina as someone who cares about people first and foremost, not about selling AI."*

**—Michelle Hawkins-Collins, Ageing-well activist, researcher and Gerontologist**

*"More than ever, people are beginning to recognize now that the process of aging, and in particular our ability to maintain health throughout it, is inextricably bound to our collective health as a society.* Live Longer with AI *details how AI and related technologies are paving the way for significant increases in healthy lifespan, and the transformative effects this can have on our economy, personal lives, and ability to resist all diseases – infectious or otherwise. In Tina's skilled hands this critically important topic receives the care and attention it most certainly deserves."*

**—Keith Comito, President of Lifespan.io – Life Extension Advocacy Foundation**

*"This new book by Tina Woods is an amazing achievement and one of the most important books of 2020 as it provides a comprehensive overview of longevity, an industry that is at its inflection point today and will become the "new industrial revolution" of the 21$^{st}$ century. It covers a broad range of tangent verticals from healthcare AI to precision medicine and reads like a detective story"*

**—Anton Derlyatka, Co-Founder and CEO, Sweatcoin**

"Most of us want to live longer. Can AI help us? Tina's visionary book answers this question by synthesizing a vast amount of cutting-edge scientific information and providing insights through interviews with today's leading AI thinkers and practitioners. Instructive and analytical, and densely packed with info while being engaging and accessible, reading this book will help you get up to speed in record time. Thank you, Tina, for fast-tracking our understanding by pursuing your passion."

**—Ann Longley, Founder, Something New Together**

"This book is a wonderful riposte to the catastrophists who see doom around the corner. Tina has compiled inputs from some of the leading thinkers in the world to create an inspiring overview of the prospect for biology, AI, and government policy to greatly enhance population healthspan.

By grounding her survey with her personal experience she helps to soften the breath-taking ideas being proposed by some of her interviewees and make them more comprehensible. This is a superb book for those interested to learn about the revolution that the researchers in the longevity and healthspan field promise to deliver to all of us."

**—Brian Lynch, Serial Healthcare Entrepreneur**

"This is the antithesis of a lazy beach read. Sit up straight, deploy your concentration and curiosity genes, and get ready to grow your brain with the knowledge provided by Tina and dozens of top-tier longevity scientists, academics, and entrepreneurs. You'll learn that cancer cells are biologically immortal, as are germ and stem cells. You'll learn about the concepts of singularity, cellular reprogramming, and aging biomarkers. And Tina will help you understand how computational biology will help unravel the basis of life itself. This is a fabulous book that will clear up any confusion you have about the role of AI in building a better world. It's a tool that can help move us beyond our troubled state of human and planetary distress to a future of abundance, better health, and well-being."

**—Susan Flory – Host-producer, The Big Middle Podcast**

*"The strangeness of 2020 has made many of us reflect rather obsessively on what is truly important in life and what is not. It has made the importance of science, the importance of collective endeavor, the importance of society, and the importance of quality of life stand out in sharp relief. Tina's book is timely. It addresses all of these key priorities – and weaves a fascinating narrative, informed by the finest thinkers in the field. If you read only one book in the coming months, make it this one."*

**—Karen Lipworth, Healthcare Communications Consultant, Healthcare Writer and Contributor**

*"Life, time, health, and especially technology move at such breath-taking speed that it's hard to keep up. This book tackles a more important dimension, though – how to turn it all to the advantage of humanity through AI."*

**—Nicole Yershon, Founder & CEO, NY Collective**

*"I am normally something of a sceptic about AI, but unusually I can see much promise here. Apart from anything else, an informed, personalized approach to well-being and health seems essential if we are to encourage people to focus on the perfectly manageable number of new behaviors which will be of greatest benefit to them personally, rather than bombarding people with every single statistical finding. Many of these may work at the aggregate level, while being mostly ineffectual at the level of the individual. The price you pay for issuing too many instructions is often that people do nothing at all."*

**—Rory Sutherland, Vice Chairman, Ogilvy Group**

*"Live Longer with AI showcases the latest exciting developments in artificial intelligence and how they will help us live longer, healthier, and better than ever before. From exploring AI's potential in managing the global pandemic to personalizing healthcare for every single person on the planet, the book creates a mind shift that allows us to see aging and our partnership with technology in a fresh, new light!"*

**—Sergey Young, Founder of Longevity Vision Fund**

# Contributors

## About the author

**Tina Woods** is a social entrepreneur and innovator in health. As CEO and Founder of Collider Health (`https://www.colliderhealth.com/`), she builds ecosystems connecting government, business, and academia to align thinking and take action to solve real-world problems in health.

Tina is the Secretariat Director of the All Party Parliamentary Group for Longevity (`https://appg-longevity.org/`), has co-authored *The Health of the Nation Strategy*, (`https://appg-longevity.org/events-publications`) and is now helping to implement key actions in the Strategy made more urgent as a result of COVID-19.

Tina supports UK Research & Innovation on the Healthy Ageing Industrial Strategy Challenge Fund, NHSX, and the National AHSN AI Network to support AI-and data-driven technologies in health and care.

*My biggest thanks go to my dear husband, Nick, and my wonderful sons, James, Gabriel, and Noah; really, I will always love you more than my work.*

*There are so many others to thank for their generosity, knowledge, and inspiration on this journey of discovery in how technology can help us live longer, healthier, and better lives, many of whom are interviewed in the book. The entire team at Packt have been stupendous too. And finally, an important message to Marcos, Jasmine, and other young people I have been so lucky to work with—your optimism, spirit, and greatness give me such hope for the future.*

## About the consultant editor

**Melissa Ream** is a leading health and care strategist in the UK, leveraging user-driven design and artificial intelligence to design systems and support people to live healthier, longer lives.

# About the reviewer

**Dr. Devin Singh** was one of Canada's first physicians to specialize in clinical **artificial intelligence** (**AI**) and is a practicing Pediatric Emergency Medicine Doctor at **SickKids** (the Hospital for **Sick Children**) in Toronto, Canada. He completed his undergraduate degree at the University of Western Ontario in medical sciences and went on to work for the Ontario Provincial Government. Afterward, he attended medical school at the University of Sydney, Australia, followed by a Pediatric residency and Emergency Medicine subspecialty training at SickKids Hospital. His fellowship in clinical AI was completed at SickKids and he is finishing a Master's in Computer Science degree (2020) at the University of Toronto, Canada. His research focuses on the use of machine learning to solve some of healthcare's biggest problems.

Devin is also the founder and CEO of Hero AI, a tech start-up with a mission to empower patients and healthcare providers with AI to enable increased equity and access to care globally via clinical automation.

# TABLE OF CONTENTS

# Preface

An algorithm led Packt to me in January 2019.

This was life **Before COVID (BC)**. I got a message on LinkedIn: "Would you author a book on health tech? It would be something looking at AI in the NHS, and maybe the AI hospital."

Like many people who use LinkedIn, I get a lot of messages from people I don't know. This was one of them and I thought it was harmless spam. I whizzed back a slightly flippant message:

"Thanks for the idea but probably not for me right now as just too busy!"

Well, after a few more exchanges, I realized it was a serious approach by a leading international tech publisher. Within a week, we had agreed terms. And that was the same week I was invited to 10 Downing Street for breakfast, to talk about the Ageing Society Grand Challenge with the Secretary of State for Health and Care (for non-Brits, Number 10 is where the UK Prime Minister lives). Two days before that, I had published my first article on Forbes.com: *'Longevity' Could Reach Billions In 2019 - And Is No Longer Just The Preserve of Billionaires.*

Fast-forward to April 2020—at the height of the global COVID-19 pandemic. We put a freeze on the book's publication because it wasn't right to talk about living longer when the entire world was grappling with how to deal with the worst public health crisis in our lifetime.

We are now living and experiencing this murky, strange period of a patchwork "new normal." We have moved from BC, but have absolutely no idea when we will reach **After the Disease (AD)**. COVID-19 has changed everything: our lives, our plans, our hopes, and our future. And there is still no end in sight.

But we are learning a huge number of lessons that will form part of an enduring legacy AD. For one thing, the pandemic has brought renewed attention to how humanity's destruction of biodiversity may have created the conditions for new viruses and diseases such as COVID-19. The discipline of "planetary health," the intricate and finely balanced ecosystem of humans and all other living things, has been put into the limelight.

I have tried to capture some of the lessons we're learning in the pages ahead.

So, first, back to January 2019. How did this algorithm identify me? What criteria was it using? Was it using the right criteria?

After the algorithm found me, a human being did, of course, check me out before approaching me. The one thing everyone should know about algorithms is that, for now, they are only as good as the data they draw from, and the rules that humans set (at least until AGI—artificial general intelligence—hits us; that is, when machines take over what humans do. But that's still a little way off. More on this later).

On the face of it, I am hardly an "AI expert" at a technical level. I speak to many who are, and certainly now have enough experience to know when so-called "AI experts" really have no clue at all (knowing what you don't know is a very underrated skill, but I use it all the time!). What I am becoming an expert in is how AI will affect society and drive change.

As you will see in this book, artificial intelligence is influencing, and indeed driving, far more things in our lives than most of us realize. And technology is moving fast, and far faster than many C-suite industry executives, think tank leaders, or policymakers realize.

But the entrepreneurs and the scientists do realize it. I spend a lot of time with these people. And it is thanks to them and their knowledge that I find myself in the privileged position of writing this book. I've interviewed some of them, but I didn't interview the two people I'm about to mention. Without them, I would not have been found by that algorithm over a year ago.

Melissa Ream is the first one. She is an AI and digital expert in healthcare, and that's why I asked her to help me with this book. She gave me my first big opportunity to work in AI—with the Academic Health Science Network AI program, then with the Department of Health and Care and NHS England, and more recently with NHSX, helping to build the UK's AI ecosystem for health. I talk about this in *Chapter 4, Moving Sickcare to Wellbeing, Through Prevention*.

Eric Kihlstrom is the second one. We met about five years ago and we've collaborated on many projects involving our shared interests in data innovation and longevity. He invited me to help build an ecosystem of "unusual suspects," companies to come together in transformational bids for the Healthy Ageing Industrial Strategy Challenge Fund (backed with £98 million of government money), when he was interim director for the fund at Innovate UK.

There is a famous quote (that Eric uses a lot!) by the writer William Gibson: "*The future is already here—it's just not very evenly distributed.*"

The future is definitely not evenly distributed at the moment.

In many ways, prosperity in the Western world has become more accessible to wider sections of society, with better cars, better-quality housing, and high-quality healthcare. Consumer technology has become ubiquitous, and many of the most deprived people in both the developed and developing world have a smartphone. However, we have seen rather alarmingly that despite growing economies and the many developments in science, technology, and medicine, life expectancies have been dropping in the USA and stalling in the UK. Inequalities in health are increasing.

Something is going wrong. And it has to do with inequality, the uneven, unfair ways we are sharing the benefits of the future. The COVID-19 pandemic has brutally exposed this.

I was invited to speak at a recent event run by the UK chapter of Singularity University, a hotbed of exponential thinking in California. I imagine many attendees expected me to speak about how science is getting us a step closer to achieving immortality, but I started with a question—why aren't we fixing this problem of health inequality? How can we share the benefits of longevity democratically, so that we can all benefit from the "longevity dividend?"

Why is it that the treatment we receive in hospitals (accounting for a mere 10% of what keeps us healthy) gets the most attention and budget, when it is the 90% of the other determinants of our health (including the environment, genomics, and socio-economic factors) that matter far more?

This conundrum is what I have been trying to unpack with many experts in *The Health of the Nation: A Strategy for Healthier Longer Lives*, a strategy we created on behalf of the All-Party Parliamentary Group for Longevity. The strategy was published in February 2020 with proposed actions on how all UK citizens can gain five extra years of healthy life expectancy by 2035, while minimizing health inequalities between the richest and poorest. This goal is part of the current government's manifesto but was initially drawn up by Theresa May, the former prime minister, in 2018. May's deputy prime minister at the time was Damian Green. Damian, who is still an MP, chairs the All-Party Parliamentary Group for Longevity, which is now getting international attention. There is so much to thank him for in terms of his hard work in getting the *Health of the Nation* strategy to where it is now.

Many of those involved in the strategy have been interviewed for this book. But this strategy would not have been possible without the extraordinary expertise and energy of Lord Geoffrey Filkin CBE, who, among his many other accomplishments, set up the Centre for Ageing Better. Together, Geoff and I have led the strategy, and it has been a terrific partnership of social entrepreneurship since we first spoke in March 2019.

The strategy is focused on closing the health inequality gap. When we emerge from COVID-19's massive impact on society and the economy, the priorities and recommendations we have set out will only become more urgent and more pressing. And with all the work I have been doing in AI, data, healthy aging, and now in longevity, one key thing keeps coming up over and over again: our citizens.

The public will shape the future. Ordinary people need to be brought more into the debate on how technology could be more powerfully deployed as a force for good, to cope far better when the next pandemic hits, and until then, to help us live longer better. We all need to participate in decisions that could ultimately shape a better society—at all levels—whether individually for personal reasons, at a community level for civic duty, or through votes at a national level. And I think we need a societal system more focused on social capital, on the value of human contribution.

We also need to scale solutions at an international level. That's especially true when it comes to sharing knowledge in science and harnessing data, but also to learn what is working best to engage communities, prevent ill health, and care for our most vulnerable.

At the time of writing, Ipsos Mori published a poll showing that scientists are the most trusted profession in the world (politicians come last). It is no surprise that politicians have insisted on being "guided by the science" during this devastating pandemic.

It is clear we need to involve scientists in decisions affecting our future. And there seems to be an appetite for it. A public program I ran before the pandemic on the science of aging for How To Academy was a sell-out, and had to move to a bigger venue. I invited four leading scientists (two of whom were interviewed for this book) to speak and the audience couldn't have been more mixed (as were the questions asked afterwards)—young students, middle aged, and older people—all interested and curious to know more.

My curiosity about science began as early as I can remember in childhood, when I first started asking the questions most kids ask, like "where do we come from?" This curiosity propelled me to Cornell University, where I studied genetics at the time that the Human Genome Project was first being conceived—30 years ago. Now in my mid-50s, I am starting to ask many more questions about how we can harness science to help us live a good life, not just from the beginning, but right through to the very end, aided by technology that was unimaginable just a few years ago.

So, starting with the science of "our beginning," let's start answering some of those questions.

# Get in touch with Packt

Feedback from our readers is always welcome.

**General feedback**: Email `feedback@packtpub.com`, and mention the book's title in the subject of your message. If you have questions about any aspect of this book, please email us at `questions@packtpub.com`.

**Errata**: Although we have taken every care to ensure the accuracy of our content, mistakes do happen. If you have found a mistake in this book, we would be grateful if you would report this to us. Please visit `http://www.packtpub.com/submit-errata`, selecting your book, clicking on the Errata Submission Form link, and entering the details.

**Piracy**: If you come across any illegal copies of our works in any form on the Internet, we would be grateful if you would provide us with the location address or website name. Please contact us at `copyright@packtpub.com` with a link to the material.

**If you are interested in becoming an author**: If there is a topic that you have expertise in and you are interested in either writing or contributing to a book, please visit `http://authors.packtpub.com`.

## Reviews

Please leave a review. Once you have read and used this book, why not leave a review on the site that you purchased it from? Potential readers can then see and use your unbiased opinion to make purchase decisions, we at Packt can understand what you think about our products, and our authors can see your feedback on their book. Thank you!

For more information about Packt, please visit `packtpub.com`.

# CHAPTER 1

# INTRODUCTION

The search for the secret of eternal youth and the quest for immortality have endured since humans life began—some would say this is part of our intrinsic survival instinct and is hardwired into our genetic code, which has evolved since life on earth began, about 3.6 billion years ago.

How did life begin? Where do we come from? Where do we get this insatiable curiosity that drives us, making us want to live longer, and for some of us, even forever?

These are questions I have been fascinated with ever since I was a little girl. I used to draw a lot, which helped me work out my ideas and process my obsessive curiosity about life. My drawings were everything from religious images depicting Jesus and Mary to anatomical drawings from textbooks on obstetrics showing the birth process. I thought I was destined to be a doctor, but then fell into a very different path after studying genetics.

Years later, with three sons born, through complete serendipity, I saw Sir Ken Robinson's wonderful TED Talk "Schools Kill Creativity." Seeing this 20-minute talk resulted in an epiphany moment—I suddenly realized what was "holding back" my middle son in school (hyperactivity, it turns out, which is a gift in so many ways, but not necessarily at school when you have to sit still at a desk for hours!). Compelled to read Robinson's book *The Element*, I realized for myself what was holding me back and what I was really interested in too.

Fundamentally, it is what drives people, and how they can either be blocked (though archaic educational systems, stultifying workplaces, or slow-moving institutions, for example) or be released, enabling them to achieve big things from seemingly small and inauspicious places when they find their purpose and their passion.

Just look at Greta Thunberg! Most people know her as the climate change activist that she is—most recently named by *Time Magazine* as the "Person of the Year." But did you know that she has Aspergers, was very depressed, and had no interest in eating, until she found her cause?

Will and purpose are what drive us to want to live longer. And I am not sure this is hardwired into our genes, like the survival instinct clearly is.

For me, I re-discovered my purpose when I hit "middle age" by going back to my entrepreneurial proclivities and becoming a sort of social entrepreneur. I started a social enterprise to inspire young people in science and technology; two years later, I started an innovation business in health, and then a year later I co-founded another venture in longevity.

A lot of what I do is about making connections with ideas and with people to drive change. Some of the stories from the extraordinary people I have met are in this book. I talked to scientists, entrepreneurs, corporate leaders, politicians, activists, and even the world's strongest man.

We all have our own exquisitely unique way of figuring out the path we take in our lives—and our personalities shape whether we follow, create, or destroy these paths in this most intricate map of life.

So back to the first question: how was life first created? Let's turn to the science.

# Life's beginning

Theories still abound. The leading contender, detailed in the BBC's wonderful program *The Secret of How Life on Earth Began*[1], explains that it all started in hydrothermal events in the deep sea.

The water was tepid enough, and alkaline enough, for precursor organisms to form in the porous sections of the rock, which in effect acted like "cells." These cells contained essential chemicals, and when a natural proton gradient developed, so that the proton concentration was higher outside the inner membrane than inside the membrane, it enabled cells to store and release energy (protons are subatomic particles occurring in all atomic nuclei, with a positive electric charge equal in magnitude to that of an electron). These cells were the ideal place for metabolism to begin and for the first molecules, like **ribonucleic acid** (**RNA**), to form by harnessing the energy created by the gradient, which also created the conditions for a cell membrane to emerge.

Many scientists have been involved in solving the mystery of life. Most people have heard of Charles Darwin, who developed the theory of evolution, and he, together with other lesser known figures like the Russian Alexander Oparin, proposed various versions of theories that life started with chemicals that began to form microscopic structures in a "warm little pond."

In 1953, one of the greatest scientific discoveries of the 20th century, that of the double helix structure of the DNA code by Watson and Crick, redirected the search for the origin of life by revealing the extraordinary structure inside living cells.

All living things are made of cells, which contain DNA, the instructions that tell a cell what it will become. Most forms of life are made up of just one cell. Bacteria are the most well-known group and are ubiquitous, included in almost all the branches of the "tree of life," as published in *Nature*[2] in 2016. An analysis of the tree suggests every living thing—including humans—descended from a bacterium.

More recent research[3] by Gustavo Caetano-Anollés shows that viruses emerged before bacteria, supporting the idea that viruses stemmed from the cellular domain, which may shape the ongoing debate over when viruses first existed. Caetano-Anollés came up with this theory by exploring protein folding and the origins of **transfer RNA (tRNA)**, which is central to every task a cell performs and thus essential to all life. He discovered that tRNAs of each of the super kingdoms diverged from the overall tree, allowing him to determine the order in which viruses and each of the super kingdoms diverged.

Caetano-Anollés also studied how viruses swap genes with a variety of cellular organisms[4]. His findings suggest that viruses share genes with organisms across the tree of life.

Driven by such exponential developments in understanding the biological assets codified in life on the planet, scientists are now racing to put together what they call the "book of life[5],"the genetic sequences of all complex species on the planet and the relationships between them. So far, they have only decoded 0.28 percent of the relevant DNA, but with DNA sequencing seeing a million-fold decrease in costs since 2003 (when human DNA was first mapped), this has made it viable for Juan Carlos Castilla-Rubio, chairman of SpaceTime Ventures, to launch the Earth BioGenome Project. This project aims to fully sequence everything on the planet, on land and in the oceans, that has cells with nuclei, over the next 10 years. When it reaches full sequencing capacity, the project will be generating about 1,000 to 2,000 times more data than that produced by Twitter and YouTube combined.

Significant advances in AI and causal machine learning will be needed to decode the many complex networks at work in this most extraordinary book of life, which will provide a new foundation for biological discovery and innovation at an unprecedented scale.

Castilla-Rubio's aim is to create a new inclusive bioeconomy that can help solve the majority of humanity's problems in energy, water, food, materials, healthcare, and transport in a rapidly changing climate. Preserving life on the planet is not only critical to our own survival as a species, but also to preserving nature's vast biological intelligence, which has been codified in the book of life over the past 3.5 billion years of evolution.

Today, biology has become fully digital, so DNA information can effectively be coded as ones and zeros and can thus be programmed to unleash a powerful nature-inspired innovation engine. In Castilla-Rubio's view, biology will be the most valuable enterprise in the 21st century, and far more valuable than monetizing people's data, but it depends on sharing the value of the assets fairly between and across nations. This is the dual mission of the Earth Bank of Codes[6] that the Earth BioGenome Project launched in partnership[7] with the World Economic Forum.

---

*What is AI?*

AI is generally defined as the ability of a machine to show intelligent behavior. It is often confused with "machine learning," which is the ability of an AI system to analyze raw data and from that learn how to make predictions from new data.

Deep learning combines AI with machine learning and was inspired by how the human brain works, with its system of neural networks. An artificial neural network is literally a computer program or algorithm that organizes millions or billions of transistors in a similar way to how a brain's neurons interconnect to transmit nerve impulses.

Deep learning is being used widely in consumer technology and increasingly in health and medical applications.

---

Castilla-Rubio makes the crucial point that to maximize the societal value and public benefit from decoding the book of life, we need to engineer governance on data access, data sharing, and the use of protocols[8] to avoid the vast concentration of wealth and power in a few companies, and to proactively identify and manage the risks and the many unintended consequences that the book of life will certainly unleash. Engineering longevity is a case in point, and we will explore the ethical considerations and social and economic disruptions that it may bring to society at large in this book.

# Living forever

All this talk of life assets being reduced to ones and zeros would have been heresy before the 1800s, when most people believed in "vitalism"—the notion that living things were endowed with a magical property that distinguished them from inanimate objects. In religion, vitalism was thought to be responsible for animating the first humans, and also perpetuating the immortal soul.

This vitality—energy of life—is still the subject of so much research today. Scientists are busy trying to understand this life force of cells, and how to unlock the elixir that could keep us going, potentially forever.

Ever since becoming "human," we have sought to understand how we can become immortal—how to bottle up vitality. This is the stuff of ancient myths, Greek legends, and modern literature.

The "Epic of Gilgamesh" is an ancient Mesopotamian poem that tells the story of Gilgamesh, king of the city Uruk, who tragically loses his beloved friend Enkidu—this compels him to find the solution to prevent or overcome old age and death. On his journey, Gilgamesh discovers a flower that can achieve rejuvenation, but in the end doesn't use it. The moral of the story is that the king becomes wiser as a result of his journey and achieves a different kind of peace.

Gilgamesh has survived the ages and is enshrined as a character in popular culture too—as one of the Marvel Avengers with eternal powers including virtual indestructibility, limitless stamina, superhuman strength, and, of course, extreme longevity. But there are many other stories throughout the ages: Herodotus' Fountain of Youth, Rowling's philosopher's stone, Barrie's Neverland, and Ovid's Cumaean Sibyl. The list goes on in the search for eternal youth.

Fast forward to the present day and eternal youth may soon move out of the realms of myth[9] and into reality thanks to developing technologies. Three main technological shifts are driving the innovation in biology and longevity (according to Alex Zhavoronkov, a pioneer in AI and CEO of Insilico Medicine, who I interview in this book):

1.  DNA sequencing and synthesis: The cost of genetic sequencing has come down to $100 per person (compared to $24,000 only a few years ago[10]), so decoding our DNA is becoming accessible to the masses.

2.  AI, machine vision, and machine learning is rapidly developing.

3.  Biological data collection and manipulation in the lab is increasingly automated.

Combining these three applications presents a very powerful tool for AI, which can be categorized in the following ways according to Zhavoronkov[11]:

- Machine learning refers to algorithms that can learn from and make predictions on data.

- Deep learning is a subset of machine learning and is based on neural networks.

- **Reinforcement learning (RL)** is a method of directing unsupervised machine learning through rewards and penalties.

- **Generative adversarial networks** (**GANs**) are structured, probabilistic models for generating data and consist of two entities—the generator and the denominator. The denominator checks the authenticity of the data produced by the generator, whereas the generator tries to trick the denominator—it's kind of like learning to lie without getting caught.

- Transfer learning is a machine learning method where the set of learned features of a model for a specific task is reused, or repurposed.

The applications of these tools within the field of aging research[12] offer tremendous opportunities.

# AI and understanding health and aging

Aging is an almost universally unifying feature possessed by all living organisms, tissues, and cells, which I will describe in the next section.

Insilico Medicine uses GANs and RL to research "biomarkers of aging" and to deploy novel methods for analyzing the most important features underlying the aging process.

These techniques can also produce diverse synthetic molecular and patient data, and help to identify novel biological targets and molecular compounds with desired properties in much less time than traditional methods used by pharmaceutical companies.

In fact, using these techniques, Insilico Medicine managed to generate and validate a novel small molecule in just 46 days, designing the drug from scratch—compared to in *two to three years* by pharmaceutical companies following "accepted" practice. This was considered the "AlphaGo" moment in health and was published in *Nature Biotechnology* on September 2nd, 2019[13].

Insilico's work shows that AI can reduce the 99% preclinical failure rate in pharmaceutical and expedite the time it takes to go from R&D in drug discovery to real treatments. Not surprisingly, these developments are all of high interest to pharmaceutical companies that are threatened themselves by technological disruption, especially as AI talent is being siphoned by tech companies.

Modern AI will continue to drive the longevity[14] biotechnology industry, and contribute to the convergence[15] of countless areas of research across the course of a human life. Better use of public data, combined with digital tools and an understanding of the wider determinants of health, will give us the ability to better identify risks and help the people most in need before they become patients, which is a big focus of this book.

At the moment, AI devices work independently of one another, with data flowing through each device. The true power of AI can be unleashed when these devices are connected and algorithms can analyze datasets across these devices. The datasets collected from multiple sources can be described as "multimodal datasets." When these multimodal datasets are consolidated into one model, and algorithms can generate completely novel insights, spotting the patterns that would otherwise not be spotted in individual datasets, this is called "multimodal learning."

The two main benefits of multimodal learning lie in more robust predictions (since multiple sensors analyzing the same information can act as a double-check and make predictions more precise) and new pattern recognition (by combining multiple sensors).

The potential of multimodal learning to develop predictive and preventative health strategies is colossal. Insights from genetics, biological, behavioral, environmental, and financial data are currently under-utilized and there are significant opportunities to use AI and multimodal learning to predict disease and incentivize healthier living through harnessing such "life" data.

The opportunity for tech developers is getting these devices to learn, think, and work together to produce novel insights. This is the basis of research in aging biomarkers, for example, which could lead to the development of strategies to minimize the risk of dementia, or, indeed, cure it.

There are billions of petabytes of data flowing through AI devices every day and the volume will only increase in the years to come, which is why edge and quantum computing are so important. "Edge computing" is a distributed computing model that brings computation and data storage closer to the location where it is needed, such as devices and sensors. This dramatically increases processing times and will help with managing the proliferation of data that will only increase in years to come.

Indeed, 2020 marks the start of what's been called "our trillion-sensor world[16]" and data is quite clearly fueling the economy—healthcare, finance, insurance, education, and beyond. Big Tech knows this, which is why companies are investing so heavily in health.

## The Big Tech takeover of our health

Leading tech futurist Peter Diamandis[17] predicts Apple and Amazon will come up with a service where a person pays a company to keep them healthy, rather than to cover the cost of illness, based on their health history and daily activities. This approach makes so much sense. This is where China and other Asian countries are ahead of the game: the basic philosophy of Chinese medicine that has been practiced for over 3,000 years is that prevention of disease and maintenance of health is the main priority of doctors. The doctor is paid a retainer to keep their patients healthy.

But do we want Big Tech to "take over" our health? As the use of technology in our lives becomes more widespread, social, legal, and ethical issues will grow in importance[18].

Amy Webb, professor of strategic foresight[47] at New York University's Stern School of Business, warns of scenarios in the future when Amazon, Google, and Apple could run our households, as well as our health. One day, smart refrigerators, for example, could be calling you out for snacking between meals and smart garages could start telling you to walk to work on a sunny day!

Amazon has big plans in healthcare with Alexa, which is already helping people with dementia in their homes to live independently for longer. The company has also launched its own health clinic[19] for employees, a program called Amazon Care that provides virtual and in-person urgent care, preventative care, and medication delivery for Amazon employees enrolled in its Amazon insurance plan. Amazon is also working on a health project with JP Morgan and Berkshire Hathaway called **Haven**[20].

Amazon has also been active in its response to the pandemic, from prioritizing delivery for high-need items to launching a $20 million AWS Diagnostics initiative. Amazon Care also announced a partnership with the Gates Foundation-sponsored Seattle Coronavirus Assessment Network to deliver home testing kits for coronavirus in Seattle.

Just recently, Amazon announced it is getting into the health gadget market with a new fitness band and subscription service called Halo[48]. Unlike the Apple Watch or basic Fitbits, the Halo Band doesn't have a screen but comes with an app with standard fitness tracking functionality but also two novel (some would say disturbing) features: creating 3D scans of your body fat and listening to the emotion in your voice.

Google is active in health and healthcare through the Alphabet company Verily[21] and its Google Fit ecosystem for wearables[22]. One of its most notable commercial activities has been the recent $2.1 billion acquisition of Fitbit.

Google's core expertise in search is being applied to make it easier for doctors to search medical records, and to improve the quality of health-related search results for consumers across Google and YouTube.

On the technological side, some of Google's innovations are mind-blowing. DeepMind recently announced a new deep learning tool called AlphaFold[23], which can predict the innumerable ways in which various proteins fold by analyzing their amino acid sequences. The ability to predict a protein's shape is useful to scientists because it is fundamental to understanding its role within the body, as well as diagnosing and treating diseases believed to be caused by misfolded proteins, such as Alzheimer's[24], Parkinson's[25], Huntington's[26], and cystic fibrosis[27]. Understanding protein folding using tools like AlphaFold will aid drug discovery to fight today's most intractable diseases, including COVID-19.

Apple is getting into healthcare through its on-site employee medical clinics, Apple HealthKit, and Apple Watch. It is putting its efforts into harnessing the value of lifestyle data to help understand what keeps us healthy and develop the technologies to keep us well.

Some interesting Big Tech partnerships have formed in response to COVID-19. For example, Apple and Google announced in April 2020 that they are partnering to develop and deploy an automatic, anonymous, Bluetooth-based contact tracing technology for COVID-19, which is now being used in many countries, including the US and parts of Europe.

Big Tech companies can easily build risk profiles based on all the metadata they have. Apple and Amazon can already see what we buy, how active we are, and what we eat via Apple Pay, Apple Watch, Amazon Fresh, and Whole Foods. But Big Tech still can't really learn the same way humans learn. Our intelligence is still greater than theirs, but maybe not for long.

In July 2019, Microsoft invested $1 billion[28] in the Elon Musk-founded AI venture OpenAI, helping toward its efforts to build **artificial general intelligence** (**AGI**) that can rival and surpass the cognitive capabilities of humans. OpenAI's mission is to ensure that AGI—which they mean as, highly autonomous systems that outperform humans at most economically valuable work—benefits all of humanity. In its charter, the venture states that it will actively cooperate with other research and policy institutions to create a global community working together to address AGI's global challenges. In an open letter, it said: "We cannot predict what we might achieve when this intelligence is magnified by the tools AI may provide, but the eradication of disease and poverty are not unfathomable."

Once AI can learn and solve problems in similar ways to humans, it throws up more questions than answers in fundamental areas, and especially ethics.

In his book *Superintelligence*, Professor Nick Bostrom, director of the Future of Humanity Institute at the University of Oxford, analyzes the steps needed to develop superintelligence, and the ways in which humanity may or may not be able to control what emerges, along with the kind of ethical thinking that is needed. Bostrom suggests[29] that creating AI to understand human values is essential to ensuring we will be safe. But inputting individual lines of code to teach a superintelligent robot what humans care about would be a nearly impossible task due to the complexity of human emotions and cultural differences.

Cultural differences are at the heart of how AI is being developed around the world, and the starkest differences are between China and the US, which are both on a quest to lead the world in AI.

# China winning the global AI race

So far, China is winning. The rise of China as a leading player in AI research has been revealed by new figures showing how quickly the country is gaining on the US[30]. The 2019 AI Index Report, put together by US academics and researchers, found that Chinese companies are on average receiving millions of dollars more in investment than their Western counterparts.

Why and how is China becoming so powerful here? For a start, China has developed a completely different version of the internet than the one the Westernized world is using. And it is all based on phone technology using WeChat, a messaging platform that is very much like WhatsApp. WeChat was developed by Tencent, a social media giant, and it has quite literally exploded, becoming ubiquitous in Chinese business, culture, and society. WeChat has become completely integrated into people's lives simply because all transactions can be accomplished using a tool in the palm of your hand.

Its rise has been quick and is accelerating. WeChat now has more than a billion monthly active users (1.17 billion as of Q1 2020[31]) and a significant portion of all Chinese data traffic. It is the "app for everything," acting as a social network, a payment system, a communication medium, and, perhaps most ambitiously, the infrastructure for business transactions through its "mini programs," which resemble Facebook pages.

The number of these mini programs is fast rising—it includes big companies like McDonald's as well as the many tiny businesses run in local communities—and on last count is equal to half the number of iOS apps available in Apple's App Store[32]. Because the mini programs run inside WeChat, business customers don't have to sign up, log in, or add their credit card numbers, so it is easy and seamless. It is supremely clever.

In 2017, the Chinese Government published its ambitious national plan to become a global leader in AI research by 2030, with healthcare listed as one of four core research areas during the first wave of the plan. WeChat will be a core part of this plan, with the majority of China's 38,000 medical institutions registered on the platform, enabling patients to engage digitally.

WeChat is now used to self-diagnose, look up drug information, search medical information, schedule doctor appointments, and process healthcare payments.

Not surprisingly, WeChat gave China a significant advantage in managing the COVID-19 pandemic too. This includes its "Health Check" app, which takes self-reported data about places visited and symptoms to generate an identifying QR code that is displayed in green, orange, or red, corresponding to free movement and 7-day and 14-day quarantines.

In parallel with the explosion of WeChat, the Chinese Government is building a so-called "social credit system[33]" that aims to collect and analyze information on its 1.4 billion citizens and rate millions of corporations, both domestic and foreign. Its goal is to keep local governments, businesses, and people in compliance with national directives.

Many Western commentators talk of social credit policy only in very negative terms, through its potential to abuse human rights and control citizens' behavior too heavily. This, of course, is a valid, justified position in many respects.

However, on the technological front, it is clever as a gigantic data sharing platform, with a universal "national API" allowing data from over 1 billion citizens to be accessed, shared, and leveraged. Adding in the magic dust of multimodal learning and edge computing, you can easily understand why China is leading the race in AI.

Through its social credit policy, China guides its citizens' behavior in ingenious ways—just like Big Tech does, but in the context of a completely different cultural, political, and ethical framework.

Businesses are imaginatively nudged to behave as model companies. Using AI, the system can rate firms for "credibility" or "sincerity." The higher the score, the more benefits companies have access to, but it goes the other way too—with blacklisted companies potentially being denied access to cheap loans or facing higher import and export taxes. For international businesses, the system looks at business contracts, social responsibility, regulatory compliance, and how many Communist Party members they employ to give a score.

In the West, China's Government is typically seen as a "citizen controller," but in China, they see the Government through a different cultural lens—as a record keeper, whose central job is to consolidate Government files. Keeping a central database of social credit records means that important information can be accessed by state agencies, city governments, banks, industry associations, and the general public, and data on individuals and companies can inform their own evaluations.

While China's Government does not issue social credit scores to every individual (as of September 2019, it has not issued a social credit score to any Chinese citizen), what it is doing is encouraging local governments to use social credit data to develop their own scoring systems for local residents.

Several cities in China have already rolled out such systems on a trial basis, and many more are gearing up. "My Nanjing" is a good example, tying together city transportation, environmental data, hospitals, utility providers, civil affairs bureaus, courts, schools, local financial institutions, and charitable organizations into a one-stop shop for citizen services. Once logged in, citizens are able to view certain aspects of their social credit files, including records of any state-issued awards and honors, unpaid bills, traffic violations, and any legal violations and administrative penalties received.

While My Nanjing doesn't issue social credit scores (yet), it does include a points system that nudges and rewards people for behavior that protects the environment, while improving their health. "Green points" are assigned to users based on their public transportation choices, with points earned for walking, biking, taking the bus, or riding the subway. Citizens can earn double points for not driving on heavily polluted days.

Doesn't this sound like something the West should have in place?

# The EU as a leader in "ethical AI"

Indeed, the features on the My Nanjing app look remarkably similar to what Estonians are able to access via their e-Estonia program. Estonian citizens can access all their records, including health records, and choose to share them with anyone they wish.

Note the words "citizen" and "choose"—this is the point of difference between how China and the **European Union** (**EU**) deal with data. It is the citizen's choice in the EU—enshrined by the **General Data Protection Regulation** (**GDPR**)—that stipulates that citizens are the custodians of their data and can choose how and with whom to share it.

While the EU is rarely considered a leading player in the development of AI, certain EU countries like Estonia and Finland are pioneering ethical ways of accessing and sharing data in a social contract between the citizen and state that is very different to that in the US and China.

I visited Estonia and Finland in April 2019 as part of a study tour with Melissa Ream (an AI expert in health and adviser for this book). We organized the study tour for senior health stakeholders as part of the National Academic Health Science Network AI Program in 2019 to see what we could learn and take back into the UK scenario.

We learned a lot, but, most important of all, we learned how important trust is before data sharing can generate true rewards for people and society. The extraordinary potential of data lies in its value as a tradable public asset or societal good for the benefit of all.

Estonia is a digitally enabled society through its e-Estonia program. Nearly every one of Estonia's 1.3 million citizens has an ID card, which is much more than simply a legal photo ID. Technically, it is a mandatory national card with a chip that carries embedded files, and using 2048-bit public key encryption, it can function as definitive proof of ID in an electronic environment.

Citizens have unparalleled access to a range of digital services through a trusted data exchange (called the "X-Road"), built on an open and secure data architecture. Citizens can lock and unlock access to a range of services and see which professionals have logged in (after granting access).

Estonia was the first nation in history to offer internet voting in a nationwide election in 2005. The i-Voting system allows citizens to vote from any internet-connected computer anywhere in the world. In health, over 95% of the data generated by hospitals and doctors has been digitized, and blockchain technology is used to assure the integrity of stored electronic medical records, as well as system access logs.

Finland is piloting the use of Estonia's X-Road to adopt as its trusted data exchange, enabling it to collaborate beyond borders (why have borders in a digital utopia, right?). It also passed a law in April 2019 allowing for secondary use of data, which will significantly accelerate innovation, particularly with AI.

SITRA, the Finnish innovation agency, is pioneering an ethical open data ecosystem through its work on the **IHAN (International Human Account Network)**[34], a "human-driven data economy" involving the creation of a method for data exchange and a set of European-level rules and guidelines for the ethical use of data.

The IHAN standard is the "human" equivalent of the IBAN banking standard. Finland has a strong well-being culture, empowered through access to data; citizens take far more personal responsibility for their health than most other developed nations as a result.

Overall, these data models all highlight how culture will influence the use of AI in our lives and the role of the citizen versus the role of the state in issues linked to privacy, security, fairness, justice, liberty, and human rights. There is something to learn from all of them.

Countries are paying increasing attention to the ethics of AI. For example, the UK set up the Centre for Data Ethics and Innovation[35] in 2018. Singapore is establishing an advisory council on the ethical use of AI and data[36]. Australia's chief scientist has called for more regulation of AI[37], and the National Institution for Transforming India, an Indian Government think tank, has proposed a consortium of ethics councils[38].

In March 2019, the Leverhulme Centre for the Future of Intelligence published a survey of the EU's AI ecosystem[39], which highlighted the key differences between the EU, US, and China. The report revealed how the EU is more focused on ethics compared to the US and China, but also flagged how its leadership in AI is being hampered through less **Venture Capitalist** (**VC**) investment and startup funding. The EU is beginning to address the funding challenges through such initiatives as the VentureEU fund and the European Fund for Strategic Investment, which may also ease the "brain drain" of talented researchers and developers going to other continents that are able to afford higher salaries through better-funded ventures.

It is clear that brain drain, skills, and jobs will all be impacted by the AI revolution. According to Yuval Noah Harari[40], poorer countries will suffer as there will be less demand for the unskilled labor they've typically provided and the more developed countries will be able to invest in the specialized skills to meet higher demand for jobs in the digital era.

More than a decade ago, Thomas Friedman[41] argued that the force of technology is the key driver in flattening the world. However, according to futurist Azeem Azhar[42], far from flattening the world, technologies have fractalized it, and location matters. Indeed, there are complex geostrategic maneuvers at work between China and America in a world where existing institutions, such as the G7 or United Nations, have less impact.

After months of slogging it out against the US trade sanctions, some of China's most profitable tech companies are looking to reduce their exposure to the US[43]. Recently, the US succeeded in changing Britain's decision to include Huawei as one of its core partners to bring in 5G technology—much to the anger of China. The COVID-19 pandemic is significantly exacerbating these tensions.

# The move from global to local

Azhar predicts that national governments will increasingly insist on adhering to local laws and standards. Indeed, "localism" seems to be in vogue. For example, India is insisting that critical data relating to its businesses and citizens reside within India[44]. In the UK, there are interesting local initiatives being developed through the Connected Health Cities program, which uses a data sharing "consent wireframe" devised and overseen by local citizens, who decide how their data might be shared for anonymized, pseudonymized, and identifiable purposes. The level of transparency enabled through an audit feedback loop (which confirms when personal data was used and what it was used for) has been central to developing and maintaining trust in the system.

Will such examples of "localism" swing the pendulum away from "globalism"? Could we ever create global open standards? Would nations adhere to them?

These are important questions as nations build their capabilities in data and AI to solve the world's problems.

The experience of COVID-19 has also thrown up big questions on state authoritarianism versus citizen empowerment—and privacy is a big concern for many. But the issue at the heart of everything is trust—people need to trust science, business, the government, and the media. People need to trust those institutions that hold such power and influence over their lives.

Taiwan's response to the pandemic is a shining example of how tech can build trust, accountability, and democracy by harnessing citizen action[45]. In the earliest stages of the crisis, a month before the **World Health Organization (WHO)** declared COVID-19 a global pandemic, Howard Wu, a clever "citizen coder," developed a crowdsourcing app using Google Maps where people could input stocks of masks in pharmacies to help people find them. As the app went viral, an equally clever government digital minister, Audrey Tang, spotted the opportunity to extend the availability of masks by distributing them through pharmacies affiliated with Taiwan's **National Health Insurance (NIH)** system, keeping track of them in real time. Tang then created an open-source portal for mask data to be open to the general public and invited other tech activists, in addition to Wu, to contribute too. Taiwan's collectivist approach to dealing with the pandemic is being recognized globally as a leading exemplar showing what open data, open governance, and collaboration between citizens and government can achieve.

# Professor Baron Peter Piot

*World expert in global health; Director of the London School of Hygiene and Tropical Medicine; Handa professor of global health*

I met Peter at the National Academy of Medicine Healthy Longevity Global event that took place on 3-4 February, 2020, in Singapore. I had been asked to speak about the work we were doing with the APPG for Longevity, 10 days before we were due to launch The Health of the Nation Strategy, and I met Peter in one of the breaks.

COVID-19 was definitely "in the air," so to speak, and on people's minds—we had to use sanitizer before entering the conference suite and I remember feeling distinctly uneasy when someone started coughing in the row in front of me at one of the sessions.

Back from Singapore, I followed up with Peter to arrange a coffee in London, and a date was set for 23rd March to meet at his office. This, of course, was a week after the first day of the official UK lockdown on 16th March. Unsurprisingly, Peter was getting immersed in the UK Government's response to COVID-19, and his office asked to reschedule the meeting.

I followed up in April and was told that Peter was unwell, but I did not realize that at the time he was battling the COVID-19 infection himself, suffering terribly from "the revenge of the virus" as he described it when he had recovered.

He wrote about his experience very movingly in *Science* in an article headlined "Finally, a virus got me." He was compelled to publish the piece by a desire to communicate that COVID-19 is about people first and foremost, not just about the statistics that dominated the headlines. He also wanted to highlight that it is potentially far more serious than flu, with chronic morbidity and other long-term sequelae for some.

It turns out that Peter started suffering from the symptoms of COVID-19, including fever and a sharp headache, on 19th March (he had started working from home on the 16th). He tested positive in a private clinic on the 25th March, as he had suspected. Peter initially thought the infection would pass in a straightforward manner, being fit and healthy, with his age (71) being the only risk factor. He continued his work for a while as a special adviser to the European Commission President, Ursula von der Leyen.

But the fever persisted, and complete exhaustion set in and was getting progressively worse. On the recommendation of a doctor friend, Peter went to get examined on 1st April, and discovered he had severe oxygen deficiency and severe pneumonia typical of COVID-19, as well as bacterial pneumonia.

He was hospitalized but tested negative for the virus at that time (this is also typical: the virus disappears, but its consequences linger for weeks).

Peter says this in his personal account: "I shared a room with a homeless person, a Colombian cleaner, and a man from Bangladesh—all three diabetics, incidentally, which is consistent with the known picture of the disease. The days and nights were lonely because no one had the energy to talk...but I always had that question going around in my head: how will I be when I get out of this?....after fighting viruses all over the world for more than 40 years, I have become an expert in infections...they got me, I sometimes thought. I have devoted my life to fighting viruses and finally, they get their revenge."

My interview with Peter was on the 29<sup>th</sup> June. By then, he had been interviewed by many newspapers and broadcasters around the world, including the *New York Times* and the BBC, on his personal experience and what the pandemic is teaching the world. I was obviously very grateful to Peter that he kept our appointment!

Peter has an extraordinary background. His official biography is rich with the numerous prestigious posts he has held over his 40 years as an expert, but what stands out is his pursuit of access to health for all.

Peter co-discovered the Ebola virus in Zaire in 1976 while working at the Institute of Tropical Medicine in Antwerp. He was one of the leading critics of the UK, UN, and WHO's response to the Ebola outbreak in West Africa in 2014, which he thought was too slow. In 2014, he was named "TIME Person of the Year" ("The Ebola Fighters").

He also led research on HIV/AIDS, sexually transmitted diseases, and women's health, mostly in sub-Saharan Africa. He was the founding executive director of UNAIDS and Under-Secretary-General of the UN from 1995 to 2008, and an associate director of the Global Program on AIDS of WHO.

Under his leadership, UNAIDS became the chief advocate for worldwide action against AIDS, also spearheading UN reform by bringing together 10 UN system organizations.

Peter is the first chair of Her Majesty's Government's **Strategic Coherence of ODA-funded Research (SCOR)** board and is also a special advisor to the president of the European Commission on research and innovation for COVID-19. He is a member of the board for the **Coalition for Epidemic Preparedness Innovations (CEPI)**.

Peter has published over 600 scientific articles and 17 books, including his memoir *No Time to Lose* in 2012 and *AIDS Between Science and Politics* in 2015.

**Tina Woods**: You've been in the field of virology for so many years. You've seen viruses grip communities and nations, and then suddenly you caught COVID-19 yourself; what surprised you about the experience? Did your experience as a patient match up to what you would have expected as a professional?

**Peter Piot**: Good question; I actually never expected I would get ill! I've never been ill in my whole life, or seriously sick, so I've been lucky at 71. I never thought about it. I didn't assume I was invincible or immune to COVID-19, but getting sick was just not on my radar screen. When I got it, I thought—as I believe the majority of people thought, as the consensus was then—that I'd be OK. I thought that with COVID-19, either you're asymptomatic or it's a bit like the flu, or sometimes a bad flu; 1% of those infected die, and they're older people anyway, and they have pre-existing conditions.

We were primed to think of it as if those deaths don't count. The more I thought about it afterward, I got really angry at some points. It's a very eugenic discourse and that's reflected in how in many countries—including the UK—care homes were treated seriously, or not. That's actually one of the reasons I came out of the shadows to talk about this.

I told the world that there is a lot in between. This disease is much more nuanced, and there's a lot of chronic sequelae—chronic conditions that could be with you forever that hang around as a result of this disease.

On the other hand, once I was admitted to the hospital, I became a patient 100%. I didn't try to be the doctor. I've said before that I'm not the type of person who tells a taxi driver which route to take.

**Tina Woods**: Yeah! You let them look after you, then?

**Peter Piot**: I let them do their job, yes.

I was also so exhausted, and actually quite confused, so I was not capable of thinking clearly. I think, retrospectively, it was a good experience. I mean, it was a terrifying experience, yes, but it was good to feel the virus inside, and not just look at it and try to defeat it, in some way or another, from the outside.

My mother tongue is Dutch, and we have this term "ervaringsdeskundige," which means "experience expert." It comes from the social side of government, from social policy-making. You wouldn't dream of developing policies for, let's say, the elderly, by only speaking to experts and not by involving people who are old. I come from the AIDS movement, and people living with HIV have been involved from really quite early on as part of our reaction to HIV/AIDS.

I think what getting infected has also done for me is make it clear that the official communication on COVID-19 has not been about people; it's been about flattening the curve. Certainly, the UK was probably an extreme example; you had ministers, even the Prime Minister, giving lectures about the reproductive rate ($R_0$) and flattening the curve. It was about saving the NHS, and so on; and then, as an afterthought, it was about saving lives.

That's why I think there was so much interest in my story. I gave the first interview to a Flemish weekly magazine, because I'm very well known in Belgium, and that was to help raise awareness. Then, when the interview was taken up by *Science*, it got millions of views. That was very interesting to me; it showed that there was a gap in the whole communication strategy and the storytelling.

**Tina Woods**: Where do you think, internationally, the public health messages were right? I know we certainly have got it wrong in the UK on a number of fronts, but what do you think the message should have been?

**Peter Piot**: Well, of course, the benefit of hindsight is always there. I'm probably a bit milder than many other people about all the mistakes we've collectively made, but the most important message is that the severity of this epidemic is unprecedented. I think that the communication of that message wasn't very well done.

I gave some talks about this with non-health experts in Singapore, but I don't think people internalize how contagious it is. Because of that, acting early is one of the most important things. That's one lesson that's particularly true for anything that's contagious; if you can nip it in the bud, you basically prevent not only the next generation of infections but the $n^{th}$ generation. In essence, by preventing transmission in the beginning, you can prevent the whole chain that comes afterward.

COVID-19 also illustrates how important it is to prevent the development of obesity, diabetes, and cardiovascular disease through healthy lifestyles. I probably was lucky because I am not ill; I have no underlying conditions.

On the other hand, I got some messages from friends saying, "You'll be fine; you're a strong person."

In the hospital, I'm there thinking, "Well, there are certain things that your body does that are not under your control." You can't do anything at that moment of crisis, but you can make yourself more resilient as an individual or as a society.

The most important lesson for a government is to act early and at a scale that makes a difference, and an accompanying issue is maintaining enough trust in the government to do that. That's a big difference in what we've been seeing in Eastern Asia compared to Europe. There's one thing they had in Singapore, in Hong Kong, in Taiwan, and in South Korea: the SARS experience.

**Tina Woods**: Of course, they learned a lot from that.

**Peter Piot**: Yes, but we've also had lots of events to learn from. Afterward, we always say, "No, never ever again," and so on, and then we start again as if it were erased. Where SARS hit, those people learned from it, but more importantly, they set up a system to be ready when the next thing happened. It's not enough to learn and to say that we'll remember; you need to institutionalize that.

Internalizing the necessary changes, and making them part of the culture, is another essential element in making these changes stick. For example, in Japan, since the Spanish flu, people wear face masks even when they have a stupid cold to avoid infecting others. It's become part of the collective consciousness, and part of what's considered good behavior for the community.

**Tina Woods**: The masks are worn in a sense of collectivism, for the public good, then?

**Peter Piot**: Yes, the collective good. When in Japan, or in Singapore, people wear a face mask or a mouth mask, but it's not to protect themselves: it's to avoid infecting others. It took me a while to understand that; I've been going to Japan and East Asia for a long, long time, and at first, I thought, "These are people who are scared of others." I was completely wrong.

I've had a very hard time understanding the resistance to face masks and mouth masks. It's there in individuals as well as governments. I think in the UK, they still haven't said that it's compulsory [*this advice has partially changed since this interview*] and you can even hear resistance from scientists who say that the evidence is weak, and so on and so forth.

But they're cheap, there are no side effects, you can even make it yourself, and it can be sexy!

**Tina Woods**: I have seen some sexy face masks and some real creativity there! I think, if nothing else, it's a reminder of the fact that this is serious. That's what I found when I put the face mask on; initially, I found it very odd, but it's a very good reminder.

**Peter Piot**: I wear it as a reminder, too. I'm not contagious to anybody, and I assume I can't be infected because I have immunity.

**Tina Woods**: Is that true, though? Do we know for sure how long the immunity lasts?

**Peter Piot**: There's a lot we don't know, but frankly, if that's not the case, then a vaccine is impossible. In any case, I wear my mask whenever I go into a cubicle or an inside space in a shop because we go every morning to buy bread and vegetables, and what have you. I also always wear it on public transport, just as a way to let people know that hey, this change is coming.

**Tina Woods**: I think the key messages in what you've said are that governments and individuals need to act early, and that prevention, by remaining in good health, is important. Is there anything else you want to add to that?

**Peter Piot**: We need to be ready, meaning that we have a combination of systems in place: real-time intelligence on what is going on, cultural attitudes, and mental preparation. I think that these are the key issues. As a general reflection, you can assume that societies that are more cohesive are more resilient and are therefore better prepared for shocks like this.

**Tina Woods**: The sheer level of infections and deaths in care homes was a bit shocking, wasn't it? What do you think it told us about our values as a society?

**Peter Piot**: It was very shocking. As I've said, my work on HIV and epidemics has revealed how they exacerbate the fault lines in society, and make inequalities worse.

With COVID-19, the fault line that worsened the most in my opinion was how we treat our elderly; on the other hand, it revealed once again the higher vulnerability of ethnic minorities. Although we haven't totally understood why that's the case, in the US, a big part of that vulnerability is due to limited access to care. In the UK, that factor's a bit less important because we've got the NHS, but there are still maybe some genetic factors, as well as social discrimination and other social factors that are relevant. However, we've seen the higher vulnerability of ethnic minorities being exacerbated by different epidemics before.

The way the elderly have been affected by COVID-19, though, is something new. I mean that in the sense that I can't think of anything else that has revealed just how badly we are dealing with our elderly citizens. I've been in elderly care homes, though I'm not familiar with the British system. I know the Belgian system, because my parents were part of that before they died. My mother died in September, but she died with dignity, at a moment that she had chosen to die, which is something that's been possible in Belgium since '96. The economic situation and the housing situation mean that for most people, it's no longer possible to have, say, three generations in one home as used to be the case. So, what do we do when you're no longer productive, or when you become a bit of a nuisance for everybody? We park you in a pre-mortuary type of institution.

If you've got the money, then you can have even a butler and all that. There is an enormous class dimension in the quality of these institutions. But if you seriously think about it, this is how your old age is going to be; how comfortable you are in it depends on whether you have the money to affect it. Plus, of course, it depends whether you're abandoned by your family, and so on. Another revealer of this problem we have with how we treat our elderly citizens was the heatwaves in France in 2019. I read articles about old people who died during those heatwaves on their own, and it took two or three weeks to find out they were dead. It's so sad, this loneliness.

I think that it's interesting in the UK that the Department of Health changed its name to the Department of Health and Social Care in 2018. I never got a sense that social care was taken seriously budgetary-wise, and I'm a bit surprised when you look at it politically because older people are first in politics. They vote the most; they put pressure on their MPs; and they're well organized in many countries. Despite that, social care has been absent from the agenda of the politically active older generation. I never understood that. It may be completely unfair what I'm saying because it's a field I'm only viewing from the outside. I don't know for sure, but I've never seen a campaign in the media, or people testifying to how bad it is.

**Tina Woods**: All the data shows it's the most vulnerable who are hardest hit by COVID-19: those in deprived areas, the elderly, and the already unwell. Do you think there are any long-lasting changes that will come out of this pandemic?

**Peter Piot**: Well, I always have hope, I'm an optimist. Experience shows that it's not always the case. That's why it's important, I think, to understand that today we're in the midst of a crisis. It's not over. With this pandemic, we're only at the beginning; we're right in the midst of it. That means it's definitely worthwhile to take stock now and learn for the next wave. We need to put in place now, or start a discussion about, what we need not only for this next wave but also for the next epidemic, in 5 years' or 10 years' time. We need to start now, and not wait until it's all over, and when it no longer has any use.

**Tina Woods**: There's been a rise in nationalism and putting one's own country first during the pandemic, but there's a culture of openness that we need in terms of data sharing to help stop future pandemics. What do you think nations, and the global community of nations, need to do moving forward?

**Peter Piot**: First of all, we need to take a good and hard look at what happened. That's not about who's to blame—I don't think that's very useful—but about what the lessons are that we can learn.

We need to consider the immediate future, and the next outbreaks and waves. Next, we can start thinking in the longer term. For example, take Germany in Europe. I think Germany and Denmark probably had and have the best responses, and that's reflected in the lowest death rates and the lowest infection rates.

Part of that might be the backgrounds of the leaders—the German leader is a physicist. I'm not saying that people with a medical or scientific background make better politicians, but I do think there is an immediate understanding there of what needs doing; there is far more resolute leadership early on. There's been an interesting combination of strong national leadership and local implementation in the individual Länder, the federal areas of Germany. The central leadership gave a lot of resources and authority to local authorities.

In the UK—I knew this, but I hadn't understood how bad it is—it's a hyper-centralized country. No wonder Public Health England wanted to control everything to do with testing, and no wonder they were unable to do it, particularly since it was a home-based test. They weren't working with businesses, or with private firms, or with universities and labs. It's all about logistics, organization, and coordination when dealing with pandemics; it's all about communication. Government test stats show that these are not strengths of governments in general. Letting go is essential. By that, I mean that the UK Government needs to provide the resources, have the policies, take the decisions, and then let people do things. That's what's happened in other countries.

**Tina Woods**: That's something that we're also exploring in the All-Party Parliamentary Group that we're doing with the Health of the Nation: building up resilience for the next epidemic, with this concept we're calling decentralized health resilience. It's about health in our communities, starting individually with taking care of ourselves and building up from there and mobilizing local and regional networks to act quickly. There's a role for central leadership, but the implementation is very much driven from the ground up. Which countries are effective models that we could look to for inspiration, moving forward?

**Peter Piot**: National leadership is the easier one in a sense, because countries that have done well have seen strong leadership at the top. That's why when people say this is a public health crisis, I say no, this is a societal crisis, which requires the leadership of whoever is in charge in the country—prime minister, president, or whatever. We've seen it in Singapore, in Thailand, in South Korea, and in Vietnam.

There's another interesting lesson in the transition to the second part: Vietnam is a hyper-centralized society and politically controlled, yet the response has been very locally driven. Rather than to go for a nationwide lockdown, they did it sometimes as locally as by neighborhood, by company, by factory, or by schools. Rather than go for the bulldozer approach, which we've been using in Europe, they went for a more granular, more targeted or tailor-made approach. That's, I think, where we are now. This consensus is what we need to cope with the second wave and with particular local outbreaks. You used the term "localized resilience," is that correct?

**Tina Woods**: Decentralized health resilience. It's an approach where you're building from the bottom upward; it's this notion of decentralized networks.

**Peter Piot**: I like that a lot. I mean, it's nice to have the NHS, but it's also problematic to have the NHS as it is now with the hyper-centralized system. When you go to procurement and action, it's too slow and it's too heavy. And I never understood why one of the strengths of the NHS, primary care and GPs, who are much more connected to the community than hospitals, were excluded from the response.

**Tina Woods**: What key legacy points, moving forward, do you think we need to take on board as a country?

**Peter Piot**: I think we need to mobilize resources, not just money, to invest in new systems. In the UK, we can see that Public Health England is not fully equipped to the task. Frankly, its budget—the budget for public health and for the prevention of disease—has been cut. (*Since this interview, the decision was taken in August 2020 to disband Public Health England; in its place will be the formation of* **National Institute for Health Protection** (**NIHP**) *that will absorb the pandemic response unit of PHE and combine it with the NHS Test and Trace service and the Joint Biosecurity Centre.*) This is not recent. This has been going on, I think, from even when Labor was in power. I think it's been going down every year, because there's pressure to put money into the NHS into curative things, rather than prevention (since 2014, it is estimated that £850 million has been cut from public health budgets in England[46]). That's also why care for the elderly and for others has been left out. Then, we spend all that money when someone from a care home has to be hospitalized, at enormous cost.

It doesn't make sense. Working out how to fix that, in political terms, is massively important.

**Tina Woods**: Is it fair to say that one of the key takeaways from the pandemic is that we need to focus more on prevention?

**Peter Piot**: Absolutely. But then, you see the rhetoric again; the UK Prime Minister, Boris Johnson, said, "We are going to build 100 new hospitals." I'm not sure that we need that, but that's very concrete. Compare that to saying, "We are going to cut obesity and diabetes and so on, by doing this and that." They're not very popular measures, but would contribute far more to the health of the nation than 100 hospitals. I am pleased to see that the PM and the Government are now going to tackle obesity.

**Tina Woods**: Do you think viruses sometimes get overlooked when we talk about planetary health and respecting the environment?

**Peter Piot**: Of course. I'm biased because I've spent much of my professional life dealing with viruses, but they do, it's true.

I remember when I was in my last year in medical school in Ghent in Belgium, and I did some of what today would be called career counseling; I don't think that term existed in '73! I said I wanted to study infectious diseases, and I wanted to specialize in that. All my professors said, "No, no, no! There's no future in infectious diseases. We've got antibiotics. We've got hygiene and vaccines." I still went for it, being a bit stubborn and thinking that you need to follow your passion.

There are cancers caused by viruses. When you think of liver cancer, you should think of hepatitis C; cervical cancer is caused by human papillomavirus. We have a cancer that's preventable through a vaccine, and really, isn't that wonderful? Looking at the take-up of the HPV vaccine in some countries, Britain is doing very well on that one.

I think we will see that more and more things are linked to viruses, and not only viruses but the whole microbiome (this is the aggregate of microbes—bacteria, fungi, and viruses—and potentially harmful ones, but mostly helpful ones). It's not just that an evil virus is attacking us—we need to understand it in the context of the wider microbiome. There is a kind of harmony of microbes in our guts—and there are more and more indications that something like that harmony exists with viruses as well.

**Tina Woods**: When it comes to the human impact on biodiversity, what do you think is the most important thing to understand from the general citizen's perspective?

**Peter Piot**: One extreme perspective is that these epidemics, these emerging infections, come from animals. In large part they come about because of risky interactions between animals and people, and sometimes extremely risky ones in poorer parts of the world. That's true in Central Africa, where everywhere people eat the proteins that are surrounding them, but also in China with the consumption of even threatened species. There's that, plus the whole modern food industry.

I'm not a vegetarian, but when you think about it, the way that food is produced and sold in the modern era is a very high-risk business. In the old days, when a small farmer had a few chickens dying from a microbe, that was bad for him and for the chickens. Today, you have literally a million chickens in one farm and they're sent all over the world. Industrial farming increases our risk of exposure, and the potential for novel viruses. That's one aspect.

On the other hand, we live in a completely obesogenic environment. That's certainly the case in Western countries, but also, increasingly, elsewhere. Think of the fact that even in Africa now—in South Africa—the percentage of women who are obese is as high as in the US.

All that together, plus the ever-looming threat of climate change, means that we really need to question, fundamentally, how we live and what we do and don't do. This is where planetary health is becoming very important as a concept. The question is how to translate that into action in the environment.

**Tina Woods**: So, if you had to pick one core message that you would want to say to the average punter about planetary health, what would you say?

**Peter Piot**: In order to have a better future for everybody, we need to not only work on our own health but also respect the health of the planet. That means thinking about biodiversity, how we consume food, how we produce it, and respecting the environment. I learned a lot about that from the Navajo and Hopi, and it had a big impact on me, particularly since they are so poor. I think that the core message is moving away from thinking we're the masters of the universe and everything around us. We need to stop thinking the universe is at our disposal and we can do whatever we want with it.

**Tina Woods**: Going back to health resilience: we've seen how huge a risk poor health is, on its own but also with the epidemic. Do you think we need a risk management framework for health like we have for climate change? Health is where the climate change agenda was 10 years ago—shouldn't we be guiding investment and innovation decisions by ESG mandates, like we do for climate change, and applying them to health?

**Peter Piot**: This seems essential. In terms of risk management for COVID-19, I think that there's some serious cognitive dissonance around it; there's this idea that we're going to end this epidemic, eliminate it, wipe it out with a vaccine, and so on. I don't think it's realistic. We need to see, as a society, that it's about harm reduction and about risk management. I think that's true for everything because I'm also realistic enough to know that we need jobs and employment. People need to move around. It's something I'd like to read more about.

**Tina Woods**: One final question: how have you changed your lifestyle since getting ill, and what is your secret for a healthy, long life now that you've gone through what you have?

**Peter Piot**: I think I'm looking for a better work-life balance—although I've not been very successful! Right now, frankly, I'm still in recovery. I'm rebuilding strength. There's no qualitative difference in my lifestyle yet, but I'm trying to do more exercise. I'm paying more attention to all kinds of things. I lost seven kilos with COVID, which is more than I ever succeeded in doing with exercise and diet, so I will try to keep it that way. I think that's a question to ask me again at the end of the year, to see whether I actually followed up on my intentions!

# Final thoughts

Citizens have a crucial role to play ahead in shaping the "new normal" and choosing between nationalist isolation or global solidarity. The epidemic itself and the resulting economic chaos are a global problem that can only be addressed through collaboration—and we should take stock of how more "collectivist" countries are weathering the pandemic storm far better than the more "individualist" countries are to date.

In order to beat COVID-19 and minimize future viral threats, we need to share information globally. But we also need to act locally to harness trust from our citizens, building individual and community resilience—and from there national health resilience. The concept of decentralized, or distributed, health resilience is something we will explore in this book.

Scientific cooperation has exploded in the quest to understand what puts people at risk of infection, why some suffer more than others, and what treatments and vaccines might be able to prevent further deaths. The next chapter will lay the groundwork on the science of aging, including the role of genomics and regenerative medicine, as well as more ethereal considerations on what gives us the "will to live."

# References

1. *The Secret of How Life on Earth Began, Michael Marshall, BBC,* 31 October 2016, `http://www.bbc.com/earth/story/20161026-the-secret-of-how-life-on-earth-began`

2. *A new view of the tree of life, Hug et al, Nature,* 11 April 2016, `https://www.nature.com/articles/nmicrobiol201648`

3.  *Researchers see history of life in the structure of transfer RNA, University of Illinois*, March 7 2008, https://phys.org/news/2008-03-history-life-rna.html

4.  *Viruses share genes with organisms across the tree of life, University of Illinois*, December 6 2017, https://phys.org/news/2017-12-viruses-genes-tree-life.html

5.  *The Book of Life will be the century's most valuable enterprise, Financial Times*, https://www.ft.com/content/e45fd96a-d3a9-11e9-8d46-8def889b4137

6.  *Engineering an Inclusive Bioeconomy, Khanna et al, Harvard Faculty & Research*, August 2020, https://www.hbs.edu/faculty/Pages/item.aspx?num=56652

7.  *New Partnership Aims to Sequence Genomes of All Life on Earth, Unlock Nature's Value, Tackle Bio-Piracy and Habitat Loss, Fon Mathuros, World Economic Forum*, 23 January 2018, https://www.weforum.org/press/2018/01/new-partnership-aims-to-sequence-genomes-of-all-life-on-earth-unlock-nature-s-value-tackle-bio-piracy-and-habitat-loss/

8.  *Data trusts raise questions on privacy and governance, Jane Croft, Financial Times*, September 13 2019, https://www.ft.com/content/a683b8e4-a3ef-11e9-a282-2df48f366f7d

9.  *New Tech Is Giving Humanity Many Potential Paths to Immortality, Tom Ward, Futurism*, August 17 2017, https://futurism.com/new-tech-is-giving-humanity-many-potential-paths-to-immortality

10. *DNA Sequencing Costs: Data, National Human Genome Research Institute*, 2020, https://www.genome.gov/about-genomics/fact-sheets/DNA-Sequencing-Costs-Data

11. *How is AI decoding aging?, Alex Zhavoronkov, medium. com,* May 3 2019, `https://medium.com/faces-of-digital-health/f036-how-is-ai-decoding-aging-490bd8524675`

12. *Artificial intelligence for aging and longevity research: Recent advances and perspectives, Zhavoronkov et al, Science Direct,* November 2018, `https://www.sciencedirect.com/science/article/pii/S156816371830240X?via%3Dihub`

13. *Deep learning enables rapid identification of potent DDR1 kinase inhibitors, Zhavoronkov et al, Nature,* 02 September 2019, `https://www.nature.com/articles/s41587-019-0224-x`

14. *Longevity, Thomas Theodore Samaras, Epigenetics of Aging and Longevity,* 2018, `https://www.sciencedirect.com/topics/biochemistry-genetics-and-molecular-biology/longevity`

15. *Binocular Convergence, An Osteopathic Approach to Children (Second Edition),* 2009, `https://www.sciencedirect.com/topics/biochemistry-genetics-and-molecular-biology/binocular-convergence`

16. *IoT Supporters Envision A Trillion-Sensor World, Matt Bail, Informed Infrastructure,* 2013, `https://informedinfrastructure.com/6547/iot-supporters-envision-a-trillion-sensor-world/`

17. *Amazon and Apple will be our doctors in the future, says tech guru Peter Diamandis, Ruth Reader, Fast Company,* 12 November 2019, `https://www.fastcompany.com/90440921/amazon-and-apple-will-be-our-doctors-in-the-future-says-tech-guru-peter-diamandis`

18. *Gartner highlights AI among its top 10 strategic Internet of Things trends, Anasia D'Mello, iot-now,* 8 November 2018, `https://www.iot-now.com/2018/11/08/90245-gartner-reveals-top-10-strategic-iot-technologies-trends-itxpo/`

19. *Amazon launches Amazon Care, a virtual medical clinic for employees, Christina Farr, CNBC,* 24 September 2019, `https://www.cnbc.com/2019/09/24/amazon-launches-employee-health-clinic-amazon-care.html`

20. *Everything we know about Haven, the Amazon joint venture to revamp health care, Christina Farr, CNBC,* 13 March 2019, `https://www.cnbc.com/2019/03/13/what-is-haven-amazon-jpmorgan-berkshire-revamp-health-care.html`

21. *Google Life Sciences Rebrands As Verily, Uses Big Data To Figure Out Why We Get Sick, Sean Captain, Fast Company,* 12 July 2015, `https://www.fastcompany.com/3054352/google-life-sciences-rebrands-as-verily-uses-big-data-to-figure-out-why-we-get-si`

22. *Google Fit gets ready to take on the Apple Watch, Jared Newman, Fast Company,* 21 August 2018, `https://www.fastcompany.com/90222193/google-fit-gets-ready-to-take-on-the-apple-watch`

23. *AlphaFold: Using AI for scientific discovery, DeepMind blog post,* 15 January 2020, `https://deepmind.com/blog/article/AlphaFold-Using-AI-for-scientific-discovery`

24. *Protein misfolding and aggregation in Alzheimer's disease and type 2 diabetes mellitus, Ashraf et al, National Library of Medicine,* 2014, `https://pubmed.ncbi.nlm.nih.gov/25230234/`

25. *Misfolded protein transmits Parkinson's from cell to cell, Virginia Hughes, Nature*, 15 November 2012, `https://www.nature.com/news/misfolded-protein-transmits-parkinson-s-from-cell-to-cell-1.11838`

26. *Revised view of Huntington's protein misfolding mechanism, Stu Borman, C&EN*, 2 October 2017, `https://cen.acs.org/articles/95/i39/Revised-view-Huntingtons-protein-misfolding.html`

27. *Cystic fibrosis – a multiorgan protein misfolding disease, Fraser-Pitt & O'Neil, Future Science OA*, 1 September 2015, `https://www.ncbi.nlm.nih.gov/pmc/articles/PMC5137970/`

28. *ELON MUSK'S AI PROJECT TO REPLICATE THE HUMAN BRAIN RECEIVES $1 BILLION FROM MICROSOFT, Anthony Cuthbertson, Independent*, 23 July 2019, `https://www.independent.co.uk/life-style/gadgets-and-tech/news/elon-musk-ai-openai-microsoft-artificial-intelligence-funding-a9016736.html`

29. *Nick Bostrom on Superintelligence and the Future of AI, Nick Bostrom, Freethink*, 3 December 2019, `https://www.freethink.com/shows/uprising/future-of-ai-superintelligence`

30. *China on verge of becoming AI superpower as investment closes in on US, Olivia Rudgard, The Telegraph*, 12 December 2019, `https://www.telegraph.co.uk/technology/2019/12/12/china-verge-becoming-ai-superpower-investment-closes-us/`

31. *WeChat Revenue and Usage Statistics (2020), Mansoor Iqbal, Business of Apps*, 30 July 2020, `https://www.businessofapps.com/data/wechat-statistics/`

32. *China's internet is flowering, and it might be our future,* Yiren Lu, *New York Times,* 13 November 2019, `https:// www.nytimes.com/interactive/2019/11/13/ magazine/internet-china-wechat.html`

33. *China's social credit system, South China Morning post* `https://www.scmp.com/topics/chinas-social- credit-system`

34. *IHAN – proof of concept pilots, SITRA,* `https:// www.sitra.fi/en/projects/ihan-proof-concept- pilots/`

35. *Consultation on the Centre for Data Ethics and Innovation, UK government,* 20 November 2018, `https://www.gov.uk/government/consultations/ consultation-on-the-centre-for-data-ethics- and-innovation`

36. *Artificial Intelligence Governance and Ethics Initiatives, Singapore Government,* 8 November 2019, `https:// www.imda.gov.sg/news-and-events/Media-Room/ Media-Releases/2018/artificial-intelligence- governance-and-ethics-initiatives`

37. *Australia's chief scientist calls for AI regulations, Beverley Head, ComputerWeekly.com,* 5 June 2018, `https://www. computerweekly.com/news/252442528/Australias- chief-scientist-calls-for-AI-regulations`

38. *India is a latecomer to AI, Here's how it plans to catch up, Utkarsh Amitabh, World Economic Forum,* 14 June 2018, `https://www.weforum.org/agenda/2018/06/ india-latecomer-artificial-intelligence-niti- aayog/`

39. *Writing, Charlotte Stix, Personal blog,* `https://www. charlottestix.com/european-union-ai-ecosystem`

40. *Who Will Win the Race for AI?, Yuval Noah Harari, Global Thinkers,* `https://foreignpolicy.com/gt- essay/who-will-win-the-race-for-ai-united- states-china-data/`

41. *The World is Flat: Some Second Thoughts, Thomas Friedman, address to Williams College,* April 2006, `https://www.youtube.com/watch?v=4kTXwxwO8hY`

42. *The world is spiky, Azeem Azhar, Exponential View,* 13 December 2019, `https://www.exponentialview.co/p/-the-world-is-spiky`

43. *Chinese companies boost self-reliance as trade war with US rolls on, The Straits Times,* 12 December 2019, `https://www.straitstimes.com/business/economy/chinese-companies-boost-self-reliance-as-trade-war-with-us-rolls-on`

44. *Are data localization norms in sync with India's Cloud vision? IANS, New Indian Express,* 18 October 2019, `https://www.newindianexpress.com/lifestyle/tech/2019/oct/18/are-data-localisation-norms-in-sync-with-indias-cloud-vision-2049482.html`

45. *How Taiwan's Unlikely Digital Minister Hacked the Pandemic, Andrew Leonard, Wired,* 23 July 2020, `https://www.wired.com/story/how-taiwans-unlikely-digital-minister-hacked-the-pandemic/`

46. *Hitting the poorest worst? How public health cuts have been experienced in England's most deprived communities, Chris Thomas, IPPR,* November 2019, `https://www.ippr.org/blog/public-health-cuts`

47. *Amazon could soon force you to go on a diet, according to one futurist, Katharine Schwab, Fast Company,* 21 March 2019, `https://www.fastcompany.com/90322180/amazon-could-soon-force-you-to-go-on-a-diet-according-to-one-futurist`

48. *Amazon announces Halo, a fitness band and app that scans your body and voice, Dieter Bohn, The Verge,* August 2020, `https://www.theverge.com/2020/8/27/21402493/amazon-halo-band-health-fitness-body-scan-tone-emotion-activity-sleep`

# CHAPTER 2

# WHO WE ARE –
# AND WHAT
# DRIVES US

*"Gilgamesh went after death itself... It's the original hero's journey, which everyone in modern society is familiar with whether that's through Marvel movies or Star Wars.... It's literally the story of humanity, and we are blessed to be alive in this unique pivotal moment. We shouldn't take that for granted."*

*– Keith Comito, President, Lifespan.io*

*"It's important to look at biomarkers or aging clocks.... They are the predictors of biological aging at every level: molecular, psychological, and societal. AI will give us the ability to identify specific areas where we can intervene.... Once you realize what kind of impact this field can have, and what kind of tragedy a delay could cause, stopping due to ethical arguments would be a crime against humanity."*

*– Alex Zhavoronkov, CEO, Insilico Medicine*

So, where do we begin?

Curiosity has driven humans to understand where we come from, who we are, and where we want to go in future. Right now, it seems we are in a race to catapult Homo sapiens into "Homo extraordinarius," and there are respected thinkers with astonishing predictions for the near future.

According to Yuval Noah Harari, author of best-selling *Sapiens: A Brief History of Humankind*[1], human beings are all algorithms, and AI will overtake human beings. He reckons Homo sapiens will continue to evolve in the age of digital in one of two ways[2]. The first is that we use technology to augment ourselves into "superhumans." The second is that we become something completely distinct from what we are at the moment—a new species spawned through AI. This new species would be inorganic but still living, breaking all the rules of life that has evolved organically for over four billion years. If this new non-organic living entity became more powerful and more intelligent than humans, Darwinian evolutionary theory says this new species would take over. Is this science fiction or could it actually happen?

Peter Diamandis is best known for being the founder and chairman of the X Prize Foundation, as well as the co-founder and executive chairman of Singularity University. He says we are moving from "simple Darwinian natural selection to intelligent direction and meta-intelligence"[3]. Diamandis has a theory of the next stage of humanity's evolution in four stages with parallels to previous evolutionary stages of life on Earth: 1) progression of our interconnected world; 2) development of brain-computer interface (BCI technology); 3) application of BCI with AI for 'meta-intelligence' in which we are all highly connected brain to brain via the cloud; and 4) man becoming an interplanetary species reaching the final frontier of space. He argues that in the next 30 years, humanity will move from the first stage—where we are today—to the fourth stage.

I believe the idea of creating Homo extraordinarius, or a new superintelligent species is still a little way off despite Harari's and Diamandis' prognostications. Today, most of the AIs we use are "narrow." Machines can perform particular tasks (such as beating a human at Go) but we are yet to create machines which have broad general intelligence, which is to say machines that can turn their intelligence to novel tasks. We've not yet created consciousness in an AI; we have not yet created intelligent life. However, scientists think that day is not far away, creating excitement for many, but concerns for others such as the late Stephen Hawking.

Before we delve into where we might be going, I want to talk first about where we have come from and what we are born with: our genetic code. Our understanding of what makes each of us exquisitely unique has exploded in recent years, and expanded exponentially with the help of AI. But AI isn't just a dream for the future that might create new forms of life—it's a tool in the present, capable of changing the lives we lead right now.

In this first chapter, I want to take you from a baseline appreciation of genomics, including what our genes can and cannot tell us about our future, and show you how advances in computational biology and epigenetics are taking us into a new zone of understanding the aging process and exploiting opportunities to live much longer. Some are trying to conquer immortality, but most of us are still trying to understand what makes a good mortal life.

# The Genomics Revolution

*"I think the number one thing you can do for your happiness is look after your health. People invest in mobile phones; they invest in cars; they invest in holidays; but people neglect their own health.*

> *I've seen people happily spend a couple of hundred*
> *pounds for a tracksuit. But for that same money, you can*
> *go and get a full blood works test... I think that putting*
> *a little bit of money aside every month to put into your*
> *health is probably one of the best things you can do."*
>
> *– Eddie Hall, World's Strongest Man, Epigenetics*
> *Evangelist*

The genomics revolution is here, and the research is being accelerated by the use of AI. Literally every day, new ways are being discovered in which we can make the most of our genetic inheritance.

My mother used to take pride in the fact that I was quite tall. At the age of ten I was already taller than her, and she's 5'3". I am now 5'11", and of my three sons the shortest is 6'3" and the tallest is 6'7". I remember at the age of ten someone asking my mother "what is in her genes?" I had heard "jeans," so of course worriedly looked down, blushing, to see if there was some visible rip or stain about to humiliate me in public.

Fast forward a few years later and I was studying genetics at Cornell, fascinated with the "recipe" we get from our parents, and their parents, and so on, the instructions for what makes us. I have always been fascinated with this idea that we are created from this intricate blueprint of life. At university I remember countless trips to the lab, grouping and counting drosophila flies; I didn't come up with anything ground-breaking then, but years later in 2017, researchers discovered that a genetic mutation called the **E(z)** gene leads to increased lifespan in fruit flies[4] by up to 20%.

The genetic blueprint for drosophila—let alone humans—has been years in the making. Billions of years. The earliest prokaryotic life (simple, single-cell creatures without even a nucleus) appeared about 3.5 billion years ago; even if we look at a closer ancestor, it's been 400 million years since the first vertebrate fish species emerged from the ocean, bringing complex life out of the water and onto the land.

I heard Laura Deming, the Founder of Longevity VC, speak recently, and immediately afterwards introduced myself to her. She has a personal obsession with understanding this evolutionary process and its connection to longevity. The first point she makes on her excellent website (`https://www.ldeming.com/longevityfaq`) is that "As you get older, the chance that you will die goes up." So simple, yet so true. When she was living in her native New Zealand she became fascinated by the fact that mutant genes could make nematode worms live longer, and at the age of 12 (when I first discovered the difference between "jeans" and "genes") she had already been accepted into Cynthia Kenyon's lab in Silicon Valley to study this in more detail. After helping Dr Kenyon for 2 years Laura went on to study at MIT before starting Longevity Fund (`https://www.longevity.vc/`), the first VC firm dedicated to funding high-potential longevity companies, in 2011. Laura is a child prodigy and an incredible person. I wonder if she has done a DNA test to try and understand where she gets her curiosity from?

## Testing your DNA

Testing your DNA is now mainstream. According to MIT Review[5], more than 26 million consumers in the USA alone had added their DNA to four leading commercial ancestry and health databases by the start of 2019. One of the reasons DNA testing kits have taken off is because the cost of genome sequencing has come down to about $100, which has enabled a torrent of companies to get in the business of offering DNA testing to the masses who can now afford them. I personally know the CEOs and founders of quite a few of them, like Chronomics and Muhdo.

So, what can you learn about yourself when you take a DNA test? And what can you do as a result of this information?

Your DNA is what is also called the genome—think of your body as hardware, and DNA as the software that runs the machine.

Our DNA comprises a sequence of 3.2 billion letters made up of the nucleotides adenine, thymine, cytosine, and guanine, or As, Ts, Cs, and Gs; DNA determines everything from the color of your eyes, hair and skin to your risk of disease, and even affects the type of personality you might have.

People are now using it to set their diet and even for dating! Further down the line, as more studies are conducted and more data is analyzed with the help of AI, "polygenic risk scores" will help us rank our genetic potential for everything from getting Alzheimer's to being a genius (and you can imagine the ethical minefield already happening around the idea of "designer babies").

Polygenic risk scores are metrics that collect information from tens, hundreds, thousands or even millions ("poly") of your genetic variants ("genic"), and condense that information into a score that measures your genetic predisposition to specific diseases or complex traits such as depression, schizophrenia, dementia, and even educational achievement.

Even your sense of taste is affected by your DNA. People who possess a specific gene are repulsed by certain vegetables, which will provide a "ruin-your-day level of bitterness"[6] when tasted, according to scientists. The same gene also makes people averse to dark chocolate, coffee, and beer.

Genes influence, and are influenced by, sleep. Margaret Thatcher was known to only need four hours of sleep a night, and Tim Cook reportedly[7] wakes up at 3:45 am to start work. Barack Obama said he only sleeps about 5 hours; Donald Trump and Elon Musk have both said[8] they sleep only a few hours a night. Perhaps it is in their genes; recent research[9] shows that there exists a DNA mutation which lets some people live healthy lives on only 4 hours of sleep. In the other direction, according to Mathew Walker[10], who wrote *Why We Sleep*, lack of sleep can also influence your genes.

Missing sleep can increase your risk of death via disrupting the production of the sex hormones estrogen and testosterone, and also by accelerating the aging process.

Genes are also implicated in your risk of heart disease, the leading killer in the developed world. Recently, the science journal *Nature*[11] reported a study analyzing data from 420,000 individuals in the UK Biobank. That study showed that a simple blood or saliva test could identify babies born with a high genetic chance of having strokes in later life, allowing doctors to help them to reduce their risk. About one in 400 people has this genetic risk. Scientists have said that the test provides a more accurate assessment of stroke risk than traditional measurements based on family, environment, and lifestyle factors.

What about a "longevity gene?" Recent research published in the journal *Cell*[12] showed that the gene **Sirtuin 6** (**SIRT6**) is linked to longevity through conferring more efficient DNA repair—seen in species with longer lifespans. The research reveals new targets for anti-aging interventions and could help prevent age-related diseases (and by the way, being tall, I was pleased to read recently that longevity was positively correlated with being tall, slim, and female in a recent study conducted in the Netherlands![13])

## Influencing your genes

Understanding your genome will help us understand how to make the most of what you have inherited from your parents. But new scientific research is also showing how important our environment and lifestyle are in terms of influencing the expression of these genes—meaning we can dial up or down the expression of our genes, through our actions and choices. This is known as "epigenetics" and refers to external modifications to DNA that turn genes "on" or "off"—not changing the DNA sequence, but rather by influencing how cells "read" the genes and respond, through altering the physical structure of DNA.

One example of an epigenetic change is DNA methylation. DNA methylation is the addition of a methyl group, a tiny chemical flag, to part of the DNA molecule; this methyl group prevents certain genes from being expressed (we will come on to this later when we describe "aging clocks"). Epigenetics is the reason why a skin cell looks different from a brain cell or a muscle cell. All three cells contain the same DNA, but their genes are expressed differently, which creates the different cell types.

As we accumulate more knowledge from research into genomics and epigenomics, this will help us guide the development of personalized health plans unique to each of us, making the most of our personal genetic blueprint. Imagine a dashboard that could tell you the best foods, the most appropriate drugs, the most suitable exercise regimen, and the right supplements to achieve your optimum health? Imagine being able to predict your response to the microbiome, identify the gut flora best suited to you, and provide a calculation of your risk of disease. Most importantly, imagine you could be told how best to prevent these diseases, through choices and decisions that lie within your control.

Personalized health is already here and developing fast. I have been a guinea pig for two DNA lifestyle companies. After sending off my saliva to the first company, they came back later with a very dense report showing a long list of my genetic variants, coded green, amber, and red. Red was supposed to mean "genetic variant alert"; I was alarmed to find quite a few of these alerts! For example, the **ADIPOQ** variant gives me a tendency towards weight regain, and **IRS1** is involved with insulin regulation. It was only when I spent two hours with their scientific director, who holds a PhD in genetics, that I was reassured that no, I was not going to die young.

Acting as my personal genetics coach for the day (genetic counsellors are in very high demand these days) she drew a number of very elaborate metabolic pathways with big arrows showing where I had potential enzyme deficiencies, and after the session I walked away with a list of about 8 supplements to address them.

My sons and husband teased me that I was spending a fortune on these supplements. A year on, they asked "how do you know these are working? Are you getting younger?" This is actually a good question! This is where the "biological markers of aging" come in, which we will explore later. Of course, I had no idea whether these supplements were working or not, but I felt good anyway!

This is why I took my second DNA test, which provided the ability to track my progress through regular epigenetic assessments. After sending off my saliva again, I was subsequently issued with a less daunting personal dashboard, which showed that my biological age was 47! (I was 55 at the time.) Maybe all those supplements were working? The dashboard showed that I was more of a "worrier" than "warrior," so I have a propensity to worry, and also that I was "highly gifted" with regards to my muscle stamina (that sounds impressive but there are two categories above this: "elite" and "super elite"). Certain key results concurred with the previous DNA test, including my slight propensity for a "yo-yo diet response" (the weight regain from the **ADIPOQ** genetic variant) and slightly higher risk of type 2 diabetes (the altered insulin regulation from the **IRS1** genetic variant).

Apparently, my eye and hearing age was much lower than my chronological age, and my inflammation markers were bang on normal for my age. Worryingly, my "memory" was a year older; this reminded me that the genetic coach from the previous test said she could tell that dementia was in my family, when I asked her. Worried about this memory finding, I promptly did a cognitive assessment with another company and found that on 5 measures my "cognitive fitness" was okay—it was my only my episodic memory that needed a bit of training.

This finding made complete sense of why it is that I can never remember books I have read, movies I have seen, or places I have visited!

A "nutrigenomics coach" advised me on what I should do to keep up "age 47," which included a range of changes in my diet, including taking Omega-3 oil and eating nuts, avocado, flax seeds, mackerel, salmon, and cold pressed olive oil saturated fats to keep my inflammatory markers in check—as well as folate from foods like raw green vegetables important for DNA methylation and emotional stability (relating to my serotonin levels). To address my memory, I was advised to take glutamine and do lots of exercise, as research shows that this improves **brain derived neurotrophic factor (BDNF)**, a protein that among other things helps maintain nerve cells in the brain.

I submitted another saliva sample about ten months later; my biological age came back measured at 49 despite taking the recommended supplements. On the positive side, my "memory age" had improved to "healthy," but my inflammation score had worsened. They say stress is linked to chronic inflammation, so this would make sense, given my intense work schedule and pressure over the last year.

While this genetic information is fascinating, it is important to stress that information gathered from DNA tests cannot give you the full picture on your health trajectory. Genetics and/epigenetic data needs to be combined with many other data points (like biomarkers in blood, hormone levels, cognitive assessment, and lifestyle and environment factors) and this is where AI and aging biomarkers, we explore later in the book, are so important.

When you ask people what they fear most about getting old, more often than not it is getting dementia, especially since there is still no cure for it.

However, this is where the latest research using AI is so exciting as it is beginning to unravel the complexities of the interplay between genes, environmental factors, and, most importantly, the interventions which might minimize your risk of dementia, delay the progression of dementia, or even treat dementia directly. As citizens we need to face our fears and get involved in a massive global data sharing effort, which will one day find the answers we seek.

## Unravelling the genetics (or not) of dementia

Alzheimer's disease is the most common form of dementia, an umbrella term for a decline in mental ability severe enough to interfere with daily life. Genetic risk factors have been shown to play a role in the development of Alzheimer's. There is a lot of debate about whether you would want to know if you have a risk or not as there is no treatment to slow, cure, or prevent the condition, yet. Defining and quantifying this risk is the subject of intense research at the moment. There is still a lot you can do right now to reduce your risk of Alzheimer's, though according to a recent poll by Ipsos Mori only 7% of people even knew that lifestyle affects your risk of developing the disease. Despite this, a recent report[14] by Alzheimer's Research UK showed that 74% of people would want to know they had Alzheimer's disease before any symptoms appeared; 4 in 10 people say they would want to know even 15 years before showing symptoms.

For most people with Alzheimer's, no single gene is responsible for the disease. Rather, a combination of factors plays a role in influencing an individual's risk; genetic variants can sometimes come into play in ways that scientists have yet to understand. Evidence[15] suggests that a **single nucleotide polymorphism (SNP)** of **apolipoprotein E (APOE)** is the most significant risk factor for developing late-onset of the disease.

That's a single substitution of a single nucleotide that occurs at a specific position in the genome, affecting a single protein. In addition to APOE, recent genome-wide association studies[16] have identified numerous other Alzheimer's-associated SNPs, most of which have a small effect on disease risk.

Researchers in the US[17] have devised a new scoring system based on a **polygenic hazard score (PHS)**—similar to a polygenic risk score—to assess an individual's total risk of Alzheimer's disease. In the case of Alzheimer's, it seems that there are 31 genetic variations associated with an increased risk, and that individuals with the highest PHS are the most likely to develop Alzheimer's. A patient's PHS can even predict their age of onset of the disease.

Do we want to know this information, if there is not yet a cure for Alzheimer's? This is an individual decision, fraught with ethical and personal dilemmas, but if we consider from a wider point of view the health of the whole population, understanding how genetic and lifestyle factors interact to affect each person's overall risk could lead to more targeted risk reduction strategies. This could allow the development of precision, individualized medicine to prevent or even treat Alzheimer's disease. It is very important to note that there is a lot of research out there showing what you can do to keep your brain healthy and there is a lot you can do to reduce your risks. One thing is clear: living a healthy lifestyle may help offset a person's genetic risk of dementia, according to research conducted with data from 196,383 UK Biobank[18] participants.

About a third of dementia cases could be prevented if all nine of the condition's risk factors for dementia were eliminated, according to a report in medical journal *The Lancet*[19]: these include low levels of education, midlife hearing loss, physical inactivity, high blood pressure, type 2 diabetes, obesity, smoking, depression, and social isolation.

Research shows that changing our lifestyle can help to support a healthy brain. The best current evidence, according to Alzheimer's Research UK[20], suggests that as well as staying physically and mentally active, eating a healthy balanced diet, not smoking, drinking only within the recommended limits and keeping weight, cholesterol, and blood pressure in check are all good ways to support a healthy brain as we age. Sabina Brennan's book *100 days to a Younger Brain* is an excellent primer in this area, and gives top tips.

These lifestyle interventions will also reduce chronic inflammation, which is associated with autoimmune diseases and common conditions like heart disease and diabetes, in addition to dementia. People who have high levels of chronic inflammation at midlife are more likely to suffer memory loss and other cognitive issues later in life according to a recent study in the journal *Neurology*[21]—the first long-term study exploring the link between inflammatory blood markers (such as **CRP**, **C-reactive protein**, a key indicator of inflammation in the body) and brain health. How exactly chronic inflammation is linked to Alzheimer's, including the role of the gut microbiome, is a huge focus of research at the moment[22] and we'll cover it in more detail later in this book.

The link between sleep and dementia has also become a focus of research. A recent study in *Science*[50] suggests that both cerebrospinal fluid and brain wave activity may help to flush toxic, memory- impairing proteins from the brain. As people age, it appears that their brains tend to generate fewer, slower brain waves. This, in turn, may affect blood flow in the brain and reduce the pulsing of cerebrospinal fluid during sleep, leading to a build-up of toxic proteins, and a decline in faculties such as memory. Previous studies involving animals have indicated that one of the waste products removed from the brain during sleep is beta amyloid, a protein closely associated with Alzheimer's disease. The brain-rinsing occurs during what is known as non-REM sleep, soon after a person drifts off.

Meanwhile, scientists are also looking at other theories—and this is where the power of AI can be used to spot patterns and trends that we cannot. For example, several studies[23] show clear evidence that **herpes simplex virus type I (HSV1)**—the virus which causes cold sores—may be a potential trigger. Scientists have known since the 1990s that HSV1 infection causes a greater risk of developing Alzheimer's for people who carry a specific variant of a gene called APOE4.

This ability of AI to spot patterns using data has led to a new form of data for research called "**digital biomarkers**," which will accelerate our understanding of Alzheimer's disease. A digital biomarker is a quantifiable measure of a person's physiological and/or behavioral state captured through connected devices, including wearables (such as blood pressure monitors or sensors), implantable devices (such as pacemakers or continuous glucose monitors), or smart devices in the home (such as voice assistants or gait sensors). They're also sometimes referred to as digital "signatures" or "fingerprints," because their exact values tend to be unique to us. Identifying those digital biomarkers or combinations of biomarkers that indicate early risk of Alzheimer's, such as certain sleep patterns, nocturnal blood pressure dipping, or changes in voice analysis, will help design possible interventions—whether lifestyle or drug—to delay, or one day even cure, the disease.

Recently, Alzheimer's Research UK announced a major study, with funding from the Bill Gates Foundation, to analyze digital data captured from wearable devices such as smart watches to develop these digital fingerprints. AI can be used to identify new insights into the early signals of disease, by combining digital fingerprints with traditional sources such as brain imaging and memory tests.

Dementia highlights how complex the interplay between genes and our environment is, and how individual our risks and responses are to those factors.

# Understanding aging, mastering longevity

*"Any living organism is a far more complicated machine than anything that's man made, but that doesn't change the fact that the concept is still the same. Any machine's function is determined by its structure, and therefore, if you can restore the structure, then you're also going to restore the function."*

*– Aubrey de Grey, Chief Science Officer, SENS Research Foundation*

We are now entering a new phase where we can be in the driving seat of our genetic code. So, how does understanding genetics and epigenetics help us understand and influence the aging process?

I had the pleasure of meeting Professor Thomas Kirkwood at Newcastle University recently. He framed the question of why we age in terms of an organism's available resources. Known as the **"Disposable Soma Hypothesis,"** it is based on the notion that there are always limited resources available to species: energy, nutrients, water. Organisms therefore evolve with the choice of either breed fast and die young, or breed slowly and maintain your soma, or body, to die later. In the history of life, any line of creature with a mutation that caused it to live fast and attempt to die old soon ran out of resources and was thus deleted from the gene pool. Kirkwood's hypothesis explains why a mouse lives for 3 years while some birds can live to 100.

Since Kirkwood's original hypothesis, research in aging has grown exponentially, aided hugely by AI, particularly with the discovery that the rate of aging is controlled, at least to some extent, by genetic pathways and biochemical processes conserved in evolution. Interestingly, these pathways share similarities with cancer.

Intuitively, cancer and aging can be seen as two conditions at opposite ends of the spectrum—with cancer caused by cells gone "wild," and with aging caused by cells losing their fitness and ability to replicate. However, research has shown that cancer and aging are actually two different manifestations of the same underlying process—namely, the accumulation of cellular damage. This is summarized below in the nine hallmarks of aging, published in *Cell*[34] in 2013:

1. **Genomic instability**: As we age, damage is caused by the environment (for example, radiation or toxic compounds) but also through normal cellular processes.

2. **Telomere attrition**: Each strand of DNA in the body is wound into a chromosome. Each chromosome is capped by "telomeres." These short snippets of DNA are designed to protect the bulk of the chromosome, much like an aglet, the plastic end of a shoelace. Telomeres shorten as our DNA replicates. Once a telomere reaches a certain critical shortness, a cell will stop dividing, and this hastens the incidence of disease.

3. **Epigenetic alterations**: Over time, environmental factors will change how our genes are expressed; this is a significant focus of research at the moment. Nutrition, pollution, stress, smoking, alcohol, and other environmental factors are all known to affect genetic expression.

4. **Loss of proteostasis**: When proteins fold properly, your body runs like a well-tuned machine. But under stress, or with age, protein folding stops working so well and begin unfolding or misfolding. There's good evidence that misfolded proteins play a major role in aging, as well as in Alzheimer's, diabetes, cancer, and a variety of other common diseases. Understanding how proteins fold is one of the most difficult challenges known to science, but algorithms are being used to understand protein folding and protein structures faster than ever. Google DeepMind has developed a program called "AlphaFold" to predict how proteins configure themselves, and how they can be as stable as possible[51].

5. **Deregulated nutrient-sensing**: Nutrient levels influence various metabolic pathways. Critical proteins in these pathways include IGF-1, mTOR, sirtuins, and AMPK; they are implicated in longevity and are a huge focus of research at the moment.

6. **Mitochondrial dysfunction**: Mitochondria, our cellular power plants, begin to decline in performance as we age. Decreased performance results in excess fatigue and other symptoms of chronic illnesses associated with aging.

7. **Cellular senescence**: As cells age, they stop dividing, cannot be removed from the body, and increase inflammation as they build up in the body. These senescent cells are often called "zombie" cells, because they refuse to die and continue to emit signals that inflame surrounding cells. Immunosenescene, or senescence of our immune cells, is a big factor in the aging process; developing targets to decrease immunosenescence is a huge focus of research at the moment to build up people's resistance to COVID-19.

8. **Stem cell exhaustion**: As we age, our supply of stem cells begins to diminish between 100 to as much as 10,000-fold in different tissues and organs. Stem cells can also mutate, which reduce their quality and effectiveness at renovating and repairing the body.

9. **Altered intercellular communication**: The efficiency of communication between cells decreases as cells age, and information between cells becomes progressively disrupted.

David Sinclair, Professor of genetics at Harvard and expert on aging, published the excellent book *Lifespan : Why We Age - and Why We Don't Have To*[52] which outlines a foundational theory unifying the 9 hallmarks called "**Information Theory of Aging**." Put simply, it is based on the notion that aging is caused by a loss of information.

In his book, Sinclair argues there are two types of information in biology, and they are encoded entirely differently. The first type of information is digital, based on a finite set of possible values—using not binary coded as 0s and 1s, but quaternary, coded as adenine, thymine, cytosine, and guanine, the nucleotides A, T, C, G of DNA. Because DNA is digital, it is a reliable way to store and copy information, and can be copied again and again with tremendous accuracy (no different in principle from digital information stored in computer memory or on a DVD).

The other type of information in the body is analog information, now more commonly referred to as the epigenome (described in more detail in the next section), a record of the chemical changes to the DNA[35], which can be dynamically altered by environmental conditions. In the same way that genetic information is stored as DNA, epigenetic information is stored in a structure called chromatin.

The Information Theory of Aging starts with the "survival circuit" we inherited from our distant ancestors, like the sea snail *M. superstes*, but which have evolved since then into some two dozen longevity genes within our genome, including sirtuins. Sirtuins are named after the yeast **SIR2** gene, the first one to be discovered, but there are seven sirtuins in mammals, **SIRT1** to **SIRT7**, made by almost every cell in the body. Sirtuins are a major focus of aging research at the moment. They have evolved to require a molecule called **nicotinamide adenine dinucleotide** (**NAD**) to function; the loss of NAD as we age, and the resulting decline in sirtuin activity, is thought to be a primary reason our bodies develop diseases when we are old but not when we are young.

## The hopes for gene editing

Soon after I completed my genetics degree in 1985—I remember telomeres were all the rage—we started to hear about the Human Genome Project.

The Human Genome Project is a gargantuan project that began in 1990, and in 2004[24] the first human genome sequence was published at a cost of over $3 billion.

Since then, geneticists and biologists have made exponential progress in understanding how our genetic code operates.

In addition to reading the human genome, scientists can now edit a genome using a naturally occurring biological system discovered in 1987, called **CRISPR/Cas9**, which is short for "Clustered Regularly Interspaced Short Palindromic Repeats and CRISPR-associated protein 9."

Crucially, CRISPR is cheap, quick, easy to use, and more accurate than all previous gene editing methods. As a result, CRISPR/Cas9 has swept through labs around the world as the best way to edit a genome. In 2012, scientific publications mentioning CRISPR totaled 127. Since then there have been more than 14,000. Although the United States has had the most CRISPR publications—and continues to have the most cited papers—China is now a close second[25] and is investing heavily into CRISPR's uses.

Biophysicist He Jiankui[26] infamously used the genome editor in China to alter the DNA of two human embryos that would become twin girls, in an attempt to make them resistant to HIV. His results were published in *Nature* with great excitement in November 2018, but also with consternation; *Nature*[27] posed the question "when will the world be ready?" This first known attempt at heritable gene editing in humans was an effort to disable a gene called CCR5, which produces an immune-cell receptor that allows HIV to infect humans. Break the gene, reasoned Jiankui, and the children should be resistant to the virus.

However, after getting worldwide media attention he has since been convicted[28] of "practicing medicine illegally and violating Chinese scientific research regulations, as well as forging ethical review documents." He was sentenced to three years in prison and fined 3 million yuan (£330,000).

The bottom line is that Jiankui crossed the line in the ethical minefield that CRISPR represents.

Setting aside the significant ethical conversations, CRISPR will soon provide us with the tools to potentially eliminate diseases, create hardier offspring, produce new environmentally resistant crops, and even wipe out pathogens. Recently, Harvard College researchers[29] led by George Church have announced that more than 13,000 genetic alterations have been made to a single cell using CRISPR technology. This work is designed to edit genomes at a much larger scale than currently possible, potentially resulting in the "radical redesign" of animal species—or even humans.

Another recent CRISPR innovation dubbed "prime editing" can make virtually any alteration—additions, deletions, swapping any single letter for any other—without disrupting the DNA double helix. Developed by David Liu[30] at the Broad Institute in Cambridge, Massachusetts, he described the system like this: "If Crispr-Cas9 is like scissors and base editors are like pencils, then you can think of prime editors to be like word processors." According to Liu, the technique is so precise that it can correct around 89% of the mutations that cause heritable human diseases[31].

## The future of regenerative medicine

Genetic editing is one thing, but "regenerative medicine" will also be transformative in the decades to come. Regenerative medicine is about replenishing, replacing and rejuvenating our physical bodies. The "three R's"[32] of regenerative medicine advocated by Singularity University are:

1. **Replenish: Stem Cells - The Regenerative Engine of The Body**. Stem cells have the potential to develop into many other kinds of cells, so if we can keep these undifferentiated cells from tiring out, they can continue to generate all the differentiated cells necessary to heal damaged tissues and battle all kinds of diseases.

2. **Replace: Organ Regeneration and Bioprinting**. Prior to 3D printing capabilities, medical researchers were able to reproduce cells in laboratory settings, including blood vessels and skin tissue, but full organs were much more difficult because of their complex cell structures. With the advent of 3D printers, however, making organs is becoming feasible, as demonstrated by the example of a girl in Illinois born without a trachea who received a windpipe created from her own stem cells using the printing technique[53]. Such "organ on a chip" research is being applied to printing tissue samples that mimic the functions of other major organs, including the heart, liver, and lungs.[54]

3. **Rejuvenate: Young Blood & Parabiosis**. Research at Stanford and Harvard has demonstrated that older animals, when transfused with the blood of young animals, experience regeneration across many tissues and organs. The opposite is also true. Elevian is a company exploring specific circulating factors that may be responsible for the "young blood" effect, including a naturally occurring molecule known as **growth differentiation factor 11 (GDF11)**. When GDF11 is injected into aged mice, it reproduces many of the regenerative effects of young blood, regenerating heart, brain, muscles, lungs, and kidneys.[55]

When it comes to regeneration, some animals are well equipped. If you cut off a salamander's leg, it will grow back. Some geckos detach their tails to distract their predator when threatened, only to regrow them later. Other animals take the process even further. Planarian worms, jellyfish, and sea anemones can actually regenerate their bodies after being cut in half.

Recently a Harvard research team[33] discovered exactly how animals like lizards, worms, and jellyfish regenerate body parts through a master control gene called **early growth response (EGR)**, which triggers changes in a complex system of 18,000 other genes. Without the EGR gene turned "on," none of the other processes can happen. Humans express the EGR gene, too, and researchers know exactly how to control it. But the human version of EGR does not have the same switching effect that causes regeneration, and this "switching on" is what the researchers are now trying to work out in the human model.

While advances in genomics and computational biology are enabling us to explain what makes up a human being at its most intricate level, what about the spiritual elements of what makes us human? While our survival instincts may be hardwired in our genes, what drives our quest to live longer? What fuels our insatiable curiosity about immortality?

# Spirituality, Immortality, and the "God Gene"

> *"When Galileo was saying in Rome in the Vatican that it was not the sun that went around the earth, but the opposite, they almost burned him alive. These ideas are even more revolutionary than evolution or astrophysics."*

> *– José Cordeiro, Director of the Millennium Project*

Dr Dean Hamer, the director of the Gene Structure and Regulation Unit at the National Cancer Institute in America, was one of the first scientists to explore the link between religious belief and a person's genetic make-up. In his study he asked volunteers 226 questions, in order to determine how spiritually connected they felt to the universe.

The higher their score, the greater a person's ability to believe in a greater spiritual force and, Dr Hamer found, the more likely they were to share the gene VMAT2[56].

Tim Spector, Professor of Genetic Epidemiology and Director of Twins Research at King's College London, also explored the genetic basis for religious belief[36]. Twin studies conducted around the world in the US, the Netherlands, and Australia, as well as at King's in the UK, show a 40 to 50% genetic component to belief in God. Interestingly, these findings are consistent even across countries like the US and the UK, where there are significant differences in church attendance and religious beliefs. Some may argue that twin studies showing similarity for belief are just reflecting some cultural or family influence that wasn't properly corrected for in the study design. However, in one study of adopted twins, the researchers looked at religious belief in a number of adopted twins raised apart. They found exactly the same result—greater similarity in identical twin pairs, even if raised apart.

In the 19th century and for much of the 20th century, science asked hard questions of faith. But in the 21st century, faith needs to ask hard questions once again of science. The belief in an afterlife is a fundamental tenet of most faiths, but the concept of an immortal soul is not. The "soul" means different things in different religions. For example, even the various branches of Christianity do not share a unified view on the soul's immortality and its relation to the body.

The USA is a deeply religious society, based on the Christian beliefs that God created the universe, that God loves the world, and that God became human to restore us and show humans what it means to live well and reach our full potential. For some Christians, their faith reconciles their fears over death and the constraints of being mortal.

The Church of England has stepped into the debate around AI and longevity: about what it means to be human, about the ethics and limits of human endeavor.

Being human is also about weakness and imperfection. If we become superhuman, will that make us less tolerant of the frailties of the human race? I caught up with Reverend Malcolm Brown from the Church of England to explore these points in greater detail. I first met Malcolm when he spoke at a public event in 2017 on Ethics in AI, which I helped my good friend Maja Pantic, Professor of Affective Computing at Imperial College (and now also AI Scientific Research Lead at Facebook) to organize. The event was hugely popular and even had to move to a much larger venue. At this event Malcolm talked about AI and manifestations of power; questions were raised, like" is that power in the hands of the people who create the AI, or is it in those of the user? Where do responsibility and accountability lie, and how do we change that if it goes wrong?" From an ethical standpoint, these are the areas where society is floundering.

When I caught up with Malcolm to interview him for this book, two years after our first encounter, things had moved on a little. He felt that we're coming to maturity in our relationship to AI, instead of being either over-awed and over-credulous, or over-panicked and clamping down on it in a way that kills off the benefit. He said, "both of those bad approaches have risks, because we need a rhythm to cope with the new and to work out collectively how we respond to it. You learn to trust, or not to trust, after millions of encounters. We haven't had the luxury of those millions of encounters. From our point of view, AI has done the millions of encounters in the background; but the conclusions AI draws from its data may be quite problematic.... The market ideology, if that's used as the paradigm, says that there's no moral weight to the outcome because there's no moral consensus that can be represented. That strikes me as a real danger; that we're applying the ideology of the market to the way we're dealing with data."

Malcolm feels that technology could have a role to play in building communities. He said, "It's really important not to get onto a nostalgia kick about community, but to recognize that we do need more of it than we've got right now.

That's a hugely difficult trajectory for a human mind to capture; there's always the draw of the binary. I think that the distinction between liberal individualism and communitarianism is the big political fault line of the era. We need to learn how to stop swinging the pendulum from one extreme to the other, and instead understand how each is corrective to the other, rather than an alternative to the other. Negotiating that in real time, in real communities, is fascinatingly complex. There was an attempt maybe 25 years ago, a movement that tried to coin the phrase "glocal" as a combination of global and local. It never took off as far as I know. Finding solutions to questions which combine the global and the local, that don't denigrate the one in favor of the other, that don't create tribalism on the one hand or a universal monopoly on the other, strikes me as something that technology could really help with."

On the subject of religion and mortality, Malcolm said that most religions are in some sense about making sense of finitude and mortality; we haven't escaped death, but we have forgotten how to talk about it. He said, "That's not necessarily an argument for a particular narrative, but it is fascinating for instance that when I was a parish priest in the 80s, most people had a Christian funeral and it was about commending the soul of the departed person to God. It had an implicit belief in eternity, but not in this life. Now, the average funeral is a celebration of the life of a person; an attempt at immortality through history, by making your mark. It's a fascinating difference and that's right there in the religious funeral as well. They've moved from a commendation of a soul forward to a new phase, to a celebration looking back. My hunch is that if we pursue questions like longevity, purely as longevity, we'll find in due course that the religious insights probably had more to commend them than we thought, because we'll be going down a route that leads to an increasingly inhuman understanding of humanity. I may be wrong about that of course.

I'm not against long life, but the pursuit of it as an end in itself? That strikes me as so narcissistic, potentially, and so out of kilter with the whole of the material order that it could reveal all sorts of truths that we thought we'd lost."

Whether the COVID-19 pandemic has changed popular perceptions of mortality is an interesting and, as yet, unanswered question. Early in the pandemic, Malcolm was worried by the implicit narrative about the relative value of different lives. "The constant refrain that people dying generally had underlying health conditions, or were elderly, didn't state in bald terms that those lives were somehow expendable, but it did send a subtle and probably unintended message to that effect. The disparity in deaths among BAME people could have become part of that narrative, and among some extremist groups it definitely has done. As a response to that, the emergence of the very prominent Black Lives Matter protest during lockdown may help to make it clear that disparate valuation of people's lives is just not acceptable. But we're not out of that particular wood yet by any means."

As a counterpoint to the Christian perspective, transhumanism is a growing but controversial movement which believes in the scientific method rather than having faith in its own version of religion. The movement is built around the core idea of evolving and enhancing human beings by integrating biology with technology[37]. Transhumanism welcomes anyone who aspires for super-longevity and is prepared to experiment on themselves and others, using vitamins and prescription cancer drugs, as well as compounds not licensed for human use but procured creatively through underground suppliers: extropians and brain uploaders[38], artists keen to paint in virtual worlds, and do-it-yourself biohackers[39] ready to have electronic chips implanted in their bodies.

Zoltan Istvan[40] is one of the best-known transhumanists, who wrote *The Transhumanist Wager*[41] and was a candidate in the 2016 US presidential campaign, when he drove around the United States in a bus in the shape of a coffin.

Although Zoltan did not expect to beat Trump, he was betting that the "immortality bus" and his campaign might help inject more science, technology, and longevity research into the political discourse, or at the very least spark a more serious conversation around the future of our species.

James Clement[42] is another transhumanist who runs BetterHumans, which he calls "the world's first transhumanist research organization." He has financed and supervised four small studies, in volunteers, of treatments found to extend the healthy lives of rodents—the immune drug rapamycin, the supplement NAD+, a combination of compounds that kill off aged cells, and injections of plasma concentrated from umbilical cords. His aim is "to do as many small trials as possible" to generate and publish basic information on safety and possible benefits. Clement sees his job as bringing that day closer and making sure it's affordable to everyone, "not just billionaires."

Ray Kurzweil, Google's Director of Engineering, is a well-known futurist with a track record of being able to make accurate predictions[43] 86% of the time. Arguably his most famous prediction is that we will reach "**the Singularity**" by 2045[44], that point in time when all the advances in technology will lead to machines that are smarter than human beings. This concurs closely with Softbank CEO Masayoshi Son's prediction that super-intelligent machines will emerge by 2047[45]. Kurzweil says that the process towards this singularity has already begun, with computers having human intelligence (akin to Peter Diamandis "meta-intelligence" concept[46]) and humans starting to implant computers into our brains, like Elon Musk's controversial neuralink[47], which is a device to connect the brain with the internet and one day merge with artificially intelligent systems.

Should we fear the singularity? Or embrace it? Reaching the singularity will enable us to reach "**longevity escape velocity**" (a hypothetical situation in which life expectancy is extended faster than time passes), meaning that we could also effectively achieve immortality by 2045, too.

The possibility of immortality could have profound effects[48] on the individual, as well as society as a whole. Proponents of immortality would say it could mean that we would no longer suffer the fear of death, we could do more with our lifetimes, and the world's greatest minds could continue to develop their thoughts.

The cynics, however, would argue there could be a strain on resources, serious psychological problems associated with extreme age, and stress on societal structures such as marriage and parenthood.

The great strides we are seeing with AI and computational biology are making the idea of achieving immortality more achievable, even to the diehard cynics.

There are many AI experts who worry that **artificial general intelligence (AGI)** will be a threat to human life by replacing humans. However, according to Alex Zhavoronkov, CEO of Insilico Medicine, making AGI a partner could help our quest for better, longer lives if we create a set of values for AGI focused around the maximization of human **quality adjusted life years (QALY)**—a generic measure of disease burden, including both the quality and the quantity of life lived.

Zhavoronkov argues that an AGI could be taught to maximize global longevity and the human healthspan, and achieve the ultimate form of altruism[49]. As Zhavoronkov says, "If anyone is counting up there, they are likely counting the actions you take to make the world better rather than the actions you don't take by following the restrictions outlined in the religious texts. And to me, it only feels logical that the actions that maximize the number of QALY for everyone on the planet will yield the most points. The longevity biotechnology industry—the convergence of aging research, biopharmaceutical industry, regenerative medicine, and AI—is likely the most QALY-rich area. So people who believe in any form of afterlife or karma should consider these areas when making career choices."

Taking together all the viewpoints across religious, spiritual, and humanist perspectives, I can't help feeling that we need to make sure we see imperfection as a core ingredient of what keeps us human. Apart from anything else, it means there can be no authority on what makes "perfection"! It seems to be our moral compass is remarkably consistent across cultures—and this is something I am not sure can be replicated by machines any time soon. Humans are still unique in the animal kingdom, with a need for some element of spirituality to guide us, or help us make sense of our place and purpose in the world. Having a finite end to our life also helps put things in sharp focus, like any deadline does; hopefully, we learn to focus on what really matters to us.

## Interviews

The interviews coming up reflect an extraordinary blend of perspectives on life, death, and immortality, from civic, scientific, and societal viewpoints. José Cordeiro and Keith Comito carry the torch for living as long as possible with transhumanist flair and a deep sense of public service, while Aubrey de Grey and Alex Zhavoronkov represent some of the most unconventional, provocative, brilliant minds in science—uncompromising in their approach to challenge entrenched orthodoxy. Eddie Hall, the world's strongest man since 2017, has had a fascinating personal journey to understand what gave him his "superhuman" gifts—which helped wrench him from a dark period of depression as a teenager to a fulfilled life, aided, in part, by his fascination with how epigenetics can optimize health and well-being.

Since this book started development, we've had our lives turned upside down by the emergence of COVID-19 and the stunning impact of the pandemic it's caused. Most of these interviews were carried out before the pandemic- where I could get back in touch, I asked them an extra question:

**What have you learned from the COVID-19 pandemic?** The answers to this question have been added to the end of each interview.

# Eddie Hall

*World's Strongest Man, Epigenetics Advocate*

Eddie Hall is also known as "The Beast" and he won the World's Strongest Man in 2017 when he deadlifted 500 kg under Strongman rules.

I first met Eddie Hall at a lunch held by Muhdo, the epigenetics company, in November 2019. I had come across the firm a year earlier after having been introduced to them by my good friend Omar Fogliadini, serial entrepreneur and managing partner of LIFEdata AI who was advising them on their platform (I had met Omar the year before and was a guinea pig for the DNA epigenetics product he was launching in the UK at the time). I met Nathan Berkley, CEO of Muhdo shortly after Omar connected us, and he offered me a place on their study. They were doing one for athletes and one for the media, and I grabbed the chance to be one of their "journalists on trial."

A year on, and two epigenetic test results later, I went to the company's lunch announcing their latest product innovation, and encountered a room full of real journalists and athletes. Helen Glover, Team GB rowing double gold medalist, three-times world champion, twice European champion, and multiple world cup gold-medal winner was there. So was Sam Quek, winner of an Olympic gold medal for GB Hockey. I sat across from her at lunch, and was fascinated by her journey, story, and reasons for doing the DNA test. Engrossed in conversation, I hadn't realized that Eddie Hall, world's strongest man since 2017, was at the table opposite from me.

He arrived late and had to leave early; while he was saying his goodbyes, he came to our table (you couldn't miss him—he has presence!) and I caught his eye. Two weeks later I was interviewing him for this book.

I have to confess, I'd never heard of Eddie Hall before the lunch. But when I mentioned I was due to interview him to one of my sons it started a flurry of excitement in my household, and before I knew it had my three sons showing me various YouTube clips of Eddie lifting half a ton, and performing the most unbelievable feats of strength and power imaginable.

Eddie is arguably the most famous strongman of the last decade, having won Britain's Strongest Man five times in a row from 2014 to 2018, winning the UK's Strongest Man six times in a row from 2011 to 2016, being named the World's Strongest Man in 2017, and for setting the world record for heaviest dead-lift (500Kg) the previous year. Few people know that he started out as a champion swimmer.

Eddie has an interesting personal story and for him, achieving excellence as an athlete swimmer and then setting his sights high on being the world's strongest man helped save him from depression in his teenage years. He is the youngest of three boys, and being the mum of three sons we talked about the endless competition that ensues in a household full of testosterone. Obviously devoted to his kids, we spoke about how to motivate kids to eat more healthily and become happy in themselves. He is now an ambassador for Muhdo and becoming sought after in Hollywood.

**Tina Woods**: Tell us a little bit about your journey: I know you started as a swimmer and you became the World's Strongest Man, and now you're a Muhdo ambassador, and I understand you're seeking fame as an actor as well. Where did that all start?

**Eddie Hall**: So, I'm from Stoke-on-Trent. I'm the youngest of three brothers, grown up in a somewhat poor family. All of us were very sporty, so we're all very competitive—swimming, and rugby, and whatever else.

We all got very heavily into the competitive side of swimming. We represented our area, and I actually swam at the Nationals and won the Nationals three years in a row, setting British records. I was on the World Class Potential squad, which is basically the junior Olympic team; it's government funded, and comes with gym memberships and a bit of money, as well as nutritionists and coaches. I was pretty gifted—I was basically a professional athlete at 11 years old.

**Tina Woods**: And better than your brothers?

**Eddie Hall**: Yes. Much better. Much better.

**Tina Woods**: I've got three sons. I know exactly what it's like having three boys, all competing against each other all the time!

**Eddie Hall**: Well, there you go! Having two older brothers made me the competitive monster I am, because growing up everything was a competition. When we were eating food at the table, we'd see who could eat the most; when we were walking to school, we'd see who could get there the fastest. Even fighting, we wanted to know who was the hardest. It was like a constant battle. Being the youngest put me in a very difficult position, where I had to be the best at everything to survive. That set the blueprint for the rest of my life, I believe. When I got into swimming, my brothers were replaced by new people to compete against; the Ian Thorpes, the Michael Phelpses.

Then, when I was 13, I started suffering with very bad anxiety attacks. That then stemmed into depression, which meant I had to withdraw from school; well, I was expelled from school. A number of other things happened to me at that point, and I became very depressed. I was on Prozac and seeing a psychiatrist for a couple of years. I got to about 15—I was being home tutored and doing nothing with my time, and I decided to join a gym.

That's when I found that going to the gym gave me that sense of well-being, that euphoria. It made me feel better, and it became an obsession to combat the depression. When I started the gym, I eased off the Prozac very quickly.

Fast forward to 19 years of age, and I'd been doing weightlifting for four years, since I was 15. I discovered that I had a hell of talent. I was one of the strongest men in the country—I discovered this from social media, YouTube, and so on—and started doing Strongman. I did my very first Strongman contest when I was 19. I came 5<sup>th</sup>, and got the bite for it. I decided that day, there and then, that I was going to be the World's Strongest Man.

I said it out loud, put it on social media, and I went on this hell of a journey. 10 years later, to the day, I became the World's Strongest Man.

**Tina Woods**: Were you surprised at yourself, or did you know that one day you were going to be the World's Strongest Man?

**Eddie Hall**: I think, when I won at the swimming, it gave me that belief that with hard work and dedication you can achieve anything in life. That taught me a huge lesson going into the Strongman. Everyone said: you'll never win the World's Strongest Man. You're too small, you're not tall enough. You haven't got the right genes; blah, blah, blah. I just thought "screw you"—no-one's going to tell me what to do. I made sure it happened. I put my whole heart and soul into doing it. Basically, I was obsessed with becoming the World's Strongest Man. There's no other way to put it.

**Tina Woods**: You were very determined—it's almost like the mind over matter, isn't it? I know you're often doing film now. Are there any movies that we should be keeping an eye out for?

**Eddie Hall**: Well, I've got a movie I'm doing next year, I'm starring in the film, but that's all I can say right now. I've also got a few backburners going on in Hollywood as well, maybe a few appearances coming up, but honestly my ambition right now is just to concentrate on building my empire.

I do TV shows, I'm getting into the movie side of things, and I've got quite a few businesses, Official Strongman being one of them. I want to grow Strongman from the roots up. I've got a lot ahead of me, a lot of plans, and I'm doing pretty well with it all.

**Tina Woods**: Excellent. So, tell us about Muhdo, and the epigenetics testing you did with them. I suppose that's also part of your journey, discovering what it is inside you that makes you?

**Eddie Hall**: Yes—after I won the World's Strongest Man, I did the test, and it opened my eyes to my genes. I realized how blessed I was to have these genes and to have gone into strength athletics, because I was actually built for strength from my genes up.

**Tina Woods**: So, even before you did a genetic test, you knew that there was something special about your physical makeup?

**Eddie Hall**: 100%. I've always been the biggest kid—not just tall. I've always had a big chest, big arms, abs. I mean, yes, it came from the swimming, but even in the swimming world, the other swimmers looked like pencils compared to me. I always knew I must have had some genetic variation where I was more gifted in that way. I was able to put more down on the table, and get better results back. So, after I won the World's, I did the DNA test with Muhdo and it opened my eyes to my genes.

**Tina Woods**: Did you find Muhdo, or did they find you? And did you know anything about epigenetics before the test?

**Eddie Hall**: I think they found me, to be honest. But I was 100% keen to try it out. The depth of knowledge you could get was completely new to me. I knew you could check your ancestry, but I didn't realize you can break down your DNA, you know, to define whether or not you have fast slow-twitch fibers, to define what deficiencies you may or may not have. It was a big eye-opener to me.

**Tina Woods**: Were there any particular surprises in your results?

**Eddie Hall**: One of the biggest surprises was they found out I had an MSTN gene deficiency, which is the same as is found in Belgian Blue cows, this breed that just has muscles on muscles on muscles. I discovered that I've got a type 2 deficiency, and that's why I'm able to carry more muscle mass than any other human; they call it the Hercules gene. It's a super, super rare gene, and it just so happened that I have this gene and I got into strength sports. That was the biggest shock.

In Belgian Blue cows this gene was bred into them but in humans it's incredibly rare. It's so rare that there aren't any precise measures, but it's definitely rarer than one in a million. A bit like the cows, it sometimes follows in a family, and I will say that my Mum was adopted from Sweden. Perhaps it's a sort of Viking gene—the Scandinavians are renowned for breeding big people.

**Tina Woods**: I've got a bit of Viking genetics myself—my oldest son is almost 6'8"!

**Eddie Hall**: Jeez! There you go. There you go.

**Tina Woods**: What else did the test tell you about your propensity for strength?

**Eddie Hall**: I'm not the most absolutely gifted person for strength, but the Hercules gene gave me the capability to go above and beyond what other people could. There are genes out there which will make you big and strong effortlessly, but the gene I have gave me instead the capability to be big and strong. Without any effort, I'd be like my brothers and my dad. My dad's 6'3" and very slender, about 14 stone in body weight. I've had to work super, super hard, and pump huge amounts of food into my body to reach a body weight of 32 stone—I needed that mass to lift half a ton off the floor and win the World's Strongest Man, and that muscle mass is what my genes gave me the capability to build.

**Tina Woods**: From what I understand, there's something in your genes about your ability to convert arachidonic acid, and that increases muscle mass. Does that ring a bell?

**Eddie Hall**: It does. I can't remember all the details, but there's something in there that gives me a defense against these acids. They're made when you exercise, and I recover quicker. My muscles recover faster, and of course, that in turn makes you bigger and stronger.

**Tina Woods**: Has knowing what you now know about your genes influenced what you eat or how you exercise?

**Eddie Hall**: It actually came in very handy to confirm that a lot of the things I was doing in my training were the right thing for me. It turns out I have very, very good resistance to lactic acid. That means high weight, high rep work is good for me; and in the competitions, I was always good at those events. I'd always win the high rep, high volume events, and getting this information about my genetics reiterated to me that I know how my body's built in this world, and what I'm meant to be good at. Having lighter weights or super, super high weights wouldn't be my forte; but it's a bit weird how it all works, because Strongman can be suited to your strengths and weaknesses, and the results from this helped me to work on my weaknesses.

**Tina Woods**: What were your weaknesses?

**Eddie Hall**: I've had to work super, super hard on my cardiovascular health for example, to bring my fitness up to match my strength. Apparently, my body is very against being cardiovascular fit—I'm more drawn to being the guy for lifting weights. I work hard on my endurance, in that respect, but I couldn't go out and run a marathon.

**Tina Woods**: From looking at pictures, it seems like you're much fitter now than you were two years ago. Was that just through doing the work you wanted to, or was that because of what you discovered from Muhdo?

**Eddie Hall**: A bit of both. I wanted to change my look. I was sick of being called a fat bastard on the scene.

They say you shouldn't let it bother you, but it does, when you've been called a fat bastard your whole life. So, I decided to take a step back and kept myself in shape.

It wasn't only for vanity, of course. I needed to take my body weight down, to give my organs a bit of a break and give my heart a bit of a relax for a few years, after having put it through such a hard regime for such a long time. I decided to trim up, basically; get as healthy as I could. I definitely took the suggestion from my genes on what diet would work best for me. I've found that I work better on a high-fat diet than on a high-carb diet.

**Tina Woods**: I know you eat a lot of meat, don't you? The Game Changers film has opened up a conversation about the pros of a vegan diet, but you're certainly not vegan, are you?

**Eddie Hall**: No, not at all! I watched that Game Changers film, and I took some points away from it. I think in general, it was a load of shit, but it's got some good points in there. In general, the human race could make a bit more of an effort to eat less meat, and the human race would benefit from that.

That's another thing I took away from the DNA test, you know: protein. The need for protein is quite overexaggerated in the bodybuilding and strength world. You don't actually need as much as some people say you need to build muscles, and I find you can get just as good quality from protein shakes and broccoli as from meat. Taking a step back, I definitely eat less meat now; I'd say half what I used to eat.

**Tina Woods**: I've heard you talk about taking Omega-3 oil, which is generally considered good for most people. Do you still take it?

**Eddie Hall**: One of the biggest alterations I made to my diet in 2016, leading into the World's Strongest Man, was quadrupling my Omega-3 and my Omega-6 and fish oil intake. When I did the test with Muhdo in 2017, it confirmed that I'd made the right decision; my body, my genes, don't let me absorb these oils like any normal person.

I have to take far higher quantities to get the same intake as a normal person would. I happened to have done this on the advice of a doctor anyway, but the DNA test reconfirmed what the doctor said; that my genes mean I can't absorb it as well as other people.

**Tina Woods**: Does that influence your cardiovascular profile as well?

**Eddie Hall**: Yes, exactly. At home now, I've got a bottle of fish oils that I keep by the fridge. First thing in the morning, I neck a bit, and last thing in the day, last thing at night, I neck a bit. Honestly, the difference it's made to my well-being and performance is astounding. That was a big, big change for me. The DNA test underlined how important that is for me, and I'll definitely be doing that for the rest of my life now.

**Tina Woods**: So, it really has made a difference to you, having that information. What would you say to other people who struggle with their mental health, who suffer from anxiety or depression?

**Eddie Hall**: Well, I think diet is a huge part of mental health. It's a bit like a car. If you're putting shit fuel and shit oil into a car, it's going to run like shit. I think the body is exactly the same thing. If you're filling it full of shit food and shit drink all the time, you're going to feel like shit.

That was another big moment for me, to take a step back and realize how big an impact your diet can have on your mental health. It affects your mental health just like it affects your physical health. I wouldn't say I used to eat badly, but I used to eat a lot of crappy foods just to get the volume of calories I needed into myself. I realize, now, that I could have done it in a lot of better ways. Perhaps saved myself a lot of dark nights.

**Tina Woods**: As I'm sure you know, there are huge issues with childhood obesity and poor diet in the UK and other countries in the developed world. Knowing what you know now, do you think it would have helped you earlier on? How has it affected the food, and the advice about food, you give to your own children?

**Eddie Hall**: We try and influence them to always eat a good portion of vegetables. We have vegetables every day, and for the rest, I think it's similar for every kid. I think sometimes you've got to just give them what they like! Chips and chicken nuggets are quite a common meal in our house for the kids; but then again, so is spaghetti bolognese and other healthy stuff, so they get a good mix. We always try our best to give the kids good variety in their diet, to make sure they're getting all the minerals and nutrients they need in there.

**Tina Woods**: When it comes to dietary supplements, do you think Muhdo and other services like that can help you focus on what you really need? There's a lot of talk about money going into supplements being mostly wasted.

**Eddie Hall**: I completely agree. There are so many supplements on the market, but the key word there is "supplement." It's a supplement to food, so food's still number one. If you can, you want to get all your nutrition, protein, or carbs and fats from food, but the problem is that everyone's so busy. Everyone's got busy lives, and that's why supplements were created. They exist to keep us healthy, to keep that healthy intake of amino acids, that intake of protein and carbs.

I think it's a good idea to take a step back and ask yourself what your body needs. Write it down, make sure you get it one way or another, from your diet or a supplement if you can't stretch your diet to it, and then I wouldn't do any more than that. I think it's best to just take the bare necessities when it comes to supplements, and don't get too worked up about it. Be relaxed with it. Enjoy your food, eat a healthy balanced diet, and if you need to supplement it then go ahead and supplement it.

**Tina Woods**: Finally, what do you think is the secret to a long, healthy, happier life?

**Eddie Hall**: I think the number one thing you can do for your happiness is look after your health. People invest in mobile phones; they invest in cars; they invest in holidays; but people neglect their own health.

I've seen people happily spend a couple of hundred pounds on a tracksuit. But for that same money, you can go and get a full blood works test, that might tell you that you're deficient in vitamin K or vitamin D. I think that putting a little bit of money aside every month to put into your health—through professionals—is probably one of the best things you can do.

For me, that's what makes me feel good about myself, and in turn I feel good about myself with everything. I feel good about my work; I feel good about my family.

There are a few things you carry around with you these days. One is your health. Another is your mobile phone, and there's lots of ways to use your phone to keep healthy. There're apps like the Fitbit apps and the Muhdo app that I use quite regularly. Because it's in my phone, it's in my pocket, so when I'm on a plane or a train, I can pull it out, I can look at it, and absorb a little information about how to be fitter, healthier, and live a longer life. The technology means the professionals are everywhere now, and you can always use what's around you to invest in your health.

About eight months after my initial interview with Eddie, I caught up with him again in July 2020 to see how his life changed as a result of the COVID-19 pandemic.

My three sons had mentioned that his 500 kg deadlift world record had been beaten and that he was turning to boxing! Intrigued, I contacted Eddie to get the full low-down.

So, here it is, straight from Eddie. At the height of the pandemic, on 2 May, Icelandic Hafthor Bjornsson, who played Ser Gregor "The Mountain" Clegane in Game of Thrones, deadlifted 501 kg in his home gym. There were arguments as to how the deadlift world record should be set, and Hafthor launched an onslaught against Eddie, offering to fight him in the ring.

They will now be fighting each other in a Las Vegas boxing showdown next year.

In preparation, Eddie is following an intense training regime to transform from strongman into boxer, switching his workouts and upping his cardio to build speed as well as strength. He is also eating about 10,000 calories a day.

His routine comprises a number of elements, doing 4 strength and conditioning sessions a week along with 4 boxing sessions, 2 high intensity training (HIT) sessions and hours and hours of recovery such as massage, hot'n'cold treatments, and even cryotherapy treatments, all at home.

Eddie has been so busy locked down in training he has hardly noticed that lockdown extends beyond his training and recovery at home!

## Aubrey de Grey
*Chief Science Officer of the SENS Research*

I first heard about Aubrey de Grey in 2016. This was before I started to get heavily involved in healthy aging and longevity. I was immersed curating a 3-day conference (the GIANT Health event) and crowdsourcing potential speakers. At one of our editorial board meetings Aubrey's name came up as "the lead provocateur, maverick, and godfather of aging." Always one for mavericks, I was of course intrigued.

Perform a quick Google search and you will be inundated with items including of course a Wikipedia entry, which describes him as an English author and biomedical gerontologist "known for his view that medical technology may enable human beings alive today not to die from age-related causes."

He is the Chief Science Officer of the SENS Research Foundation and VP of New Technology Discovery at AgeX Therapeutics. He is editor-in-chief of the academic journal *Rejuvenation Research* and author of *The Mitochondrial Free Radical Theory of Aging (1999)* and co-author of *Ending Aging (2007)*. The Wikipedia entry also summarizes some of the controversies around Aubrey's main theory of SENS, or "strategies for engineered negligible senescence."

In a nutshell, the SENS theory describes seven types of molecular and cellular damage caused by essential metabolic processes, and ways to repair this damage. These seven processes align with the nine pillars of aging published by *Cell* described earlier.

Aubrey is regularly in the media, including TIME, CBS 60 Minutes, the BBC, The New York Times, Fortune Magazine, The Washington Post, and TED, with journalists tantalized by Aubrey's claims on radical longevity including, for example, that the person who will live to 1,000 has already been born and may be 50 or 60 already. Aubrey is 56 (and so am I!).

He studied computer science at Cambridge (where he met his friend Demis Hassabis, the co-founder and CEO of DeepMind), and applies engineering principles to understand aging often using the analogy of a car. Cars need regular MOTs to assess wear and tear over time, and you need to repair any damage to keep the car on the road. It is the same with a human body.

When I approached him to speak at an event in 2016 I thought we would hit the brick wall of a "celebrity scientist" requiring a heavy-duty speaker fee and all expenses paid (business class of course). We had nothing as a start-up. This didn't matter an iota; Aubrey supports anything new, different, grassroots, even underground. He agreed without question to support us.

Many times since then I have been struck by Aubrey's generosity and support for the underdog (not just relating to myself, but others who have said the same thing about their encounters with Aubrey). It probably comes from being someone who has had to get round obstacles many times himself over the years, battling entrenched thinking and prevailing scientific dogma, and wanting to lend a helping hand to any newcomers. Interestingly, the name of his latest spin-out is Underdog (which he talks about in our interview)!

At our interview we talked about when the tipping point will be reached about the science of aging and treating aging as a disease to move from "underground" to "mainstream'. Now that aging is included in the International Code for Diseases (ICD code) and the FDA is now on board with a trial looking at metformin's "anti-aging" effects—it seems that we will soon reach this stage. Aubrey talks to scientists and investors all the time, and big pharmaceuticals are starting to get interested.

The public is too. This is what we need to catalyze attention further. Since our interview, Aubrey helped by being one of the 4 scientists, along with Nir Barzilai, Lynne Cox, and Sabina Brennan, to speak about the Science of Aging at a public event, run by the How To Academy, in November—it was so popular the event had to move to a different venue.

**Tina Woods**: What do you think are the key points and messages that people should understand about living longer with AI?

**Aubrey de Grey**: I would say that there are really two aspects to this. First of all is the number of ways in which AI is going to participate in the actual creation of medicines that will allow us to stay healthy longer, and allow us to stay alive longer.

The second is the other improvements in AI that are going to happen in parallel, which will impact and interact with the benefits to life that will be delivered by these medicines.

With regard to the first of those, AI is already in fact helping to deliver these technologies. The improvements that have been seen in machine learning over the past decade have been absolutely mind-blowing, but most of the publicity that has revolved around those advances hasn't been about the medical realm; it's been about things like getting computers to play Go better than humans can. Even if the publicity isn't there yet, right now there's certainly a lot going on with regard to using machine learning to identify new medicines.

One particular area of progress is not so much about new medicines, but about the repurposing of existing drugs that are being found to have more wide-ranging benefits for the health of the elderly than they were originally designed for. Of course, the more we can use existing drugs the better, because it's a good deal quicker to get an old drug approved for a new purpose than it is to get a completely new drug through the system, mainly because the safety of the drug has already been established.

It's also often cheaper. That's not always a good thing; the clinical trials that need to get done sometimes have difficulty getting funded if people don't know whether or not they can make money out of a drug being repurposed. But this is still definitely happening in a big way right now. A number of the best-funded and leading companies in the anti-aging space right now are pursuing precisely this approach; Insilico Medicine is a great example of this.

**Tina Woods**: Insilico Medicine have had their own AlphaGo moment recently, haven't they?

**Aubrey de Grey**: I guess that's true! They've certainly been publishing an enormous amount lately and their progress is extremely impressive.

On the other side of all this progress is something that I want to emphasize because people overlook it a lot; whenever I give public talks or interviews or so forth, I always end up spending a lot of time trying to alleviate people's concerns about the problems that might be created, and the consequences of solving the problem we are having today, the problem of aging.

A number of those problems really misplaced, because they arise from unwarranted assumptions about how the world is going to be. The most important misconception people have is a terrible tendency to think about a post-aging world as if everything else in that world were pretty much the same as today, whereas what's actually going to happen is that we're not going to have a post-aging world for another 15 or 20 years at least, and by that time an awful lot of other things are going to be very different from how they are today.

In relation to AI, the big thing that I always have to point out is that we're not going to have any work to speak of, in the sense of having to do stuff that we would not do unless we were being paid for it, because of the enormous advances in automation that will have occurred by that time. That means that it's really wrongheaded to be thinking in terms of, "How will I survive with my pensions running out, because I'm living longer than I was expecting to?" Wealth will simply not be distributed in the same way that it is today.

There will need to be a lot of work to be done to redesign society so that wealth is distributed in an equitable manner, but it will not look anything like the way things work today, where there's the assumption of full employment up to a particular point, and then retirement.

**Tina Woods**: You're describing a world that's very different from our current one; hopefully better as well. I'd like to talk a little more about that—are you talking about things like Universal Basic Income? What will the world look like in this sort of future?

**Aubrey de Grey**: Things like that, exactly. Universal Basic Income sounds like a very blunt instrument to address this thing, and I'm quite sure that there will be plenty of refinements of that concept that will come to the fore over the coming years, but it's certainly a start. We definitely need not to hang about or hesitate, we need to actually figure out good ways to cope with a post-work world because that's going to come even sooner than a post-aging world.

**Tina Woods**: What technology or advancement do you think is going to have the biggest impact, when it comes to extending our healthy lifespan, in the next five or ten years?

**Aubrey de Grey**: There's not really going to be one single dominant area of medicine, or area of research, that's going to be at the center. The reason for that is because the whole approach to keeping people healthier later in life that's working and is going to work is the divide and conquer approach. It's basically to do with rejuvenation, with actually repairing the various types of molecular and cellular damage that the body does to itself throughout life. By definition, because there are so many different types of damage, we're going to have to give people a whole variety of different treatments, all at the same time. If we leave anything out, if there are types of damage that we're not addressing, then they're going to kill people more or less on schedule however well we've met all of the others.

This has really been the dominant determinant of how we at SENS Research Foundation prioritize our work. We always look to see what areas are being most neglected by the research community and by funders, because those are the things that need to catch up and not be allowed to fall by the wayside, and that's certainly happening now. The first few years, especially the first couple of years, we've seen that even the most challenging, most difficult areas of damage repair have started to yield to the efforts that we've been putting in. Progress is being made that actually seems likely to deliver real medicines and get into clinical trials over the next couple of years.

Moving on to the private sector, picking the time when something becomes investable, depends on your investor. We, of course, tend to talk to those investors who are much more involved with the early stage, the seed stage; angel stage investors, people who are comfortable with high-risk/high-reward stuff. They tend to be happy to get into an investment opportunity when the science has maybe still got a couple of years to go before it's even going to be in the first stage of clinical trial, which in other words means that there's only preliminary animal data.

Our connections with that kind of investor are very good news, and certainly that's why we have so far succeeded in spinning out half a dozen of our projects into start-up companies. We're definitely going to carry on doing that. That's basically our business model now and it's not just us; the industry really is an industry now. Karl Pfleger, one of the more active small investors in this space, did an enormous public service recently for the community and created a pretty comprehensive spreadsheet of all of the investment opportunities that currently exist (it can be accessed via agingbiotech.info). There were more than a hundred in that list already and it's growing every week, so life is good.

**Tina Woods**: Could you talk us through a handful of the exciting projects you've been working on?

**Aubrey de Grey**: Let's start with the most recent spin-out, which is called Underdog and is focused on eliminating the main toxic agent that drives atherosclerosis, the number one killer in the Western world.

It's been understood for a long time that the real thing that goes wrong in atherosclerosis is that modified cholesterol, oxidized cholesterol in particular, accumulates in certain cells in the walls of our arteries. It especially accumulates in white blood cells, and it poisons them. They become pro-inflammatory, and attract more white blood cells which can't cope with the problem either and so they become part of the problem, and the whole thing just gradually spins out of control.

Our approach is to use an ingeniously modified version of a very well-known old drug called cyclodextrin to extract this oxidized cholesterol and thereby to allow white blood cells to do what they're trying to do, namely to actually cause the atherosclerotic plaque to regress. We've just spun that out into a new company, courtesy of investment coming from a number of folks in our community.

As another example, let me talk about our mitochondrial project. This is one that hasn't yet reached the point of spinout, but it may only be a year or two away from that. What we're doing there is addressing the problem of accumulating mitochondrial mutations. Mitochondria are an essential part of the cell where the chemistry of respiration takes place, combining oxygen with nutrients in order to extract energy from the nutrients. They're the energy powerhouse of the cell, and they've even got their own DNA.

Mitochondria are the only parts of the cell that have their own DNA outside of the nucleus, where our chromosomes are, and it turns out that inside a mitochondrion is a really bad place for DNA to be. The chemistry of respiration is a hairy process that produces toxic molecules, free radicals that damage DNA. That means mitochondrial DNA accumulates damage much more rapidly than nuclear DNA.

What we've been trying to do about that for the past decade or more is that we've been trying to put backup copies of the mitochondrial DNA into the nucleus, into our normal chromosomes, so that even if the mitochondrial DNA gets damaged then the proteins that it encodes—and there are only 13 of those proteins— those proteins will still be available, so that the mitochondrion itself will still be able to function.

This isn't actually our idea. It's an idea that was first put forward more than 30 years ago by a group in Australia. There was some initial optimism that it might be able to work, but people hit obstacles and they basically gave up.

We decided that they'd maybe given up a little too easily, so we would have a bit of a go, and it took us a long time to get anywhere but a couple of years ago we published our first real breakthrough in that area. We've actually got a paper in review right now which demonstrates very substantial progress over and above that. We could be getting fairly close to being able to spin that project out as well, and that's one of the most challenging of all.

Another spinout that we have done is called Revel Pharmaceuticals, and they're focusing on stiffening of tissues; especially the artery walls and major arteries, but also the skin. It happens through a reaction called glycation, which is essentially the creation of unwanted chemical bonds between long-lived proteins. The chemistry of what's going on there has been reasonably well-understood for quite a long time but the question of what to do about it, in particular how to destroy these chemical bonds and thereby restore the elasticity of these tissues, that is something that nobody was really even trying to do because they thought it was too hard.

We said, "That won't do," and so we funded a group at Yale University for a number of years to work on this and they were extremely successful. They eventually identified a variety of enzymes that appear to be able to do exactly the job we needed, and that has now gone far enough along that we've been able to spin that out into a private company as well.

**Tina Woods**: Can you tell us a little bit about how all these inventions go back to the **strategies for engineered negligible senescence (SENS)**? The Seven Pillars of Aging is the backbone of this, isn't it?

**Aubrey de Grey**: It's nearly 20 years ago now that I first started to talk about SENS, and that was based on the realization that we hadn't really discovered anything new about what aging is, and the levels of molecular and cellular damage in aging, for nearly 20 years before that.

The most recent examples were from the early 1980s. I thought, "That's pretty good news, but what does it actually mean?" Does it mean that we're close to being able to actually develop therapies that would work?

That was what led me to the realization that damage repair therapies, which don't stop damage from being created, but rather eliminate damage before it gets to the point that causes us to get sick, that approach was much more practical than anyone had really appreciated. I certainly wasn't going to say it was easy, but I did claim that maybe it was easy enough that it was worth having a go.

The gratifying thing is that even though, initially, scientists were by and large not terribly convinced of this, and most of my colleagues actually didn't think it was particularly scientific at first, nevertheless the idea gradually caught on. People eventually realized that the only real reason they were so pessimistic was because I'd brought in a lot of ideas that had been developed elsewhere in biology, for reasons that had nothing to do with aging, and so it was just stuff that they weren't up to speed on.

Time went on, and this decade we've seen the whole idea essentially being reinvented by a variety of groups, in somewhat different forms but essentially the same concept, and it's now become very mainstream and orthodox. That's very nice to see, and certainly the science is standing the test of time. We haven't had any new discoveries in the past couple of decades that show that the problem is harder than we thought it was, or anything like that. It's all very gratifying, and that's why we've been able to push things along.

The reason that we set ourselves up initially as a charity, rather than as a company, was precisely because these things were very early-stage, too early for even the most risk-friendly investor to be interested. It's really over the past four or five years that that has progressively changed and one by one we've been able to take our companies private.

**Tina Woods**: Is it accurate to say that you approach aging as an engineering problem that needs to be solved? Is it as simple as thinking of the human body as a machine you can restore, in the same way that you can with as with a car; you just need to tinker around and repair the bits that have stopped working?

**Aubrey de Grey**: It really is, yes. Of course, any living organism is a far more complicated machine than anything that's man made but that doesn't change the fact that the concept is still the same. Any machine's function is determined by its structure, and therefore, if you can restore the structure then you're also going to restore the function. Showing that it was a feasible thing to do, in other words that the complexity of the problem of the machine was not an insuperable barrier, that was really the purpose of classifying the damage of aging. I classified it into these seven strands that I talk about, the Seven Pillars of Aging.

The classification has the value of demonstrating that even though the damage itself comes in many, many forms, we only need to develop a very manageable number of repair strategies to actually eliminate this damage. For example, one of the types of damage that I talk about is the loss of cells, where cells die and they're not automatically replaced by cell division. The generic repair strategy for that is stem cell therapy. The cells are repaired in the laboratory, so that they know what to do to divide and differentiate to replace the cells that the body is not replacing on its own.

That sounds pretty simple. Of course, it's not really simple because every tissue, every organ that loses cells needs its own specific stem cell therapy, but that's kind of okay. Once you've got a couple of stem cell therapies working for a couple of tissues, you can essentially reuse all of the knowledge that you gained in getting those ones working, and you can get the next one working a lot more quickly than the previous ones. Even though each stem cell therapy is different in its details, all stem cell therapies have a great deal in common.

**Tina Woods**: The work that you're doing is so cutting-edge, and you're one of the first to really innovate in this whole sort of arena. How have you managed to quell some of the cynics who threw up their hands and said, "Oh, what is this all about?"—what has been your approach? As you get more evidence, is that helping convince the doubters?

**Aubrey de Grey**: It comes at many levels. First of all, absolutely it's the evidence, the actual progress that has been made, not just the progress made by SENS Research Foundation itself but also by other people who are pursuing the same strategy or parts of the same strategy and are themselves having success. It's partly that. It's also what I mentioned earlier, essentially just the community becoming more educated about what I was suggesting.

When I was first talking about this, most of my colleagues didn't understand a word that I was saying. That's not their fault particularly, it's just that it was a big paradigm shift. Really, it's taken no longer for these ideas to be accepted than this kind of thing normally takes. First of all, the concept has stood the test of time as people have been continuing to understand it, and secondly there's actual progress being made in the most challenging and the most difficult components of the whole thing.

**Tina Woods**: Over the past ten years with the developments of the Human Genome Project and understanding of the human genome, how has that helped your work?

**Aubrey de Grey**: Lots of inaccurate things were said back then, when the human genome was being sequenced, to do with how much it would revolutionize medicine. It has revolutionized medical research, in the sense that there are many things that can be done more rapidly now as a result of having the human genome. Of course, the same applies to the manipulation of the genome, genome editing with things like CRISPR. These are technologies which don't specifically allow us to do things that we couldn't do at all before, but they make it much easier to do them.

They make the things we do much quicker, much cheaper, and much more effective, and that is very important.

**Tina Woods**: What we're really trying to understand is how to keep people healthy and well across their life course, from pre-birth through to the bitter end. How do you see what you are doing through that lens?

**Aubrey de Grey**: Thank you for mentioning prenatal health, because that's actually a really important factor. The life expectancies that we see in the West today are at least two or more times the age that they were couple of hundred years ago. Most of that progress was made as a result of simply eliminating infant mortality, which used to be like 40%, even in the wealthiest countries in the world. There was also, of course, death in childbirth and so on, and that's been reduced to an absolute fraction of what it once was, which is great. But the point is that those improvements had already pretty much been made by World War Two. Hardly anybody was dying really early in life by then, yet we have seen continued improvements in life expectancy throughout the industrialized world.

The big question is why? How has that been happening? And it's been because people have had a higher probability of survival—in other words a lower probability of death—at older ages, which has allowed their life expectancy to rise. It turns out that, at least in most people's view, that change has arisen in very large part from good prenatal nutrition and perinatal nutrition. A century ago, eighty years ago, there was still a progressive improvement in prosperity going on, and prosperity of course translates into better nutrition. It turns out that if you have been well-nourished in the womb, then this stays with you throughout your life. You essentially are born biologically younger than you otherwise would be and you stay that way. This is a large part of why people are now living longer than they were even after World War Two.

**Tina Woods**: I was struck by the epigenetics aspect, how even that can be influenced by how you live your life and what you eat, that the lifestyles of the mother and father can actually influence epigenetic expression in their offspring.

**Aubrey de Grey**: The laying down of our epigenetic information prenatally is a very complicated network of chemical reactions, and those chemical reactions need reagents. If, for example, there is a shortage of some important micronutrient, then that process won't happen entirely correctly, and that can end up being problematic.

**Tina Woods**: How do epigenetics and the environmental pressures on our health influence the work that you've been doing, in terms of keeping people healthier and also living longer?

**Aubrey de Grey**: It does not actually influence our work directly. Our work at SENS Research Foundation is restricted to the hardcore molecular biology and cell biology that's involved in the early stages of developing new medicine. That's in no way to imply that we don't think environmental factors are important; they certainly are important.

In fact, a large part of the incentive to look after one's life, one's health as best one can today is to improve one's chances of making the cut, so to speak. Surviving long enough, in a good enough state of health, to be able to benefit from these therapies that don't yet exist, that people like us are developing. That's only one reason, of course, to stay healthy—it has its own benefits in the meantime as well—but it is certainly important.

I think the only thing I always want to make sure people understand here is that they mustn't go too far the other way, in the sense of thinking that they can really have a big influence on their health through longevity with things that already exist. That can lead to the conclusion that the research we're doing to develop those essential components of healthy longevity that don't yet exist isn't very important.

That's a tendency to come to that conclusion that some people have, and we need to fight that by keeping a sense of proportion about this.

**Tina Woods**: There's this notion that you can probably get to 80 or 90 in decent health, like in the Blue Zone countries. That's through being socially connected, through eating well, getting your exercise, having a sense of purpose and so on. Is it getting beyond that, getting to 120 and older in decent health, where some of the strategies that you are pioneering really kick in?

**Aubrey de Grey**: That's pretty much exactly right, yes. The amount of impact that one can have on one's own longevity with what exists today is certainly pretty limited. In fact, even in the Blue Zones, life expectancy is only a few years longer than in neighboring areas; that's despite the fact that in many cases, those populations have spent their entire lives living a different kind of lifestyle than the neighboring areas, and that lifelong difference is inevitably going to have more of an impact on a person's longevity than if they only started trying to look after themselves starting in middle age, for example. Even with that lifelong healthy lifestyle, the difference is only a few years.

**Tina Woods**: Whether or not aging should be classified as a disease is a discussion that's gone round and round—obviously, it would be useful when looking at things from an FDA perspective, trying to get drugs approved and interacting with the very precise classification systems involved with that.

Do you think the classification of aging as a disease or not poses a risk to any of your research?

**Aubrey de Grey**: To be honest, I think that we've pretty much passed the point of the question of whether aging is a disease being relevant to the regulatory process.

A lot of that progress is thanks to the work of Nir Barzilai and some of his colleagues, who have, through a very painstaking process of negotiation with the FDA, got to the point of developing this thing called the TAME trial, which is a clinical trial to determine the impact of the drug metformin on aging.

The reason why it took so long was precisely what you're saying. The FDA needs something that they can then take as a hard and fast clinical endpoint, that will stand up to scrutiny, where you can actually say whether the thing was achieved or not. The difficulty was that aging isn't clearly defined in many cases; if you ask 10 specialists what aging is, you'll get 10 different answers. What had to happen was the development of a very sophisticated combinatorial definition of the endpoint of the trial, that the FDA could be happy with because they could in a concrete way say whether it had been achieved. From the point of view of the biologists, it was aging in all but name. That was the requirement.

So that has happened and the key thing to understand about that is that no-one's going to make money out of metformin, because it's generic now, but that's okay. The trial has now been fully funded. That took a long time because no one is going to make any money out of it, it had to be done philanthropically but that's now happened. That means that this clinical endpoint, that was so laboriously agreed with the FDA, is something that can now be used in the future just by copying and pasting from the TAME trial, for any other trial that that might happen for a drug that's new and that could be coming. That's a really big step forward.

The other thing that's happened much more recently, just this year, is the release of the latest iteration of the ICD code, the International Classification of Diseases, which has now included a qualifier—called an extension code—defining something to be aging-related. This is a very clever way of achieving the required goal; rather than saying that aging is a particular type of disease, that one would say that someone has aging rather than having Alzheimer's or having cancer or whatever, instead this qualifier can be added to an existing disease code.

This changes the incentive structure a great deal, in terms of what big pharmaceuticals may be tempted to actually invest in the research to treat. Altogether, the question of whether you want to call aging a disease is no longer an important question. I think personally it's always been a distraction, whether or not we should call aging a disease. Aging is quite clearly a medical problem—in other words it is amenable, in principle, to medical intervention—but whether you call it a disease or not is not honestly very important.

**Tina Woods**: You've been quoted saying that the first person to reach 1,000 may already be alive, and we hear about concepts like longevity escape velocity, or the idea that in 2045 we may even achieve immortality. Do you believe we will reach immortality?

**Aubrey de Grey**: I don't like to use the word immortality because it has too many connotations. Of course, what you're really asking is if I think we're going to reach this thing I called longevity escape velocity, which is the concept that we can, before we reach the stage of absolutely 100% perfect damage repair therapies, still stay one step ahead of the problems, and keep improving the therapies fast enough that people never actually have as much damage in their body as they would need to have in order to get sick.

This is a concept that is pretty easy to understand, it's pretty straightforward, and I believe that at this point we have at least a 50/50 chance of getting to that point, of getting the therapies that are good enough to start staying one step ahead of the problem, within the next 17 years or so.

Of course, it could take longer. That's a very speculative prediction, because any pioneering technology is obviously speculative. We may hit additional problems that we don't know about yet; there's maybe a 10% chance that we won't get there for a hundred years, but that doesn't really matter. What matters is we've got at least a 50/50 chance of getting there pretty soon. That would of course certainly mean that most people alive today, never mind just one person, most people alive today would be likely to benefit from this technology.

They will be young enough 17 years from now not to be at death's door quite yet.

**Tina Woods**: Do you think that everyone will benefit from this technology? What do you think society will be like if we achieve this much longer sort of longevity—what do you think are some of the ethical issues, and how might it impact society?

**Aubrey de Grey**: There are many questions that people constantly raise with regards to how this would actually work, and I guess you could call them some of them ethical; people sometimes say, "Doesn't death give meaning to life?" Honestly, I've got no time for that kind of stuff. It seems to me that you can only say such things with a straight face if you've just not really taken on board that aging is a medical problem in the first place.

As far as I'm concerned, people just have to pay attention and remember that it is a medical problem; people do not say "Alzheimer's gives meaning to life." There are other issues which I would say are not so much ethical exactly, but rather, sociological. Questions like where will we put all the people, or won't awful people live forever or stuff like that. I honestly don't have much time for any of those things either, for two reasons. First of all, it's really easy to see how these problems won't really arise, or even if in some worst case scenario they do arise, how they can be addressed.

Secondly, it's really easy to see how even if they were to arise, and not be addressed, there's no way that they could be anywhere near as bad as the problems that we have today. The problem we have today is 110,000 people every day dying of this thing worldwide because most people are dying after a long period of decline and decrepitude and pain.

It is painful to have to keep going on repeating the same rebuttals of these concerns. A time will come when we don't have to do that anymore, because the only reason that really people are so resistant to the argument that this is actually quite a good idea is because they don't want to get their hopes up. They are terrified of getting emotionally invested in all of this.

**Tina Woods**: When do you think we will reach the tipping point? What do you think it will take to get the public to wake up to what you're trying to say?

**Aubrey de Grey**: I think it is really the same kind of thing; a combination that first of all caused the scientific community to wake up, maybe less than ten years ago, and that similarly got the investment community to wake up in the past few years. I think it really is just a matter of both the actual progress that's happening in the laboratory that's being reported in the news every week, every month, together with the repeat advertising, the fact that people have been saying this thing for a long time, and I am still getting away with it. Nobody has come along and provided solid reasons why this either can't be done or shouldn't be done.

**Tina Woods**: Taking all this together, what's the secret to your life? What are you doing yourself personally, to live longer and better?

**Aubrey de Grey**: I'm not actually doing very much, to be honest. First of all, I'm a lucky guy. I seem to always come out much younger than I really am when my biological age is tested, but also because I figure I've just got to work as hard as I can to get this done. I probably do myself a bit of harm by not getting enough sleep! But, no, I don't really do anything. I'm just one of those people—I can eat and drink more or less exactly what I like, and nothing seems to happen. I don't need to do any exercise to speak of.

**Tina Woods**: It sounds like you've got a very strong sense of purpose. That's keeping you going isn't it?

**Aubrey de Grey**: Yes, I think that certainly helps. I do feel extremely privileged to have been able to get to this point in making such an important contribution to the world's most important problem.

**Tina Woods**: What have you learned from the COVID-19 pandemic?

**Aubrey de Grey**: The pandemic has greatly impacted the work at SENS Research foundation, with an extended period when only two people could be in the lab at the same time, rising only to five at the time of writing. We've been doing the best we can within that constraint, but for sure it has delayed a lot of research—and of course the same applies across the medical research world. I shudder to think how many lives will end up having been lost as a result.

For me personally, the lockdown has been quite pleasant, but that's not much compensation. The only positive is that maybe, just maybe, policy-makers will learn the lesson that prevention and front-loaded investment in early stage research is actually quite a good idea.

## Alex Zhavoronkov

*CEO, Insilico Medicine*

I first met Alex at the CogX AI Festival in 2018. I was chairing a workshop on AI in health for the work I was doing for the Academic Health Science Network and was introduced to him and his colleague Polina Mamoshina afterwards by Dmitry Kaminskiy.

Alex gave me a 5-minute presentation and I was blown away by the work he was doing. I invited Alex to a workshop I was running (with Maxine Macintosh) a week later on harnessing consumer datasets for aging research and the mind-boggling potential of using multimodal AI to leverage insights across disparate datasets to aid research in aging became clear—including to some of the big companies who were there like Mastercard.

Alex founded Insilico Medicine in 2014. He studied computer science initially and decided to go into biotechnology with his interest in slowing down the aging process. He received his Master's from Johns Hopkins and then got a PhD from Moscow State University, where his studies focused on using machine learning to look at the physics of molecular interactions in biological systems.

Insilico Medicine is regarded as a game changer in AI-driven drug discovery and longevity research. His company uses computers to simulate how certain drugs will affect specific tissues—without the need for animal testing or clinical trials. Their approach is based on using bioinformatics to model human bodies and entire populations and provide a testbed for therapeutic interventions and evaluate their ability to restore the body's homeostatic capacity and ultimately delay or even prevent aging.

The company's original philosophy was based on using deep learning to train neural networks on large gene expression datasets to identify novel drug targets and then go through large libraries of molecules to find promising drug candidates with certain properties. However, Alex realized that he could get machines to imagine new molecules with particular properties and in so doing completely disrupt the current pharmaceutical R&D drug discovery and development process.

Insilico makes use of **generative adversarial networks (GANs)** and **reinforcement learning (RL)** in a lot of their work. Recently, they had their "AlphaGo" moment published in *Nature Biotechnology* on 2nd September 2019 showing that its deep learning system could create new unpatented molecules for a protein target implicated in fibrosis. That system, called **generative tensorial reinforcement learning**, or **GENTRL**, was used to design new molecules for a kinase target that was nominated by a partner company conducting a challenge. The molecules were easy to make and were then synthesized in under 10 days and were successfully tested in human cells and one was even tested in mice. It took about 21 days for the AI system to design molecules, and the total time for design, synthesis, and validation was about 46 days. Although none of the drugs designed by GENTRL appear to be more effective than inhibitors developed by the traditional research method, the traditional process to develop drug candidates may take years and millions of dollars to develop, compared to the handful of weeks and approximate $150,000 cost of Insilico's method. It was also the first substantial experimental demonstration for the generative RL approach in drug design. Many pharmaceutical companies decided to focus their efforts on this technique after this paper.

You can tell by now that Alex is, quite simply, a genius. But more important, he applies his incredible brain for the good of many. Alex is guided by a philosophy of "effective altruism," that is, using research to have the most positive impact on peoples' lives; he has published his views on creating values for AGI focused around the maximization of human QALY globally, which are seeded in his book, *The Ageless Generation: How Advances in Biotechnology Will Impact the Global Economy*. In 2017, Insilico was named one of the Top 5 AI companies by NVIDIA for its potential for social impact.

When the COVID-19 pandemic started to strike, Alex was one of the first scientists to look at how to bring AI and the science of aging together, focusing on target discovery, drug repurposing, and de novo drug design for the SARS-CoV-2 targets.

He recognized early on that COVID-19 does not treat all age groups equally, and that many of the expected interventions such as vaccine, therapeutic, and symptomatic treatments will not work as well in the elderly population. He is now planning clinical trials for low-dose rapamycin for prevention of COVID-19 and possibly even for treatment as single agents or in combination with metformin, NAD+ boosters (commonly sold as supplements), and possibly other geroprotectors.

When I interviewed Alex it was 4 am his time—he was in Hong Kong and it was my evening in London. He was so busy he was not going to go to sleep that night anyway and slotting in an interview was no inconvenience. Alex clearly does not seem to need a lot of sleep. He is driven by an energy and deep sense of purpose and belief in sharing the benefits of knowledge to as many people as possible.

**Tina Woods**: You're one of the preeminent leaders in this space. In your view, what are the key messages that people should know about living longer with AI? Why should people care about this topic?

**Alex Zhavoronkov**: Living longer is pretty much inevitable at this point. The only way to live better, and perhaps even reverse all the age-associated processes, is to apply AI to aging research at scale. Using AI, we can accelerate aging research in pretty much every aspect, from hypothesis generation and drug discovery, all the way up to regenerative medicine and real-world evidence collection.

Due to the breakthroughs in AI, we're going to enjoy an accelerated pace in this new longevity biotechnology industry. There is a massive convergence of various technologies from very different angles. For example, we've got mobile devices now that enable **Internet of Things** (**IoT**) and massive connectivity. We can track pretty much everything in our daily lives. We can also reduce risk by preventing a lot of human error, malevolent behavior, and malevolent events. As Peter Diamandis puts it, we just need to ensure that we don't die of something stupid!

When I entered this field 16 years ago, I left a lucrative job at a company that is now powering AI through **graphics processing units (GPUs)**. That's one area that has contributed to the emergence of AI in recent years. At the time, I thought that I needed to become an expert in biology and completely switch into biology. If I had the choice to live my life over again, I wouldn't have quit that job; I would have continued working in computer science and doing research on aging from that perspective alone trying to steer the company into biotechnology.

Right now, the boundaries between computer science and biotechnology are blurred. That convergence is leading to massive increases in productivity. There are new ideas coming from all over the place: electronics, the consumer industry, entertainment, cars, and so on. Everything in healthcare, safety, and security that is powered by AI is contributing to increased longevity.

**Tina Woods**: Does anything have the potential to halt this progress?

**Alex Zhavoronkov**: The only thing that could really impede progress is an economic collapse, which actually might be caused by aging itself. Governments aren't prepared for the silver wave (aging populations).

Most economies are unsustainable. The US has accumulated a massive amount of national debt and there is massive unfunded fiscal imbalance. This is true for many other developed countries too. The only way to get the economy to grow again is to increase productive longevity. That can only be achieved through AI. It's a catch-22 because from one perspective, increasing lifespans is bad for the economy in the short term. On the other hand, productive longevity will definitely result in unprecedented economic growth.

**Tina Woods**: The US seems to be lagging behind in terms of policies and being proactive in this area. The UK, however, is trying to lead the way. Singapore and Japan are also wrestling with these situations as we speak. Which country would you say is most at risk from the silver wave?

**Alex Zhavoronkov:** The US is the most susceptible developed country to this silver time bomb because of the unfunded fiscal imbalance but also because of its healthcare system. The US Government's Medicare program begins at 65. Medicare, Medicaid, and Social Security programs total about $35-40,000 per capita. The net tax income that the country derives per capita is much smaller than that, so it's unsustainable in just these basic terms.

However, I would say that despite being the most susceptible to this time bomb, the US will also be the most resilient to it. The US economy is the most technologically driven economy in the world and the US dollar is the strongest currency in the world; it's the beating heart of the world's economy. If the US goes into a silver crisis that leads to a devaluation of the US dollar, that will kill the world's economy in an instant so all other economies have no choice but to play along.

The US is also the leader in longevity biotechnology. It's home to the National Institute on Aging, which spends over a billion dollars a year on aging research. The National Institutes of Health also spends an enormous amount of money on other areas of medical research that contribute to aging research.

When thinking about the future, one risk for longevity is war. If you look at the history of the world, you can spot very similar trends from the previous century. The first two world wars were preceded by massive advances in technology, and population growth. The governments were not prepared for that. We've now got hyperinflation, along with economic and political instability in many countries. The massive global wars pretty much exterminated the elderly because they just couldn't survive. We don't want to have that happening again; we need to break the cycle.

**Tina Woods:** Due to this economic time bomb that's looming, we face societal and ethical dilemmas. If we break responsibilities down in terms of roles, what should governments be doing?

**Alex Zhavoronkov:** The world is now very democratic; only a few countries are dictatorships. However, most politicians focus on staying in power. Their policies appeal to the masses and to people who are mostly uneducated about economic theory. People are not willing to sacrifice their current benefits for the future good. They continue to steal from future generations and continue to borrow. There is an intergenerational war going on. If you look at the US, the last two presidential candidates had one thing in common: their age. Both are over 70. They appealed to the older layers of the population and the same is true for the UK where it resulted in Brexit.

Politicians appeal to what is important currently. People are very distracted by the current state of affairs. Our world has actually never been better in terms of the general net utility per capita. We have more enjoyment in life, and more benefits, than any person, even a royal, did 200 years ago. We have fresh running water and options that would seem magical to people in the past. At the same time, we are also very depressed as a society because the world is changing very quickly. To combat that depression, we start focusing on current events.

Governments need to look at longevity as an opportunity and then teach that to the masses. Politicians don't do that currently because saying unappealing things isn't going to help them to be elected. Only one government is stepping up: China. In Europe and the US, there are no leaders who want to take the painful pill that is telling people to stop spending. We need to stop spending on the military, for example. Military spending has one of the highest economic multipliers and it's not actually a very altruistic thing to invest in; it's an egotistical thing.

Politicians say that a particular country is a threat to make people want to invest in safety. The truth is that the politicians are simply appealing to the electorate. Voters are influenced through the media or by big oil, banks, or pharmaceutical companies.

It's very difficult for the politicians in a democratic world to think further into the future than their current time in office. That's why the most altruistic and benevolent government is actually in China. Whether we're talking about China, Russia, Iran, Saudi Arabia, or any other country that is seen as following a different life cycle paradigm, if the people in those countries accept the ethical framework where longevity is seen as the ultimate good, they will, in turn, do good.

**Tina Woods**: China is often presented very negatively in the media in terms of its social credit policy. In fact, there are some very interesting aspects of the social credit policy surrounding incentivizing people to behave well for the collective good. Do you agree with those ideas?

**Alex Zhavoronkov**: Yes, I think the social credit policy is one of the most amazing inventions out there and it could eclipse both communist and democratic thought going forward. The policy takes the best of both worlds and puts it into action. From one perspective, you really do count the opinion of every individual because you're looking at everybody under the microscope and understanding their desires.

From another perspective, you're making people conform to rules. But if you're trying to argue against the social credit policy, you're basically trying to argue against rules being enforceable. The policy would definitely separate the bad people from the good people because bad people don't conform to the rules.

At a very basic level, if there is a street sign telling people not to cross in a certain place, crossing there will get their social credit score reduced. There is likely a good reason for that sign to be there. However, if the AI that monitors this activity sees people crossing the street en masse, even if a penalty is associated with that, there clearly needs to be a place to cross. This gives governments democratic feedback very quickly.

If people want to smoke, their credit rating will be reduced. There is nothing good about smoking. A lot of people are trying to quit and it's actually a very good thing for us to quit as a society. Smokers create a burden of healthcare costs later on. If you are contributing negatively to your health, should you be punished? Continuing this idea of social credit, you might not be able to access the healthcare system in the same way as a person who doesn't smoke in the future. That's democracy in action.

**Tina Woods**: I agree with you. The National Health Service in the UK spends 10% of its budget on diabetes treatment. Diabetes, for the most part, is caused by lifestyle and food choices. All the resources that go toward treating people with diabetes take away resources from other people who, through bad luck, became ill. There's a huge debate about the best way to incentivize individuals while also communicating a message about the consequences of their behavior, not just for themselves but also for the wider community.

It's very interesting what you're saying about the Chinese. I visited China 25 years ago and I remember that everyone smoked. Has the social credit policy resulted in a lot fewer people smoking?

**Alex Zhavoronkov**: I don't think that the social credit rating system has been widely implemented yet. There is more talk about it than action. Journalists are taking the sensationalist position only because they want their stories to sell. As the visionary entrepreneur and educator Peter Diamandis points out, our brains are designed to react to negativity much stronger than to positivity.

People start a debate only if something is seen as evil or a threat. If somebody implements a new policy, they are seen as the enemy; people mobilize against this. The idea of social credit is to create a feedback loop where the decisions are made collectively. Instead of elected leaders, we could navigate policies through voting on a massive scale.

**Tina Woods**: What will be the role of businesses in all of this?

**Alex Zhavoronkov**: Businesses, I think, will play a greater role than the governments, at least if we're talking about businesses outside of China. In the corporate world, the really large corporations, such as Google, Amazon, Apple, and Microsoft, take a longer-term view than governments because the CEOs are elected for longer periods and are given a chance to build on consumer spending. People vote for established models, but companies and CEOs can explore new models.

Nowadays, it's very difficult to sell something to the consumer if you're a smaller company. Most consumer needs are satisfied by the top companies that cater to pretty much all our digital and physical needs. For those large corporates, they control so much of our lives that the only thing that isn't currently available for them to sell to us is more life.

These companies invest in all kinds of health-related consumer products, such as the personalization of nutrition and healthcare. Since our greatest need is healthcare, there is no other direction for these companies to go in; there is no other way for them to grow. That's why Google is investing in companies like Verily, Amazon is now going into insurance by partnering with Berkshire Hathaway on healthcare programs, and Alibaba is taking a leap of faith with some of the healthcare apps.

These companies can take on the role of a government by creating healthcare as a service and maybe longevity as a service. Corporations will be able to really make a difference. Many of them are doing so already, but it's not for altruistic reasons, despite what they may say.

**Tina Woods**: What will have the biggest impact in helping people to live longer and better lives in the next 10 years? What are your predictions?

**Alex Zhavoronkov:** AI will have the biggest impact on longevity. AI is essentially the glue that sticks every other technology together. That's why I chose this area to focus on.

Drugs to combat muscle wasting will probably be one of the first frontiers in our fight against aging. That's one area where if you show that your drug works, it will immediately be used off-label for purposes such as bodybuilding.

Secondly, senolytics is a topic that we're improving our understanding of immensely right now by using AI. We're able to target the cells that are senescent. Essentially, they sit there and pollute the environment around them. One scientist who managed to categorize these sources of damage better than anybody else is Aubrey de Grey. He's a very famous British biogerontologist who has had a large impact on our field. He came up with seven sources of damage and repair. AI taps into every one of those seven areas by making things happen faster and learning from those areas. We can eliminate the damaged cells, replenish those cells with muscle regeneration, and build muscle through a combination of factors.

I think the low-hanging fruit right now is fibrosis. That's what my company is focused on. Fibrosis is a driver of aging. We naturally just scar and lose function. Mineralization of the connective tissue and all kinds of connective tissue damage is another great field that can be addressed through intervention by AI.

It's important to look at biomarkers or aging clocks, as we call them. These are the markers of biological aging at every level: molecular, cellular, tissue, psychological, and societal. AI will give us the ability to identify specific areas where we can intervene. This will help us understand the rate of aging and the causes of aging. Other areas of interest are gene therapy, regenerative medicine and AI-driven diagnostics.

I have my own ethical framework, as you know. I think that anything outside of life extension is a waste of time at this point.

Once you realize what kind of impact this field can have, and what kind of tragedy a delay could cause, stopping due to ethical arguments would be a crime against humanity.

**Tina Woods**: What have you learned from the COVID-19 pandemic?

**Alex Zhavoronkov**: We used our generative chemistry platform to generate 100 molecules targeting the COVID-19 3C-like protease. Our generative chemistry platform can handle multiple scenarios with varying amounts of input data available. Here we used the homology modeling approach, where we used the protein sequence to model several variants of the binding pocket, and generated a number of template molecules that are likely to bind the protein. Then we expanded the chemical space using these template molecules and generated tens of thousands of molecules with different medicinal chemistry properties.

We then used our deep learning medicinal chemistry filtering system to narrow down the generated molecules to just a few. Another scenario handled by our platform was the actual 3C-like protease crystal. There, instead of homology modeling we used the actual crystal structure obtained from Dr. Rao's lab from ShanghaiTech. That crystal also had a small fragment that we used as a template to generate multiple molecules with a similar structure using ligand-based generation, a third scenario handled by our platform. In the end, we ordered the synthesis of seven of these molecules.

But we were faced with another challenge—our FTE chemists were quarantined. Now we got one molecule synthesized and are waiting for the binding and cell-based assays to become available. This work is available via a dedicated page on our company's website: https://insilico.com/ncov-sprint/.

Since the many medicinal chemists liked the generated molecules, we got a large number of inquiries. We did not publish the code for the generative chemistry platform as it is a $20-million system that took four years to develop but we are offering it to a limited number of our big pharmaceutical partners to deploy on their premises and get similar capabilities in AI along with the licenses to our extensive patent portfolio covering generative chemistry work.

## José Cordeiro

*Futurist, Transhumanist, Director of The Millennium Project, Vice chair of HumanityPlus, Fellow of the World Academy of Art and Science*

José Cordeiro is an extraordinary human being, full of joy for life, wearing a multitude of hats and possessing a long list of credentials and accolades which would literally take pages to describe. He is one of the founders and professors of Singularity University, counts among his friends Ray Kurzweil (Google's Director of Engineering and author of the famous book, The Singularity is Near), is a Director of the Millennium Project that connects futurists around the world to improve global foresight, and is also a transhumanist, author, and political activist, among many other things.

I first came across José at a longevity conference in 2018 when he was a late addition to the panel I was chairing. Not having his biography to read beforehand I was admittedly a little unprepared when he announced that the longevity escape velocity (the point at which life expectancy is being extended longer than the time that is passing) will be reached in 2030, meaning that by 2045 we will be immortal.

This was quite left-field at a panel otherwise replete with policymakers and business leaders prepared to discuss "The Business of Prevention and the Future of Wellbeing"—but oh no, José was able to shift gears quickly to their level, explaining how developments in geroscience and biological computing are fast surpassing governments' ability to keep up with policy frameworks to maximize the opportunities of living longer. Compelled to act with the dawn of immortality in sight within our lifetime, José announced he was creating a new political movement "from the future" and running as an MEP for the newly created MIEL ("honey" in Spanish) Party in the European elections in May (he didn't win). At the end of the conference I was a proud owner of a signed copy of his latest book, La Muerte de la Muerte ("The Death of Death") and can now call him a dear colleague and even friend. I can imagine calling him up on my next El Camino walk.

Full of optimism, zest, and hope, José represents a glass not only half full, but full and exponentially overflowing. When I interviewed him I could tell he was walking briskly—and that of course is how he gets a lot done while getting his exercise too! Interviewing someone like José can make your head hurt after an hour—trying to keep up with a gigantic brain that is making all sorts of creative connections on the go and taking you to places that you haven't even thought of, ever (no matter how many MIT Technology Reviews, Abundance 360 newsletters, Azeem Azhar Exponential Views and other super-intelligent magazines you scour weekly in the hope you don't fall behind).

The clever question I had up my sleeve for José was on when we would achieve "super-humanity." I should have known of course that he would get there before me, within minutes expounding his views on the hardware and the software of human beings: with our memories, ideas, dreams, and loves as impulses that can be harnessed to create augmented brains and expanded lives. Imagine that as the next Christmas present you can order from Amazon!

**Tina Woods**: What are the key messages that people should understand about living longer with AI?

**José Cordeiro**: Well, I'm an immortalist, but I'm also a transhumanist and a singularitarian. I believe in indefinite lifespans, radical life extension, and even immortality as a concept, but from two points of view; the biological point of view and the computational point of view. Or, as I call it sometimes, the hardware and the software.

When you talk about AI, we might actually be able to wire up our brains to a computer and upload our knowledge within the next 20 to 30 years. In fact, I'm pretty sure you've seen that Neuralink and Elon Musk announced that they hope to begin trials with humans to read their brains by 2020. When we can read our minds, basically, we will be computationally immortal.

This is important to me because I believe in both immortalities: biological immortality, and also computational immortality. I'm a good friend of Ray Kurzweil, who also more or less believes in that, but he thinks computational immortality is probably better because we would be able to increase our memories, our brain capacity, our overall knowledge, and the speed at which we communicate. We communicate very inefficiently and very slowly. Going back to the biological part, I think AI will also help us to discover many things about our biology, and therefore change medicine forever.

**Tina Woods**: What do you see, both now and looking ahead, that will help us with our healthspan as well as our lifespan?

**José Cordeiro**: Well, of course, the objective is to increase both, but healthspan is relevant because we want to be living longer and also healthier lives. The objective is that they are eventually both equal and indefinite.

Right now there are many exciting things happening, like stem-cell treatments, gene therapies, senolytics, CRISPR; all these things are relatively very new.

What we understand now as epigenetics and the famous Yamanaka factors have shown that in principle, we can take an old cell and turn it into a new cell: this is something absolutely amazing, incredible, exciting.

David Sinclair's book is called *Lifespan*, and he talks about cellular reprogramming. He thinks this is the next big thing in medicine and I find that I agree. In terms of our biological parts, this is going to be revolutionary. The proof of concept is there; if we can do it at the organism level, not just at the cell level as we can today, that will change everything.

**Tina Woods**: Where do you think reprogramming's really going to take off at that next level, the organism level?

**José Cordeiro**: Well, it's not even beginning. This has been done at the cell level and hopefully, some people are working at the organ level, but talking about a whole organism just isn't happening yet. The concept is there; the proof that it can be done is, I think, there. We just need more time. These things are moving exponentially, so it might be possible in 5 years or 10 years to do some of that.

That is why I'm personally interested in reading David Sinclair's book, because he's at the frontier of some of these developments; him, all the people at Harvard, and also George Church. George Church is incredible—he participated in the Human Genome Project and now in the Human Brain Project, and that is why I want to talk about both parts: not only the biological, but also the computational part of what we are.

**Tina Woods**: Could you expand a little bit more on the computational part, just so that people can understand what you mean by that?

**José Cordeiro**: This is basically, as I mentioned, the hardware and the software of what we humans are. Most of our memories, our ideas, our dreams, and our loves are electrochemical impulses in the brain.

If we can read the brain, reproduce the brain, and—even better—expand the brain, increase the brain, augment the brain, we will not only be able to live longer, but we will also have bigger lives, in a way.

This is not just life extension but life expansion. Expansion meaning that we expand our brains and our capabilities; this is what I mean by computational immortality. If we think about this in evolutionary terms, we have a brain which is about three times as big as a chimpanzee's brain. So, imagine if we had a brain which is bigger than our biological brain. Google have in fact said that Google wants to be the third half of our brain. I think this is a very deep concept because after adding the third half of the brain, we can add the fourth half of the brain and the fifth half of the brain; we will soon have more brain outside our brain than inside our brain. This is also what is called sometimes the exocortex. We will move from the neocortex into an exocortex that will give us a lot more capabilities: a superintelligence, probably.

**Tina Woods**: So, are we talking about a superhuman stage of humanity?

**José Cordeiro**: Yes. Just like we are super-chimpanzees, I think we'll move into the superhuman level. The important things that we believe in in transhumanism are superlongevity, superintelligence, and superhappiness. If we increase our brains, we will have superintelligence; if we increase our healthspan, we will have superlongevity; and if we expand our lives—not only extend, but expand our lives—we might have superhappiness.

**Tina Woods**: How would you describe life as a superhuman, when we get to that point?

**José Cordeiro**: We'll have more capabilities, and we'll have more time to do more interesting things. Imagine all the languages that we could learn, all the foods that we could try, all the books that we could read and write, all the art that we could create, all the planets that we could visit.

In fact, I just came back from a Mars simulation last week. I'm very excited about going to other planets.

We're not just talking about outer space, but inner space too. Not only can we go to other planets; we can also go into our inner space, that we will increase. With augmented reality and virtual reality, new worlds are opening within our own minds.

**Tina Woods**: You've started your own political party, the **Movimiento Independiente Euro Latino** (**MIEL**), and you ran as a candidate for the European Parliament. To what extent have these possibilities driven you to engage on the political front the way you have?

**José Cordeiro**: Well, politicians aren't really leaders, but followers. Most of the time, they just follow the trends. My idea was to push these ideas about healthy lifespans, more intelligence, better lives, increased capabilities. Since politicians weren't talking about that, I said "Well, why don't we create a political movement that talks about these ideas, not just for a single party, but also to get other parties to copy our ideas?"

I think it has been successful, not only because we got 7,000 votes as a first-time campaign, but also because other people are beginning to talk about these ideas. I used words like superintelligence, superlongevity, and even—sometimes—immortality. I did have to make it clear, however, that immortality can never be reached because we never know what is going to happen in the future.

Immortality is like infinity. It's hard to imagine and hard to prove or disprove. We never know if an asteroid or a comet is going to hit planet Earth, or if the heat death of the universe is coming. We don't know what will happen in millions or tens of billions of years into the future. I'm happy if we can extend our lifespans from 100 years to 300, or even 200, even though the ultimate goal is much, much higher.

**Tina Woods**: How do you think we need to work together, as citizens, businesses, third-sector workers, to really make this world you're describing a reality? What role do we each have?

**José Cordeiro**: I believe we have to be more active. It is, after all, our lives, our own lives, and for the first time in history we have the possibility of extending and expanding our lives thanks to science and technology.

This has never happened before, and that's also why some cynics or some skeptical people don't believe in any of this. But I'm not just optimistic; I'm an engineer myself, from MIT, and I believe in science and technology. We are advancing very fast. The things we have seen in the last 20 years are absolutely amazing, and what we will see in the next 20 years will be even more amazing because we're moving exponentially quickly.

People need to understand if they want to live longer, better lives they have to be more active. In fact, I believe even politics will be transformed thanks to technology. We will have more e-government, for example; we might be able to have a robot president in 10 years. It is a possibility. Artificial intelligence might make a better president than a human president.

**Tina Woods**: Once people are really convinced that this is on the horizon, how will that balance against the existing status quo?

**José Cordeiro**: This is the biggest disruption in human history and nothing compares to this in terms of longevity increases. There are always people from the previous system that oppose changes, because they're afraid and because they don't understand. For example, when Darwin was talking about evolution, most people thought he was crazy. When Galileo was saying in Rome in the Vatican that it was not the sun that went around the earth, but the opposite, they almost burned him alive.

These ideas are even more revolutionary than evolution or astrophysics.

This has been the number-one dream of humanity from the very beginning. Our dream has been immortality. We know it from literature; the first book in human history, the Epic of Gilgamesh, is about immortality. The pyramids of Egypt were built because the Pharaohs wanted to be immortal. Really, there's nothing that compares to it. That means there will be a lot of opposition to it at the beginning, and that's OK.

This happens with all revolutions throughout history. Groups will oppose these developments, some because of religious reasons, and that's my real concern, that some people for badly understood ethical reasons or badly understood religious reasons will oppose some of this development. Nonetheless, people need to be aware this is to benefit their lives. This is like medicine. Why do we want to cure cancer? Why do we want to cure Alzheimer's? Because people don't want to be sick.

There are some perverse interests. Some pharmaceutical companies lean on products that just keep you sick instead of curing you, and this is obviously bad. The same is happening in other industries, like the oil industry. They don't want electric cars because they live off providing oil. There is a huge battle, I would say, between the old system and the new system. However, eventually, I'm very much convinced that electric vehicles will be the norm throughout the planet, maybe as soon as in 10 years, because they're better. They're cheaper, they're environmentally friendlier, and so on and so forth.

The same will happen with these pharmaceutical companies because someone will develop treatments not to keep the diseases at bay, but to actually cure the diseases. Eventually, this will be unstoppable.

**Tina Woods**: Is there a tipping point that we need to see happen before the idea of living longer through AI really disrupts the paradigm that we have today?

**José Cordeiro**: It is hard to say there's a single factor that will be the tipping point. It might be a combination of many different factors, but I think something will happen that will basically begin a new game for all these industries. It's happened in the oil industry—for example, the Indian company Tata now is positioning itself as a solar energy company, moving from fossil fuels into renewables. Maybe the same shift will happen with pharmaceutical companies. They will evolve, and I hope they will; and I think many of them will because they see people want to be healthy, and there is good business in making them completely healthy.

**Tina Woods**: In your view, is there going to be a day of the death of death? Do you think we'll ever have a so-called pill to cure aging?

**José Cordeiro**: Yes. As Aubrey de Grey says sometimes, the idea is to have either one pill or one injection that will make you stay young. This is the objective by some of these companies and some of these visionary people: to have a single treatment like a pill or injection. I think the longevity industry will certainly be the largest industry in the world in maybe a decade, and AI will be one of the main drivers of that. It will be bigger than the phone industry, the travel industry, any industry, because at the end of the day everybody wants to be healthy.

Longevity/escape velocity are some interesting ideas popularized by Aubrey de Grey and Ray Kurzweil, and Ray Kurzweil puts dates to these ideas. He says by 2029, we'll be able to reach longevity escape velocity, but still be aging. However, by 2045, we will be able to reverse aging to make people younger. Those two dates are important: 2029 for longevity/escape velocity, and 2045 for immortality, even though we need to understand what immortality means in this context.

**Tina Woods**: Do people really want to live forever?

**José Cordeiro**: I think people want to live indefinitely so long as they can be young. The problem is if they're old, if they're sick, some people might not want to live. But even when people are 90 or 100 years old, even if they're a little bit sick, most people would say they would want to live one more day, one more week, one more month, one more year. The problem, again, is that we are aging. We get all these diseases, and that is why we need to attack. We need to conquer these diseases and people need to understand that this is possible.

I consider aging the mother of all diseases. If we cure aging, we won't develop most types of cancers or neurodegenerative diseases or cardiovascular diseases. Cancer is the number one enemy of humanity; today in the developed world, over 90% of the people die because of aging. Aging is the enemy. It's not other nations or other tribes or other religions, or even the environment, or viruses. No, no. The enemy today is aging.

There are two examples I like to give. The first is that we discovered that cancer is basically immortal in 1951. Cancer cells are considered biologically immortal, but if you go out in the street and you ask people, 99% of people don't know that. There is a lot of missing information and misinformation. Besides cancer cells being biologically immortal, there are other cells that are considered biologically immortal, like stem cells and germ cells. Germ cells and stem cells are considered biologically immortal, and they can live indefinitely.

The second example is that besides independent cells, we have organisms like hydras. Hydras are also considered biologically immortal, and there are some other species that can live for hundreds of years. People need to understand that this is real, this is happening, even though we didn't know it before. We didn't know about immortal animals like hydras, or immortal cells, until last century. This is all new.

People need to know that this is possible. That we will be able to live young, not live old. No-one wants to be old. We work towards youth, towards an indefinite lifespan of people being in good health at a good age.

**Tina Woods**: What do you think is the secret to a long life? Do you do it for yourself?

**José Cordeiro**: Ray Kurzweil talks about the three bridges to immortality. Bridge number 1 is right now, in the 2010s. It's doing the things that your mother told you to do: eat well, exercise, don't drink too much, don't smoke and so on. That's bridge 1, and I try to do bridge 1.

Bridge 2 will be in the 2020s, with the first biotechnology treatments and the first drugs. For example, I personally take metformin, which is a very cheap and available drug that has already shown good results for longevity. Some things like metformin can be taken right now, and they certainly help you to live a little bit longer. That will take us into bridge 3.

Bridge 3 is nanotechnology and that's going to be around in the 2030s. If we do bridge 1, bridge 2, and bridge 3, we'll eventually reach the 2040s when we should be able to reach immortality after passing the longevity escape velocity. I try to do everything in bridge 1 and then that will allow me to live long enough to live forever.

**Tina Woods**: We often hear of Blue Zone countries, where people tend to be living longer. Do you think what they're doing now is for the most part in bridge 1?

**José Cordeiro**: Yes, actually. In Spain, people eat the famous Mediterranean diet, and this is a big part of a healthy lifestyle; the same is true in Okinawa in Japan, some places in South America, and so on. To me, that's all part of bridge 1.

**Tina Woods**: Behavioral change seems to be one of the biggest, difficult barriers that we face to getting people onto bridge 1. Do you think technology will help us get over that?

**José Cordeiro**: Yes. That is a very, very important issue, and let me just remind you that many people still smoke. Many fewer than in the past, but some people still smoke. The trend is that this will continue decreasing and maybe with technology we can help them to do this faster, make this transition from an unhealthy to a healthy lifestyle.

There are also things related not to behavior but to mental state, which is also very important. People commit suicide today; and maybe in the future, even if they're not sick, they will still commit suicide. So this is an important consideration: why do people commit suicide? Sometimes obviously this is related to sickness—if people are terribly sick, they may decide to commit suicide. Therefore, if we stay healthy, my hope is that the suicide rate will decrease.

**Tina Woods**: Where do you see AI and technology tackling the other aspects of what keeps us unwell—behavior, genomics, social determinants, and the like?

**José Cordeiro**: AI will be like electricity. It'll be everywhere, and it'll help us with everything—for example, in medicine, and especially in genomics. The human genome is quite big. We are talking about 3 GB of data—twice that if you consider both your parents. 3 GB of data is something that a normal human cannot process, but AI can do that and can process the interactions between different genes. AI can do all of that; we can't. AI will be important in eliminating genetic diseases and discovering new treatments, new drugs, new pills, and new injections. I'm very hopeful about AI.

**Tina Woods**: Do you think technology will help solve the problem of the really difficult, gritty issues of health inequality, relating to economic and social considerations?

**José Cordeiro:** Yes. Economic distress is one of the biggest problems humanity faces. Thanks to technology—AI, yes, but also robotics, drones, and general automation of just about everything —we will move from an economy of scarcity into an economy of abundance, and that's really revolutionary.

With nanotechnology and 3D printing, we'll be able to make any product very cheaply, anywhere on the planet. This is absolutely revolutionary. People will basically have almost anything they want, very cheaply. If we can go from the distress of economic scarcity to a world of more abundance where people are freer to do what they want and be more artistic, more creative, I think that people will be happier.

**Tina Woods:** What are the ethical considerations that need to guide us ahead to make sure that we can address issues about longevity?

**José Cordeiro:** I think the ethical issues are very straightforward. Who could be against living healthier, longer lives? When people talk about overpopulation or when people talk about pensions, or when people talk about environmental disasters and things like that; I don't think they will be problems in the future, but if they are then they would be good problems. These kinds of good problems are better than the old problems of the past.

How could anyone be against living longer and healthier? To me, it's inconceivable that some people could be against it, especially if they understand we are moving into a world of more prosperity and more abundance. I see no ethical issues in living better, healthier lives.

**Tina Woods:** One potential criticism is that these pharmaceuticals will only get into the hands of those who can afford them. How do we cope with that sort of scenario if we really want the longevity dividend to be accessible to all?

**José Cordeiro:** It's like mobile telephones or sequencing the human genome. When any technology begins, it's very expensive, and it's for the elite.

They are also very bad in the beginning—they don't work properly. However, when technologies are democratized, when they are popularized, when they are mass produced, they become very good and very cheap. They're reliable and they do even more things than you expected.

I think that this longevity field or this longevity injection will be available to everybody who wants it, because it'll become very cheap. With nanotechnology and AI, we might be talking about $1 per day of treatment; absolutely nothing. Everybody and anybody who wants it will have it. Like today, anybody in Africa or in India who wants a mobile phone owns a mobile phone because you can buy Chinese mobile phones for $10. It will be available to everybody.

Going back to the ethical issue, the real ethical issue is that some groups won't want these technologies. Many religions don't want certain medical treatments. Jehovah's Witnesses, for example, don't want blood transfusions. Some people are still horrified about heart transplants, about having the heart of a dead person. The problem isn't that these technologies will not be available to everybody, because I believe they will, and very cheaply. The problem is that some people, for ethical reasons or religious reasons, will not want them.

For example, consider the Amish. The Amish live in the 18th century. They don't want cars, they don't want telephones, they don't want the internet, and so on and so forth. I believe the real ethical problem is actually the opposite of your question. The real ethical problem is that some of these treatments will be prevented from reaching people because some suppose a moral highness, or ethical highness, or religious goodness, which to me is absolutely crap.

**Tina Woods**: You mentioned cheap Chinese mobile phones—China are leapfrogging rest of the world in terms of technology and AI, using the sheer amount of data they have accessible from their citizens to create things like the social credit policy.

Where do you think that's going to head, and what do you think we can learn from what's happening there with technology?

**José Cordeiro**: That is an excellent question, and let me give you two answers. Firstly, the ethics and morals of China are different. Think about self-driving cars and when we give a choice to the self-driving car: you can kill a baby or you can kill an old person. According to Western societies you should kill the old person and let the baby live. In Eastern societies like China, because they revere older people, they actually let the baby die so that you can keep the old person. It's an interesting example of how different ethical points of view have arisen on the planet today from different cultures.

Going back to the fear of China for the second answer, to me it's like the fear of a Terminator AI. It's an unreal scenario. I'm actually very happy about China's progress because they are changing the world. One of the most interesting programs they have is to sequence the genomes of their most intelligent people and their most long-lived people, people who are over 100 years old. They are going to discover what makes us live longer and what makes us more intelligent. So, if people in Western countries don't want to live longer and they don't want to be more intelligent—well, too bad, but the Chinese will do it.

**Tina Woods**: In terms of your upcoming projects—you've mentioned Mars, but are there any other relevant projects that you're looking at?

**José Cordeiro**: I'm focusing on four areas: biological immortality, computational immortality, outer space, and inner space. In the next 20 years, we're going to be looking at more changes than the last 200 years—not 20, but 200 years—in the past. It's incredible.

**Tina Woods**: Are there any final remarks that you want to make?

**José Cordeiro**: There are a few sentences I like to say all the time: We live in the most incredible times.

We are between the last human mortal generation and the first immortal generation—this is the best time to be alive. It is never a good time to die, but now is certainly the worst time to die because we are so close to being basically immortal.

**Tina Woods**: What have you learned from the COVID-19 pandemic?

**José Cordeiro**: Although it might seem difficult to believe now, thanks to the great exponential advances in science and technology, I hope that there will be some antivirals in a few weeks and the first vaccines against this coronavirus in a few months. It is quite possible that this terrible pandemic will be remembered in the future for having been overcome with unprecedented speed. The situation is providing a great lesson for humankind. It has shown that we must work together because global problems require global solutions. This experience will eventually serve as a model for tackling other global challenges such as climate change and terrorism.

There will be new pandemics in the future, but we will be more prepared to overcome them quickly thanks to exponential technologies. It is highly likely that we will sequence the next pandemic virus in just two days, and the next one after maybe in two hours, and not in two weeks like in the current situation, or two months for SARS two decades ago, or more than two years for AIDS. Not only are the timescales for fighting these diseases being reduced exponentially, but the costs also are falling dramatically.

# Keith Comito

*President, Lifespan.io*

My interview with Keith was at Think Coffee, a trendy hangout in the west village in New York City. Keith has an eclectic background, bringing together his education in computer science and mathematics in a variety of ways to provoke thought and promote social change. He has created video games, bioinformatics programs, musical applications, and biotechnology projects featured in Forbes and NPR. He has developed high-profile mobile applications such as HBO Now, MLB At Bat, and most recently Disney+.

Alongside his day job as a senior engineer at Disney, he also works to accelerate and democratize longevity research efforts through his role as President of **Life Extension Advocacy Foundation** (**LEAF**). Keith is passionate about public engagement and sees the citizen as a key stakeholder in working out the problems of the disease of aging. His main role at LEAF is focused on exciting the public that extending healthy human lifespan is a very worthwhile goal, that it's desirable, it's feasible, and that it isn't about extending a period of decrepitude, but more about extending increasing choice made possible by science.

Many of the projects at LEAF are crowdfunded with public support and are based upon the idea that change will happen more quickly as a bottom-up movement—just like what we have seen with the climate change emergency—so that the powers that be can no longer ignore it.

Since LEAF launched their research fundraising platform in 2015, they have raised over $390,000 for aging research, working with institutions including Harvard Medical School and SENS Research Foundation. These funds have supported eight studies, including topics such as mitochondrial repair, DNA damage, visual biomarkers of aging, and senescent cell clearance.

In 2018, LEAF launched the Rejuvenation Roadmap, a curated database tracking the various therapies targeting the aging processes in order to delay, prevent, or even reverse age-related diseases. The roadmap breaks down aging into nine categories of damage (the "hallmarks of aging").

Keith fundamentally agrees a positive narrative is needed to change the mindset around aging and growing older. Feeling hopeless needs to change to feeling hopeful, harnessing the potential of science and technology. LEAF believes that everyone has the right to a long and healthy life that is free from these diseases, and by developing rejuvenation biotechnologies that target the aging processes directly, diseases such as Alzheimer's, Parkinson's, heart disease, and cancer could become a thing of the past.

I had a fascinating hour with Keith. Our discussions touched on history, philosophy, politics, society, and science, which shows how many facets there are to drive a social movement to engage the public on the topic of healthy longevity!

**Tina Woods**: Just before we start, can you give us an idea of who you are and what you do?

**Keith Comito**: My background is in mathematics and computer science, but I started crossing over into biotech 6 or 7 years ago. That's because, like many people in this space, I've come to realize that working on the problem of the disease of aging is the most important thing that we can work on as a society.

Starting about 6 years ago, I helped to found the **Life Extension Advocacy Foundation** (**LEAF**), which has been working to raise funds and awareness for research aimed at extending the healthy human lifespan. Our main role is essentially positioning ourselves between the research and the public, helping to educate the public and, frankly, excite the public that this is something that is very worthy to work on, that it's desirable, it's feasible, and we need to work on it.

**Tina Woods**: What are the key points or messages that people should understand about living longer with AI?

**Keith Comito**: I think the first point is a broader one that doesn't just cover the AI aspect. It's that, as I mentioned earlier, living extraordinarily long and healthy lives is feasible. That's the first thing that people need to understand, that it's totally a tractable problem: it's not magic, and part of that feasibility is that the way that it will happen is by extending healthy human lifespan.

There's a little bit of undue pessimism with some people in the field in believing that the public isn't on board, but I think if you present these ideas in the right way, the large percentage of the public actually is on board. They just need to be informed that this isn't about extending a period of decrepitude. This is health. This is life. This is extending choice to you.

There have been Pew research polls and YouGov polls that show that if you frame the issue in slightly different ways, you get very different answers. This is especially true if you question people about their desires directly. If you say "hey, do you want to be immortal" or "do you want to live forever," you get strongly negative results, especially among women. I think it's maybe a 20% positive in that case.

If you instead frame it as "are you in favor of curing the diseases of aging, like Alzheimer's, heart disease, and cancer?" obviously you get a much higher percentage. Then you can point out that if you accomplish one, you take steps towards the other. That's just one example, but this is something that again, we deal with a lot.

There's a whole slew of misconceptions, and there are two ways to engage with them. You can demonize the public, saying if you don't understand that this is the most important issue, you're an idiot. You don't really win any people to your side that way. The other way to engage is to talk, to say let's understand why you might think that way, and then maybe there's some data that presents against your objection.

A classic example is overpopulation. That's one of the objections that you see most often; what about overpopulation? Well, it's very easy to show historically that as life expectancy has gone up, birth rates have gone down. I'm not sure what the causality there is, but that serves against the point that it's a foregone conclusion that life extension will lead to overpopulation.

**Tina Woods**: What's the biggest role for AI when it comes to living longer, and how are you realizing that potential at LEAF?

**Keith Comito**: Concerning AI specifically, the important role for AI is that big data and proper application of AI can be a vast boon to not every aspect of biotechnology—to say that would be a little bit of an overhype—but certainly to some aspects. There's drug discovery, combing through medical literature, and isolating findings that maybe humans have overlooked. We could use machine learning to develop classifiers for physiological and chemical biomarkers, which is probably one of the most important things. We could put actual metrics on your process of aging that are not just anecdotal.

This will become the hugest role for AI: helping to provide actionable data and information to the public on how they're actually aging, and how that can be modified. This is part of our crowdfunded work at LEAF.

We have a crowdfunding platform called Lifespan.io that helps to raise funding for novel aging research projects. We try to go to the root causes, the things that will really help aging. Things like end-stage cancer projects are more downstream; while it should be worked on, that's not our remit. We're looking at the root causes of aging, and assisting technology that would help with that.

Specifically, we've funded two projects that are in this sphere, each relating to biomarkers. One of these projects uses AI directly, the other is a little downstream. The one that's most related to AI is one that we did as a partnership of a variety of organizations, including Insilico Medicine and Beauty AI. This was called the MouseAge project.

The MouseAge project has a simple concept. It uses machine learning for facial recognition, just like your iPhone would do, building a classifier of large image sets to analyze; but it does it for mice. The end goal here is to have the ability to take a picture of a mouse and know how well it is biologically aging compared to its chronological age.

For example, if you're doing an aging therapy trial, you can find out if the therapy's having an effect before waiting 5 years to find out when the mice die. It has an ability to vastly increase the circular pipeline of research. That's one project that's just straight-up machine learning and AI.

The other project is called the AgeMeter. So, this basically a smartphone application that will measure various physiological biomarkers of aging like your reaction speed. Attachments can connect to it to measure things like your lung capacity. Some of the best biomarkers we have to predict mortality are simple things like how well you can get up from a cross-like position without leaning on things.

While AI isn't involved in the collection of that data, you can see how it could be very useful in the amalgamation and analysis of the data, and in pairing that data with genetic data and other data pools. I think it's very extendable to a large sector of the public because there's already a movement of early adopters called Quantified Self.

The only problem is that there's a bit of a barrier to entry. You have to supply a lot of data on yourself, maybe do a cheek swab or have a blood sample taken, and whenever you have that sort of friction, you're never going to get widescale adoption. As someone with a computer programming background I'm well aware of the pipeline of friction. If you add any extra one step to filling out a form, you cut your response down to about 10%. Add a couple of those and the response goes down two orders of magnitude.

If you have something that's literally in your pocket that's already measuring, for example, your walking gait, you don't really have to do anything. Maybe if you want to go above and beyond, you can get a little bit of extra data by doing a lung capacity test, or something similar.

You could see how eventually that just becomes part of an app that you have on your phone, where you see these nice graphs that show things like how your walking speed has been modified. I think that has the possibility to almost gamify it and become more fun, because then you would be able to notice all sorts of interesting outliers. You might see that, for some reason, when you listen to Mozart your stress levels are way lower. Then maybe you'd do that more often.

**Tina Woods**: Are there any other crowdfunded projects that you've got in the pipeline?

**Keith Comito**: As far as crowdfunded projects go, the next project is a follow-up to a successful one we did for the MitoSENS team at the SENS Research Foundation. The project is centered on essentially backing up the mitochondrial DNA into the nucleus, which is a process that evolution has largely started but hasn't quite finished yet. The first leg of that resulted in a successfully published paper that made a lot of waves because 2 of the 13 genes were successfully backed up.

If the full goal can be accomplished, that will solve a lot of mitochondriopathies, and those are one of the reasons that many things go wrong as we age. Mitochondriopathies are one of the 7 or 9 pillars of aging—there's some debate about whether it should be 7 or 9.

Defining those pillars is one of the major reasons why the field is blossoming. Instead of just having this amorphous thing called aging and asking what do we do about it, it's been codified into 7 to 9 types of damage that accumulate in the body.

I wouldn't say that the theory is 100% slam-dunk yet, but it paints targets and we can craft therapies to take aim at those targets.

I'm not sure if there was an earlier formulation, but Aubrey de Grey gets a lot of credit for his book *Ending Aging* in 2007, which included a list of the "seven deadly things," the types of damage that make up aging as we understand it. Then, many years later, there was a Hallmarks of Aging paper that very much leaned on that, adding a category here and subtracting a category there, and that has, I believe, become one of the most cited life science papers. That's become a great entry point into engaging the mainstream public in this talk. It's a super credible paper and it's very intelligible.

**Tina Woods**: The **International Disease Classification** (IDC) now includes aging; how does that relate to the pillars of aging?

**Keith Comito**: That's a big win, and it's the end stage of something that's been building for the past 4 or 5 years. One of the things that we're trying to do at LEAF is catalyze huge society-wide changing paradigm shifts about aging, and I believe one of the most instructive models to look at is what anti-cancer advocates did in the past. This was very well detailed in the book *The Emperor of All Maladies*.

To make a long story short, what worked for them was a 1-2-3 process of one, find some credible research; two, build a grassroots movement around that; three, build that growing pressure into a lever that can influence policy. For the anti-cancer advocates, it was the Jimmy Fund. They did telethons and all that charitable work, and then took out full-page spreads in the New York Times and The Washington Post that basically said: Nixon, what the hell are you doing? We're dying here.

That catalyzed the 1971 Cancer Act—the war on cancer. We're trying to emulate that process. The research that we're crowdfunding is groundwork for step one there.

We know that we're never going to crowdfund the amount that the government could one day release, but in a sense it's a PR endeavor; this very public visible thing that captures people's interest. We're building up a movement, and then as that goes on there are a couple of policy targets that the movement aims towards.

One of those targets was the classification of aging in the IDC. Beforehand, the IDC didn't have any useful codes for aging. I believe it had some sort of generic catch-alls. Without the classification, there was a follow-on effect on government departments and policies, on the codes that you could use to apply for grants, and therefore what you actually worked on.

I believe the change was a tag team effort by two organizations that we work with; the Biogerontology Research Foundation and the International Longevity Alliance. They helped to catalyze this change. It's not a straight-up definition of aging in the ICD, but it's more useful sub-classifications that can be directly targeted for grants and so on. It's definitely perceived as a monumental win.

**Tina Woods**: Healthspan is a term that's started to enter this discussion. What's your take on how language is best used in this field? How can we adopt the right language to really engage people?

**Keith Comito**: Effectively communicating what we're doing as a field is probably the most important aspect of our work, in terms of how fast we can get useful therapies to happen. You really need to bring the public along with you. Not only to build the pressure that catalyzes policy change, but also because if it's not there you risk catastrophic pushback, like when the stem cell lines were banned.

I think it's super important to have a sense of PR consideration. How do you say things in the right way, and how do you present the right version of your authentic message to the right audience at the right time? I'll try to explain with two examples that are polar opposites. On the one hand, you have the immortalists, and on the other hand you have the term healthspan.

The immortalist mindset is that we want to live forever. We want to put our brains into robot bodies; all this kind of stuff. Now, coming from a background of computer engineering, mathematics, and a strong hobby of philosophy, I'm interested in that. But I don't think that it's the right time to try and sell the mainstream public that this is definitely doable and definitely desirable. I think coming at it from that angle will actually prolong your timeline on things like curing Alzheimer's disease. It's putting the cart before the horse.

On the other side, with concepts like healthspan; I think that's totally fine. I understand why that's the term being chosen. But in my opinion, you can be a little bit too gun-shy, too cowardly. You need to be bold if you want to inspire people.

There are many prominent people in the field that get the big question. They might be in the middle of a great interview, giving all the right answers about societal issues, really getting their points across. And then, at one point, because they have to, the interviewer will ask: What about you? Do you want to live longer? Do you want to live to be 200, Mr Person or Miss Person? And invariably, the longevity movement leader will say something like: Oh, well, you know. It's not about me. It's about health, and better living, and this and that.

I think that's a great answer, don't get me wrong. But I think it's more authentic to say: Listen, the whole reason why I'm doing this at all is because I believe life is worth living, and that the choice to extend it should be given to everyone in the public. I'm not ashamed to say that I am one of those people who would want to live longer; but even if I wasn't, I think it's valuable to work on this for all of the other good reasons we've talked about. I think that's a much more honest approach.

That really is just my opinion, though. When it comes to the right terms to use, I think terms like healthy life extension strike that right balance because you're qualifying that life extension comes with health. You're pre-emptively disabusing the listener of the notion of the Tithonus myth of being decrepit, decrepit, decrepit.

You're being clear that if this all works, then yes: you will have an extended healthy life.

**Tina Woods**: What research do you think will have the biggest impact in helping people with this healthy life extension in 5 or 10 years from now?

**Keith Comito**: I imagine you'll get this answer a lot, but the research on senolytics is looking extremely exciting for multiple reasons. Unlike some other therapies that might be coming down the pipe, I believe senolytics has the chance to foment a non-negligible increase in healthy lifespan, something that people would really notice. Maybe even up to 10 extra healthy years.

As you go through your life, your body builds up this burden of what's called senescent cells. You can think of them like zombies. They're in some senses similar to cancer; in some senses, they're the opposite of cancer. They're opposite in the sense that they don't reproduce out of control. They don't actually reproduce at all. They're similar in the sense that they are harmful to the body.

Senescent cells secrete these toxins, this soup sometimes called **senescent-associated secretory phenotye** (**SASP**), that can turn other cells around them into them. A zombie bite is actually a really great analogy for that—these are zombie cells.

Senolytics kill the senescent cells, the zombie cells. Aside from the research utility and the efficacy senolytics are going to have, they're also very easy to understand for the public. I like that. It's a very engaging way to say: Hey! This is one of the things that goes wrong. We know aging isn't all flowers and roses, you're building up these zombie cells in you and here's how you can get rid of the zombies and be healthier. And that in itself is useful.

**Tina Woods**: How do you think, in order to make that kind of research accessible so that as many people as possible can benefit from it, we can work together to make it happen? Who has the biggest role: government, business, or individual citizens?

**Keith Comito**: I think the answer is all of the above. I will say that the part that I think would get most easily left out is the citizenry. I think that if this happens as a bottom-up movement, it will happen faster. Take any example of action that's happening for other causes now, like climate change. It's always from the ground up, and there becomes a great outcry until the powers that be can no longer ignore it. I think there's a way to position aging so that that happens.

The silver bullet as far as this tactic goes is Alzheimer's disease. Last month, I was at a meeting with the XPRIZE group, who potentially want to put up a prize for longevity projects. Our goal there was to come up with projects that they might be able to use to galvanize all these groups, businesses, governments, and citizenry, to get behind the problem of longevity. Of the 20 or so projects that were raised, the one that I raised was meaningful remediation of dementia by 2030. That was the one—or one of the two—that I believe they are picking and going forward with.

One of the reasons why I was able to convince the room is that Alzheimer's is unique in the pantheon of diseases. It is absolutely a specific disease, like cancer. But unlike every other disease, it is intrinsically bound in the public consciousness with aging in a way that cancer isn't. You can be a kid and have cancer; but if you think of aging and what you don't want to have happen to you, you think of Alzheimer's.

This is very useful as a soft way of pulling the general public into extending healthy human lifespan. Nobody wants Alzheimer's disease. I also think that psychologically, society has a sort of Stockholm syndrome around death. It's always been so hopeless. I think most people would be raring to go if they thought living extremely long, healthy lives was very much feasible. When people don't think it's feasible, they don't want to get their hopes up. They don't want to think about it.

I think Alzheimer's plays a key role in this because I've had this conversation with people where I'll be talking to them about aging research, and there's a sense that people think it's foolish. They think, come on. You guys are going to cure aging, and you can't even cure Alzheimer's disease? It creates a sense of learned hopelessness. If we can take that chess piece off the board, in my opinion it would send a shockwave through the whole world.

**Tina Woods**: How can we tackle the social determinants of health as well as funding research like this? How much weight do we need to put on all these different approaches to really make the biggest impact?

**Keith Comito**: I would say a massive amount of weight needs to be put on every approach. I think that's the only way that this kind of change happens. Certainly not enough weight is being put on the longevity movement space and we could really be the tip of the spear.

Putting weight on every front is why we run one of the largest news outlets on aging research, focusing on credible, feasible stuff and what it actually means. A lot of what we do on our site Lifespan.io is to educate the public on social determinants and how they can affect health. For example, one statistic that most people in the field didn't know but that was very useful in that conversation with the XPRIZE is that most of the health decisions for a family are made by women. Most caregivers are women.

We know it's very important to make sure, whatever message you're trying to sell, that you engage the primary stakeholder. If you're not aware that that's women when it comes to healthcare, it's a potential faux pas but more importantly you miss out on amazing strategies. If you're aware of who makes the health decisions, then you can start to make alliances, start aiming the discussion at the right people. That's one aspect of why education of the social aspects of aging is a core tenet of what we do at LEAF.

I think what's very important is to always keep your ear to the ground, to the rumblings that are happening. With something like aging that affects absolutely everybody, there is a great chance to pair that mission with almost any other mission, especially ones that are really in the public consciousness now.

For example, right now in America, everyone is very clear that the current healthcare system is incredibly broken regardless of what their prescription for that is. That de facto knowledge creates a hunger; it begs the question, what do we do to make this better, because we know it can be? There's talk of medicare for all, universal healthcare, ideas like that. That allows an opportunity for us.

If we can get someone like Bernie Sanders or Alexandria Ocasio-Cortez in a room, it would be very easy to put forward the idea that if universal healthcare is your goal, because of the population aging demographics, no current plan is going to be sustainable long term. That's objectively bad, and it also opens you up to legitimate political attack. If you want this to work, here's our data; if we can age healthier as a society, that has to be a core tenet of any kind of universal healthcare. Allocate a trillion dollars to core research into aging as part of whatever proposal you have.

We can circumvent all of those conversations about whether transhumanism is good or not. We don't even need to have that conversation.

**Tina Woods**: Given the impact of lifestyle, nutrition, pollution, fitness, and all these social determinants of health, what are the things that we can actually do ourselves to help our bodies age better?

**Keith Comito**: For right now, if you want to extend your healthy lifespan, the things that you should be doing are the things that your mama always told you should be doing. Sleep well; keep your stress low; don't eat crazily. All that is largely true.

I forget what the actual statistics are, but something like 51% of your health determinants are that stuff, it's the majority of what matters; and a lot of us fail, honestly. That begs the question: why do we fail at this basic stuff? I don't like to point fingers here because I think this is one of those situations where everyone is responsible.

The government can help by really pushing the focus on preventative healthcare. Cuba is an interesting example; it's a country that doesn't have as many resources as we do. They're super focused on preventative healthcare because they have to be, they don't have the resources not to be; but that can teach us a lot of lessons as far as the socioeconomic benefits of preventative healthcare.

On the flip side, we all bear responsibility for how we eat, how we exercise. I think part of what we need to do as well, and this is what LEAF can hopefully help with, is to build a culture of healthy life extension, or just health in general.

What you can do yourself is form healthy communities. That touches other aspects of policy or social groups. In my opinion, we don't do too great here in America as far as respect for the elderly is concerned, compared to other cultures. I really feel like it's quite a sad story; once you reach a certain age, you're essentially obsolete in our society. You're not considered, and I think that is a great tragedy.

It's not just a loss in terms of human suffering, but also because we miss the value the elderly can bring to society. There's a great waste of talent. As healthy life extension becomes the norm, co-present with that should be initiatives like retraining the elderly who maybe want to try another career or mentorship programs.

**Tina Woods**: How are we going to make sure of a future where AI-powered life extension treatments are available to everyone? What guiding principles do you think we need to keep in mind as a society?

**Keith Comito**: I think we need to be aware that this is a shared socio-political endeavor. We have to decide as a society what we want our goals to be, and part of that is getting in the streets and shouting for what you care about. Part of it's putting the right people into office that will put those things into action.

For example, let's consider the idea of healthcare, or just health, as a human right. It's up to us to make a decision to say that's a thing we want as a society. It's our choice, and if we make that choice in society then obviously there are so many downstream things that happen to make sure this idea can be realized; laws that companies have to adhere to and so on, like tributaries that trickle down from this idea.

That's the value, in my opinion, of pushing these ideas. An example in an adjacent area that has borne fruit very quickly is Sci-Hub. Sci-Hub is kind of a Pirate Bay for research papers, created by the computer programmer Alexandra Elbakyan. It exists to solve the problem that, especially in America, we pay with our tax dollars for public research to be conducted but then we do not get to see that research unless we pay. It's a co-present problem to healthcare and health data, there's a clear overlap there.

It's one of the biggest open secrets in science, that everybody uses Sci-Hub. You just don't tell the publishers that you do it.

And here's what got really interesting about it. She's not just saying: Hey, science should be free, and so on. Which I agree with. She actually—you know, I'm paraphrasing this. You can look this up later; you know? But she came at it through an ethical governmental lens, that not doing this is actually a violation of our rights, like the First Amendment and things like that. It stands in the way of the pursuit of happiness because you're denying knowledge that's owed to the public, right, which is very interesting.

A friend of mine, Jason Schmitt, made a documentary called *Paywall: The Business of Scholarship* that he showcased at the UN about this.

This resonated with the UN's "sustainable development goals" initiative; the movie was shown in many different countries, and that helped to catalyze legitimate policy change. For example, there's an initiative called Plan S in the EU which is driving legislation to make open science the law of the land.

That's a good example of how clearly identifying a principle and stating it as a right, as "scientific information should be public," can quickly shift the paradigm and affect the law.

**Tina Woods**: How do you think that squares with the reality that we have, where Google, Apple and other tech giants are making significant investments into "owning" health?

**Keith Comito**: Personally, I think that in the letter of FDR era antitrust law, many companies in the US right now are in huge breach of that, and that law's just not being properly enforced. I think if enforcement doesn't start to happen in the next administration, there will be an increasing public outcry for it.

I think the change that will happen will be some sort of paradigm shift from the legislative side that makes data harvesting illegal, where it'll move data ownership so that you own your health data. You can choose to sell access to your data, through a company like Facebook, but you're in control of that just as you are with other aspects of your marketing data. I think it's important that that happens. I think it will happen. I think you're starting to see companies that are filling that need now, that are jumping ahead of the government.

Blockchain is a technology that's jumping ahead here. Blockchain can decentralize and anonymize your data; give you power to choose who you give access to. George Church from the Human Genome Project recently created Nebula Genomics, which is a genome-sequencing business like 23andMe, but the data is securely stored on the blockchain and you own it. You can see how if the government doesn't do this, the door will start to be opened.

I think the government will eventually need to get there because I think otherwise it'll get so Black Mirror bad that people just won't stand for it anymore.

**Tina Woods**: How do you think that paradigm shift in privacy might compare with what's happening in China, which of course is absolutely stealing the market in AI and installing things like the social credit system?

**Keith Comito**: The dichotomy here is between transparency and privacy. How we square that is a totally worthy debate to have; and obviously, as we get there, the balance is going to seesaw.

Let me just go on the record that I'm not in favor of an over-policed surveillance state. I think the right way to do this is through a technology like the blockchain where you can give access, but in an anonymized way. I'm not going to say I have the answers to all the minutiae of that, but that kind of technology is what allows transparency without the state getting into your personal business.

We have to figure out where exactly as a society we want to draw that line. I think that this crosses over into the philosophical issue of Jean-Paul Sartre's idea of bad faith. It's the concept that when you're an object in someone else's world, your behavior changes. Because you're putting on an act, you're not really your authentic self. In the panopticon of modern society, with the pervasiveness of technology—iPhones in your pocket, everyone on social media—at all times you can be acting as an object for others, acting in bad faith. It's constantly happening to everybody. You're always conscious of how you look, and that can't be healthy.

I think at some point we need to make a decision about what's public and what's private. That's a co-issue that we're going to have to figure out.

Another point here is that if you look at how much money Facebook actually wrings out of you from all the advertising it shows you over the year, it's shockingly low.

I think it's about $20. It's worth considering that aside from new technology, that's also a decision that we could have made as a society with Facebook. Their business model could have been that people subscribe for $20 a year, and then they don't have any advertising. They'd still make a lot of money upfront.

That's one of those examples where I think it's not necessarily an evil overlord or malfeasance. It's just that the system's landed in a very stupid configuration and we forget that we could just make the decision to have a different configuration.

**Tina Woods**: What if AI has the effect of changing that configuration by removing or replacing jobs that we currently think of as necessary? Many people have fears about how that might change our economy.

**Keith Comito**: Well, this is more speculative, a little bit beyond just the conversation of aging and AI, but there's a similar objection that I hear all the time on the frontlines of longevity advocacy. It's the concern that longevity might be bad for us, because we really need aging and death to light a fire under our ass.

Even in mythology and fiction, this concern arises. The Lord of the Rings is a classic example. Elves don't get much done because they have very long lifespans, but humans with their short lifespans; they get stuff done. They've got to get more stuff done. It's absolutely pervasive in fiction and it's seen as an absolute truth, but the data actually doesn't bear that out.

There are lots of studies about things like the hedonic treadmill and how boredom works. It doesn't seem like the data supports the idea that longevity would be bad for us. I see a commonality between that idea that you need this restriction of a short life in order to have a good life, and the objections some people have to completely different sounding topics, like some idea of universal healthcare or universal basic income.

There's a sense that if you have basic restrictions removed from you, you're going to not do anything and be lazy. This is based on the idea that human beings are inherently lazy, that we somehow need these restrictions to give our life structure. That's totally a valid philosophical proposition, but it's one that I personally don't think is true, and I don't think existing data bears out.

It goes back to a Hobbes vs Locke dichotomy; do you believe a human being at their core is shit, that they need a rod to keep them in order? Or, do you believe that human beings are basically good if they're not suffering? Are we going to become the *WALL-E* future, where everyone's in a robot chair because they don't move enough?

My own spin on this, which is totally speculative, is that if you remove restrictions on basic needs, people will not necessarily become lazy. They will become a more fully actualized version of what they truly already are. This certainly holds true for my own life, and to many people that I've talked to who have an entrepreneurial bent. I think that if you are lazy with a guaranteed minimum income, you can be lazier. But if you have ambition, if you want to make the rocket go to the moon, now you don't have to work 30 years for the man before you can do that. Right now, by the time you are able to, you're so disillusioned and tired you can't even do the thing you had the ambition for anyway.

That's certainly true for me. I spend 8 hours of my day on life extension, but if I didn't have to survive by working some other job, I'd be able to spend 16 hours a day on life extension.

**Tina Woods**: What role could AI play in this broad kind of reorganization of society?

**Keith Comito**: AI can help with this, but I think this is a broader conversation that goes back before AI to general automation. This was the whole dream—we were supposed to work a 15-hour week, have the robots do all the boring stuff, and be free for creative endeavors.

Then my field—Silicon Valley culture in the '80s—we took a hard-left turn completely, and embraced the idea that you should work 80 hours a week, and isn't that great? No! It's not great!

I think that if we can reconcile the coming future of automation with policies that make it so the average person doesn't need to work as much, if we can reap those benefits, we end up in a future like Star Trek, which I don't think is unfeasible at all. It's like that classic William Gibson quote: "The future is already here. It's just not evenly distributed."

It may sound glib, but I think these problems are logistically simple to solve. They're politically hard to solve and I don't even necessarily think that's always due to some sort of malfeasance. It's just ignorance or entrenched ways of doing things. We need to supplant that, and that's a burden. That's work.

**Tina Woods**: Do you think we'll ever have a pill to cure aging?

**Keith Comito**: I think that that's way too simple a formulation. It's never going to be a silver bullet, a single pill. Aging is a super-complicated, super-multi-factored process. So, the solution, the "cure" for aging is going to be a combination of a lot of different things, only some of which would be ingestible. I do think in the future we will see something in the supplement kind of space that will be part of the puzzle.

**Tina Woods**: Do you think we'll ever reach a point where we become immortal?

**Keith Comito**: Immortality is a very loaded term, so I'd like to pick it apart. When you say immortal, it pulls in other causes of death, and you could still get hit by a bus even if you stopped aging. The most conservative flavor of immortality we can discuss would be something like indefinite life extension, which is a little bit more of a precise term. It's indefinite.

I believe there's been some statistical studies that have shown that if all of the diseases of aging were cured and there were no infectious diseases, you would live something like 9,000 years before some horrific and unpredictable accident would kill you. You'd get hit by an asteroid or something.

Now, let's say we really could wave a magic wand and cure all those diseases of aging right now, put ourselves into that zone of statistical death due to accidents. I would like to think that in the average 4,500 years or so we'd get before we had our unpredictable accident, technologies would develop to make us more robust against other causes of death.

Perhaps instead we'd get a really good definition for consciousness that allows the idea of mind-uploading to happen in a more informed way. That's definitely way downstream though, and I'm not going to predict where we'll be 2,000 years in the future.

**Tina Woods**: Taking everything that we've just talked about into account, what do you think is the secret to a long life?

**Keith Comito**: The, perhaps overly simplistic," answer is that the secret thing is your mindset. If you don't want to live, if you can't enjoy life, you will probably hasten your death.

Perspective shifting is the most important near-term thing. If you shift yourself into a mindset of really appreciating and loving life, you will want to preserve your own life, and preserve life for society and those you love. If you don't have that mindset, then the story ends and nothing else is worth it. You're not able to have a real conversation about any of these other things.

One thing that is always left off the table in these conversations is the spiritual component, especially because a discord can be perceived there that I don't think is really present. Some transhumanists deal with religious organizations in a very antagonistic way, which I think shows a lack of understanding.

One thing that I think is always helpful is to contextualize what we're doing in terms of history. It's part of making people realize they're already on your team.

Immortality isn't some freaky new idea. I love the Epic of Gilgamesh. It's one of my three favorite stories, not just because I like the themes but because I like the rhyme of it. It's important to say that this is literally the first great work of literature that we produced as a species, that we found it on clay tablets—and it's all about the idea of conquering death.

It's all about looking at this problem directly, and saying: No, this is objectively bad. I just watched my best friend have maggots come out of his eyes. There's no way that I can rationalize that and pretend it's a good thing. No platitude is better than it would be to have my friend with me right now, so we could laugh together. It's why Gilgamesh goes on his journey, this goal he has, to overcome the death of his beloved friend.

In a very real sense, every other epic after that is a version or a sublimation of that same story. Gilgamesh went after death itself, the thing itself. It's the original hero's journey, which everyone in modern society is familiar with, whether that's through Marvel movies or Star Wars.

Here's where we have a way to really bring it back home to people. This is the first hero's journey, and you and I get to finish it, perhaps, or make real significant gains. That's super exciting and it's not something that's new. It's literally the story of humanity, and we are blessed to be alive in this unique pivotal moment. We shouldn't take that for granted.

I feel like there's a critique that older generations might have towards the Millennials and Gen Z, which is that they're vapid. Imagining that they have their heads in their cell phones and they don't care about anything deep.

I don't think that's true at all. I think you can see signs of this hunger for meaning everywhere in modern society. Even in Candy Crush, what does it say when you do well? Sublime.

That's funny, but I think there really is that hunger for the sublime. In modern society, maybe because of post-modernism, it is hard to find that. It's easy to enter into a kind of existential despair. Whereas in the olden days, if you blindly believed in whatever your theology was, you had that sense of the eternal. You would work on long-term projects like a church that would take 500 years, even though you knew you weren't going to reap the benefits, because you knew you were helping with the universe.

I honestly feel that if we can succeed in our goal here, we can almost bring that back to society. Wouldn't you be a better steward of the earth—climate change-wise, and in other ways—if you believed that you and your family were going to be around in 500 years? Things would be less ephemeral. You'd care more. I would like to think that we would become wiser with more years.

Maybe it's optimistic, but I'm optimistic.

**Tina Woods**: What have you learned from the COVID-19 pandemic?

**Keith Comito**: There are decades where not much changes, and then there are events which can catalyze decades of change all at once. The normal operations of my life, like everyone's, have been profoundly disrupted by the COVID-19 pandemic. But beyond this, and beyond even the incredible tragedy of the lives lost and irreparably damaged during these past few months, it is important to recognize that this moment also presents opportunities to save lives.

We see this in our work at Lifespan.io: now more than ever, people are aware that existing systems of healthcare do not fulfill the promise of their name. They understand that the time has finally come to fix them. Coupled with the fact that aging is the single greatest risk factor for COVID-19, as well as almost every other disease known to humankind, this energy is creating an opportunity to engage an ever-increasing amount of the public in our work.

Perhaps because infectious diseases are perceived as outside assaults to be dealt with, rather than a seeming inevitability like chronic diseases, the current situation is allowing us to clearly illustrate the value proposition of longevity research as the ultimate preventative healthcare. In addition to the moral good of alleviating the suffering of ill-health, a scenario where we maintain our fitness with age will bring about vast socio-economic benefits, which include that of younger immune systems significantly mitigating the effects of any pandemic. Press, policy makers, and everyday citizens alike are waking up to this potential, and seeing how the goals of our movement directly relate to current issues and struggles.

As a response to this new socio-political landscape, LEAF has accelerated plans to launch a sweeping initiative focused on clarifying the above value proposition, building broad coalitions, and catalyzing policy change. This will be centered on updating the concept of the "Longevity Dividend" and involve collaborations with the research community, press, popular social media influencers, and the public via crowdsourcing to rally around very clear policy prescriptions.

Countless lives are at stake, which makes it incumbent on all of us to make what we can of this opportunity. Yes, we must focus on overcoming the current pandemic as quickly as possible, but we should be sure that we don't just apply band-aids. We must take this moment to re-evaluate our priorities and build healthcare systems that will not only protect us from pandemics like this, but will make us truly healthier as a society.

It's up to all of us, and the time to act is now.

## Final thoughts

The COVID-19 pandemic has exposed the fracture lines of society and we need a new social contract founded on a more sustainable and compassionate value system. Our combined experience from the pandemic also shows just how connected planetary, animal, and human health is, and we need to factor this into all of our decision-making. To make sure everyone has access to the benefits of living longer healthier lives—the "longevity dividend"—will require a concerted action from all stakeholders in society. That includes you, me, and every single one of us.

The latest developments in science and technology will certainly give us more options for us to lead a healthier, longer, and hopefully happier life. But big questions remain on access to these developments, to translate potential into reality. How will we ensure everyone benefits? How can we ensure equitable distribution of the longevity dividend? To answer these questions, we need to understand the fundamental inequities in society that impact our health. New research is putting the spotlight on how our biology is affected by the "wider determinants of health," and we will explore this in the next chapter.

## References

1.  *Yuval Noah Harari, Sapiens: A Brief History of Human Mankind* (November 2019): `https://www. albin-michel.fr/ouvrages/sapiens-edition- limitee-9782226445506`

2. *Yuval Noah Harari, Homo Deus: After God and Man, Algorithms Will Make the Decisions*: `https://www.ynharari.com/homo-deus-after-god-and-man-algorithms-will-make-the-decisions/`

3. *Futurism, Dom Galeon, Peter Diamandis Thinks We're Evolving Toward "Meta-Intelligence"* (January 2017): `https://futurism.com/peter-diamandis-thinks-were-evolving-toward-meta-intelligence`

4. *Nature, Alexey A. Moskalev et al., Transcriptome Analysis of Long-lived Drosophila melanogaster E(z) Mutants Sheds Light on the Molecular Mechanisms of Longevity* (2019): `https://www.nature.com/articles/s41598-019-45714-x?fbclid=IwAR1bKMmRmPPhz5Nm3qIkK60CXYi7nTpYv06LVPx-KYMx9VRQEUrh9mxLhGU`

5. *Technology Review, Antonio Regalado, More than 26 million people have taken an at-home ancestry test* (February 2019): `https://www.technologyreview.com/2019/02/11/103446/more-than-26-million-people-have-taken-an-at-home-ancestry-test/`

6. *The Times, Kaya Burgess, Broccoli aversion 'all in the genes'* (November 2019): `https://www.thetimes.co.uk/article/e0a1160c-047a-11ea-872c-a98e8bfab8fc`

7. *Wanda Thibodeaux, I Got Up at 3:45 A.M. Like Apple's Tim Cook for a Year. Here's What Happened* (September 2017): `https://www.inc.com/wanda-thibodeaux/i-got-up-at-345-am-like-apples-tim-cook-for-a-year.html`

8. *Market Watch, Catey Hill, Do you sleep a 'normal' amount? This chart reveals how much shut-eye we really get* (March 2019): `https://www.marketwatch.com/story/its-world-sleep-day-heres-how-much-shut-eye-donald-trump-jennifer-lopez-and-marissa-mayer-get-2017-03-16`

9.  *New Scientist, Alice Klein, DNA mutation lets some people live healthily on only 4 hours' sleep* (August 2019): `https://www.newscientist.com/article/2214505-dna-mutation-lets-some-people-live-healthily-on-only-4-hours-sleep/#ixzz68DLI3Fk3`

10. *Wired, Emily Dreyfuss, You're Not Getting Enough Sleep—and It's Killing You*: `https://www.wired.com/story/youre-not-getting-enough-sleep-and-its-killing-you/?CNDID=49968855&CNDID=49968855&bxid=MjM5NjgxNzMyMjI0S0&hasha=6032b8dba112b7af18c5765ed8278a34&hashb=d6e2b03400f3771bc45580e20effb5e45695ac24&mbid=nl_041919_daily_list1_p4&source=DAILY_NEWSLETTER&utm_brand=wired&utm_mailing=WIRED%20NL%20041919%20(1)&utm_medium=email&utm_source=nl`

11. *Nature, Conor A. Emdin, Analysis of predicted loss-of-function variants in UK Biobank identifies variants protective for disease* (2018): `https://www.nature.com/articles/s41467-018-03911-8`

12. *Cell, Xiao Tian et al., SIRT6 Is Responsible for More Efficient DNA Double-Strand Break Repair in Long-Lived Species* (April 2019): `https://www.cell.com/cell/fulltext/S0092-8674(19)30344-7#secsectitle0020`

13. *Lloyd Brandts and Piet A van den Brandt, Body size, non-occupational physical activity and the chance of reaching longevity in men and women: findings from the Netherlands Cohort Study* (2019): `https://jech.bmj.com/content/73/3/239`

14. *The Times, Four in 10 would choose to get early diagnosis of Alzheimer's*: `https://www.thetimes.co.uk/article/four-in-10-would-choose-to-get-early-diagnosis-of-alzheimers-c39n5h9vk`

15. *L A Farrer et al., Effects of age, sex, and ethnicity on the association between apolipoprotein E genotype and Alzheimer disease. A meta-analysis. APOE and Alzheimer Disease Meta Analysis Consortium* (October 1997): `https://pubmed.ncbi.nlm.nih.gov/9343467/`

16. *Rahul S Desikan et al., Polygenic Overlap Between C-Reactive Protein, Plasma Lipids, and Alzheimer Disease* (June 2015): `https://pubmed.ncbi.nlm.nih.gov/25862742/`

17. *Rahul S Desikan et al., Genetic assessment of age-associated Alzheimer disease risk: Development and validation of a polygenic hazard score* (March 2017): `https://journals.plos.org/plosmedicine/article?id=10.1371/journal.pmed.1002258`

18. *UK Biobank, Healthy lifestyle may offset genetic risk of dementia* (July 2019): `https://www.ukbiobank.ac.uk/2019/07/healthy-lifestyle-may-offset-genetic-risk-of-dementia/`

19. *The Lancet, Prof Gill Livingston MD et al., Dementia prevention, intervention, and care* (July 2017): `https://www.thelancet.com/journals/lancet/article/PIIS0140-6736(17)31363-6/fulltext`

20. *Alzheimer's Research UK, A version of a gene linked to key Alzheimer's protein* (November 2019): `https://www.alzheimersresearchuk.org/a-version-of-a-gene-linked-to-key-alzheimers-protein/`

21. *Neurology, Keenan A. Walker et al., Midlife systemic inflammatory markers are associated with late-life brain volume* (November 2017): `https://n.neurology.org/content/89/22/2262`

22. *Estella A. Newcombe et al., Inflammation: the link between comorbidities, genetics, and Alzheimer's disease* (2018): `https://jneuroinflammation.biomedcentral.com/articles/10.1186/s12974-018-1313-3#Sec21`

23. *The University of Manchester, New study highlights Alzheimer's herpes link, experts say* (July 2018): `https://www.manchester.ac.uk/discover/news/new-study-highlights-alzheimers-herpes-link-experts-say/`

24. *Nature, Jeremy Schmutz et al., Quality assessment of the human genome sequence* (May 2004): `https://www.nature.com/articles/nature02390`

25. *Science, Jon Cohen, China's CRISPR revolution* (Aug 2019): `https://science.sciencemag.org/content/365/6452/420.full`

26. *Science, Jon Cohen, China's CRISPR revolution* (Aug 2019): `https://science.sciencemag.org/content/365/6452/420.full`

27. *Nature, Heidi Ledford, CRISPR babies: when will the world be ready?* (June 2019): `https://www.nature.com/articles/d41586-019-01906-z`

28. *Independent, He Jiankui: Scientist who edited babies' genes jailed for three years* (December 2019): `https://www.independent.co.uk/news/world/asia/he-jiankui-baby-gene-editing-crispr-dna-aids-prison-sentence-a9263966.html`

29. *MIT Technology Review, Genome engineers made more than 13,000 CRISPR edits in a single cell*: `https://www.technologyreview.com/2019/03/26/103248/genome-engineers-made-more-than-13000-crispr-edits-in-a-single-cell/#:~:text=Expand%20menu-,Genome%20engineers%20made%20more%20than%2013%2C000%20CRISPR%20edits%20in%20a,with%20large%2Dscale%20DNA%20changes.&text=Since%20its%20invention%2C%20CRISPR%20has,made%20one%20at%20a%20time`

30. *Wired, Inside a Chemist's Quest to Hack Evolution and Cure Genetic Disease* (June 2010): `https://www.wired.com/story/inside-a-chemists-quest-to-hack-evolution-and-cure-genetic-disease/`

31. *Wired, One Scientist's Quest to Bring DNA Sequencing to Every Sick Kid* (August 2019): `https://www.wired.com/story/one-scientists-quest-to-bring-dna-sequencing-to-every-sick-kid/`

32. *Peter H. Diamandis, Longevity & Vitality - Part 5: The Three R's of Regenerative Medicine* (March 2019): `https://www.diamandis.com/blog/longevity-and-vitality-part-5`

33. *The Harvard Gazette, The genetics of regeneration* (March 2019): `https://news.harvard.edu/gazette/story/2019/03/harvard-study-unlocks-a-key-to-regeneration/?utm_campaign=Abundance%20Insider&utm_source=hs_email&utm_medium=email&utm_content=71057214&_hsenc=p2ANqtz--jOj16mWybI0W7-5knoZx5An8t2KsFhbnuV3NzbuFi1tiVUuPYWa20fZLpB8SNvIteepge1-MqSHoG5A1kIL5KI77zTOLAVfZSaX-welODEcbpJ-A&_hsmi=71057216`

34. *Cell, Carlos López-Otín et al., The Hallmarks of Aging* (June 2013): `https://www.cell.com/fulltext/ S0092-8674(13)00645-4#secsectitle0010`

35. *Wikipedia, DNA:* `https://en.wikipedia.org/wiki/ DNA`

36. *Popular Science, Tim Spector, What Twins Reveal About The Science Of Faith* (August 2013): `https:// www.popsci.com/science/article/2013-08/what- twins-reveal-about-god-gene/`

37. *SingularityHub, Vanessa Bates Ramirez, Biohacking Will Let You Connect Your Body to Anything You Want* (September 2016): `https://singularityhub. com/2016/09/01/biohacking-will-let-you- connect-your-body-to-anything-you-want/`

38. *MIT Technology Review, Antonio Regalado, A startup is pitching a mind-uploading service that is "100 percent fatal"* (March 2018): `https://www.technologyreview. com/2018/03/13/144721/a-startup-is-pitching- a-mind-uploading-service-that-is-100-percent- fatal/`

39. *MIT Technology Review, Antonio Regalado, Don't change your DNA at home, says America's first CRISPR law* (August 2019): `https://www.technologyreview. com/2019/08/09/65433/dont-change-your-dna-at- home-says-americas-first-crispr-law/`

40. *SingularityHub, Zoltan Istvan:* `https:// singularityhub.com/author/zistvan/`

41. *The Transhumanist Wager, Zoltan Istvan* (January 2013): `https://www.amazon.com/dp/B00AQQSY60/`

42. *MIT Technology Review, Antonio Regalado, The transhumanists who want to live forever* (August 2019): `https://www.technologyreview. com/2019/08/16/133364/transhumanists-live- forever/`

43. *Futurism, Christianna Reedy, Kurzweil Claims That the Singularity Will Happen by 2045* (October 2017): https://futurism.com/kurzweil-claims-that-the-singularity-will-happen-by-2045

44. *Futurism, Roey Tzezana, Singularity: Explain It to Me Like I'm 5-Years-Old* (March 2017): https://futurism.com/singularity-explain-it-to-me-like-im-5-years-old

45. *Futurism, Dom Galeon, Softbank CEO: The Singularity Will Happen by 2047* (March 2017): https://futurism.com/softbank-ceo-the-singularity-will-happen-by-2047

46. *Futurism, Dom Galeon, Peter Diamandis Thinks We're Evolving Toward "Meta-Intelligence"* (January 2017): https://futurism.com/peter-diamandis-thinks-were-evolving-toward-meta-intelligence

47. *Futurism, Jolene Greighton, Musk Is Preparing to Release "Brain Hacking Tech," And He's Not Alone* (January 2017): https://futurism.com/elon-musk-set-to-release-plans-about-the-neural-lace-next-month

48. *Futurism, Tom Ward, New Tech Is Giving Humanity Many Potential Paths to Immortality* (August 2017): https://futurism.com/new-tech-is-giving-humanity-many-potential-paths-to-immortality

49. *Science Direct, Alex Zhavoronkov et al., Artificial intelligence for aging and longevity research: Recent advances and perspectives* (January 2019): https://www.sciencedirect.com/science/article/pii/S156816371830240X?via%3Dihub

50. *Coupled electrophysiological, hemodynamic, and cerebrospinal fluid oscillations in human sleep (November 2019):* https://science.sciencemag.org/content/366/6465/628

51. *AI protein-folding algorithms solve structures faster than ever (July 2019):* https://www.nature.com/articles/d41586-019-01357-6

52. *Lifespan: Why We Age – and Why We Don't Have To (September 2019):* https://www.amazon.com/Lifespan-Why-Age-Dont-Have-ebook/dp/B07N4C6LGR/

53. *Groundbreaking Surgery for Girl Born Without Windpipe (April 2013):* https://www.nytimes.com/2013/04/30/science/groundbreaking-surgery-for-girl-born-without-windpipe.html

54. *Organs-on-a-Chip: A Fast Track for Engineered Human Tissues in Drug Development (March 2018):* https://www.sciencedirect.com/science/article/pii/S1934590918300730

55. *Replenish, Replace and Rejuvenate, the Three Rs That Will Alter Human Existence (July 2020):* https://www.21stcentech.com/replenish-replace-rejuvenate-three-rs-alter-human-existence/

56. *Experimenting with Spirituality: Analyzing The God Gene in a Nonmajors Laboratory Course (2008):* https://www.ncbi.nlm.nih.gov/pmc/articles/PMC2262126/

# CHAPTER 3

# NATURE VERSUS NURTURE AND THE EXPOSOME

*"AI is a chisel that could affect both the speed and the capability to better carve that stone called our 'future life'. It's still a black box full of mysteries, but these technologies, with the amazing capabilities of researchers all over the world, will help us to progressively illuminate this darkness and connect dots we are still not able to see today."*

*— Nic Palmarini,*
*Director, National Innovation Centre for Ageing*

## The determinants of health

There are extraordinary developments taking place in the science of longevity, as detailed in the previous chapters. So why haven't people been living longer, better lives?

Health is influenced by factors in five key domains[1]—the "non-sick" domains include behavioral patterns (40% of the influences on your health), genetics (30%), social circumstances (15%), and environmental exposures (5%). The "sick" domain encompasses healthcare (10%). While the exact percentages between the five domains may be disputed, most people will agree that when it comes to reducing early deaths, healthcare (that is, the quality of care you receive in a healthcare setting) has a relatively minor role, yet it consumes most of the attention of policymakers, corporations, and budgets.

The circumstances in which we are born, live, and age are the strongest influences on health, and are often called the wider determinants of health[2]. These factors are the underlying drivers of health, and if measures are taken to positively influence them, they can enable individuals and societies to flourish. But, these wider determinants of health are also the root cause of inequity in health; they are behind the avoidable and unfair differences in health that we see between different countries, and between different areas and communities within countries.

The COVID-19 pandemic has highlighted how we have taken our health for granted for too long. It has also exposed the health inequalities that exist in society in a horrific fashion, and how this links to social divides too. So far, the majority of deaths have been in the most vulnerable groups—older populations, those with underlying health problems, and in deprived communities.

For the third year in a row[3] (before the pandemic), life expectancy in the U.S. has fallen, according to the most recent statistics and analysis from the **Center for Disease Control (CDC)**. The U.S. spends about twice as much as other rich countries on healthcare, but it has the lowest life expectancy among those rich countries[63]. As the U.S. has become richer, inequality has also soared—inequality in wealth has become inequality in health[4].

Data from the UK's **Office for National Statistics (ONS)**[5] shows that the UK is heading in the same direction. The latest figures show that improvements in life expectancy have stalled (it will be interesting to see the figures post-pandemic). Life expectancy in the UK is lower than in several other European countries, including Italy, France, and Spain.

There is significant inequality between the most and least deprived communities in the UK. Recent research using objective NHS data (not subjective assessments used by the ONS) published by Outcomes Based Healthcare[6] show that men and women in the poorest areas are being diagnosed with a significant long-term condition when they are on average only 49 and 47 years old, respectively. The reasons behind these figures are complex, but the recent publication *Marmot Review: 10 Years On*[7] advises that the UK Government addresses the areas that have the most impact on people's health and well-being, such as poverty, employment, housing, and education.

The New Zealand Government recognizes this, but, much more importantly, it is doing something about it. On taking office as Prime Minister, Jacinda Ardern focused her attention on the fact that many New Zealanders were not benefiting from New Zealand's growing economy in their daily lives, with growing disparity between the haves and have-nots. So, in May 2019, the government unveiled its "world-first" well-being budget[8] charged with looking after the country's most vulnerable people. New Zealand is the first western country to make well-being priorities, including poverty, mental health, and violence, the center of its budget. New Zealand's ministries have been instructed to design their policies around this concept of improving the well-being of the populace.

It is perhaps not surprising that New Zealand has shown similar leadership during the COVID-19 pandemic. It implemented an elimination strategy that was highly effective in minimizing deaths from the virus. This has been attributed in large part to Ardern's humane and transparent leadership style that focuses on the health of its citizens first and foremost.

The UK should take lessons from New Zealand, both in terms of its quick action against COVID-19 but also its focus on overall societal well-being. It is early days for the new UK government, which so far has shown its commitment to care and compassion in its response to the pandemic, not least from its action to minimize the economic hardships in the immediate term through its multi-billion bailout announced early into the pandemic for the business (£330 billion) and charity (£750 million) sectors affected by lockdown.

As the world learns to live with the epidemic as part of a "new normal", the problems that existed beforehand will remain and will only become more acute. The UK Conservative Manifesto makes a commitment to the goal of delivering five extra years of healthy life expectancy while minimizing inequalities in health by 2035[9]. This was initially set by the government in 2018, and Boris Johnson made a pledge after being elected to "level up" poorer communities. However, the impact of the epidemic will make this even harder as the most deprived struggle with lockdown, social isolation, and a sharp drop in economic activity.

*The State of the Nation: A Strategy for Healthier Longer Lives*[10] was published in February 2020, just before the epidemic hit. It identified nine core recommendations to achieve the UK Government's goal, making the case for reducing premature ill health and widening health inequalities linked to deprivation. The fallout from COVID-19 will only make these recommendations more compelling and urgent.

The strategy proposed a much bigger focus on preventative health (requiring more budget and the metrics to measure it), and recognizes, like New Zealand, that "health-in-all" policies—with all government departments working together—are required to tackle ill health, reduce health inequalities, and improve national well-being.

The UK had started to look at the national rate of well-being[11] in its Prevention Green Paper[12] (out for consultation at the time of writing, but delayed due to the pandemic) with reference to a new Composite Health Index, designed to track the health of the population alongside GDP. As we emerge from the pandemic, there will be a greater appreciation of health as a key societal asset that we need to develop and protect, contributing not only to happiness but also to the economy.

First and foremost, like Ardern in New Zealand did, we need to help people who are most vulnerable. Sadly, the statistics from the pandemic have so far shown that deaths have been concentrated in the most deprived communities, including certain ethic groups. In the "new normal" UK ahead, it is the people "left behind" who need to be the focus of government policy, and this will be a critical part of rebuilding the nation's economy and the "health of the nation."

The same applies globally, too. Policymakers will need to start concentrating on how the poorest segments of society can benefit fairly from improvements in health that richer citizens are benefiting from. Social and economic factors are at the core, and there is exciting scientific evidence on how genes are influenced by the wider environment. This new research is all being accelerated exponentially using AI.

## Nature versus nurture

*"What experts are telling us in terms of living a healthy life hasn't changed much in decades: it's about moving more and not being sedentary. We also need a diet that is rich in nutrients, with a wide variety of plants that help us to develop a healthy gut and a diverse microbiome.*

*Sleep is probably one area that we should also prioritize. We're sleeping worse and less than we need, and I don't think we're going to do away with the need for eight hours."*

*— Thomas Balkizas,*
*EMEA Healthcare and Life Sciences Lead,*
*Amazon Web Services*

Historically, debates about human behavior, health, and biology have often focused on the difference between the contribution of nature, and the inherited characteristics with which we are born, and nurture, which is all those influences that enter our lives after we're born. However, most diseases involve many genes, engaging in complex interactions[13], in addition to environmental factors. You might not be born with a disease, but instead be at high risk of acquiring that disease. We call this a genetic predisposition, or a genetic susceptibility. Having a genetic susceptibility to a particular disease, whether it's due to the presence of gene mutations, a set of recessive alleles, or a combination of those, need not necessarily be considered abnormal, however.

Biomedical research overwhelmingly focuses on the genetic side— the "nature" of the nature versus nurture debate[14]. Our knowledge of both our nature and the tools we have to affect our nature is far more advanced than our knowledge of our environment and the tools that affect our environment, but this is starting to change. Research aided by AI is starting to find patterns in very large datasets in "non-sick" domains.

Robert Plomin, who recently wrote the book *Blueprint: How DNA Makes Us Who We Are*, provides convincing evidence that what we care about is heritable, and what are often thought of as "environmental effects" are shaped by our natural genetic inclinations.

Plomin is currently conducting the Twins Early Development Study[15], which is a study of all twins born in England from 1994 to 1996, focusing on developmental delays in early childhood and the association of those delays with behavioral problems and educational attainment. This ongoing study of 13,000 twins studied longitudinally for over 20 years has involved collecting over 55 million items of data from the twins, their parents, and their teachers during this time.

His research shows that genetics has the most influence in shaping who we are, and that genetic differences account for more of the psychological disparities between us than everything else put together. He has proposed that important environmental factors, such as families and schools, account for less than 5% of the differences seen in mental health or academic performance, for example. Far more important are genetic factors that account for 50% of all psychological traits, from our personality to our mental abilities to how well we do at school. Most of the traits that make us "who we are" result from many genes interacting with each other, rather than single genes that code for schizophrenia or intelligence or extraversion.

Plomin explores the potential of polygenic risk scores (as detailed in the previous chapter). While the predictions these scores provide are probabilistic, rather than certain, they're improving in accuracy all the time and can predict things about you from the start of your life. He argues that school attainment is now better forecast by a polygenic score than any other method of prediction—it is even more accurate than how your parents did at school or the type of school you go to (which turns out to have little effect, once controlling for the fact that selective schools tend to select more innately talented children).

Not everyone agrees with Plomin's conclusions, which run counter to what most of us have been taught in life: that our behavior and intelligence are mostly shaped by our parenting, and by our social and educational environments. The idea that our environment "is king" is more palatable, too, since these factors are more within our control. Government intervention and policies can modulate our environment, with the goal of producing a fairer and more equitable society.

Continued advances in "omics," which is the collective term for those fields of study in biology ending in -omics, such as proteomics, metabolomics, or genomics, will continually inform this debate of nature versus nurture. Omics aims to characterize and quantify the dynamics of the biological molecules that are transformed into the structures and functions of our bodies, and will help us understand and address the way environments affect human health, both individually and at the population health level.

Scientists at Stanford University School of Medicine in California have recently published in *Nature*[16] that we have individual biological patterns of aging—or an "ageotype." Led by Professor Michael Snyder, the chairman of the Department of Genetics, a team studied in unprecedented detail the physiological changes in 106 participants aged between 29 and 75. To determine precisely how each individual was changing, and in which organs, Snyder's team regularly measured groups of molecules in their subjects' blood—proteins, metabolites and RNA (a nucleic acid that can carry genetic information)—and the microbiome in their samples, as well as conducting clinical tests. From the results, his team identified four main ageotypes based on where in the body the cellular aging process is most active: immune, liver, kidney, and metabolic. One person was classified as a "cardio ager," but each had their own personal aging profiles.

# Aging clocks and biomarkers

*"I showed the FDA that we're going to target and then delay or prevent a cluster of age-related diseases...you don't need to call aging a disease...epigenetics is a huge opportunity. It describes the way that the environment interacts with our genes and that there is a lot to learn from understanding that."*

*– Nir Barzilai,*
*Director, Institute for Aging Research,*
*Albert Einstein College of Medicine*

New research shows that epigenetic clocks, as described in the previous chapter can provide insights into why certain tissues age faster than others, and why those tissues may be more cancer-prone. These clocks rely on the body's epigenome, which comprises chemical modifications, such as methyl groups, that tag DNA. The pattern of these tags changes during the course of life, and they track a person's biological age, which can lag behind or exceed chronological age.

Scientists can construct epigenetic clocks and Steve Horvath, a bioinformatician at the University of California, Los Angeles, has developed one of the most accurate ones[17]. His "Horvath clock" was published in 2013 and was aimed initially at detecting "age acceleration" or the difference between a person's epigenetic and chronological age, in one particular part of their body or more generally. However, Horvath and other researchers soon discovered that epigenetic age acceleration is linked to mortality, even after controlling for chronological age and other risk factors.

Since then, epigenetic clocks have been finding increasing application in measuring the effectiveness of interventions to delay or prevent aging.

In September 2019, a small clinical study in California was published[18] that suggested for the first time that it might be possible to reverse the body's epigenetic clock. In this study, nine healthy volunteers took a mix of three commonly prescribed drugs for one year—growth hormone and two diabetes medications—and on average shed 2.5 years of their biological ages while also showing signs that their immune systems were improving. The researchers were surprised by these findings but Horvath probed further using four different epigenetic clocks to confirm the effect of the treatments on enhancing each patient's biological age.

Aging clocks can be used to help us measure the effects of other interventions besides drugs too. Metabolomics can help us identify the optimal set of markers, including metabolic biomarkers and general health parameters, to monitor the metabolic effects of intervention. A significant part of a person's average lifespan is determined by environmental exposures and lifestyle choices. As we aim to eat better, and eat less, to live longer, will this make us look younger too? Greying hair and wrinkles are external signs of aging, but can they signal the state of our internal health and aging process too?

Anastasia Georgievskaya, CEO of Haut.ai, is doing groundbreaking work in skin health, using skin as a unique biomarker of aging. It turns out that wrinkles, especially around the corners of your eyes, are very accurate in predicting chronological age. She uses AI to understand how lifestyle factors (such as nutrition) and environmental triggers (such as allergens and pollutants) impact skin biomarkers—and how these biomarkers relate to the state of a person's health and can measure the aging process.

Skin is the biggest organ of the body and is very influenced by the state of your internal health. A professional dermatologist can tell from skin tone or radiance how well, for example, your liver is functioning. Professional dermatologists can identify some diseases just from the color of your skin.

Unsurprisingly, Haut.ai is working with cosmetic companies to guide people with recommendations to improve their skin biomarkers (wrinkles), which can act as a proxy for how healthy you are and where you compare to others in the aging process.

Haut.ai has devised a "photo clock" that can assess your age from a selfie, using algorithms trained on 20 data points, including bags under the eyes, tightness, wrinkles, and skin spots. The intention is to use this as a tool to motivate people to stick to their healthy lifestyle regimens, measure progress, and improve compliance (whether it is exercise, drugs, supplements, and so on).

I asked Georgievskaya whether skin biomarkers could tell whether the food, exercise, and supplements I have been taking on the recommendation of my nutrigenomics coach were helping to improve my biological age (or at least delay the aging process).

Georgievskaya said that a combination of biomarkers used to identify personal "health signatures" may be a more potent way of measuring health and aging—and this is the focus of research at the moment. She added that biomarkers, whether they are wrinkles, aging spots, heart rhythms, or proteins in the blood, change qualitatively and quantitatively as you age, and the most useful biomarkers are linked to mortality. Scientists like herself are trying to find the most reliable biomarkers to track health and aging.

There are many aging clocks based on various biomarkers, such as blood biochemistry, or, in Georgievskaya's case, skin aging, but the Horvath clock is still regarded as one of the most important biomarker clocks.

The real potential of AI is looking at the relationship between these biomarkers and understanding the specific reasons why everyone ages differently; once we understand the underlying reasons, we can then begin to design highly personalized interventions to help people stay healthier, age better, and live longer. Just recently, new company Deep Longevity launched its iPhone app Young.ai which crunches biometric data to interpret your biological age and provide you with a personalized "longevity strategy"[64].

We will explore the wide range of environmental and lifestyle influences that impact aging clocks in the next section.

# The exposome

> *"In AI and longevity, or AI and disease, we have so much to learn from genetic markers. So much is tied to our genes and how we interact with our environment. There's a lot of potential there and it's a very unexplored area. What is more common in mental health is the long-term impact that nurture and environment can have on a child. When looking at genotypes and phenotypes, different individuals have different levels of resilience in terms of their ability to cope with difficult situations. If we can identify these factors early, can we intervene early? Social determinants are also important in the elderly... the big social determinant is isolation and its impact on different individuals."*
>
> *– Paul Dagum,*
> *Founder and Vice Chair, Mindstrong Health*

A new concept known as the "exposome" is challenging widely held beliefs and assumptions that have guided our understanding of human biology for decades, if not centuries. So, what is the exposome? It represents the complex environmental exposures we are subjected to throughout our lives, including our diet, lifestyle factors, and social influences, and our body's response to these challenges. The exposome encompasses much of what we refer to as nurture, and was first coined by Dr Christopher Wild[19] at the International Agency for Research on Cancer, World Health. The exposome consists of three overlapping domains:

- A general external environment, including the urban environment, education, climate factors, social capital, and stress

- A specific external environment with specific contaminants, radiation, infections, and lifestyle factors such as, tobacco, alcohol, diet, physical activity, and so on

- An internal environment that includes internal biological factors such as metabolic factors, hormones, gut microflora, inflammation, and oxidative stress

The exposome catalogs and integrates the complex factors into a model[20] that can also help us understand the effects of the environment on longevity.

Paul Shiels, Professor of Geroscience at the University of Glasgow, is an expert on epigenetics and the exposome of aging. I caught up with Shiels while writing this book and had a fascinating discussion. My main personal takeaway was that despite all the genomics research underway and the availability of DNA testing kits, "gait speed" (how fast you can walk) measured at age 45 is still regarded by most as the best predictor of how well you will age in the future. However, this will all start to change with what we are starting to uncover with new evidence in omics and the exposome.

For example, the level of **C-reactive protein** (**CRP**), which can be measured in the blood, is linked to chronic inflammation seen in aging (also known as "inflammaging"). In general, a low CRP level is better than a high one, because it indicates less inflammation in the body. According to Shiels, CRP is also a measure of "gut leak"— leaky gut is a measure of how well your kidneys are functioning, which is now accepted as a proven risk factor for morbidity and mortality in the aged. The latest research shows that biological aging in the kidney is influenced directly by nutrition, inflammation, the gut microbiome, psychosocial factors, and lifestyle factors[65].

The impact of the microbiome on our health and how well we age is a fast developing area of research. According to research presented at the European Society of Cardiology Congress 2020[21], bacteria and other microorganisms in the digestive tract are linked with dozens of health conditions including high blood pressure, high blood lipids, and **body mass index** (**BMI**).

## You are what you eat

Hippocrates, the Greek father of medicine who died in 377 BC, said, "All disease begins in the gut"—and he may be right. A significant amount of research these days is on the role of the gut, microbiome, and nutrition as key determinants of age-related health and resilience. And all this is being driven by AI, making research easier to do and helping with spotting patterns in the data.

The evidence is certainly there to back up the old saying that "you are what you eat." It seems there are very good reasons why grandmothers through the ages have told us to eat our greens. Many who have watched the recent Netflix *Gamechangers*[22] documentary about the benefits of plant-based eating for athletes will have sworn never to eat meat again. I have started to become a convert to vegan food myself. I'm currently obsessed with oat milk thanks to my son's girlfriend!

Is eating too much red meat actually bad for your health? The jury is out but recent research has shown[23] that too much red meat can lead to high phosphate levels in your blood (known as "hyperphosphatemia"), and it can also disturb gut flora, leading to subsequent inflammation. This, in turn, leads to adverse effects on renal function, which is linked to accelerated aging. Interestingly, big cats (like lions and tigers), who consume large quantities of red meat, are also prone to hyperphosphatemia and subsequent renal toxicity.

## Living greener and living longer

While eating less meat and more plant-based foods may enhance your health and boost your longevity, did you know that it could save the climate too?

Linking living greener with living longer is driving the "meat-free" movement. This has spurred innovation in all sorts of ways, and the latest technologies in AI, gene editing, and cellular techniques are being used to grow protein in the lab, in the hope of lessening our dependence on livestock.

Sales of red meat fell more by value than any other category in supermarkets last year, down by £185 million, according to research by Nielsen[24]. Beef sales declined by 4% and pork by 6.4%. By contrast, sales of meat-free alternatives rose by 18% to £405 million, the highest growth rate of any category. Some consumers switched to eating more poultry and fish, which are often perceived to be healthier, with sales up 1.4% and 1.2%, respectively.

Wanting to be healthier[25] was the most popular reason for giving up animal products, and was mentioned by 55% of people. Concern for animal welfare was mentioned by 49% and protecting the environment[26] by 30%.

According to CB Insights[27], Beyond Meat and Impossible Foods are two of the main players currently commercializing plant-based beef, and they have deals with a wide variety of restaurants to provide their plant burgers as a replacement for beef burgers to consumers. Unilever and Nestle are two other big players investing in plant-based food, recognizing that alternative dairy and vegan options are becoming popular with consumers. Alternative milks, like soy, almond, and oat milks, are finding their way into big brand ice creams too.

According to George Monbiot, an environmental journalist, food grown from cells in a lab will soon make plant- and meat-based foods irrelevant[28]. For example, Perfect Day is growing ice cream in the lab using gene sequencing and fermentation. Another company, Solar Labs, based in Helsinki, is able to concoct a "primordial soup of bacteria" (remember how life started?) taken from the soil and multiplied in the laboratory; the process involves extracting hydrogen from water as its energy source, and it multiplies selected micro-organisms to produce the desired products in factories.

So-called "farm-free" food could foster rewilding[29] and carbon drawdown[30], leading to cheap, nutritious, and abundant food for everyone.

Interestingly, a survey by Censuswide for Aviva[31] into greener lifestyles found that people aged 55 and over were ahead in "living greener" in every category measured except the vegan diet—nine percent of 16- to 24-year-olds say they are vegan, compared to just 2% among the over-55s. However, younger people are not as good at reducing their carbon footprint on a few measures compared to their older counterparts; for example, they are more likely to buy cheap clothes from ASOS, take Ubers, and order fast food from Deliveroo—all of which negatively impact the environment.

## Longevity diets

Tim Spector, Professor of Genetic Epidemiology at King's College London, is one of the world's leading experts on personalized health and the gut microbiome and has published many books, including the best-selling *The Diet Myth*. His latest book, *Spoon Fed*, explores the latest scientific evidence showing that almost everything we've been told about food is wrong, with little scientific evidence for many of our deep-seated ideas. What's more, he argues, the food industry is influencing our choices, along with many medical and government recommendations, towards less healthy options. Labeling, for example, is being used to give the impression that foods are "healthy," when, in fact, they are laden with calories and heavily processed.

Cynical marketing tactics and lax licensing laws are huge issues too, and are heavily linked with obesity, which has reached epidemic levels and reduces healthspan. The recent report on childhood obesity[32] by Sally Davies, former Chief Medical Officer for the UK Government, shows just how urgent this problem is to address. This is now being set in motion by the UK Government through its latest anti-obesity campaign spurred by the COVID-19 pandemic.

Many diets being hyped at the moment to promote healthier living and longer healthspans involve "intermittent fasting." Calorie restriction has been known for years to extend lifespans of mice; however, more recently it has been found that it is the interval between eating that leads to this longevity effect, not the extent of caloric restriction. This is the basis of intermittent fasting and practically every person involved in longevity research I have met does it (and so do I, now).

The evidence is interesting here—and sure enough, the day after the most calorie-laden day of the year (Christmas Day, when on average, most consume over 6,000 calories) the New England Journal of Medicine[33] published *Effects of Intermittent Fasting on Health, Aging, and Disease*, presenting the accumulating evidence that eating in a six-hour period and fasting for 18 hours can trigger a metabolic switch from glucose-based to ketone-based energy; this, in turn, can increase stress resistance and decrease diseases, including cancer and obesity, leading to increased longevity.

## Exercise as the "killer app" for healthspan

According to Graham Lawton, who has just published *This Book Could Save Your Life: The Science of Living Longer Better*, we should look to our ancestors, the hunter-gatherers, to work out how much exercise we need to live longer. Lawton says our bodies evolved for hunting and gathering, and that people who live much like our ancient ancestors, such as the Hadza people of the Rift Valley and Serengeti in Tanzania, are a good guide to how much exercise we need. They typically get about two hours daily, mostly from fast walking over hilly terrain, dragging firewood, hauling water, and climbing trees. They have healthy hearts, no diabetes, and stay strong into old age. We can deduce from this that the optimum dose of exercise is two hours of brisk walking each day. In the age of the personal fitness tracker, with an ambitious daily target of 10,000 steps (the daily UK average is 1,500), the number of steps equivalent to two hours' walking is nearer 15,000.

This is quite different from the World Health Organization's recommendation of 150 minutes of moderate-intensity activity (equal to a brisk walk, at a pace of 3 miles per hour) or 75 minutes of vigorous-intensity activity (makes your heartbeat and breathing faster, and makes you sweat) each week, preferably spread throughout the week.

A study led by American Cancer Society[34] researchers has found that even low levels of walking are linked with lower mortality. This concurs with a recent study published in November 2019 in the British Journal of Sports Medicine[35], which showed that runners who turn out more often, and who run faster in longer sessions, do not reduce their risk any more than those who hit the road gently once a week. Analysts from around the world, including the Institute for Health and Sport at Victoria University in Australia, looked at 14 studies on the link between running and a reduction in "all-cause mortality." The studies examined 232,129 participants, tracking their health for between 5.5 and 35 years. Almost 26,000 of the participants died during the study periods.

Pooling the study results, researchers found that any amount of running was linked to a 27% reduction in an early death from any cause, with a more pronounced effect among women, when compared with those who led a sedentary lifestyle and did no running. The analysis found that running reduced the risk of death from cancer by 23% and death from cardiovascular problems by 30%. Intriguingly, one study[36] found that older women who walked about two miles a day, or a little more than 4,000 steps, lived longer than women who covered only about 2,000 steps, or a mile.

Multiple studies have shown that very short but intense workouts—known as high-intensity interval training—improve fitness to about the same level as more moderate exercise.

Overall, exercise generally positively affects aging[37]: in various recent[38] studies, active older people's muscles, immune systems[39], blood cells, and even skin[40] appeared biologically younger, at a molecular level, than those of sedentary people. Their brains also tended to look and work differently. Studies also show that physical activity lowers people's risks of dementia or, if dementia has already begun, slows memory loss[41], increases brain volume[42], and improves the quality of connections between neurons and different portions of the brain[43].

Exercise also improves mood, with observational studies showing that physically active people are much less likely to develop depression or anxiety than sedentary people[44].

These positive benefits of regular exercise can have a significant impact on economic growth, workforce productivity, and life expectancy too. Research by Vitality[45], a life insurer that uses behavioral nudges to improve people's health and reduce healthcare costs, and RAND, a United States-based not-for-profit research group, concluded that if every Briton walked only 22 minutes a day, the economy would be permanently £6.2 billion larger (the figures globally[46] were in the order of $100 billion with just 15 minutes each day). Improvements would come from longer lives, reduced time off work with illness, and greater productivity. Workers would gain up to five additional days of productive time each year, the study suggested.

Companies like Peloton, Strava, and Sweatcoin are showing how fitness tech might shape the future of health and wellness more broadly, including diet and nutrition, mindfulness, and sleep. Recent innovations in fitness technology also have the potential to create an entirely new platform for interconnected health and wellness. Could connected devices streaming fitness content directly to homes also connect you with doctors, physical therapists, or other medical professionals to save you from the hassle of going to a health center?

How might wearables integrate biometric data with connected fitness devices to build personalized fitness regimens, or provide a real-time data feed for primary care physicians to help them make smarter and faster recommendations for a patient remotely? In the short term, boutique gyms and fitness apps might help us reach our summer body goals. However, in the long term, fitness startups might unlock a more connected, informed, and effective health and wellness future, especially as the world moves increasingly online post-pandemic.

My friend Anton Derlyatka, co-founder and CEO of Sweatcoin, has a very interesting vision for the future of fitness. Sweatcoin is a digital platform that motivates people to keep active by converting steps from walking into a virtual currency called a "sweatcoin." Steps are verified through algorithms (that can catch cheating!) and whatever is "earned" can be spent on products and services. Users can choose their personal goals, and it doesn't have to be 10,000 steps; a recent report in JAMA, for example, showed that as little as 4,400 steps per day significantly lowered the risk of death in older women.

Sweatcoin is taking learnings from tax incentives that work well in the financial sector to incentivize human behavior in the health context. Derylatka says that while most people understand what they need to do to keep healthy, less follow through on their actions. The problem is that humans are "lazy by design" and the market responds to this with products and services that make life easier and more convenient, feeding our pleasures and vices, rather than promoting good, healthy habits.

Derylatka was inspired by the book *Nudge* by Richard Thaler, and Sweatcoin uses technology to nudge people gently, by using incentives to promote healthy behaviors. Incentives can work on a variety of different levels, mostly emotional, to encourage people to make the "right" decisions for their health and well-being.

So far, Sweatcoin has made more than 40 million people around the world more active, and has been named as one of the fastest growing health and fitness apps in history, alongside the likes of FitBit, Nike, MyFitnessPal, and Strava. My three sons were some of the first to use it four years ago. They would regularly receive Graze snacks through our letterbox purchased with their sweatcoins.

Sweatcoin is free and aims to reach as many people as possible, including less privileged sections of society. It is focused on creating incentives that work well in different social demographic groups; for example, it could be handbags for an older woman, or a mountain bike for a 14-year-old.

Sweatcoin has expanded into partnering with local authorities and local branches of the NHS in the UK to test how the platform can tackle inactivity through social engagement, as well as promote local businesses and help local communities. Sweatcoin has been particularly effective in appealing to those social demographic groups that are typically "left outside"—people from less privileged communities, who may not be able to afford going to a gym, and who governments find it hard to engage with. Academic research shows that people with a high BMI react even better than an average user and become more active.

Derylatka predicts that these incentives will start to influence city design, to promote more public transport and less cars, leading to better air quality and increased "active travel." Derylatka suggests that cities of the future will have more social spaces to enable people to interact more, as social isolation and loneliness are major causes of poor health, especially mental health. With suicide rates increasing in the Millennial and Generation Z populations, more connected social environments with greener spaces will become more important, and support the climate change agenda too.

## New age mobility and transport

Some futurists predict that the car will increasingly be a place to help us monitor our health, where basic health parameters and vital signs could be determined using sensors located in the seats or the safety belt and analyzed with supercomputers such as IBM Watson in the cloud, instead of a doctor's clinic. If something is wrong, the patient could receive a notification to see their doctor.

Car-makers such as Ford and Honda have started developing heart monitoring technology, using real-time data to identify potential medical problems before they happen. UK-based B-Secur[47], for example, has developed a biometric-based authentication technology called HeartKey that identifies users by their unique heartbeat. The sensor is integrated into the steering wheel, where it can track changes in heart rate and rhythm (including atrial fibrillation, which is one of the biggest silent killers), stress levels, and fatigue. These metrics can provide drivers and passengers with real-time insights into their health, and can also prevent accidents by detecting drivers who are sleepy or ill.

In this way, cars may evolve to become more like "wellness pods." Technology is already being developed to enhance well-being using sensors that can interpret drivers' moods and make adjustments to seat posture, lighting, temperature, and sound. Hyundai, for example, recently launched "Mood Bursts" to help drivers: a Calm Burst helps the driver to relax if sensors sense the driver is feeling anxious and an Alert Burst can stimulate the driver if the driver is becoming sleepy.

"Micromobility" is an emerging field and is likely to expand quickly, especially post-COVID as people look to other forms of transport to travel with less risk of infection. Scooters and bikes are expected to become popular alternatives to buses, for example, and have the added benefit of providing exercise, reducing pollution, and preventing traffic jams, thus increasing health and lowering the environmental footprint.

Dan Burden[48], Director of Innovation and Inspiration at Blue Zones, is America's top walkability expert[49] and is a pioneer in people-first urban planning. He sums it up: "What if economics is not based around the car? What if it was based around the human? We could build a stronger economy, much greater health, and work at a much quicker pace towards sustainable life on the planet."

## Connected cities and communities

The use of AI will accelerate our understanding of the impact of the exposome, but it depends on the availability of datasets in the wider environment. AI can be used to look at the impact of exposure to pathogens and toxins (for example, sensors can readily measure pollution), but it is more difficult to measure the impact of family relationships or green spaces on stress.

All this is changing, and it will change quickly with developments in **smart cities**. Big Tech is heavily involved and placing big bets on smart cities using AI, sensors, and data analytics to manage urban resources. Urban centers around the world, including in Egypt (New Cairo), China (Hangzhou), and Italy (Milan) are gearing up.

Toyota recently revealed plans[50] to build a prototype city of the future on a 175-acre site at the base of Mount Fuji in Japan. Named "Woven City," it will be powered by hydrogen fuel cells and act as a lab to test and develop technologies in a real-world environment. People, buildings, and vehicles will all be connected and communicating with each other through data and sensors to create better living and mobility for all.

Until recently, a network with sufficient speed and scalability did not exist, but 5G networks have the speed and scalability necessary to make city-wide sensor networks feasible. Edge computing, which brings computation and data storage closer to the location where it is needed ("the edge"), will massively increase capacity and speed, and is on the horizon.

From smart parking to AI for public safety, startups are making cities smarter and hopefully, more human too. Identity technologies like Yoti—an app that provides a secure way to prove your identity online and in person—will play an increasingly important role in the smart cities of the future.

According to CB Insights[51], public spaces such as parks and other soft targets may soon utilize AI cameras and UAVs to monitor and flag suspicious activity or to identify known criminals. City airspace is increasingly crowded and **Internet of Things** (**IoT**) tech will help to manage airspace to prevent autonomous drone collisions, coordinate CPG delivery, support travel, and so on. Smart city municipalities will have the ability to crowdsource real-time mobile data on citizens' behaviors and views of city-wide planning efforts.

Valuable lessons about how not to build smart cities from scratch can be drawn from Songdo in South Korea and Masdar in Abu Dhabi, both of which were designed to be smart, eco-friendly cities, but which remain ghost towns as no one wants to live in them.

This resembles the situation hitting many current communities too with the death of the high street, for example, making many town centers bleak and desolate. The move to online in shopping, banking, and postal services, for example, has removed a key reason why people used to visit the high street as a social, "human" place to go (and this was *before* the pandemic, which is also leaving city centers empty as people work increasingly from home).

Tim Cook, the chief executive of Apple, talks about the future of retail being around education, entertainment, and entrepreneurship—and the pandemic will only increase innovation in this respect. In the UK, an often-cited example of this is Brighton, with its street art and bohemian mix of culture. But look also at Wallasey in the northwest, where the Rockpoint Leisure estate is embodying a quiet revolution that would have been almost unthinkable a decade ago.

Led by Daniel Davies, a local businessman, the area has an open-air art gallery, which has 15 large abstract art murals. People come to visit to see the latest art but also to shop at the independent retailers. Before the pandemic, the local greengrocer, who has been there since long before the murals, said that footfall has increased as a result of the local artwork.

Another example[52] is on the streets in east London, where residents are converting unoccupied parking spaces into small community gardens where neighbors can sit and socialize—in effect reclaiming space from polluting cars to create "parklets" filled with plants and benches for people to sit on and to create greener streets. It is this restoration of civic pride in rundown areas that needs to happen across the UK in the quest to "level up" communities between the "rich South" and the "poor North."

The pandemic has also created a movement towards "low-traffic" neighborhoods in the UK, where citizens are literally reclaiming the streets, which has been made possible through a £2 billion package announced by the UK Government in May 2020 to boost cycling and walking. Councils are granting the right for citizens to close off traffic on their local roads to allow more space for shared gardens to emerge and kids to play safely outside their houses without fear of cars running them over, for example.

New ways of getting people to the town centers will be needed—especially to lure them from their houses when the risk of the pandemic ceases—and innovation in retail and community services will be part of the solution. We could revitalize communities by making it easier for social entrepreneurs and community leaders to start new services and providing a reason for people to leave their houses by rebuilding community spirit, inspiring civic action, and tackling the biggest killer of older people, social isolation.

## Home smart home and age tech

At the core of a future smart city is a layer of open digital infrastructure that provides ubiquitous connectivity for all, offers new insights on the urban environment, and encourages creation and collaboration to address local challenges.

This will help smart homes to develop too. The global smart home market is expected to reach $175 billion[53] by 2025 according to Venture Beat[54], and all the Big Tech companies are investing heavily in the industry. Google sells a host of connected contraptions under its Nest brand, Amazon has created everything from connected speakers to microwaves and clocks, and Apple is continuing to invest in its Siri-infused HomePod smart speaker[55].

Given that consumers may procure a range of connected devices, apps, and cloud services for their home from multiple companies, a common standard is in everyone's best interests. And this is exactly what Google, Amazon, Apple, and other technology companies have teamed up to do: develop a smart home connectivity standard that makes it easier for software and devices to play ball across the smart home ecosystem. Called Connected Home Over IP[56], this group will be spearheaded by the Zigbee Alliance[57], a group of companies that develop and maintain the Zigbee standard, which enables close-proximity devices (for example, light switches, smart speakers, and locks) to talk to each other in the home.

While it's too early to say what will emerge from this collaboration, the fact that the major players spanning hardware, software, and the cloud have elected to participate is something to watch.

Smart housing harnessing quantum technology is, meanwhile, on the horizon. One UK project, Quest, using quantum sensor technology and quantum-inspired imaging, and combined with AI, is being funded as part of a £5.6M, five-year, EPSRC Healthcare Technologies 2050 Program Grant.

It will provide new sensor systems using quantum-inspired imaging to diagnose and screen non-communicable chronic diseases, such as dementia, stroke, and heart disease—creating "intelligent homes." This takes the concept of precision medicine and extends it to overall physical and mental well-being for "precision healthcare" to be delivered to the home.

## Dementia-friendly smart homes

People diagnosed with dementia and their families typically face the agonizing decision to sell the family home and move the dementia sufferer into care (which, in Britain, costs on average £40,000 a year). There must be another way. The **Building Research Establishment (BRE)**[58], a UK-based world-leading building-science research center, has teamed up with experts from Loughborough University to create the "ideal" dementia-friendly home. Working with architects, health and well-being experts, academics, building physicists, space planners, technology providers, and product manufacturers, they are educating housebuilders, careers, and relatives on how to better support those living with dementia.

They have distilled the following key features for creating a dementia-friendly home:

- Clear lines of sight towards specific rooms
- Good natural lighting, to help people stay alert during the day and sleep better at night
- Automatically controlled ventilation
- Noise-reduction features to reduce stress
- Simple switches and heating controls, plus safety sensors in high-risk areas
- A homely and familiar design to encourage relaxation

Now IKEA is moving this new thinking into the mainstream. Working with Queen Silvia of Sweden, whose own mother suffered from dementia, IKEA has drawn up plans[59] for the first prototypes of low-cost modular flats to ensure that patients and their carers can continue to live in their own homes.

The six model apartments in Stockholm are a pilot for a concept that is intended to be spread across Scandinavia and into the UK over the next few years.

Smart technologies can enable dementia sufferers to live in their own homes for longer. The **Technology Integrated Health Management (TIHM)** Test Bed Project[60] in Sussex is equipping individuals and their carers with sensors, wearables, monitors, and other devices to improve communication, share insights, and send alerts to healthcare staff who, in turn, can deliver more responsive and effective services. The project aims to prevent or delay costly long-term care in nursing homes, reduce the need for unplanned hospital admissions or GP visits, and improve the care for vulnerable patients.

There are many pioneering startups in this space that are using AI and other technologies to help people live in their homes for longer. Alcove[61] has developed care technology using AI to support individuals living at home and assists local authorities, social housing associations, and retirement villages to deliver more efficient and higher quality care. "Self-learning" algorithms analyze data to automatically detect emergencies and behavioral changes that might otherwise go unnoticed.

MySense.ai[62] installs a range of non-intrusive sensors around the home to understand an individual's movements and habits, allowing their appointed carer to monitor and respond to their needs. A wristband sensor can measure heart rate for drops or elevations that could indicate stress, illness, or other abnormalities.

Door sensors can monitor unusual or even a lack of activity on front doors or fridges that could be signs of mental or physical issues. Seat sensors can check an individual's physical activity outside of normal levels, like prolonged periods spent in a chair. Plug sensors can shows usage of a kettle, TV, or other electrical devices that could flag unusual behavior patterns. Tap sensors can highlight changes to an individual's water consumption that could point to dehydration. A toilet sensor can enable a carer to compassionately raise issues that an individual may find too sensitive to share. A shower sensor can signal decreases in personal hygiene that could be a sign of mental decline or depression. And, finally, a bed sensor situated under the mattress can measure prolonged periods lying in bed or erratic movement during sleep, which can alert the carer about support that might be needed.

MySense runs machine-learning algorithms against the data to search for patterns and anomalies. Indicators of concern or patterns of behavior auto-update the individual's status. Alerts notify the individual via a MySense Home Hub or, if the situation is more serious, a relevant responder via text message or the MySense app.

# Conclusions

Our genes do not define our risk for disease on their own. The exposome is a new concept that encapsulates the environmental, nongenetic drivers of health and disease, including the range of chemicals and toxins that enter our bodies through the air, water, or food, but also our body's response to our environment, including the built environment and social circumstances, through effects as wide-ranging as inflammation, oxidative stress, infections, and gut flora.

My interviews with the following experts shed light on the extraordinary progress that scientists and entrepreneurs are making in understanding how we can influence the complex interplay between genes, our physiology (including metabolism), and response to the environment. Developments are unfolding at breakneck speed and governments, businesses, and society are struggling to keep up with how this can be harnessed for individual self-care and also wider public health benefits, including in the design of transport, homes, communities, and cities.

# Interviews

The following interviews reflect expertise at the cutting edge of aging: Nir Barzilai, who has convinced the FDA to completely change how it categorizes indications to trial the diabetes drug metformin for its ability to delay aging, the main risk factor for many chronic diseases; Paul Dagum, a pioneer who uses digital biomarkers to help diagnose and manage mental health conditions, which are on the rise as a result of the pandemic; Thomas Balkizas, who combines his Big Tech experience working with Amazon Web Services with the ability to sniff out the next disruptors on the horizon and his perspective as an investor who founded Alpha Tech Capital; Teemu Sanu, founder of Nightingale Health, which uses blood-based molecular data and AI to predict disease risk, aiming to abolish chronic diseases through prevention; and Nicola Palmarini, who was formerly with the behemoth IBM as its head of ethics and aging, and is now director of the National Innovation for Ageing in the UK, focused on harnessing AI for business to capitalize on the longevity economy.

## Nir Barzilai
*Professor of Medicine (Endocrinology) and Genetics, and Director, Institute for Aging Research at Albert Einstein College of Medicine*

I met Nir Barzilai initially through his involvement with the Scientific Advisory Board of the APPG for Longevity. I caught up with him to interview him for the book at his office at Albert Einstein College of Medicine in the Bronx. As soon as he came down to greet me in the lobby, he said we would grab a bite to eat at his favorite sushi place. He had been fasting and was ready to tuck into some sashimi.

On the way there we talked about the research supporting the theories behind intermittent fasting (and, of course, the many diet books like *The 5:2 Diet Book* that have based their methodologies on this research). I knew that mice lived longer when their calories were heavily restricted but what I hadn't realized was that it was the interval between eating food that had the effect, not the reduction in calories per se.

Nir and I had a great lunch—and left feeling completely nourished and replenished in mind, soul, and body. Nir is an amazing person: pure and simple, warm, generous, and with an unmatched sense of humor, fun, and adventure.

Nir was born in Haifa in 1955 and credits a lot of his success to his army training in Israel. By his early 20s, he had been decorated for his military service and had become chief medic of the Israeli army. Nir eventually settled in the US and developed a specialty in endocrinology and metabolism.

He has been involved in fascinating research studying "super-centenarians"—people who live extraordinarily long lives in a state of good health literally right until death. For the most part, these people get the same illnesses as everyone else—they just get ill a few decades later. Nir wanted to understand why.

Nir has been hailed as the first person to find a "longevity gene" through his Longevity Genes Project, studying more than 750 healthy elderly people between the ages of 95 and 112 and their children.

He hopes that by identifying longevity genes, it will be possible to develop new drug therapies that might help people live longer, healthier lives and avoid or significantly delay age-related diseases such as Alzheimer's disease, type 2 diabetes, and cardiovascular disease.

Nir has been in the media a lot recently for his work leading the **Targeting Aging with Metformin (TAME)** trial, which has now received all the funding to go ahead. This is a double-blind study of roughly 3,000 elderly people; half will get a placebo and half will get an old drug for type 2 diabetes called Metformin, which has been shown to modify aging in some animal studies. Because there is still no accepted biomarker for aging, the drug's success will be judged by an unusual standard—whether it can delay the development of several diseases whose incidence increases dramatically with age: cardiovascular disease, cancer, and cognitive decline, along with mortality. Metformin was chosen because its safety profile, widespread use, and length of time as an approved drug make it hard for the FDA to object to on technical grounds.

If the trial is successful, it could profoundly change the approach to aging and its diseases and affect healthcare delivery and costs; in particular, if metformin shows it can modulate aging and its diseases beyond its current indication in diabetes, it would pave the way for the development of next-generation drugs that directly target the biology of aging.

I have met Nir a couple of times since our initial meeting: during Longevity Week in London in November 2019 and then again in Singapore at the New Academy of Medicine Healthy Longevity Global Challenge meeting in February 2020 (just days before COVID-19 was announced as a global pandemic and the world changed. Nir is now working at breakneck speed to see how countering cellular aging can help to boost resistance to COVID-19).

In Singapore, Nir's colleague S. Jay Olshansky, a biodemographer of aging from the University of Illinois, Chicago, showed a video for *National Geographic* that told the fascinating story of how they took on the FDA and convinced them to change all convention and rules to authorize the TAME trial to test a drug to specifically target the process of human aging. In effect, they wanted the blessing from the FDA to make aging itself a legitimate target for drug development. What they did was incredible—they took on the prevailing orthodoxy and persuaded the FDA to accept clinical trials that target the mechanisms of aging, rather than specific named age-related conditions.

**Tina Woods**: How has the way you speak about aging, longevity, and anti-aging technology changed as your career has developed?

**Nir Barzilai**: When I started, I used to talk about aging and about the fact that we went from hope to promise. We just see aging as a biological process and it can be targeted. "Aging" wasn't a good word to use, because no matter what you told people, aging meant diseases and death. Death is inevitable, but aging is the way we die, and it turns out it's a problem to say it.

I started using the term "longevity" because it sounded better. My field of study is people with exceptional longevity. What was nice about them was that they not only lived longer, but they were healthier for longer. They were healthier 30 years more than their cohorts, and sometimes even more than that; not only that, but they had a compression of morbidity, and that's something that is very important. In other words, there was very little time at the end of their lives when they were sick.

This was confirmed by the government data from the Centers for Disease Control and Prevention which showed that the medical costs in the last few years of life for somebody who dies over the age of 100 are a third of those for someone who dies when they're 70. That was translated to a term that we're using a lot, which is the "longevity dividend."

We're calculating how much it would save the economy if we could extend healthspan even modestly. It depends on how many years you can extend it by, but it will always be trillions saved.

**Tina Woods**: How are you measuring that longevity dividend, because it's a term we've often used in the UK as well?

**Nir Barzilai**: The paper that really goes through the calculation is by Jay Olshanksy and Dana Goldman, and you can see in there how they established that and how they calculated that. It was important to us because whenever we met with the government or with other people, we had economic proof. We didn't just have the idea that people want to be healthy.

The word "longevity" didn't go well for us either in the end, because for many people it meant that they'd still get the diseases whenever they got them, and then they'd have to live longer with those diseases. The buzzword that we're using is "healthspan." When I explain it, I say that if you have a certain pill that will extend your healthspan, one of the side effects will be longevity. The longevity is more of a decided fact.

It was really interesting to discover how those buzzwords attract people and how you can make progress. That's why, at this time, it's not longevity and it's certainly not aging: it's healthspan.

When we met with the FDA, neither of us wanted to call aging a disease. There's a big argument around the world about this and I think I'm winning it in the United States. First of all, I showed the FDA that we're going to target and then delay or prevent a cluster of age-related diseases. That's aging.

Aging itself is something that the American Association of Retired People, a very strong organization, doesn't refer to as a disease. Ageism is really big now; it's one of the biggest "isms" in the world in my opinion. Elderly people are being fired and elderly people are not being hired, both entirely due to their age.

If you call them diseased too, then the next thing we'll do is send them all to a camp. It doesn't work to call it a disease, and really you don't need to call aging a disease. Not every old person is diseased. There's no need to say aging is a disease, and we have more support from the organization because we don't go into the politics, or into the "ism." Healthspan is what we talk about.

**Tina Woods**: In your view, what do you think will have the biggest impact on helping people with healthspan now and in five years?

**Nir Barzilai**: Metformin is already being used as a major healthspan targeting drug. I know that the sales of Metformin from some generic companies have increased by 20% in the last year or two. That's not because there are more cases of diabetes in the last year or two. It's being prescribed off-label.

I was in Montreal and I was invited to give a talk, and at night they opened the conference up to the public to talk about aging. There were 350 people in the audience. When some of them came into the conference, they saw me and came to me and asked, "How much Metformin are you taking?" So, before my talk, I asked who in the audience did not have diabetes but was taking Metformin? Half of the people there raised their hands. Even I take Metformin because I was pre-diabetic and my doctor prescribed it. I'm not pre-diabetic now, but I still take it for the anti-aging factor.

I realize it's a self-selected sample, but it still surprised me that there were 150 to 200 people in the audience taking Metformin. I think over the next few years more people will take Metformin; I think Metformin is going to be a relatively mild drug that will add probably two, three years of healthspan.

**Tina Woods**: In the next five to 10 years, is it access to Metformin and other sort of repackaged or repurposed drugs that will drive an increase in healthspan?

**Nir Barzilai**: I think in the next five years we'll get repurposed existing drugs. We'll have new drugs developed where repurposing is part of the business plan; drugs that treat certain diseases can get approved for treating that disease, get a reputation for treating that disease, and can then be repurposed to being primarily used to treat aging. I think really the 10-15-year scale is where things will get dramatically better, but the more rapidly we do this now, and the more companies that do it, failing and succeeding and changing targets, the more drugs will be available to treat aging within 10 years.

There are a lot of biotechs that have really big potential in five to 10 years. I'm setting a lot of them up based on the Seven Pillars of Aging in the United States and the Nine Hallmarks of Aging in Europe. All the pillars are interconnected, that's the interesting thing. In other words, we can fix one pillar and that also affects another, which is really cool.

We need to develop intellectual property and drugs that target each of the pillars. That's important because from a personalized medicine perspective, some people's health will be failing because of one of those pillars more than the others, and also because the combination of these drugs is going to deliver much bigger results when it comes to healthspan.

**Tina Woods**: How do you think that's going to affect drug companies in the pharma industry and their whole business model?

**Nir Barzilai**: Well, I've been doing the rounds in the pharma companies. I would say that 10 years ago they would show me the door. Now it's different; two years ago, I gave a talk at Pfizer at its headquarters in New York. It was televised everywhere and, after that, the company contacted me and said there are a lot of people interested and we want to bring you to our strategic meeting in Boston.

I came to the strategic meeting and clearly it clicked to them that aging is the next big thing for them. Have they been doing something about it? I'm not sure about that. Practically, I think in some ways they're waiting for the results of the TAME trial. But they've started thinking about it—and with those companies, you really can't know what decisions they're making.

Another example is Novartis. Novartis is developing rapamycin. Rapamycin is the drug that has the biggest healthspan effect on almost every animal. It's not safe in humans yet, but the company that's developing this drug has done clinical studies in humans, and it showed that if you give rapamycin for a short time to the elderly to immunize them, their immunization improves. You can already see that Novartis is thinking about aging and aging indicators. The rest of the companies are somewhere on a spectrum between 0 to 100; we don't know exactly where their focus is.

**Tina Woods**: So, it's on their radar and some are moving quicker than others, but how is it going to fundamentally affect their whole business model?

**Nir Barzilai**: That depends on people even understanding the concept. When you say how a drug's going to work and how you're going to test it, it confuses people a lot. Normally, if a drug is preventing, say, heart disease, we'll do a study for heart disease and as part of that we'll figure out how many people we need in the study in order to measure significant change in heart disease.

TAME is using 3,000 people. In an ordinary study, in order to show a successful treatment for diabetes, you have 12,000 people. So, people who are used to this say you're out of your mind, and you're not doing it properly. But they miss the point that we don't care which disease is going to happen next for the patients in the study. We're not studying a particular disease; we're studying aging. The mechanism for all these diseases is aging; we don't know, and it doesn't matter to the study, what disease people are going to get next.

If your mother was diabetic and you're obese, you're probably going to get diabetes first; if you have cancer in the family, maybe you're going to get cancer. You need aging for either one. We're looking at a cluster of diseases. We don't want any one of them to be significant. Let's say that we did a bigger, much more costly, study with 12,000 people. If we showed a statistically significant difference in, for example, cardiovascular disease, we'd have to stop the study. We could not go on with the study if people were on a placebo when we could prevent cardiovascular disease.

We don't care about a particular disease—we want to show the FDA that we can affect a cluster of diseases. We get points for every disease a person doesn't get; we're going to move the time they would get that disease into the future. It's very hard for people to understand that.

**Tina Woods**: How many of these healthspan-improving drugs do you think already exist?

**Nir Barzilai**: Over 100 drugs or combinations of drugs are being tested right now, and there's reporting on about 35 drugs. Of them, five to seven have been significant—some of them have been significant for one sex and not the other, which is really interesting. We missed that totally. We experimented on male animals because we claimed that, if females were menstruating, who knew how it was going to change something; we missed a lot of biology.

**Tina Woods**: To really make drug repurposing successful, how do you think this information and treatment can be made accessible to the general public? What role do governments, businesses, and citizens play?

**Nir Barzilai**: The field of anti-aging includes many charlatans and we get this reputation where we're trying to distance ourselves from those charlatans; it's really difficult. I worked on two articles, one in *Wall Street Journal* and one in *The Economist*, where I talked to the reporter and said don't use the term "anti-aging" because we're trying to make ourselves distinct from these charlatans; in both cases, the title had "anti-aging" in it.

I called those reporters to say I didn't understand and they said look, it's the same story. We went to the editors who made the decision to say "anti-aging" instead of "targeting aging." We said that's not how we wanted it to be named, and they said they didn't see a difference. When you say "anti-aging," there are scientists and these non-scientists who crop up. I call this out when I see it, but it's a very big challenge for us.

It goes back to the fact that we want to make really sure that we don't kill anyone on the way to our success. That's why we chose Metformin and we didn't choose rapamycin. In order to do this research safely, you have to do a clinical study. A clinical study is a controlled study, usually a double-blind controlled study; if you don't do that, you cannot really say that this is a safe drug to take. There are a lot of charlatans under the label "anti-aging" who do not do these studies, and we don't want to be linked to that. The clinical study is the litmus test, and I wouldn't suggest to the public to take anything without one.

What TAME is also providing is the template for other companies to follow: this is what you need; it's a cheaper study than what you do with other diseases; and this is what you do to get an indication. Then you can sell it to everyone.

**Tina Woods**: How do you think AI is going to play a role in all these developments?

**Nir Barzilai**: We're all using AI, but the people I deal with can be very different people and that can be very challenging. For example, I have a guy who was a systems biologist, a computer guy. He's Chinese, and his English isn't perfect; I said we should write a grant together, and we sat and talked about the grant, and agreed what parts we should write. Two weeks before the meeting, we looked at each other's work. I looked at what he had written and thought this guy had absolutely no idea what he was talking about. He looked at my work and had no idea where I was coming from.

We had to start again. It was an Alzheimer's grant, so he started coming to the Alzheimer's meetings that I was going to and he started to understand. I started to understand that I needed to ask a specific question. If you don't ask the right question, what I've found is that if you're looking for a needle in a haystack, AI just increases the size of the haystack.

To work together well we need to start talking the same language and whoever builds the AI has to ask you what to ask. If they don't—for example, there was a big study that Calico funded with Genomics England, the 100,000 genomes project. They took the genomes of 100,000 people and studied the relationship to longevity, and they basically said there is no genetics to aging; it's all assortative mating. Assortative mating describes the fact that if you're a cigarette smoker, you will probably marry a cigarette smoker. If you're obese, you will probably marry someone obese. I cannot tell you how ridiculous it is to say this is all there is to aging.

That's not how you discover the effect of aging. For example, there was a diabetes prevention trial that showed that exercise on Metformin can prevent diabetes. It was done many years ago; it was a beautiful clinical study that showed exercise with Metformin prevented diabetes by 30%. They actually stopped the study after four years because they had already showed the change was significant—it was great.

I asked the participants in this study a simple question, to see whether it impacted whether the participants got diabetes—did you have a father or mother who lived over the age of 80? And I discovered that if they had a father or mother who lived over the age of 80, diabetes was prevented by 30%. It was as effective as Metformin or exercise. You need to ask the right questions.

Another study that I'm part of showed that if you had a parent over the age of 85, Alzheimer's was prevented by 25%. If you really want to understand aging and the genetics of aging, you have to ask these kinds of questions.

Assortative mating is a major influence on the health of the population. A lot of our healthspan has to do with it. You don't need the genetic information of 100,000 people to tell you that assortative mating is important. You have such a powerful tool in AI and there's a danger of trusting the computer to give you a good answer when you've asked a poor question. The AI will tell you things that are stupid.

**Tina Woods**: Assortative mating and other social determinants of health are such huge factors in healthspan outcomes. Why is it that there's still so much attention on the 10% of the outcome that is the health side, or genomics and genetics, which perhaps affects 30% of the outcome? Do we need to change that focus?

**Nir Barzilai**: I have a very simple answer to that. Whether the effect of genetics is 20 or 25 or 5%, if we can understand this 20%, we can design a drug that will prevent the other 80% of causes. That's the strength of the genetics.

It could be hard to spot with AI. Look at the relationship between the deaths of parents and their kids when they live in different cohorts. For example, my grandfather had a heart attack when he was 68 and died. My father also had a heart attack when he was 68, but he had a successful triple bypass and died when he was 84. So, the death of my grandfather and father may not seem related, because they died due to different causes at different times. You could easily think it wasn't genetic, but it certainly was genetic.

So, rather than trying to figure out all the social determinants, if you look at exceptional longevity, it's much more about genetics. In my study, the most common answer when you ask the centenarians themselves why they think they have lived so long is "it's in my family." They say, "My grandfather was 102, my mother was 102, and now I'm here."

That's one place where you can see it. It's relevant to our work because then the chances of finding a functional mutation is higher in this population.

We've already contributed to the development of two drugs: one by Merck is a CETP-inhibitor and one for Ionis is an APOC3-inhibitor, because those drugs have the same effect as mutations that were over-represented in our centenarians. The drug companies weren't thinking about aging, but if it's over-represented in our centenarians, that means that it's a safety signal. If people have mutations that do what our drug is going to do, and those people are fine, that's a good safety signal. Companies want that genetic data.

This is an important area and it's going to happen more and more. Companies want genetic data because this idea that we'll find things in mice and then we'll tell you what's important hasn't worked for drug development. There's a drug called PCSK9, which was developed after analysis of a cholesterol-related gene in humans. It was discovered that when there was a gain of function, people had an 80% increase in coronary heart disease, and when there was a loss of function, people were protected from that by 55%. Within five years of that discovery, they developed a drug that's out there, based on human data, and it's going to be successful, unlike the others. That had nothing to do with animal studies.

That probability split, that measure of how important the social determinants of health are, came from a *New England Journal of Medicine* article 10 years ago. As we understand more about longevity, genes and genomics, our understanding of that importance could change.

**Tina Woods**: Given all these developments that we've discussed, what is the secret to a long life? Is it just in the genes?

**Nir Barzilai**: I would say that exercise, healthy food, intermittent fasting, modulating stress, and all these blue zone things will take you over the age of 80; but they're not enough to utilize our full potential as a human species.

**Tina Woods**: Can you tell me a little bit more about the intermittent fasting?

**Nir Barzilai**: In my study on intermittent fasting, we're doing intermittent fasting and not calorie restriction. We come in in the morning and we feed the mice. They're hungry, so they eat their food immediately and then they fast for 23 hours or more. If we give the same amount of food in smaller portions throughout the day, the mice are still thin, but they don't live as long. We want to up-regulate some mechanism where this fasting time has an effect, and we're looking at that.

One important mechanism is autophagy. Autophagy is our internal garbage disposal. It fails with aging, and that's why we accumulate cell garbage in the brain in Parkinson's. Really, it's all over our body—we accumulate garbage that we cannot throw away. If you can increase the rate of garbage disposal, that's good, and one of the ways to do it is fasting. Insulin immediately shuts it off, so the most important part of the fasting here is really not having carbohydrates.

Then there's another aspect to that—when you don't have carbohydrates you get ketotic, and you go to fat metabolism. If you give ketone diets to animals, they live longer, so that's part of it too. What we don't know is the time course of that process in humans. That's what I'm trying to figure out.

People have tried intermittent fasting in many ways. The one that's practiced the most is a 16-hour fast. You can still drink water and coffee and things like that; you just have no food. Then you have an eight-hour window to eat whatever you want. I have to tell you, I've never done a diet in my life, but this is so easy to do if you commit for three years, or three months, or six months. You can take a break any day. You just have a few more hours to go, so it's emotionally easy. I'm hungry sometimes, but I know I'll eat in an hour.

In any case, when it comes to 2 PM, I have so many ketones that I could push it up to a 24-hour fast easily. I'm just not hungry, and I can exercise and everything. I feel more awake during fasting days, and my exercise capacity is increased. Even on a 20-hour fast day, I exercise faster than any other day.

It hasn't really been studied well in humans. Other people do intermittent fasting differently. They do five days or seven days of fasting, four times a year. It's a different regime. Maybe it up-regulates mechanisms that affect aging, but we don't know why you'd do five days and not seven or vice versa, and that's what I'm trying to discover.

If we see that 12 hours of fasting in humans is enough, then maybe that would be easy to implement. People could just do breakfast and dinner and not eat between them, and everybody would be able to do it.

**Tina Woods**: Would this work with any diet? You mentioned this lowering your carbohydrates—do you have to eat certain types of food to make this work better?

**Nir Barzilai**: I think the main thing is the fasting part of it, not the food. There are people who think that the period when you start eating is also a very important period, so food choice certainly has a role, but the fasting part is the crucial part.

**Tina Woods**: There are, of course, a lot of other factors, like epigenetics. How does that play a role?

**Nir Barzilai**: I'm really very optimistic about epigenetics. If you take an egg from a 50-year-old woman, we can measure the age of that cell with epigenetics, for example, by examining the methylation of the DNA. We can measure age the same way in the sperm cell of an 80-year-old man. Now, people this age may not produce a lot of healthy cells of these types, but we could pick out healthy ones and fertilize the egg.

Then that egg will form a cluster, and the cells in that cluster do not remember the age of their parents. It resets the age to zero again. Nature's figured out how to do that for this one process. We'll figure out how to do it otherwise. This is an epigenetic problem to solve; it's not genetics because the genetics stay the same.

Epigenetics is a huge opportunity. It describes the way that the environment interacts with our genes and there is a lot to learn from understanding that. It's a huge field to try to understand, because epigenetics works with our genetics. There are certain sites in our genetic sequence where epigenetic regulation happens, and there are certain changes in the sequence that will suggest whether it happens.

There are people who are trying to find the genetic alterations that lead to epigenetic change because it's easier to measure that than the epigenetic site; one cell may display an epigenetic change and another cell may not display that epigenetic change, but the genetic sequence will be the same in both cells. This is a good line of research and it needs to be done in humans. I don't think animal studies are going to help much. They could help after the discovery, to go back and show the proof of concept in animals, I suppose.

**Tina Woods**: I've heard that one of the biggest game changers could be to do with fecal transplants, to change your microbiome. Do you think that might have a big effect on healthspan?

**Nir Barzilai**: Well your microbiome doesn't change much with age. It changes in people who are in an institute or hospital because they're getting antibiotics and treatments like that. Now, that doesn't mean that the microbiome has no effect on longevity, and this field is still evolving.

Everybody's very excited about this field and one day it will drop down and find its right place. I don't think it's there now. I think it's a really important area of study, but the relevance to aging is not totally clear to me.

I'm seeing a lot of papers that are repeating other studies, but cannot repeat their results. Studies like that aren't published sometimes, so how much is real and how much has been validated is a gray area.

I don't doubt that it's important. My colleagues who are working with this area in animals say every time you touch it, it does something! We know our ability to absorb vitamins A, D, E, and K is dependent on the microbiome; we knew that in the '70s. We just didn't realize the extent to which the microbiome is important. Microbiome transplants for people with ulcerative colitis and similar conditions are just a great change to treatment. This certainly may have a role to play in increasing healthspan, but we don't know yet what the role is exactly and what the treatment would be.

**Tina Woods**: In your longevity genes research, have you discovered anything in the genes that you think we need to be told?

**Nir Barzilai**: Your readers may find this personally disappointing, but you can be too tall! More than 60% of our centenarians have function mutation in the growth hormone IGF-1 pathways. We published this in *Science* last year; we found a cluster of people who had deletion of exon 3, the growth hormone receptor, who were, nonetheless, significantly taller than average.

It took me 10 years to publish the paper because we had to do a biological study and show what happened. What this mutation changes is that when there is no growth hormone in the body, there's no activation of this receptor; but with a lot of growth hormone, it is activated much more. This means that when people go through puberty, it activates and then they get taller. After that, when growth hormone goes down after puberty, it shuts off. The people stay tall, but they don't produce much growth hormone. That's relevant because we know that lower production of growth hormone is linked to aging.

**Tina Woods**: What do you think the maximal human lifespan is?

**Nir Barzilai**: I think that maximal human lifespan now is about 115 years. We argue about it—some people have lived longer than that, to 124, I think, but when you say maximal, one of seven billion will be out.

If you look at the trajectory, it starts with a paper that was published from the Einstein College of Medicine. Many people say 118 and some say 122—but let's say it's about 115. We die before the age of 80, so there are 35 years that can be realized before we even change the possibilities dramatically. I'm not against dramatic change, but there's a low-hanging fruit that we can realize because enough of us are getting to a much older age. We can do it.

**Tina Woods**: So, you don't believe in this escape velocity and immortality?

**Nir Barzilai**: No, I don't. I don't know if it's possible in the distant future, but it's not in our future now. I'll give you one example to show you the challenge. Let's say that we're doing generative work. We figure out how to create stem cells and trigger certain activities when we place tissues, so we can replace our brain tissue. That means that we start accumulating new memory, but we won't have our old memory. In other words, we won't have our old personality. What's the point of that?

So, the way to deal with it is we have to be able to download what memories we have and reload them onto new cells, and this is not going to happen in the next 5 to 10 years. I would say it'll probably take 50 years, so not in our lifetime. I'm not saying that it won't happen, or it can't happen—I actually view it as two stages.

There's new data that suggests that there are new stem cells in the brain. Eventually, you can probably have the ability to get those stem cells to start up and store your new memory. You also have to increase the connectivity between your brain and technology in order to download your old memory. Maybe we can do these things in parallel, but it's not magic.

**Tina Woods**: Some people are talking about immortality by 2045. Do you think that's a reasonable expectation?

**Nir Barzilai**: Even if it was, even if in 2045 you could live for 12 billion years—which is how long the Earth is expected to live—would you like to live for 12 billion years? I'm getting a little tired of some things now.

There is a movie, *The Immortalists*, about Aubrey de Grey and Bill Andrews, two scientists working on the problem of immortality. I was there at the premiere of this movie and I made some remarks about it afterwards. This was to an audience of about 300 people.

I said I'm going to give you two scenarios. Scenario one is that I'm going to immortalize you right now, but there's a condition. The condition is that we're just moving forward. There's no new life because we cannot afford to expand; there are no new children, no babies, no first laugh, no first love, no more weddings. We're just immortal. Scenario two is that I'm going to promise you that you will live a healthy life until the age of 85 and then that morning you don't wake up.

Only eight people chose scenario one. Everybody else chose scenario two. I thought since people came to see the movie *The Immortalists*, since that was the crowd, they would maybe be more interested in scenario one, but that's one for healthspan.

**Tina Woods**: What have you learned from the COVID-19 pandemic?

**Nir Barzilai**: It may be surprising to some, but COVID-19 has improved my personal life immensely. My life usually includes excessive world travel, jet lag, poor rest, being "on" constantly, and falling behind on many things. This has ended for now and my quality of life has improved.

I'm spending more time with my wife, who has just as demanding a job, and we're enjoying our time together, catching up on what we so often miss. A big factor in my comfort is that we both had a mild case of COVID-19, and we've donated plasma for antibodies, so fear of the disease is behind us. That's very freeing.

And now to the disturbing part. During this pandemic, the potential for targeting aging and its diseases has matured from hope to promise. COVID-19 provided us with the perfect example for us to use, to show how the biology of aging determines your health. People 80 and older die at 200 times the rate of someone in their 20s. The important thing to take away from this is that it's okay to fight the virus, but you need to fortify the host in older adults. We do have drugs that can be administered or repurposed that increase immunity, decrease inflammation, and increase the resiliency of the older body to sustain a severe disease.

The argument against these drugs, such as Metformin or rapamycin, is that they have not been studied in this situation. If I'm a doctor, I have a huge ethical dilemma. I know that clinical studies are the only way to make sure that something works, but we are at war with this lethal virus, and many elderly people will die if I do nothing. The reasons to prescribe those drugs now are twofold: firstly, the risk is low, since these drugs have already been used in humans; secondly, because we are talking about defending the host, and we have plenty of evidence for that.

My frustration is that I cannot push for this concept now and remain a careful scientist.

As Victor Hugo said, "All the forces in the world are not as powerful as an idea whose time has come." Maybe this is the time for this idea.

## Paul Dagum

*Founder and Vice Chair, Mindstrong Health*

Paul Dagum is Founder and Vice Chair of Mindstrong Health, a pioneer in developing "digital biomarkers" of brain function from human-computer interactions captured passively from a mobile device. The insight from the digital biomarkers allows Mindstrong Health to create novel care models to help people with serious mental illness.

Paul set up Mindstrong in 2013, recognizing the potential of smart phones to capture data providing a measure of cognition and emotion. There are over three billion smartphones globally and more than 75% of American adults own a smartphone (92% between ages 18–29).

In parallel, Paul also knew there was a growing need for better measurement in psychiatry and **Central Nervous System (CNS)** disorders, recognizing that the chronic nature of these disorders needs reliable serial measurements for better prognosis and prediction.

Putting these two opportunities together, Paul took the knowledge he gained from being CTO at a cybersecurity company to catch "bad actors" with behavioral analytics, using a broad array of digital information collected from a user to create a "digital fingerprint" of that individual.

Such digital fingerprints (also sometimes referred to as digital phenotyping or signatures), through the use of smartphone sensors, keyboard performance, and voice or speech features, can provide an objective, continuous, and passive measure of behavior and cognition at a global scale. Mindstrong uses this approach to detect the earliest phases of dementia, mental illness, and other medical disorders.

To identify the digital phenotyping features that could be clinically useful, Mindstrong has used powerful machine learning methods to show that specific digital features correlate with cognitive function, clinical symptoms, and measures of brain activity in a range of clinical studies.

In 2018, the company unveiled a study evaluating 27 volunteers to detect when they deviated from their daily habits. Combining those digital biomarkers with other social and environmental data helped the software to predict possible behavioral issues and performance on standard neurocognitive tests. And earlier in 2018, Mindstrong announced a partnership with Japanese pharma Takeda to identify digital biomarkers in schizophrenia and treatment-resistant depression.

I first met Paul at a workshop in 2018 looking at how consumer data could be harnessed to drive ethical research in aging, exploring the value of digital biomarkers in dementia.

**Tina Woods**: What do you think the key points are that people should understand about living longer with AI, but also living better with AI?

**Paul Dagum**: I think that there's a lot of misunderstanding around AI, but what's important to remember is that AI is essentially looking at a lot of data. What it allows us to do is understand patterns and correlations that tie—in the spirit of longevity—physiological data, current phenotypical data, or genetic data to health outcomes. It's those patterns and correlations that ultimately give us awareness of the things that we do that are good for us and the things that could potentially hurt us.

In the work that we do here at Mindstrong, we look at early predictive signals of illness. As everyone knows, the earlier we can identify any impending pathology, the better the outcome, whether that's the relapse of a mental health disorder being identified, or cancer being detected at stage 1 versus stage 4. That's where broad AI can help everyone. To get us to that point, we need to get better at capturing data, and we need to get better at capturing ecological data, which is data about us in our environment.

What's inhibiting us from achieving a vision of longevity driven by AI is the quality of the medical and wearable data captured today—we need to go from snapshot views to longitudinal measurements and from consumer-grade to clinical-grade—and we also need good target outcomes. Are we getting the sleep data, the heart rate, and the digital biomarkers from the same individual, synchronized and longitudinally? Do we have endpoints that suggest an illness or suggest the onset of an illness?

The challenge is that we don't have the target outcomes. We spent a lot of resources on just validating the digital biomarker data captured with structured clinical interviews and traditional standard neuropsychological tests.

I think, as we start to identify some of these early signals, we can take a more unsupervised approach to the problem. But at this point, we're still in that supervised phase, which means that we need quality target outcomes.

**Tina Woods**: There's supervised and unsupervised learning, as you mention. Could you explain those terms?

**Paul Dagum**: Supervised learning is where you have a target outcome. This could be a hospital readmission, a psychotic or manic episode, an ER visit, or an assessment on a structured clinical interview. That would be a measure, something that's a confirmed outcome. Supervised learning takes all the input data, whether it's digital biomarker data, physiological data, sleep data, and so on. and learns how to predict the targets from that data.

Unsupervised learning is essentially doing clustering. It doesn't take any target outcomes; it takes all the measurement data and tries to learn different homogeneous clusters. Think about a population of a million people; you can imagine that if you had data on these individuals—physiological biomarkers over time, for example—you could cluster them into different cohorts such that the persons within each cohort are similar.

That's unsupervised learning. Over time, the individuals within a cohort should behave similarly or show a similar evolution of measured characteristics. It gives us the power to improve our prognostic capabilities based on what we know about a person and similar persons in the same cohort.

**Tina Woods**: I'm intrigued about how you got started at Mindstrong because your career began in cybersecurity. Could you talk about that?

**Paul Dagum**: I have a PhD in computer science from the University of Toronto. I spent a year at Berkeley and I was introduced to the people at Stanford University working in the bioinformatics field—this was in the late 1980s—and they had created a joint program for a number of doctors with PhDs in computer science.

They were doing some very novel and groundbreaking work at the intersection of AI and medicine. I was very excited by that; I started on that program as a postdoc and I was also a medical student at Stanford.

In the 1990s, I ran a lab funded by the National Science Foundation in the US. In the late 1990s, I started my first company. I felt like I was living two parallel lives: one life was being a resident doctor at a hospital and the other was being in the lab doing some exciting work, but I couldn't bridge that gap. I realized that the best place to do that was Silicon Valley.

Three companies later, I was running product and technology at a cybersecurity company; I had deviated from healthcare. We sold the company in 2012, but we were among the early pioneers in developing what today is known as behavior analytics for cybersecurity. We looked at how users consumed online and IT resources. We would see what IP addresses, location, time of day, activity and other data. There was a whole host of information.

What we discovered was that we could create these digital fingerprints of individuals, which became powerful forensic tools. We had a list of the individuals who had legitimate access to a resource and their fingerprints. We could then identify that someone was accessing that resource who didn't line up with that fingerprint; it would mean that there was some kind of intrusion. This was exciting, of course, but after we sold the company, I was more excited to reconnect with healthcare.

**Tina Woods**: What made you want to go back into healthcare?

**Paul Dagum**: Around 2013, there was excitement about digital health and mobile health with the smartphone. Everyone had a smartphone and there were a lot of wellness apps at the time but there was a lot of promise in the smartphone becoming a clinical-grade tool for healthcare.

This area became my passion. I was very interested in brain health in particular and this covered a whole spectrum—not just mental health. I was very intrigued by anything from Alzheimer's to major depression, and how to objectively measure these illnesses. I reconnected with people at Stanford and discovered that nothing had changed in the 14 years since I'd left. We were still making diagnoses based on patient reported symptoms.

For Alzheimer's, we had pencil-and-paper tests and we used population distributions of test scores to evaluate a patient. There were huge problems with that. A patient in the upper tail of the distribution would have to lose a lot of cognitive function before we detected their illnesses in standard neurocognitive tests.

Could we measure objectively? Could we measure ecologically? Could we measure passively and more frequently? If you take measurements every day, you can tie the things that you do during the day to how they ultimately affect you, versus measuring them once a year when you're going for your test. It was my suspicion that the digital fingerprints that we had created weren't just idiosyncratic expressions of an individual.

Was there something on a digital fingerprint that was actually measuring cognitive ability or cognitive limitation? That's what I set out to find out.

We created an app, which was for the Android phone only, back then. We then launched two clinical studies here in the Bay Area. We were able to capture all of a person's touchscreen interactions with their phone. My suspicion was that reaction time to different stimuli was important. In all these repeated events, I hoped that we would find predictive signals.

We had two studies where we had 150 participants enrolled for a year each. They were tested for four hours by a neuropsychologist. He then put the app on their phones, they went away for a year, used their phones, and came back to be retested. What we discovered was that these digital fingerprints were not all idiosyncratic. In the data, there were very strong distributions of reaction times to different events by individual.

With this, we had an new way to measure people's neurocognitive function. What was exciting was not just that we could reproduce the test in the lab from the data on the phones, but that we could actually do this daily. We realized that we had 365 days of cognitive data. Interpreting the data on the day of the test was easy because we had our target, but for the rest of the year, what did it mean?

We did something very simple but clever: we got the cohort of our 150 participants, we took the first 30 days of cognitive measurement data from their phones, and we picked up one of the cognitive measures. For example, we looked at their attention scores based on our digital biomarker. Each person had 30 data points over 30 days. We sorted them from best to worst. Everyone had a day where they hit their best score and one where they hit their worst. When we looked at how well the best day compared to their test score, it turned out that the best day was actually the best predictor of the test score.

Then the predictions dropped a little bit and flattened out for most of the month. When you got to the worst day, you got very poor predictions. This taught us something very interesting. When someone came into the clinic and was tested, they were in a very nice, comfortable environment with no distractions. They had a neuropsychologist who was trained to get their best score. They were in test-taking mode.

We were not testing Stanford professors, we were getting people from all walks of life. When they went back to their real lives, they had stress, family problems, job problems, sleep problems. We all know when we're not functioning well because of illness or stress. We've all been in situations where we feel our cognitive limitations. What we were seeing was the impact of day-to-day events on an individual. That was the motivation for launching Mindstrong. We realized that we had a window into how people were functioning day to day, and that window could give us tremendous insights.

**Tina Woods:** Tell us a little bit more about the practical tools and solutions that you're currently developing. I know you've got this partnership with Takeda.

**Paul Dagum:** We started with pharma partners but today we have two businesses within Mindstrong: one is pharma and the other is our healthcare system, providing care to members that belong to US health plans.

The difficulty in drug development has always been the cost and the time it takes to develop a new drug. When we're talking about drugs for the central nervous system, whether that's mental health or neurodegenerative disorders, they take longer and cost more than drugs for other conditions. A big part of the problem is inadequate measurement. If you're creating a new drug for blood pressure, you use blood pressure readings and it's not a challenge. But for mental health, as an example, we have very subjective scales that are based on patient-reported symptoms and clinician reported outcomes.

You have a mixed bag of individuals in your cohort; your drug might work for some of them but not for others. "Depression" can be different illnesses.

Companies also struggle with reliable endpoints. The interest has been in digital biomarkers for a number of reasons: first, companies can better stratify the patient population who should be studied and second, sharp objective endpoints can assess the impact of a drug. That's been at the heart of our partnerships with Takeda and Lundbeck.

Our bigger business division deals with healthcare insurance companies. We are a healthcare system here in the US. We have licensed psychiatrists and psychologists who deliver telepsychiatry, telehealth, and therapy using the phone, videoconferencing, and asynchronous text messaging. This is all in response to the digital measures that we're capturing. Our clinicians have a panel of patients and they're responsible for those patients.

**Tina Woods:** Are these people who are already showing signs of illness?

**Paul Dagum:** Yes, these are people who have already been diagnosed; their respective illnesses are chronic. For example, once you get diagnosed with schizophrenia, it's a lifelong diagnosis, and the only thing you can do is learn how to manage it. This has been difficult for people in the past because we haven't had good measurements or good care, but we're now starting to provide that. The same is true for bipolar disorder and major depression.

**Tina Woods:** How are you engaged in the preventative health spectrum? If you ask people what they fear most about aging, dementia is often cited. Are you doing any work there?

**Paul Dagum:** We are involved in a UK program on the **early detection of neurodegenerative diseases** (EDoN) that is a global initiative developing digital fingerprints for dementia causing diseases.

**Tina Woods**: There was a news item recently covering Biogen's latest drug showing some promise for some patients with dementia. But generally, this area has been a spectacular failure for drug companies. Everyone's saying that we need to start far earlier. AI could even open up new thinking about the actual disease process itself. Is there any truth in that?

**Paul Dagum**: Once neurons are dead, there's no drug in the world that's going to bring them back, but by moving upstream and getting data early, understanding the evolution of the disease in its early phases with sensitive clinical measurements, we will develop deeper insights and better treatments. For example, we are learning that sleep disruption is key.

**Tina Woods**: Sleep, of course, affects all sorts of things and there's this whole concept of cognitive reserve and resilience. Even if they have significant disease formation in their brains, some people show symptoms and others don't. What can you say about that?

**Paul Dagum**: Just in the last few years, we've discovered the brain's glymphatic system; it opens up during sleep and cleans out your brain. If we believe that it's sleep disruption that ultimately leads to the accumulation of waste products and plaques, maybe what we need is to help people to sleep better in that early pre-symptomatic phase. It would be fantastic for something that simple to be effective.

**Tina Woods**: Matthew Walker's book *Why We Sleep* alludes to that, doesn't it? Are you working with any epigenetics companies? There's a huge fascination with the epigenetics of what is expressed and how all this will play out with disease.

**Paul Dagum**: We don't have a formal partnership, but we have started to look into this area. We have so much to learn from genetic markers. So much is tied to our genes and how we interact with our environment. There's a lot of potential there and it's a very unexplored area.

**Tina Woods**: It's fascinating because even before birth, the environment of both the father and the mother can actually have a huge influence on their offspring. Do you have any comment on that?

**Paul Dagum**: What is more common in mental health is the long-term, delayed impact that nurture and environment can have on a child. When looking at genotypes and phenotypes, different individuals have different levels of resilience in terms of their ability to cope with difficult situations. For example, a difficult family environment, a difficult school environment, poor nutrition, domestic violence, school bullying, or any number of things. What is someone's level of resilience, tenacity, and durability? Different individuals will respond differently, but any one of these factors could become a significant impediment for a child's chances of succeeding. A child with a high degree of resilience potentially does better than a child with low resilience.

If we can identify these factors early, can we intervene early? Can the school intervene? Can social services intervene? Can we really understand the impact that this is having on these children?

Social determinants are also important in the elderly; that comes up all the time in our work. The big social determinant is isolation and its impact on different individuals. Different people need different levels of social engagement. Isolation contributes significantly to someone's ability to function. Depression in the elderly is often very difficult to distinguish from dementia.

**Tina Woods**: How do you think that AI and tech will solve some of these more difficult problems around the social determinants of health?

**Paul Dagum**: AI and tech can address them in many different ways. If we think about isolation, social media is already addressing some of that by creating a more connected and holistic world. Other areas to look at are identifying agitation or stress earlier in children, whether it's through sensors or different biomarkers, or just being able to integrate data about school grades or social withdrawal from sports or activities. AI would be ideal for finding those patterns and identifying high-risk individuals.

**Tina Woods**: You've got the whole ethical issue of intervention. We had a terrible story in the UK about a young girl of 14 who committed suicide. There was a whole case where the father said that Instagram meant that she was constantly being barraged by these images of self-harm, and he felt that that was actually what tipped her over the edge. There's this concept of data custodians or data trustees who could intervene when the data signs or the digital fingerprint is indicative that there's danger lurking. Do you see a need for that?

**Paul Dagum**: I think there's a real need for that along with significant ethical and privacy issues that need to be figured out. We also need to better regulate content on the internet.

Right now, the internet, Facebook, Instagram, and so on. are unmonitored. We have children online and we have adults being exposed to disturbing content too. In the movie industry, there are ratings and age requirements, but the internet is open to everybody.

**Tina Woods**: We're sort of talking about the role of government; this is regulation, isn't it? Where do you see that going?

**Paul Dagum**: We've democratized the whole process of creating content and being able to put content online. It's almost impossible for these companies to self-police. AI could potentially be a solution because we can't have humans look at every Facebook post and Instagram post.

AI image recognition technology has advanced tremendously. I know companies are using that today to try to censor inappropriate content. As AI continues to improve, hopefully, less and less of that inappropriate content will find its way through.

**Tina Woods**: We can see Amazon being in partnership with JPMorgan/Berkshire Hathaway in terms of the pill pack pharmacy distribution. We've got Apple going into the data side. Then we've got Google focusing on life science companies like Verily and Calico. These companies are really driving the whole AI health agenda and even working with the NHS in the UK now. What is their responsibility in terms of ethics?

**Paul Dagum**: These Big Tech companies see healthcare as a massive market. In the US, it's a multi-trillion-dollar market. What's changed over the last 10 years is that healthcare moved from a traditional healthcare delivery model to a consumer led model. If you look at Apple, it wants to make healthcare accessible to all its users through its devices. Verily is straddling that line as well with Google. Medical devices, services, and information are all regulated in the US and these companies will need to comply with these regulations. Data collected and captured from any clinical-grade device is protected health information with federal and state regulations dictating how it can be used.

There's already a well-established framework for dealing with this. If you look at digital biomarkers as an example, we had to make the transition from a healthcare technology company to a healthcare delivery company. We started as a healthcare technology company but we now run a healthcare system with licensed clinicians. When our patients download the app, they consent to receive care from our doctors. If tech companies entering healthcare are not ready for that transition, then I think it will be very difficult for them to make a significant impact on healthcare.

**Tina Woods**: The European situation is a bit different. We're more regulated, of course. We've got the **General Data Protection Regulation (GDPR)**, which in some ways has been a gift because it focuses the consumer on the fact that their data is important and it has a value to it. You've then got China where, whether they like it or not, citizens have their data collected for their social credit scores. That's at the other end of the spectrum. China is leading the march on AI with that huge collection of data points on its citizens. How are we going to ensure democratic access to the so-called longevity dividend?

**Paul Dagum**: I agree with the European Union, but in terms of progress with AI, China will naturally move faster because it's not going to depend on the user consenting to provide data. AI will be extremely successful if you can consistently collect patient data with the outcome data across many individuals. Once the models have been developed in China, they could potentially be used and democratized in Europe and the US.

**Tina Woods**: Are you using the Mindstrong app yourself?

**Paul Dagum**: Yes, it's one of the things that I do to keep healthy. All of us here at Mindstrong use it. We start the week much better than we end the week!

**Tina Woods**: Has it helped you with strategies?

**Paul Dagum**: It has. It's made me more aware of the impact that my lifestyle has on me. I travel a lot to Singapore, China, and Europe, and you get to a certain point where all this travel wears you down. When you look at your data, you see it very clearly. For me, sleep and exercise are the really important, along with a reasonably good diet.

**Tina Woods**: What have you learned from the COVID-19 pandemic?

**Paul Dagum**: Part of what Mindstrong does is operate a network of value-based health systems that deliver virtual care to people with a serious mental illness. Many of our members are elderly and struggle with medical comorbidities and poor access to supporting social services.

During the COVID-19 pandemic, shelter-in-place policies swept the U.S. We quickly learned that this increased the level of isolation among our members, and made access to medical care more challenging. We responded quickly by increasing outreach to our members with education on COVID-19 and available social services including nearby testing sites. We increased on-demand access to our therapists to address negative thoughts and perceptions created by the pandemic, increased referrals to our telepsychiatrists, and expanded our provider network to include medical professionals.

We witnessed a significant jump in the utilization of our virtual care services, as we helped our members stay safe and well through the worst of the COVID-19 pandemic.

# Thomas Balkizas

*Founder of Alpha Tech Capital and EMEA Healthcare and Life Sciences Lead at Amazon Web Services*

I first got to know Thomas when he was an executive at IBM Watson in 2016. He has an interesting portfolio background, and is now working with Amazon.

Thomas holds two master's degrees in computer science, medical physics, and health economics from Imperial College London. He has worked with health systems, hospitals, and research institutes on projects ranging from genomics, cancer research, diagnostic imaging, and decision support systems to remote patient monitoring for patients living with long-term conditions.

I have bumped into Thomas at various stages of our respective journeys and he has seen the development of AI and health technology through the lens of having worked with IBM, run his Alpha Tech Capital private equity advisory firm, and now being at Amazon Web Services creating partnerships in the ecosystem.

The last time I saw Thomas was at the Biodata Congress in Basel, Switzerland in 2018. I was running a workshop on aging biomarkers and multimodal AI and it seemed that the pharma industry was just waking up to this whole new world.

Our interview focused on how AI will augment human intelligence and the important role of behavior change for any technologies to have an impact on outcomes. We also discussed the need for ethical models enabling individuals to take responsibility and have a choice about what happens to their data, along with a new social contract built on transparency and informed consent to maintain public trust.

When wearing his private equity hat, what's on Thomas' radar for investments is connectivity. Connectivity is going to be key because the value will lie in bringing data together, but data provenance and quality remain significant hurdles to overcome.

**Tina Woods**: In your view, what are the key points or messages that people should understand about living longer better with AI?

**Thomas Balkizas**: In many people's eyes, AI is this almost post-apocalyptic future where machines have taken over and they're doing functions that we've been doing for centuries, but I don't think that's the key message at all.

This is where the conversation can veer off to sometimes, and whether AI is viewed positively can change from month to month.

For me, the key message is to take what we're doing as humans and improve it. AI can be used for the automation of activities that we humans are not great at doing. However, AI is there to support us and not replace us.

The goal is to eliminate some of the functions that are preventing us from living meaningful, better lives. This could be as simple as a patient trying to get through to a doctor, or a patient trying to get through to a dentist, or a patient post-recovery trying to report their outcomes to their doctor.

All these functions today take place in very old-fashioned, manual ways. If you're lucky, you have a telephone and you can call your doctor. If they're available, they'll take the call. Many of these functions are systemic functions.

Do we need AI to do exercise? No, it's a habit, but it's been proven that if you measure your exercise, you do more. If you create the right triangle of a digital therapeutic, a group support, and targets that are pertinent to the individual, then people are more likely to stick with an exercise regime. The key message is giving people control over their health, including the data that they need to manage their health and their health options. This also has to be communicated in a language that they can understand.

**Tina Woods**: It's about information, but it's also about behavioral changes, isn't it?

**Thomas Balkizas**: Very much so. In my professional experience, I've found that most of these companion diagnostics—let's say an app—do certain functions very well, but more than 95% of them fail because they don't help people to make a behavioral change. This is because a completely different approach to self-management is required, which is difficult for people, or the technology isn't engaging enough, or it doesn't create a sense of belonging. This then leads to health apps—like most apps—being used once or twice only and then being abandoned.

What we need to do is use technology that's ubiquitous already. The key is taking the tools and putting them in the hands of the person. The biggest change that I'm seeing is around empowerment. We're giving people access to tests, information, and management systems for their conditions.

If you're a diabetic patient, not many things have changed in your care over the last few decades, but you now have a device that emits signals—sometimes in near real time—and connects you with a cohort of other patients who have similar concerns to you. This makes it more about managing your habits and getting information at the right time, with the style and tone that you prefer, as opposed to managing the insulin levels in your blood. It's about how you as a person can treat and live with your condition.

We have to manage the population and keep people healthy. With the technology that's in our hands, we're going to be able to identify risks more readily. Things will go wrong, for sure, but we will be much more proactive in trying to prevent an escalation into a full-blown episode in hospital, for example.

**Tina Woods**: Is it a paradigm shift from sick care to prevention that you're describing?

**Thomas Balkizas**: It is. This isn't new; the tools have been around for a while, but they're now easier to use and people are more accepting of them. Even the terms "machine learning" and "AI" are closer to people's daily lives. Most people use navigation systems, for instance.

I think people are much more attuned to using data and evidence that they have collected for their decision-making processes. Even if you're not measuring your blood sugar and your blood pressure on a daily basis, your phone will, at minimum, tell you how much activity you've had, and so on. In terms of the people side, this shift is already happening. I think we're behind and chasing technology, however.

**Tina Woods**: I agree that the pace with which organizations can change is always behind technology, which is racing ahead. What do you think will actually drive us towards this prevention model?

**Thomas Balkizas**: In many ways, policy has a very important part to play, but governments shouldn't take on the gatekeeper role. As a technologist, I've seen policy act as an enabler in bringing technology safely to people.

However, it's very hard for regulators or governments to get in front of technology. I would say that policy makers are trailing about eight years behind in this area.

The fact is that, currently, the barrier to creating and building something is so much lower because anyone with an idea, access to the internet, and some money in their bank account can spin a new software up, use compute power, use AI machine learning algorithms, launch a new healthcare solution, and make it available on the world's largest app marketplace. Of course, that's risky, and I think it must be giving people in positions of authority plenty of headaches.

I think that regulators are much more connected with technology now. They're employing professionals who are familiar with the technology industry. I don't feel that we have a competitive relationship, but in some cases there's still friction. That friction is mainly linked to old ways of thinking. We certainly need to embrace a new model of thinking that is much more agile, although agile and healthcare don't go hand in hand. In healthcare, you can't fail fast because you have a duty of care. At the same time, there have been instances when illness could have been prevented by a technology that's been around for years.

There seems to be this push-pull relationship: we push forward with technology, but private companies want to move faster. They are more progressive and sometimes aggressive in their approach. They want to put products and services in front of people. Governments and policy come in like a braking force, almost always causing some level of delay.

This is why we need to be very transparent. The fast pace of innovation creates an almost disproportionate response from regulators, so we need to get a bit smarter now. What we're aiming to produce is something for the benefit of society, so let's remove the mystery. These innovations sound dangerous, but they are not.

**Tina Woods**: There's increasing recognition of the social determinants of health. You've got genomics, and the social and psychological factors, which you were describing in terms of habits. The healthcare aspect of health only accounts for 10%, yet there's still so much attention on that 10%. Do you think technology now, and AI, will help us to increase our focus on that other 90%?

**Thomas Balkizas**: I think so; I'm optimistic about that. When you have your head below water as someone in the healthcare industry, it's very hard to think about what's going to happen when you're dry and enjoying your weekend. During the core hours in an accident and emergency department, with many sick patients coming in, there simply isn't enough time for people to think about keeping these patients away from hospital by providing them with the tools to manage their health at home. But on a macro level, this is already happening, although it may not be happening at the pace that we want it to.

As an example, in post-surgery recovery, we're doing a lot more away from hospitals. In the run-up to any operation, we try to keep patients informed. There is plenty of good information given. Perhaps AI is not the term for it, but there is more data being shared with patients. What we haven't been able to do is free up more time.

We're trying to do prevention, which is about lifestyle. People know by now what it is that regulates their health. They know that they need to do exercise and eat better. Machine learning has a part to play and doctors have a part to play, but there comes a point where we need to empower people and share the message that governments putting more money into acute care isn't going to help them be healthier, at least not as much as making lifestyle changes.

If someone keeps going to hospital for avoidable ailments or treatment that could be performed in the community, it is simply not sustainable. We need an alternative approach to mandating the opening of an additional 40 hospitals. If we need to do that because our population is increasing, we will, but we firstly need to encourage people to take control of their own health. We can't achieve that if we say that people can come and see their doctor whenever they like. There's got to be an element of shared responsibility and shared ownership of our health. Going to the doctor is not going to fix the fact that we haven't exercised in months or years, for example.

**Tina Woods**: A social contract is a really interesting concept, especially when it comes to the use of data. We can see what's happening in China, for example, with the social credit policy. That's one sort of model. We've also got the European model and the US model. Where do you think these data models are going to head in the future? A lot of data models are driven by the profit, but you've got some interesting concepts being pioneered on European soil that are more ethical data models. In Finland, they have a concept called IHAN, the human-driven data economy, which is about leveraging data for social good.

**Thomas Balkizas**: I think, especially based on the geographies you quoted there, it's going to be very hard to predict which model is going to win out, but my personal preference would be to have an ethical model where the individual takes responsibility and has a choice about what happens to their data. We lost our way on that for a few years; people were becoming the product.

We're not going to move towards a society where profit doesn't matter. I think that will still play a part. Businesses that seek data as their currency will still want to acquire it. I don't find anything morally problematic with that, provided that we have the transparency to discuss what they're going to do with this data. I think people are increasingly more informed about the fact that the data they produce with their activity has value.

The model I see surfacing is possibly what you're describing in Finland with a combination of factors taken into account. In the past, the information that I could get about my health was very generic. On the other side, if we have full control over our personal data, it will become extremely difficult for one person to manage all of that. That's where we need the help of technology, companies, and experts. This will be based on a mutually agreed framework.

Some people predict that it's going to be based on some form of common ledger or blockchain. I would say that the providers will put this platform out there and invite citizens to participate. I think people want something like that put in place. Businesses will play their part and life sciences companies will play their part; that's already happening. There will be much more common usage of data, but on much more robust frameworks.

**Tina Woods**: Google was in the news recently about its Project Nightingale and there's been a media frenzy over data breaches and so forth. How do you think the idea of data use will play out in this sense?

**Thomas Balkizas**: The way I see it is that the data breaches, breaches of confidentiality, and a lack of governance in some of these projects have been reported widely, and with good reason. It has taught everyone a lesson that you can't take these issues lightly. Initiatives in retail or car manufacturing, for example, need a different level of attention and governance when compared to healthcare data from clinical trials; this is the most sensitive data you can ever imagine.

As technologists in this space, we know what we need to do to be compliant. For a technology to be successful in the long term, you need to make sure that people trust it. The reverse of this, which is the level of mistrust that exists in some countries and in some ecosystems, is based on people just not taking compliance seriously. I've talked about the challenges of policy, but we need to make sure that in this social contract, we embed trust.

The technology will always push ahead. Having seen the evolution of AI in the past two decades, I'd say that much of what people are calling scary has been around for longer than the fear has been around and we've been discussing it. The fear probably depends on the latest Hollywood movie about AI and how people perceive automation algorithms to be taking over their lives.

We need to talk to people with precise language. If you went to a doctor and she was using words that you couldn't understand, that could lead to problems for both the patient—poorly informed decisions lead to poor outcomes—and the doctor. We need to use simple language and be very clear about operations, recovery, risks, and so on. We need to do the same with AI and machine learning technology. We have to explain what we're aiming for, such as improving drug discovery and shortening the time it takes to produce medications. With transparency and informed consent, everyone is going to be in a better place to utilize this technology and data.

**Tina Woods**: Do you think there's enough focus on addressing the biggest societal needs? A huge issue is the growing health inequalities between the poorest and the richest. Do you think there's enough attention on that, going back to this concept of the social contract again?

**Thomas Balkizas**: As we provide faster connectivity to more people, they can watch videos, they can listen to podcasts, and they can get a smartphone and connect through it to a number of information sources. This means that more people can get access to excellent healthcare. Giving someone a phone and a fast connection doesn't make them healthier necessarily, but we get the good-quality information to them faster.

Of course, people's habits are not the same and the outcomes will not be the same. We have to wonder, as people working in the healthcare space, what we can do to reduce inequalities. It's never *just* the role of the government to correct this. I believe that when we pass as a law, we have to give people the tools and empower them to use them well.

If you are an innovator and you're about to create something that you think is only going to be targeting the top 1% of people in the world socioeconomically, it's a moral dilemma. I don't believe that people set out to build very expensive products and services, but I like inventions and innovations that aim to lower the cost of a product or service, as opposed to getting the maximum amount out of people. However, we can't stifle innovation; it is expensive. What we can do is find alternatives that we can democratize and give to people who can't necessarily afford the most expensive innovations.

We're not able to eliminate inequality completely. We can't influence the genome as much. We're studying aging factors in some countries, and there are some really interesting studies that have shown that for some people, aging factors don't have the same effect.

**Tina Woods**: There's this whole area of looking at digital phenotypes and digital biomarkers, particularly around dementia. Do you have any view on identifying patterns in this field?

**Thomas Balkizas**: A few things come to mind. I remember a study from investigators at Insilico Medicine that summarized some of the main types of aging clocks and a range of applications in neurodegenerative diseases. I would say that most diseases, if not all diseases, get worse with aging. I'm not a bioscientist or epidemiologist; I'm a computer scientist, but my understanding is that we're not fully aware of the types of aging or the process of aging.

Part of what developing these AI biomarkers requires is a better understanding of the processes that lead to aging. I think that, especially in the space of neurodegenerative diseases, we have a lot of data on our side. We have some longitudinal studies that have increased the variety of biomarkers that we could consider as potential aging predictors. In this space, as a trend, I believe that we will see faster discovery and more experimentation. There will be more failures, but I think we will get to the biomarkers of aging faster, and if we do that, we will also be able to get the answers that we need equally fast.

**Tina Woods**: There's a lot of attention on the so-called black box of AI. What I mean by that is that we can't understand how we make decisions using the human brain, so why do we need to understand how a machine makes decisions, as long as the outcome is what we want? What's your opinion on that?

**Thomas Balkizas**: I would welcome the transparency on the "why"; I wouldn't want the "why" to be a black box. The "how" and the "what" are much more difficult. I mentioned earlier the importance of using layman's language to describe very complex technological processes. Complexity shouldn't be an excuse for not explaining a process, but at the same time, I don't think that people would expect to get into a car and know every single electronic and combustion engineering detail that makes the car move. What they want to know is why the car is built that way and whether it is safe. The same is true for healthcare and for the tools that support our decision-making about health.

**Tina Woods**: Continuing with your car example, there will be a day when they start making decisions about hitting one person over another if there is an accident. Of course, that does require some sort of ethical framework. What would you say about that?

**Thomas Balkizas**: I think this example is probably one of the most morally challenging. If we look at what's been reported so far when it comes to driverless cars, they're actually much safer. The number of accidents is so much lower that instead of debating whether they're safe to drive, we're now debating what would happen if there was a baby or an old person in the way. I don't have an answer to that.

When it comes to an algorithm that always performs in the same way, it doesn't fail. Human judgment does not, for whatever reason, behave in the same way. Statistically speaking, I would almost always rather take the algorithm built by humans than the inconsistency of human decision making. I have a reminder system so I don't have to rely on myself to wake up in the morning at the right time or schedule my appointments, for example.

However, in the example that you're giving, I would rather give that decision-making responsibility to a human because, then, there would be some level of accountability. We're driving increasingly safe cars, but we're still driving them in unsafe ways and causing accidents. If technology can bring about an improvement and still leave some room for human decision-making, then I'll take it.

**Tina Woods**: What are your predictions for future developments in AI and healthcare?

**Thomas Balkizas**: Most innovations in this area come from start-ups. I'm attracted by the companies that are achieving things in the space of patient access and experience with very simple tools.

Also, what I'm seeing increasingly is that we're now connecting many more devices. Connectivity is going to be key because we see the value in bringing data together. We've just always struggled with the provenance and the quality of that data. Companies that are able to make sense of that are certainly on my radar.

I think we will see a lot more patient-driven healthcare, but not in the sense that patients will decide to go to hospital. We will see patients becoming more aware of what their health data means. I foresee a future where doctors will be closely linked to data science as opposed to the art of medicine. We will go to them with problems, and the problems will not necessarily be health problems but data problems. They could be about understanding a pattern. Then we will jointly create a plan to change a trajectory because we know we are going to get sick. Data can help us to prevent illness, but it could also help a healthcare service that's overburdened. That's my vision.

This may be something completely novel to some people, but your personal health data belongs to you; it doesn't belong to your doctor. What that requires is education around what you could do with these metrics and indicators.

**Tina Woods**: Taking everything that we've talked about into consideration, what do you think is the secret to a long and happy life?

**Thomas Balkizas**: What experts are telling us in terms of living a healthy life hasn't changed much in decades: it's about moving more and not being sedentary. We also need a diet that is rich in nutrients, with a wide variety of plants that help us to develop a healthy gut and a diverse microbiome.

Sleep is probably one area that we should also prioritize. We're sleeping worse and less than we need, and I don't think we're going to do away with the need for eight hours.

Happiness is more complex and has no simple formula. It depends on finding meaning and being able to face challenges with resilience.

**Tina Woods**: Mental health is something we haven't touched upon. What do you think about its relationship with technology?

**Thomas Balkizas**: I'm very fortunate to be doing something that I like, and I have a family that I enjoy sharing my life with. We need something that keeps us going and gives us a sense of belonging. I think it was Malcolm Gladwell who identified that a key healthy aging and longevity determinant is a unique sharing of experiences that define a community's social structure. For the people of Roseto, PA, having someone they knew and trusted that they could turn to for support was a factor that was shown to be more important than exercise and lifestyle. Too much absorption in technology is not good for our mental health. Between spending time on a smartphone and having a meal with friends, I would take the latter.

**Tina Woods**: What have you learned from the COVID-19 pandemic?

**Thomas Balkizas**: The outbreak of COVID-19 has changed the way we work, socialize, and communicate with people around us. The COVID-19 pandemic has reminded us of how vulnerable we all are, how much we depend on each other, and about the bravery of our carers, nurses, doctors, call center employees, delivery drivers, software developers, teachers, and support staff.

The devastating effects on the eldest and BAME people in our communities have intensified calls for a more equitable public health strategy. Lessons will be learned from this multidimensional crisis, but we will never forget the shared pain we experienced.

The windows in my neighborhood were filled with posters of thankfulness; neighbors formed a music band that played songs to honor our NHS workers. A sense of solidarity was born out of the desperation of lockdown. Whatever the future holds, I expect us to carry some of that camaraderie into the post-COVID-19 era.

For those working with technology, we witnessed more transformation in the two months following the pandemic than the previous five to 10 years. Virtual hospital wards were set up and telehealth consultations took place at a rate never seen before. Millions of children connected to their first remote learning session and found creative ways to learn and stay in touch with their educators and their friends. It has been challenging at times, but we have adapted as we have always done as humans.

We discovered we can hold effective remote meetings without traveling for days and polluting the environment. Those who were unable to attend in person have now found a place at the table and their voice is heard. We still have plenty to achieve and I am optimistic that this pandemic will force us to do so faster, more effectively, and democratically. Every disaster presents us with an opportunity to reconnect with what matters the most, to change seemingly necessary evils, to protect people at risk, and to put lives before numbers.

When the human cost is so heavy and our worst fears come true, we are left with no choice but to dedicate our individual skills to serving one another.

## Teemu Suna
*CEO, Nightingale Health*

I first came across Teemu Suna, CEO of Nightingale Health, soon after TIME ran a story with this headline: "We're One Step Closer to a Blood Test that Predicts When a Person Will Die." Nightingale Health is a Finnish health tech company that's transforming preventive health with blood-based molecular data and AI to predict disease risk.

It's not every day that you meet a man who tells you he can foresee your future with the help of science. Teemu says his company is "on a mission to abolish chronic diseases by predicting a person's health risks and preventing them from happening in the future."

Nightingale's technology gives a much broader view of a person's health compared to a standard blood test. Using this technology, the company has gathered a myriad of data points from nearly a million samples. This data is backed by years of scientific research, connecting chronic diseases to the effects of lifestyle interventions. Combining technology and science, the blood test can predict the health state and risk of developing chronic diseases up to 10 years in advance. This foresight into a person's health can give people the information and motivation they need to take corrective steps to minimize or avoid illnesses.

The technology leverages the latest understanding of "omics" and the burgeoning field of epigenomics that takes into account lifestyle-induced changes that may contribute towards disease. Genomics mostly provides a static picture of inherited health information; once sequenced, there is little new information to discover from repeating the analysis. Investigating lipids (lipidomics), carbohydrates (glycomics), and other metabolites (molecules produced by biochemical reactions), however, offers new insights into the dynamic changes that occur in the body in response to lifestyle factors.

Lifestyle effects are reflected by changes in the metabolites produced by biochemical reactions (a person's metabolism), in a field of study called "metabolomics." By measuring concentrations of different metabolites in blood, Nightingale's technology can observe the effects of lifestyle factors such as diet and exercise on the health state of individuals.

Metabolomics can be used to diagnose and predict the risk of developing certain illnesses, with chronic disease prediction being a crucial area where repeating metabolic profile analyses could provide a more accurate prediction. The metabolites that indicate disease risk (also called biomarkers) can be monitored through regular metabolic profiling (for example, routine blood tests), allowing clinicians to analyze a timeline of each patient's health and detect any early signs of disease.

I caught up with Teemu to find out more about how this technology works and what role AI will play in helping people lead healthier and longer lives. We also explored what role governments and existing companies will play in all this.

**Tina Woods**: Nightingale uses AI to help predict and prevent chronic diseases. What should readers understand about living longer and better lives with AI?

**Teemu Suna**: I think the most important thing to understand here is that, with the help of science and new technology, living a healthy life is rather simple.

One doesn't need to take extreme measures to achieve good health. So, if you enjoy beer and hamburgers, living healthy doesn't mean you have to quit those and eat only veggies. Good health is all about balance—treating your body in a way that's sustainable in the long term.

Then, the question is, how does one create that balance and know what's sustainable in the long run? This is where new technology comes in, and particularly, molecular technologies such as Nightingale's.

With our technology, we can measure health markers in your blood and connect them to your daily lifestyle to show which choices are leading you towards better health.

We do this by using AI to study molecular, clinical, and behavioral data and then give simple guidance for you to follow. However, these are not generic tips, but personalized advice based on the molecular make-up of your blood and your everyday lifestyle and behavior. To summarize, we use AI to nudge you towards a lifestyle that's more sustainable and leads to good health in the long run.

**Tina Woods**: In your view, what do you think will have the biggest impact in helping people live longer, better lives, now and in five to 10 years from now?

**Teemu Suna**: Right now, people look for silver bullet solutions. However, when it comes to health, one shouldn't expect any elixir for good health from AI. It can't give you one and you don't need one.

It can, on the other hand, help provide a reliable prediction of your future health and thereby give you the power to navigate your well-being in the right direction. Think of it as getting access to the GPS system of your body. A GPS system tells you where you are on the map so that you can go in the right direction to reach where you want to be. If you take a wrong route, it alerts you and helps you get back on the right path. That's what we're doing at Nightingale—we're helping you navigate your health. We show your current health status, warn you about future disease risks, and help you take corrective steps against diseases to get you on the right health path.

**Tina Woods**: What role do you think the people have in all this, to really make use of these technologies?

**Teemu Suna**: The big revolution in healthcare, and the next "megatrend" in health, will not be driven by the current system. It will not be driven by the hospitals, or current medical doctors, or even governments. It will be driven by the consumer, and it will be driven by their need to understand personal health better.

People want to stay healthy. And now, as new technologies like wearables and molecular data are becoming easily available to everyone, I strongly believe that it's the people and communities who'll have the biggest role in defining the future of healthcare.

**Tina Woods**: How do you think that the role of the citizen is going to differ between different countries? Do you think there'll be differences, or will it broadly be the same?

**Teemu Suna**: We're seeing a change happening world over, but, in my experience, it's happening the fastest in Asia. There, people are in general very interested in using new technologies. Maybe it's because the healthcare tradition there, in many ways, is more holistic than the Western tradition of medicine. After Asia, it's the U.S. because the consumer market is very strong.

**Tina Woods**: How do you think governments and businesses will be affected by this? How do you think they'll adapt and support this?

**Teemu Suna**: As mentioned earlier, this change is going to be driven by the ordinary people, the citizens who want to empower themselves. And when this happens, it'll open new possibilities for new companies who want to think about health differently. However, this is only a fraction of the industry and there are big differences in the attitudes among companies.

The old system is driven by massive conflict of interest. The current healthcare system is an enormous business. So, many market players hope that the money-churning machinery won't change. And therefore, even though healthcare has become a macroeconomic problem for many governments, the status quo remains.

For the newer companies, there is no point in trying to integrate into the old system, but rather they want to build a new system. Here, governments should play a braver and stronger role. They should promote the idea that people should have access to better technologies to be able to take care of themselves. The only way to change the big picture in healthcare is if we put modern, advanced technologies directly into the citizens' hands.

**Tina Woods**: How do you think this will play out when it comes to the big technology businesses, and their heavy investment in health? Other sectors like the pharma sector and the insurance sector will respond to this shift in investment as best they can, but who's going to win and who's going to lose?

**Teemu Suna**: The technology companies are in a very strong position because they've been building products for people for a very long time. Their success has been defined by how people consider their products. Their problem, however, is that they are just technology companies, and that limits them. Consider Smart Watches, for example. It's very difficult to use the data provided by them to make predictions about real diseases such as cardiovascular disease and type 2 diabetes. The reason for this is that you need molecular data.

I think the big winners in this game will be companies that combine digital health (like what Apple, Google, and Amazon are doing) with real biotech. When you combine molecular biotech data with the data from wearables, and behavioral data, and you let the AI do its magic, great things will happen. I think that's the winning combination.

The companies that will struggle will include the pharmaceutical industry. They will face serious challenges if people really start to treat themselves better. There's such an enormous market for drugs, but if everyone feels a lot better due to a healthier lifestyle, there will be no buyers.

When it comes to insurance, I'd split the companies into two categories. First, there are the insurance companies that benefit when people are healthier. They can do very smart things around health. They can work with the technology companies to keep their customers in better health or pay their customers directly for using these new technologies, because, ultimately, they'll benefit if diseases are prevented.

The second category of insurance companies is those that are so integrated into the current health system that they also earn when people get sick. Those kind of insurance companies, I hope, are the losing side in the future.

**Tina Woods**: As I understand it, Nightingale's technology measures over 200 metabolic biomarkers in a single blood test. Could you tell us more about it? Also, can you discuss the current projects you're working on?

**Teemu Suna**: We use **nuclear magnetic resonance (NMR)** technology to analyze blood. How it works is that we put a blood sample inside a high-frequency magnet, which makes the blood molecules resonate. Different molecules resonate differently, and we record that resonance. Then, based on the software that we have developed here at Nightingale, we can quantify this data. So, from a single blood sample, we can quantify more than 200 different molecules.

This is a very different way of analyzing blood than other methods being used in the current healthcare system and that's what makes Nightingale's technology so interesting.

We've built our company by collaborating with the scientific community and have always promoted medical science. That's because the new molecular technologies need a solid evidence base. So far, we've measured over 700,000 samples and are constantly running many projects with leading biobanks all over the world. For instance, we've worked with the UK biobank and the Finnish National Biobank, and have run the biggest metabolomics project in Latin America—the Mexico City Study. We have done some projects in Southeast Asia as well and have big plans in Asia in the pipeline.

**Tina Woods:** Moving back to personal health, there's a theory that it's the 30% genomics, and 60% behavioral and social factors that hold the real key to keeping you in good health. What do you think about that?

**Teemu Suna:** That's correct. And there's a lot of research going on trying to understand things like what kind of molecular profiles, or what kind of genetic backgrounds, develop into diseases. In fact, the government in Finland is heavily promoting such work with initiatives like hospital biobanks and information sources. I think it's very valuable to know the progression track towards a disease from as early a step as possible.

However, I'm convinced that keeping people healthy and improving health is more appealing. One important aspect of many projects worldwide—the UK biobank, to mention one—is that the collection of population-level data allows us to understand health, as well as sickness, better. I think the key to the future is to put the data together.

In fact, we need to start putting all the data together; that is, data from the disease and hospital biobanks, the population health data (including wearable data and behavioral data), genetics, and molecular data related to lifestyle. Only then can we get the full picture—have the best possible understanding of health and sickness, so we can better help people to make the right choices at the right time and usher in the future of health.

**Tina Woods**: Absolutely. So, this is a nice segue to tell us a bit more about the "omics" revolution that's underway. What role will omics (such as genomics, epigenomics, proteomics, metabolomics, and transcriptomics) play in helping us to live longer, better lives?

**Teemu Suna**: To put it simply, it's all about understanding human biology better. Consider the Human Genome Project. The project revealed great complexities of human biology. Even today, fields like proteomics or transcriptomics keep revealing more and more about our biology. The promises and possibilities around omics almost sound like science fiction coming to life. However, the important question remains—how will these sciences help technologies that can be rolled out to help people today? This is a practical discussion that people often forget to engage in.

For instance, it was very exciting when scientists found the new genes that predict cancer. As a result of that, genetic-testing companies started putting those genes into their genome-wide panel, and you could buy the DNA-testing kits to check whether you were vulnerable to disease. Sure, that's interesting. But what happens next if you find out that you've got a high risk? What do you do? Even if you have high genetic risk for diseases in the DNA test, the information is not actionable. You cannot do anything meaningful and helpful to better your health.

We need to connect the value we put on a piece of information to the question of how actionable that information is, and whether there's something you can do to improve your situation. For example, what we do at Nightingale is provide people with data that helps them make better lifestyle choices.

Other omics—that includes genetic data, as well as data around transcriptomics and proteomics—have huge potential too, but only if the data and the knowledge they create becomes actionable.

**Tina Woods**: Is this actionable data where the solution lies to change behavior?

**Teemu Suna**: Exactly, that and constant feedback is the solution to changing behaviors. Imagine that you run every day and face the same uphill section on your route. In the beginning, you struggle. But because you keep at it, you start improving and it becomes easier with each passing day. That improvement you feel is the positive feedback that helps you stay motivated to remain on the right path.

No one can commit to any change if they don't get feedback about what they're doing. It's the same with health. When you get positive feedback for a lifestyle change, it keeps you motivated to take actions and stick to a lifestyle that leads to better health.

**Tina Woods**: Do you have evidence that your technology is implementing that behavioral change?

**Teemu Suna**: I think the evidence for feedback being a tool for behavioral change is already there, and it's not connected to any specific technology. Take, for instance, weight loss. Many studies suggest that weighing yourself every morning is a successful strategy. Here, the nature of the technology—that is, the scales—has nothing to do with actual weight loss. But the measurement, and the constant feedback every morning, helps you stay focused.

**Tina Woods**: Do you think we'll reach a day when tests like Nightingale's will become a part of regular health check-ups for people?

**Teemu Suna**: Definitely, and that's because the health system will change quite a bit when it comes to primary care. People will come for check-ups not because they are sick but because they want to take better care of themselves.

Our aim is to bring Nightingale's technology to eight billion people in the next 10 years. We'll also introduce remote testing for our blood analysis in the future. So, you won't have to come to us; we'll come to you.

**Tina Woods**: How do you think AI will be used in the future, in terms of population health management and personal health management?

**Teemu Suna**: AI will, of course, play a central role in providing people with the right information that helps them navigate their health. We'll have to combine different datasets to see whether the causalities and correlations are non-linear.

The data models and the algorithms that we combine rely on very complex mathematical models that can only be enabled with AI. We, therefore, have a solid in-house AI team at Nightingale, who mostly focus on getting extremely valuable health datasets. When we get that right, then we start building the algorithms that create the value.

**Tina Woods**: Do you think there will be a day when we can time our own death, manage it, and be in charge of when we die?

**Teemu Suna**: That's a very interesting question. I think it all always comes down to the overall idea of staying healthy. Nightingale's blood test, for instance, currently provides a broad view of a person's future risk of type 2 diabetes and heart diseases.

In the future, the key will be to develop tools to understand these risks even better, no matter what they are—be it death, cardiovascular illness, diabetes, cancer, or anything else. It doesn't matter what these risks are. What is relevant is that we devise ways to detect them on time. If we can do that, we can take preventative actions to avert them.

**Tina Woods**: Do you think we'll ever get to the point where immortality is a possibility?

**Teemu Suna**: I think what is certain is healthy aging. I feel that this idea of living to be 200 or living forever is a bit of science fiction. Would that mean growing new organs in a box and switching them when we need to? Things like that may be possible for a handful of people. But if we think about eight billion people, taking that kind of technology to everyone is quite farfetched.

What I think is more important, and where we are putting all our focus, is creating technologies that give everyone the opportunity to live healthily and age healthily. Once we can provide this basic right to everyone, we can then maybe give immortality a thought.

**Tina Woods**: What do you think is the secret to a long, healthy life?

**Teemu Suna**: Most people would be surprised but living healthily is about simple things. It's about balancing your life—sleeping enough, moving enough, and not eating too much unhealthy food. That's what it comes down to. It's also important to monitor yourself, and to use technology to understand your health better, as no people or diseases are the same.

However, all this is possible only if you have the right tools—the new technologies make this task easy and accessible to all.

**Tina Woods**: What have you learned from the COVID-19 pandemic?

**Teemu Suna**: COVID-19 has only made the case for predictive prevention even more urgent and pressing. The epidemic has painfully exposed the gaps in our current healthcare capabilities in terms of controlling the spread of infectious diseases. While healthcare professionals at the frontline have been more than efficient and even risked their lives taking care of the sick, complete lockdowns of the state and the economy are primarily a result of our current inabilities to manage infectious pandemics more efficiently.

There is a clear gap in the system—currently, no organization in any country has population-level information about who has the highest risk of being hospitalized or even dying from the virus. Due to fragmented (or even a lack of) such information, it is impossible to implement targeted restrictive measures and coordinate at the population level. Because we did not have an effective way of prevention, this left us with no option but to shut down and accept the wide-ranging socio-economic consequences.

However, it doesn't have to be so with the right predictive prevention tools and a centralized database for targeted disease management. Nightingale has been working on the prevention of chronic diseases for years and the pandemic just made the tools of prevention more needed than ever.

Quite strikingly, in addition to the chronic diseases, recent findings with Nightingale's technology show promise for preventative COVID-19 risk detection and other infectious diseases as well. As we now begin to relax the social distancing measures, such predictive and preventative health technology can be a game-changing tool for identifying high-risk people and can help in taking targeted measures in the case of another pandemic or in managing a second wave of the coronavirus.

The bigger picture (and the most effective preventive solution) is to put predictive health tools in the individual's hand to raise their awareness of their own health risks. In the case of the coronavirus, those most at risk would receive a personal warning of having high risk of getting severe symptoms (from, say, a national actor), enabling their own preventive action. This would enable the rest of the society to function nearly normally and avoid another complete lockdown. We strongly believe, in both infectious and chronic diseases, that when individuals are given the opportunity for a better and healthier life, they will take actions to improve their own health, also reducing the costs of medical care. This is a true win-win for everyone and the future of health.

# Nic Palmarini

*Director, National Innovation Centre for Ageing (formerly AI Ethics Lead and Global Manager AI for Healthy Aging at IBM Research)*

Nic Palmarini is the new director of the **National Innovation Centre for Ageing** (**NICA**) in Newcastle, a world-leading organization created with a £40 million investment from the UK Government and Newcastle University. The center brings together cross-competence professionals and researchers, clinicians, scientists, innovators, and technologists, working together with the public and sister organization **Valuing Our Intellectual Capital & Experience** (**VOICE**™), an international network of "innovation-ready citizens," in a seamless way, exchanging intelligence and background.

NICA has developed and is bringing to the market a novel approach named Ageing Intelligence™. It leverages the experience and expertise of older adults, along with stakeholders, while harnessing big data.

I first met Nic in 2018 when I was working with UK Research & Innovation on developing the ecosystem for the Healthy Ageing Industrial Strategy Challenge Fund.

I was at a meeting with a number of his colleagues to discuss IBM's potential involvement as a lead industry partner for the bids being sought for the government grant of £100 million to seed the development of a healthy aging marketplace. He was invited to the call and was at the time the global manager of AI for Healthy Aging in Cambridge (but later went on to become the program manager and ethics AI lead of the MIT-IBM Watson AI Lab, a $250 million academic-industry partnership for the responsible advancement of AI).

He joined the meeting by phone from Boston and he recounted some of his experiences in Bolzano, Italy with using IoT and analytics in a local population to promote healthy aging. This project helped inform the IBM Periodic Table for Aging, which focuses on all the elements you might need to consider from a human-centered behavioral perspective to develop solutions to care for people, harnessing contextual data versus wearables or personal data.

Nic has a far-reaching interest in understanding how technologies and AI can help address loneliness, fight ageism, and preserve independence and dignity in older people. He has been involved in various global studies and research on cultures, society, policies, language, and communication. His focus has always been on the end-user—the older person and their needs and wants.

Nic has explored the interaction of technology and humans in four books he has written, including one on the insufficient number of women in STEM careers and its impact on future society. The last book, *Immortali*, is a journey through the opportunities of the longevity revolution and the chances of a longer life provided by AI and broad research.

During our interview, I was struck by Nic's motivation on understanding the human, cultural, and societal aspects of technology. The importance of humans at the center of technological evolution and change is paramount in his view, and the importance of citizens recognizing the power they have as the "ones who are generating the data" is crucial. As he said in our interview, "We are the data that AI needs to become more intelligent and possibly help us live longer, and sharing that data is the fastest way to improve understanding."

With this power, of course, comes responsibility. We talked a lot about the importance of trust—trust in government and also in business. Governments have a crucial role in setting the rules and policies for social inclusion and the distribution of wealth. We talked about the need for a renewed pact of trust between the citizen and politics for the sake of humanity—to improve life and the planet itself, instead of destroying it.

Finally, we talked about death and immortality (the subject of one of his books). In Nic's view, we can harness technology to help preserve and transmit ideas, memories, and experiences—something that humans have been doing for eons. He said we also need boredom. As Nic so eloquently described, "My secret rule for living longer is that you just need to get bored a little. If you're bored, then you're seeking something. You're seeking love. You're seeking the next exciting thing. Being bored is probably the key to immortality—when you are happy and fulfilled, then you are ready to peacefully wait for death."

**Tina Woods**: From your work, your perspective and your philosophy, what are the key points or messages that people reading this book should really understand about living longer with AI?

**Nic Palmarini**: I think it's a very interesting question because it's combining two dimensions: living longer and AI. There is an unprecedented mass of data that is still basically unknown and unprocessed. It can literally be "liberated" in its meaning and impacts for humanity by many compelling and emerging AI-based technologies in the longevity sphere. Each one of those is playing an interesting role in accelerating the research that we are doing around longevity; I think the key word here is "accelerate."

Tom Kirkwood beautifully re-defined the process of aging, which originally had been always considered like an unchangeable piece of stone. He introduced this idea that aging is "malleable," and not fixed in a sort of an untouchable shape. The Italian word is likewise: "malleabile." It implies the action a sculptor does with a piece of stone or marble. I really like the idea that "aging is malleable" because it helps to envision the fact that we can take that stone called "life" and change it into something completely different. We can change its shape and transform it, maybe, into a piece of art. In our own piece of art, we are the artists in this process.

This idea of malleability really helps us to understand the active role of being the artists of our own life. And we can envision AI as a chisel that could affect both the speed and the capability to better carve that stone called our future life.

There has been a sort of a chain reaction around longevity and technology. We had a big breakthrough in 2013 when Google created Calico to explore research in extreme longevity. Calico was set up to try to understand why we age, what the mechanisms are around our aging process, and how we can somehow make it more malleable than ever before.

Calico somehow pushed many other companies to work in the space where technology and longevity meet each other, and I think this helped us realize that some of the upcoming technologies—mainly thanks to more and more data being available and using novel techniques to extract meaning—will help us to radically change the perception and the related possibilities around aging.

It could potentially lead us to what we define as "extreme longevity," which is something we can't yet imagine in its dimensions and impacts. We could then somehow challenge our conceptions around mortality too.

Anyway, I think it is very early now. There is still so much progress to be made in understanding the reasons behind our process of aging and therefore how to expand the boundaries of longevity. It's still a black box full of mysteries, but these technologies, with the amazing capabilities of researchers all over the world, will help us to progressively illuminate this darkness and connect dots we are still not able to see today.

As you know, AI is nothing new. It's something that has been around from 1955 at least, as we define it today. It has already had its ups and downs. We know that at least two winters have already happened. And maybe we'll face other future winters; probably we have lived through one of these disruptive seasons with COVID-19. All the technological power we thought we had available hasn't been able to solve—at least as fast as our imagination, fueled by some sensationalistic press, predicted—the deadly equation of an unknown virus.

Nevertheless, with our current computing capability, maybe we will be able to use AI as we intended to solve some of those issues and be able to answer some of the key questions around life. But it is absolutely clear that it will take a lot of time. The pandemic showed us the complexity of the domain we are trying to master. We are in a transition from what is called "narrow AI" to the so-called "broader AI" systems that use and integrate multimodal data streams, learn more efficiently and flexibly, and traverse multiple tasks and domains. But from these stages to what we define as "general AI"—AI systems capable of complex reasoning and full autonomy—someone says it will take 30 years, and others claim it to be "impossible." Recent advances in neurosymbolic systems have been exciting to the imagination. If these prove to be effective, they will have a crucial impact on society and humanity, and therefore on our longevity as well.

**Tina Woods**: Looking back, there are technologies today that, even three years ago, we would never have imagined were possible. Do you think that the pace of discovery is going to accelerate?

**Nic Palmarini**: Yes, absolutely. As I said before, the word "accelerate" should be in the middle of all the things we're discussing. I think that right now it is the great promise of AI. We want to know more, faster. Acceleration from every perspective is crucial; just think about biosciences, or technologies that could help us live better when we our body fails, just to mention a couple. There are so many aspects, and each one of those could be strongly accelerated, not only by the AI itself but also by co-operation between researchers who are working less and less in silos and are sharing knowledge more than ever before.

The "race" to develop the future through AI benefits from collaboration between the people working in this domain; they want to show the capability, the achievement, and the skills and smartness of each research center. It's a combination of factors and I think it's something that was not so obvious or possible only a few years ago.

Another reason why we can't really tell what's going to happen in the future is that we know that some problems are very, very complex to be solved by a machine. There's still a long way to go. Again, some people give 2050 as the first date at which we could probably start thinking about something that we could define as closer to general AI. Even then—and I'm saying it softly—no one can scientifically make a serious promise today about it.

You probably read the news a while ago about neuroscientist Henry Markram, who walked onstage at the TEDGlobal conference in Oxford, England, and told the audience that he was going to simulate the human brain, in all its staggering complexity, in 10 years. That was 10 years ago, and today he has mapped less than 0.01% or so. It's nothing. Probably he didn't have all the technology that we are developing today. Nevertheless, it's going to take time, even though the task appears to be doable with technologies that we can envision in the near and far future.

**Tina Woods**: In your view, what concept or device in AI or tech will have the biggest impact in helping people to live longer, better lives now, in 5 years, and in 10 years?

**Nic Palmarini**: I'd say, for sure, it is about a deeper understanding of the individual. I think that the ability to understand human behavior from its observation in a real context will be one of the most interesting things that's going to help the process of improving healthy aging, extending a pleasant longevity, and helping us to live better lives. Regarding the importance of different behaviors, let me just mention the so-called "FemTechs," which are technologies that are specifically dedicated to understanding, serving, and supporting women in their daily lives. We didn't have those as a "category" just four or five years ago, but now the pharma or the consumer electronic industries—just to mention two—have started realizing that women are different from men in their life processes, needs, and desires. The data is telling us how these trends could be enhanced in specific product or services.

By just approaching research and following development from a first main split between two genders—not considering at all the fluidity we are finally recognizing!—we can really understand the unknown landscape and the potential for innovation we still haven't even explored. I think that this way of understanding humans is somehow evident in some industries that are partnering with their customers in a sort of a mutual agreement based on data sharing, for example, insurance companies. The first that pops up in my mind is Hancock.

A couple of years ago, Hancock launched a product that basically lets clients buy an Apple Watch for a few dollars in order to receive suggestions for improvements in lifestyle and get better policy deals. This is one side. On the other side, there are companies like Nebula Genomics, for example, which claims to have a DNA sequencing technology that generates a thousand times more data than the other DNA tests on the market. Furthermore, the company is formally asking its customers to partner with it in research advancement by publicly sharing their data.

So, as you see, what previously was performed inside labs is now becoming a sort of mass mainstream. It is happening and it is part of a mutual agreement between consumers and providers; I think it is also an unstoppable process. I'm not sure how the rising privacy or ethical issues we can easily imagine could be solved. Assuming they can be solved—that is, thinking about a perfect world where the privacy of each individual is respected and data is used ethically for the enhancement of public health and to benefit the whole of society—I think that leveraging this data is, for sure, the way to accelerate the research outcomes.

Thinking about the future of AI in the next five to 10 years, there are other important elements we need to combine. I would say that explainability is one of the most important. We must be able to explain AI. Today, we have some applications of neural networks where we don't know why they're doing what they're doing. We are excited by the outcome, like children watching a painting made by throwing colors on a canvas, but we have yet to understand many of the mechanisms behind it. AI must be able to show its reasoning.

The security of AI is also important. The AI we use needs to be secure in terms of not allowing, for example, backdoors or misinterpretation of data. You can easily fake AI today using adversarial approaches that could genuinely fool the "intelligent" eye itself. Until it's secure, it can't progress in the way that we all hope for it to. It should also be ethical, but we will discuss that later, I'm sure.

An aspect that I think we don't consider most of the time is the physics of AI. There are ways we can improve AI to be more effective if we design components and information dynamics that help it to perform better, and this performance affects the whole narrative. I know it sounds obvious, but there is no acceleration in outcomes if systems can't allow this to happen. We have to invent GPUs that will require far less energy, and then perform better.

I think all of these are objectives that are maybe less sexy to discuss than the amazing possible applications of AI, but they are at the core of what we can envision from AI in the next five to 10 years.

**Tina Woods**: What responsibility do you think individual citizens have to make use of this technology? How do you think that differs from the responsibilities of governments or businesses?

**Nic Palmarini**: We are the ones who are generating the data. We are the data. We must be aware of the importance that we all, as individuals, have in this picture. We have to decide if we agree or not to sharing a part of ourselves. Any sharing has to be done properly under certain rules. We are part of the process because we are the data that AI needs to become more intelligent and this will possibly help us live longer. Sharing data is the fastest way to improve understanding around the aging process.

From a very personal and private perspective, we have to be aware. We have to be aware, first of all, of what type of data we are generating and how this data could be shared on whatever platform. Let me tell you a story: a few weeks ago, I was on stage at a conference about ethics and AI. Being part of a global organization, I was challenged by the audience as being responsible for managing their data. Or, at least, the audience believed that to be so. Their point was "we don't want you to know about us."

I asked the audience what they were doing to avoid others knowing about them. And basically 98% of the audience did nothing but were sharing everything on social platforms without any concern. No one was really aware of what about their qualified self was being shared and stored and used by these platforms. So, my first point is awareness and education.

Then it is clear that the ball is not, for sure, in the court of the citizen alone. On the contrary. That's why we have to put the same question to governments and businesses. It is my opinion that it's time for governments to take back their role, which has been somehow delegated in the name of progress and economy.

We all know there is a lot of concern from the corporations about governments controlling what's happening in their business garden, but I feel that the area of human longevity—like many others, and climate change above all—is where the governments are demanded of to fulfil their mission and duty of looking out for the good of the population. We need some control from an entity that has been politically enabled by citizens to do that job formally and ethically.

A beautiful book by Eloi Laurent titled *New Economic Mythologies* is worth reading. It theorizes how, in these troubled times of a technologically driven future, there is a need for a renewed stance on the part of governments. In Massachusetts, 45 years ago, the city of Cambridge realized that organizations were developing research around genetics. People realized it could be potentially harmful for the citizens. So, they said, "OK, let's stop the machine for a second. Let's create some clear rules of engagement."

The debates of 1976 marked the start of a five-year period that shaped the local biotech landscape. And by early 1977, the citizens committee had proposed a framework to ensure that any DNA-related experiments were done under fairly stringent safety controls, and Cambridge became the first city in the world to regulate research using genetic material. If you create clear rules of engagement, then you generate a fertile ground to then allow the growth of the crucial research that is happening here in these few square miles near where I sit in Cambridge. We have the most advanced research centers here, just because the ecosystem has been correctly designed and properly managed by the government of the city.

I wouldn't say the rules are set forever—because the rules may evolve as the science progresses—but if we keep the human being and society at the center of the evolution, than we can envision a sustainable growth model.

Again, the role of government is crucial. I'm not totally sure that GDPR or those types of regulations will be as effective as they promise to be, because they could probably become too strict as the world progresses. We'll see, but nevertheless, the intent is absolutely correct and it is a milestone we all should look at to start from to evolve ethically.

**Tina Woods**: Looking at the whole fast-moving field of AI and data, how do you think businesses need to respond? What are the responsibilities and what are the great opportunities for businesses?

**Nic Palmarini**: That's a very complicated question to answer for business in general because every entity has different angles and plays different roles. For example, pharma could take advantage of dramatically reducing the time needed to go to market with new drugs. Think about the COVID-19 vaccine race we are observing while we are discussing this. They could reduce clinical trials or do clinical trials after already having chosen the correct path to follow. This is one of the issues today because we are using drugs that were invented 20/25 years ago, which is way too long. Think about what's happened in the last 20 years!

New AI techniques applied to drug discovery and clinical trials could help to deliver new products on the market in a faster and probably safer way. For example, companies will have the amazing opportunity to combine all the experience that they have from history. That ranges from security to computing capability, to understanding data and understanding humans. If you put it all together, you see that some companies could be more equipped to answer some of the challenges that we have ahead of us. Nevertheless, every company should benefit from the combination of some of these factors.

The opportunities are fantastic, but when the opportunities are increasing, the fact you are dealing with data from people comes to the forefront. Citizens have to be aware of what's happening, and we have to have this conversation out loud because to be perfectly honest, as I said before, nobody is aware right now about the implication of the quantified self. There's still a long, long way to go to help people to understand exactly what we mean by transparency, or the ethical aspect of AI, or fairness. All these things will be probably become part of our cultural perspective in the next few years, and not in the next few weeks. And we are all called to do our part here.

**Tina Woods**: How do you think businesses are going to cope with the open, collaborative trend that we're seeing? How do you think that will change business?

**Nic Palmarini**: I think right now we are looking at a transition. Most of the AI that we have today is being trained on data that was available on the market; typically, this is pretty old data that has limitations. For example, much of this data is biased. It's clear to me that companies are seeking to start training AI with their own data. Companies are starting to generate data or process data, which is today one of the main pain points. Cleaning data and making it available for training AI systems is a tricky new business and the market of data—I envision nothing different than a stock exchange of data with prices following market rules—will grow more and more.

It opens the door to the sharing of some of this data to benefit cross-correlation or intercept different domains or, as you suggest, improve research and outcomes. It is hard to imagine a non-cooperative way of doing things since the overlapping dimensions of complex issues—let's say for a second longevity and climate change, above all—are all connected to the others. Just for the sake of the discussion: how can we correlate pollution to our hope of living longer and healthier?

These cross plays are desperately needed. If from the academic side a collaboration is happening, it is far more complicated for business ventures who are competing in gaining market share and revenue.

Ownership of data and their accessibility is for sure a key factor in today's business world and different models—collecting data directly or managing data collected by others—can have both pros and cons. But again, I don't see how we could really create smart models without cooperation. Then, for sure, it is a matter of business targets. Do we want to improve longevity in a country or engage a new consumer with the promise of providing a longer life if purchasing that drug or that service?

**Tina Woods**: I'm fascinated by your work at IBM, especially the Periodic Table for Aging and your work with older adults in Bolzano in Italy. Could you describe your work in these areas?

**Nic Palmarini**: The periodic table was something that we all realized was missing. We needed a flexible methodological approach to help us aggregate the questions that can arise along the aging and longevity process with the answers that can be provided by some technologies. The periodic table is a visual abstraction that can be understood in its dynamics by both researchers and non-professional users. The elements of the periodic table can be combined to generate virtually infinite solutions, just like chemistry. This allows us to see far beyond each simple element itself.

Aging is not only a health-related domain. We still automatically associate "old person" with "medical issue." We are completely forgetting life itself in its beauty, richness, and complexity. Aging is probably one of the few domains where you can really and properly use the word "holistic" because when you talk about aging you are really facing a multidimensional and multidisciplinary process.

We can represent the whole chemistry that rules the world with just the elements inside a periodic table; you can see the hidden power of the tool we created.

That's what we were attempting to do: to help everyone by creating a feasible chemistry to fulfill a specific individual's or stakeholder's want or need.

**Tina Woods**: Has that concept of fusing together the right elements helped you? Has it guided you in how you collaborate and how you work, for example in your Bolzano project?

**Nic Palmarini**: Yes, exactly. The Bolzano project started quite mechanically because we were working on understanding how we could know more about human behavior in order to provide insights to stakeholders. We're in the field of human activity recognition and it was a really an early project in the field of leveraging IoT and mobile technology together to harness the power of data. We studied what had been done in the UK and in Scotland a lot, because the UK was far ahead of all the other countries in the world when it came to using these types of techniques, especially in the telecare field.

But we soon realized that the context was far more articulated and complex than just putting some sensors here and there in a kitchen or a bathroom and getting some data. The seeds of the periodic table for aging go back there. Despite pretty deep experience in the field that we all transferred to this methodological tool, I don't think it is complete. There are probably many things missing, but it still gives you the sense of what things you should be thinking about when you're aiming to develop a solution for aging. It's a combination of factors; some of them that are quite obvious, but others are slightly less obvious, and still have to be considered. We had this in mind, helped by formal and informal researchers, who were designing solutions powered by some technologies to support older adults and their stakeholders. We wanted to make it an iterative tool that could be improved by the community.

The holistic approach we took, always starting from the individual and the stakeholders, helped us to develop an innovative and interesting approach focusing on understanding a behavior from contextual data versus wearables or personal data. I still think it is a very modern approach, and more respectful of privacy. It is very elegant in terms of solution design since it aims to understand a pattern from existing data sources, while trying to avoid adding new ones. For example, from analyzing $CO_2$ we can theoretically understand how many people are in one room. If we are able to understand this, we can deduct the social interactions of an individual. Did anyone visit that person in a day, in a week, or in a month? Can we suggest a better routine to caregivers serving the need of that individual from a data-driven scenario instead of using a scheduled routine driven by staffing rules? And that data is coming from $CO_2$, which is already collected from a sensor that we almost all have in our homes.

That's where we started. We shifted this idea towards the so-called "caring things" and how we define those things, so that we were focusing on how IoT could care about people. Diving down one layer, we wanted to pick out what kinds of technologies could help us to take care of people. That's what we're doing today, but we've enhanced the analytics we had 10 years ago with machine learning techniques. Now, thanks to these techniques, we can harness the time-series data, and augment it with meaning to help us read and understand the macro-and micro-trajectories of an individual. This creates a holistic behavioral footprint that can help us assess normality versus abnormality, build predictive models, and not only potentially avoid harmful events but suggest how we could promote a behavioral change.

**Tina Woods**: There's a fear of privacy concerns with this technology in terms of Big Brother and being monitored. What was your experience with that, and how did you address that?

**Nic Palmarini**: We never monitored people using intrusive or visually based technologies. We just focused on the behavior in a given context. Right now, we're developing some research that is very interesting using Wi-Fi waves over laser beams. These technologies can't understand who you are, but they can help to suggest how you are acting and allow us to develop models to understand how you are doing, which is what we are looking for. Then, we just need to assess the situation, and find out whether it is an at-risk situation.

However, to address your question, it is clear that the point of a sustainable future is exactly this. And we go back to my personal syllogism: there is no AI without data, and there is no data without ethics around it. So, it is easy to see where the syllogism loops: there is no AI without ethics.

Trusted AI is not a slogan, but a commitment to be achieved. We must endlessly ask ourselves whether the systems we are implementing are fair, are aligned with our values, are easy to understand, are robust, or are accountable. If we can answer "yes" to these questions and show users in real time how data is processed, then the Big Brother you mention is—while for sure a risk in the background—part of a venture where innovation and data are part of play.

Trust is the keyword that will help to engage people as citizens and consumers to benefit their life and society at scale. To build that trust, public and private organizations must show what they are, and how they play; they must be transparent. I think this is not a naïve mission to just gain quick goodwill; this is a strategic pillar for business success. No trust, no business. Simple.

**Tina Woods**: Do you think technology will ever get us to that place where we will live forever, and is that a good or a bad thing?

**Nic Palmarini**: You probably know I wrote a book about exploring what extreme longevity—and a theoretical immortality as a provocative concept—could lead us to both from an individual perspective and societal one. The concept around my work is beyond immortality per se—I don't care about it—and more about understanding how stereotypes around aging, ageism, and the endemic inability of brands to see the opportunity of the longevity economy could be challenged in such an extreme concept of a super-long life.

We don't really think about solutions for the older adults because we always keep death in the background. All the ideas are biased by death and this is big stopper to our imagination for a better society. People will die, so why bother too much? Just let's give them some palliatives. So, it's interesting how we could see the future from very different perspectives if life continues without an expiry date. So, it is the paradox that allows to go beyond schemes and try, finally, to imagine solutions that we typically can't see, since we refer to a pretty usual interpretation of later life always bound to disease and death.

The first idea to hold in our mind about immortality is that it is very immaterial and very tangible at the same time. Think about ideas, memories, and experiences. We've spent our lives developing technologies to help preserve and transmit ideas through every era. We have that cultural construct of ideas through history, and you can use this cultural construct as proof that we are immortal. We have just created pretty effective technologies to achieve that: from ink to GitHub. That's my main point: that we're already immortal since our ideas are. We are using ideas that were shaped by people 10, 100, and 1,000 years ago, as well as the technologies to communicate. All this is somehow the first proof that we are immortal.

We also have to be clear about what physical immortality would mean. Jonathan Swift in *Gulliver's Travels* wrote a chapter about the Struldbruggs, the immortals. Gulliver, in the beginning, is absolutely astonished by this opportunity because he thinks immediately of all the beautiful things he could do. He could become a wiser man, teach others, or explore everything; in other words, he could do everything he missed out on. But then he sees how the immortals are in such a physically bad shape. So, he immediately changes his mind. He doesn't want to be an immortal, because at the time Swift wrote the book, people couldn't imagine that potentially we could be in a physically decent shape at 90, 110, or 150 years thanks to technologies that will help us first to assess where we are going wrong and then how to fix the wrong behaviors.

Some ongoing research and some studies are suggesting we might be able to keep running on that edge: NAD+, Metformin, other senolytics, stem cells, organ transplants, CRISPR, prosthetics and robotics, fasting, gene therapy, and DNA sequencing are just few of the many rising techniques. These technologies paired with an engineering approach augmented by AI applications, and maybe quantum computing, can lead us to slowing the aging process and extending our life span.

All these don't mean that we will be young forever. It means that we could have, theoretically, a healthier life for a far longer time. I think—looking at what technology could help us achieve—we could envision extreme longevity as a concrete possibility, but personally, as I said, I'm not so much interested in that. I'm more interested in trying to understand what the impacts on society, both for individuals and organizations, could be. What will be the needs and, mainly, the wants of these humans and consumers on the planet of extreme longevity? This is a planet we haven't ever really explored.

Life can be a lot wider and not only longer! Living a healthy life isn't just a matter of how many years, but a matter of how easily you find a reason to look for another year, and then another year, and then another year. One of the key elements to life is our purpose; we've said it so many times. Purpose is strictly linked to our ability to live longer and to live a wider life. And technologies can help a lot in adding span to the length of life.

**Tina Woods**: How do we make sure that all these incredible developments are going to take us in a good direction as a society and as a world? What do you think are the critical things that we must bear in mind with all these new technological developments?

**Nic Palmarini**: I suppose we all can see the fact that these innovations that could lead us to live longer, healthier lives won't be available to all at the same time. I think that if we look at society as it is today, the idea of an extreme longevity that will been distributed equally and timely to all people is not realistic. There are areas in the world—like Hamilton, Ontario, which is a story so well documented by *The Spectator* with the CodeRed project—where the gap in life expectancy is 23 years, from a high of 87.7 years to a shocking low of 64.8 years. That's lower than the struggling African nations of Eritrea and Malawi, and we are talking about rich, progressive Canada here.

There are some interesting books in which authors envision the process to get to a wider lifespan and many suggest that to achieve that "new demographic society" we'll have to deal with some painful breakthroughs, but for sure it's a matter of money. We all know there are people today who are putting a lot of their own money into research that can help them to live longer. I'm not saying to become younger, because that's another story; they are just trying to live longer. They can afford cures or processes that could potentially help them to live longer. I say "potentially" because it's not absolutely given that they will work the way someone claims they should work, from mice to humans.

We can easily envision a "society of the rich" that would live longer than a "society of the others" that couldn't afford these techniques. But then, we also know that antacids for our stomach, for example, were very expensive 30 years ago, and now you can buy them for few cents. There is progress we can point to in the development of drugs and many other technologies and devices that could be useful for everyone and could be distributed to a wider population in less time than ever before. This is where governments come into play again with fair rules, smarter policies of social inclusion, and distribution of wealth. This is a complete revision of what we intend for retirement and work in later life through leveraging data and the knowledge derived from them. This is pure politics in a sort of renewed pact of trust between citizens and governments, and politics for the sake of humanity. I know it could sound a little visionary or cheesy, but I think that trust in the dynamic of democracy is the most powerful tool we have to take advantage of our amazing intelligence to improve life and the planet itself, instead of destroying it.

**Tina Woods**: Living longer, healthy lives is a matter of many factors: genetics, healthcare, and the social determinants of health and longevity. How do you think AI and technology will help us really address those social determinants?

**Nic Palmarini**: Well, you are talking to an Italian, so you can imagine how much I think about this from a cultural perspective. Social determinants and the other factors you mentioned are at the core of longevity of the second fastest aging country in the world after Japan, and again one of the first countries in terms of longevity. With a team of researchers, we submitted a paper aiming to explore those intangible factors that are beyond diet or exercise. We Italians know there are factors that are hard to explain but are part of our social and cultural fabric, creating a sort of invisible net that make us feel more connected and related. We called it "invisible proximity," a sort of intangible but very powerful way of living that helps us live longer.

An example: if you come to visit my village and you cross the "piazza" (the core of the village and a sort of Checkpoint Charlie that exists in every Italian village and city as well), maybe nobody stops you while you're crossing, but you basically get a sort of check-up from all the citizens who are there but are invisible at the same time; everyone is checking on each other. It can sometimes be pretty intrusive, because everyone knows about everybody else. But it's something that allows people to live their life knowing that someone, somehow is looking out for them.

This type of social network is intangible, because it's not established formally, but it's there. This thing is very complicated to measure, but that's the beauty of our challenge in the paper.

If we all think that loneliness and isolation are lethal weapons attacking our health—and it is demonstrated they are—how can we leverage AI to help us identify them before they happen? We can think about ageism as a discrimination that has lethal effects on individuals. Can we use AI to help identify one of the most dangerous types of unconscious biases? We're literally using these techniques against ageism. For example, we're developing some tools that are able to understand from natural language processing whether the language used in an online job posting is ageist and whether that's affecting potential candidates. They may feel discriminated against and not apply for that job. This is just one of the examples of how you can leverage AI for good and impact aging and longevity in a less obvious way.

**Tina Woods**: What do you think the secret is to a long life?

**Nic Palmarini**: As I was trying to describe before, I think it's a combination of factors that are very well defined by Cesare Pavese, one of the greatest Italian authors of the nineteenth century: "You need a village, if only for the pleasure of leaving it. A village means that you are not alone, knowing that in the people, the plants, the soil, there is something that belongs to you, waiting for you when you are not there. Even if it is not easy to be quiet about it."

I think this idea of the "village" (read it as a strong social construct based on mutual respect and care) is something not artificial, and something deep in the roots of the soil itself. It is such a powerful senolytic that it can't be distilled in pills. And this concept of a "new kind of village" comes out so strongly from the research we've done with the IBM Institute for Business Value around loneliness and isolation.

You find all this, for example, in Acciaroli, a village south of Salerno in southern Italy, which has the highest concentration of centennials in the world. There are 30 centennials for every 100,000 people and this has been studied by researchers all over the world. I think there is not much to extract from there; it is more in the words of Cesare Pavese than in the diet and it can't be easily exported or replicated since it is a deep cultural trait.

**Tina Woods**: Do you think there's such a thing as a good death?

**Nic Palmarini**: I attended a design-thinking workshop, one of the toughest and most interesting I was ever involved in about end of life. It covered how to deal with the end of lives of patients inside a medical facility. All the actors at my table—doctors, nurses, researchers, and mainly people used to dealing with death—were telling basically the same story: none of them was prepared or educated for this moment. No one is prepared, because most of the time, they said around 90% of the time, no one in the inner circles of a person who is going to die has any concern about his or her own death. Death is something we don't touch. It's something that we don't talk about. The key question is "do you think turning off the machine would be what this person would have wanted?" Nobody knew.

There's an interesting paper by Camillo Lamanna and Lauren Byrne about how AI could theoretically help us to shape our approach to life, our history, comments, visions, things we've seen, things we've told, things we've painted, and things we've written.

Combined together, these could create a profile about our approach to death and suggest what our wills might be in that moment, if we're not able to share a decision ourselves. I feel it's a little mechanical, but this is another interesting and less considered example about how technology could support a decision-making process even in very human and personal contexts, reinforcing the fact that some of these technologies could highlight the "other us," who is probably closer to the "real us" because they are less influenced by time and events.

**Tina Woods**: That's a very interesting philosophical point about the meaning of a good life. How do you think that this idea of a good life interacts with the idea of immortality?

**Nic Palmarini**: My secret rule for living longer is that you just need to get bored a little. If you're bored, then you're seeking something. You're seeking love. You're seeking the next exciting thing. Being bored is probably the key to immortality—when you are happy and fulfilled, then you are ready to die.

**Tina Woods**: What have you learned from the COVID-19 pandemic?

**Nic Palmarini**: That life is wide. While browsing through the graphs of the dramatic statistics on the projection of COVID-19, I have embarked on a journey. These sterile lines, day after day, tell the tale of life along the axis of time and growth, where contagion and death are silent but imposing vectors.

The lifeline is always represented as a thin one, or it takes on other geometric forms, made up of equally thin lines. That line itself means nothing; it's the parameters we plot on the abscissa and the ordinate that give it meaning. Eliminate those and it's just a simple line: naked, empty, and alone.

That's the way we've always represented "life" on a graph—a thin line. But how wide is it? What does it really contain in its shades of color when we draw it on a sheet of paper, or in the pixels flickering on a computer screen?

How wide would that line be if it could tell the stories of our everyday lives in our own voices? The stories of the dead we sadly count today—how much have we lost due to their deaths? How much "wideness" has been lost? Could we have preserved that wealth? Could we have collected it, shared it, used it, and made it good for others, for society, and for ourselves?

The pandemic taught me, once again, that knowledge is the only weapon we have to face the future, and that knowledge needs intelligence to be leveraged. We need intelligence that helps us avoid baptizing the countless superficial banalities that we celebrate as innovations without investing in the fundamentals of research. When we make that investment, it may not pay its dividends immediately, but it will lead us to a better and more inclusive humanity, instead of acting like we do; we act like a bunch of individuals only able to recognize themselves as a "society" in the case of a pandemic.

# Final thoughts

New research on the impact of the wider environment on our genetics is showing how strongly the health of humans is indeed connected to our wider environment, and of course the planet. There are certain things we can do to shape our environment, like the food we eat and the exercise we do, but so much is dependent on other factors, too, like our access to good housing, education, and jobs--the most powerful determinants.

Our genes, which are 30% of the determinants of our health, are hugely important and the rapidly unfolding "omics" field is shedding light on the complex interplay between our genomics, proteomics, metabolomics, and the wider exposome.

But what happens if despite our best efforts, whether at an individual level or wider government public health level, we fall ill and need expert medical care? The next chapter looks at the element of "healthcare," the 10-15% of the wider determinants of our health, which includes the role of doctors, hospitals, and the wide spectrum of diagnostics and treatments that are being influenced by AI and data-driven technologies.

# References

1. *The Case For More Active Policy Attention To Health Promotion, McGinnis et al, Health Affairs,* March 2002 https://www.healthaffairs.org/doi/10.1377/hlthaff.21.2.78

2. *What makes us healthy? An introduction to the social determinants of health, Jo Bibby and Natalie Lovell,* March 2018, https://www.health.org.uk/publications/what-makes-us-healthy

3. *Speed Data: falling life expectancy—an American tragedy, Angus Deaton and Anne Case,* July 18, 2019, https://www.prospectmagazine.co.uk/magazine/speed-data-falling-life-expectancy-an-american-tragedy

4. *Blame Economists for the Mess We're In, Binyamin Appelbaum:* https://www.nytimes.com/2019/08/24/opinion/sunday/economics-milton-friedman.html

5. *Health state life expectancies, UK: 2016 to 2018, Publishing team,* 11 December 2019, https://backup.ons.gov.uk/2019/12/11/health-state-life-expectancies-uk-2016-to-2018/

6. *Healthspan, Outcomes Based Healthcare*, 2018, `https://outcomesbasedhealthcare.com/healthspan/`

7. *Government must take action to level up the health and wellbeing of the population, The Health Foundation*, 25 February 2020, `https://www.health.org.uk/news-and-comment/news/health-foundation-response-to-the-marmot-review-ten-years-on`

8. *New Zealand 'wellbeing' budget promises billions to care for most vulnerable, Support The Guardian*, `https://www.theguardian.com/world/2019/may/30/new-zealand-wellbeing-budget-jacinda-ardern-unveils-billions-to-care-for-most-vulnerable`

9. *Increasing healthy life expectancy equitably in England by 5 years by 2035: could it be achieved?*, Theresa M Marteau, Martin White, Harry Rutter, Mark Petticrew, Oliver T Mytton, James G McGowan and Robert W Aldridge, *Volume 393, Issue 10191, P2571-2573*, June 29, 2019, DOI: `https://doi.org/10.1016/S0140-6736(19)31510-7`

10. *The State of the Nation: A Strategy for Healthier Longer Lives, All Party Parliamentary Group for Longevity (APPGL)*, February 2020, `https://indd.adobe.com/view/85a7129f-f900-41fa-9a9d-024d13f0aaf5`

11. *Well-being, Office for National Statistics*, `https://www.ons.gov.uk/peoplepopulationandcommunity/wellbeing`

12. *Advancing our health: prevention in the 2020s – consultation document, Department of Health & Social Care*, published on 22 July 2019, `https://www.gov.uk/government/consultations/advancing-our-health-prevention-in-the-2020s/advancing-our-health-prevention-in-the-2020s-consultation-document`

13. *Genes and human diseases, Human Genomics in Global Health,* `https://www.who.int/genomics/public/geneticdiseases/en/index3.html`

14. *The Nature of Nurture: Refining the Definition of the Exposome, Gary W. Miller and Dean P. Jones, Toxicol Sci.,* 137(1): 1-2, 2013 Nov 9. DOI: `10.1093/toxsci/kft251`

15. *Twins' Early Development Study (TEDS): a multivariate, longitudinal genetic investigation of language, cognition and behavior problems from childhood through adolescence, Bonamy R Oliver and Robert Plomin, Twin Res Hum Genet,* 2007 Feb;10(1):96-105. DOI: `https://doi.org/10.1375/twin.10.1.96`

16. *Personal aging markers and ageotypes revealed by deep longitudinal profiling. Nat Med, Ahadi S., Zhou. W., Schüssler-Fiorenza Rose, S.M., et al.* 26, 83–90 (2020). `https://doi.org/10.1038/s41591-019-0719-5`

17. *Biomarkers and ageing: The clock-watcher, W. Wayt Gibbs,* 08 April 2014, *Nature* 508, 168–170 (10 April 2014) DOI:`10.1038/508168a`

18. *Reversal of epigenetic aging and immunosenescent trends in humans, Gregory M. Fahy, Robert T. Brooke, James P. Watson, Zinaida Good, Shreyas S. Vasanawala, Holden Maecker, Michael D. Leipold, David T. S, Lin, Michael S. Kobor and Steve Horvath,* First published: 08 September 2019, `https://doi.org/10.1111/acel.13028`

19. *Complementing the Genome with an "Exposome": The Outstanding Challenge of Environmental Exposure Measurement in Molecular Epidemiology, Christopher Paul Wild, American Association for Cancer Research, Volume 14, Issue 8,* pp. 1847-1850, Published August 15, 2005, `https://cebp.aacrjournals.org/content/14/8/1847`

20. *The Nature of Nurture: Refining the Definition of the Exposome, Gary W. Miller and Dean P. Jones, Toxicological Sciences, Volume 137, Issue 1,* January 2014, Pages 1-2, DOI: `https://doi.org/10.1093/toxsci/kft251`

21. *Gut microbes could unlock the secret to healthy aging, European Society of Cardiology,* August 2020: `www.sciencedaily.com/releases/2020/08/200827101839.htm`

22. *Allostatic load and ageing: linking the microbiome and nutrition with age-related health, Paul G. Shiels, Sarah Buchanan, Colin Selman, Peter Stenvinkel, Biochem Soc Trans* 30 August 2019; 47 (4): 1165–1172. DOI: `https://doi.org/10.1042/BST20190110`

23. *The Game Changers*: `https://en.wikipedia.org/wiki/The_Game_Changers`

24. *Sales of beef and pork plunge as Britons choose vegan diet, Ben Webster, The Times,* January 2020, `https://www.thetimes.co.uk/article/red-meat-sales-hit-as-800-000-people-go-vegetarian-kpz2k3xnz`

25. *How healthy is your vegan food?, Harry Wallop,* Monday June 17 2019, 12.01am BST, *The Times,* `https://www.thetimes.co.uk/article/fake-meat-faux-fish-dairy-free-ice-cream-how-healthy-is-your-vegan-food-tgdfn9qgk`

26. *Vegan diet would slash greenhouse gas emissions, Jonathan Leake and Iram Ramzan,* January 13 2019, 12:01am, The Sunday Times, `https://www.thetimes.co.uk/article/vegan-diet-would-slash-greenhouse-gas-emissions-txs3bjv0l`

27. *11 Industries Responding To The Meatless Revolution, CB Insights,* October 15, 2019, https://www.cbinsights.com/research/meatless-transforming-industries/?utm_source=CB+Insights+Newsletter&utm_campaign=6027b8ad8a-newsletter_general_Thurs_20191226&utm_medium=email&utm_term=0_9dc0513989-6027b8ad8a-92631697

28. *Lab-grown food will soon destroy farming – and save the planet, George Monbiot,* https://www.theguardian.com/commentisfree/2020/jan/08/lab-grown-food-destroy-farming-save-planet

29. *Let's make Britain wild again and find ourselves in nature, George Monbiot,* https://www.theguardian.com/commentisfree/2015/jul/16/britain-wild-nature-rewilding-ecosystems-heal-lives

30. *The natural world can help save us from climate catastrophe, George Monbiot,* https://www.theguardian.com/commentisfree/2019/apr/03/natural-world-climate-catastrophe-rewilding

31. *Baby boomers outdo millennials in green living: study, Oliver Morrison, Food Navigator,* February 2020 https://www.foodnavigator.com/Article/2020/02/17/Baby-boomers-outdo-millennials-in-green-living-study#

32. *Time to solve childhood obesity: CMO special report: An independent report by former Chief Medical Officer (CMO) Professor Dame Sally Davies,* Published 10 October 2019, https://www.gov.uk/government/publications/time-to-solve-childhood-obesity-cmo-special-report

33. *Effects of Intermittent Fasting on Health, Aging, and Disease, Rafael de Cabo, Ph.D., and Mark P. Mattson, Ph.D.*, December 26, 2019, *N Engl J Med* 2019; 381:2541-2551, DOI: 10.1056/NEJMra1905136

34. *Study: Even a Little Walking May Help You Live Longer by Stacy Simon*, October 19, 2017, https://www.cancer.org/latest-news/study-even-a-little-walking-may-help-you-live-longer.html

35. *Is running associated with a lower risk of all-cause, cardiovascular and cancer mortality, and is the more the better? A systematic review and meta-analysis, Pedisic Z, Shrestha N, Kovalchik S, et al, British Journal of Sports Medicine* 2020; 54:898-905, http://dx.doi.org/10.1136/bjsports-2018-100493

36. *Even One Extra Walk a Day May Make a Big Difference, PHYS ED, The New York Times*, https://www.nytimes.com/2019/06/05/well/move/even-one-extra-walk-a-day-may-make-a-big-difference.html

37. *Regular Exercise May Keep Your Body 30 Years 'Younger', PHYS ED, The New York Times*, https://www.nytimes.com/2018/11/21/well/move/regular-exercise-may-keep-your-body-30-years-younger.html

38. *How Strenuous Exercise Affects Our Immune System, PHYS ED, The New York Times*, https://www.nytimes.com/2018/04/25/well/move/how-strenuous-exercise-affects-our-immune-system.html

39. *How Exercise Can Keep Aging Muscles and Immune Systems 'Young', PHYS ED, The New York Times*, https://www.nytimes.com/2018/03/14/well/move/how-exercise-can-keep-aging-muscles-and-immune-systems-young.html

40. *Facial Exercises May Make You Look 3 Years Younger, PHYS ED, The New York Times,* `https://www.nytimes.com/2018/01/10/well/move/facial-exercises-may-make-you-look-3-years-younger.html`

41. *How Exercise Can Boost Young Brains, Gretchen Reynolds,* October 8, 2014 12:01 AM, `https://well.blogs.nytimes.com/2014/10/08/how-exercise-can-boost-the-childs-brain/`

42. *For Your Brain's Sake, Keep Moving, Gretchen Reynolds,* October 4, 2017, `https://www.nytimes.com/2017/10/04/well/move/for-your-brains-sake-keep-moving.html`

43. *Running as the Thinking Person's Sport, Gretchen Reynolds,* Dec. 14, 2016, `https://www.nytimes.com/2016/12/14/well/move/running-as-the-thinking-persons-sport.html`

44. *How Exercise Might Keep Depression at Bay, Gretchen Reynolds,* Nov. 16, 2016, `https://www.nytimes.com/2016/11/16/well/move/how-exercise-might-keep-depression-at-bay.html`

45. *Vitality boss Adrian Gore is in for the long run: Meet Adrian Gore, the South African boss behind Vitality and Stanley the dachshund, Ivan Fallon, The Sunday Times,* Sunday November 25 2018, 12.01am GMT, `https://www.thetimes.co.uk/article/interview-vitality-boss-adrian-gore-is-in-for-the-long-run-9rhblkvwq`

46. *Ground-breaking study shows fitter bodies could lead to fitter economies, Vitality,* Wednesday 6 November 2019, `https://www.vitality.co.uk/media/fitter-bodies-could-lead-to-fitter-economies/`

47. *B-Secur:* `https://www.cbinsights.com/company/b-secur`

48. *Dan Burden*: `https://www.bluezones.com/about/ organization/our-team/dan-burden/`

49. *Dan Burden, Blue Zones Director of Innovation and Inspiration, Named One of "100 Urbanists of All Time, Blue Zones,* `https://www.bluezones.com/2018/01/ dan-burden-walkability-expert/`

50. *Toyota To Build Prototype City Of The Future,* Posted on 7 January 2020, `https://media.toyota. co.uk/2020/01/toyota-to-build-prototype-city- of-the-future/`

51. *The Rise Of Smart Cities, Research Webinar,* `https:// www.cbinsights.com/research/briefing/rise-of- smart-cities/`

52. *Parklets, London Living Street,* 2019, `https:// londonlivingstreets.com/parklets-campaign/`

53. *The 5 Biggest Smart Home Trends In 2020, Bernard Marr, Forbes,* January 2020, `https://www.forbes. com/sites/bernardmarr/2020/01/13/the-5- biggest-smart-home-trends-in-2020`

54. *Google, Amazon, and Apple join forces to develop IP-based smart home connectivity standard, Paul Sawers,* December 18, 2019 5:23 AM, `https://venturebeat. com/2019/12/18/google-amazon-and-apple-join- forces-to-develop-smart-home-connectivity- standard/`

55. *Apple's HomePod now supports multiple users, but it's a buggy mess, Jeremy Horwitz, VentureBeat,* November 1, 2019 11:28 AM, `https://venturebeat. com/2019/11/01/apples-homepod-now-supports- multiple-users-but-its-a-buggy-mess/`

56. *Project Connected Home over IP:* `https://www. connectedhomeip.com/`

57. *Zigbee Alliance*: `https://zigbeealliance.org/`

58. *How to dementia-proof your home, Cally Law, The Sunday Times*, Sunday March 31 2019, 12.01am GMT, `https://www.thetimes.co.uk/article/how-to-dementia-proof-your-home-wztmctqcq`

59. *Sweden's Queen Silvia joins Ikea chief to design 'dementia-friendly' homes*, Oliver Moody, Berlin, Tuesday December 31 2019, 12.01am GMT, The Times, `https://www.thetimes.co.uk/article/swedens-queen-silvia-joins-ikea-chief-to-design-dementia-friendly-homes-kjx2z99pk`

60. *Technology Integrated Health Management (TIHM), NHS Surrey and Borders*, 2020, `https://www.sabp.nhs.uk/tihm`

61. *Alcove*: `https://www.youralcove.com/`

62. *MySense: How It Works*, `https://www.mysense.ai/how-it-works`

63. *Link between health spending and life expectancy: The US is an outlier*, May 2017: `https://ourworldindata.org/the-link-between-life-expectancy-and-health-spending-us-focus`

64. *AI app reveals your biological age – and how to slow it down*, September 2020: `https://www.longevity.technology/ai-app-reveals-your-biological-age-and-how-to-slow-it-down/`

65. *The role of epigenetics in renal ageing*, June 2017: `https://www.nature.com/articles/nrneph.2017.78`

# CHAPTER 4

# MOVING SICKCARE TO WELL-BEING, THROUGH PREVENTION

*"There's no ivory tower of medicine anymore. As a patient, you are no longer just an element in a huge system of things that take care of you; you should take care of yourself with the help of amazing medical professionals and advanced technologies."*

*– Bertalan Meskó, The Medical Futurist*

*"If the premise is that there's no more money in the world, what can we do collectively? We've got to recreate healthcare in different ways. We have to reimagine healthcare to make our money go further.*

> *That's the reality of the economics of the world we're living in. We're facing an increase in population, more chronic diseases, and more burden on healthcare services. That's only going to get worse."*
>
> *— Shafi Ahmed,*
> *Futurist, Surgeon, Teacher, Entrepreneur*

Many people today don't feel in charge of their health, and expect others to manage it for them when things go wrong. Only some of us are using our biological, physiological, and behavioral data to understand ourselves, and take the steps that could help us lead healthier and happier lives. I freely admit that I am not one of these decisive few who measure everything, in the "quantified self-universe."

This is not for lack of trying. Feeling like a hypocrite for talking so much about health technology but never using the latest gadgets, I finally bought myself an Apple watch for my 55th birthday. But for 10 months, I only used a tiny fraction of the functions, and none of them had anything at all to do with my health! Yes, I loved taking calls on my wrist, and got really excited when I realized I could use my voice to transcribe a message back to my son while on the treadmill. But I had only taken an ECG reading once, after finally realizing you had to download an app for it. Thankfully, I showed no signs of **atrial fibrillation** (**AF**), the biggest risk factor for stroke. But was I tracking my sleep, my heart rate (before, during and after exercise), the number of steps I was taking? No, not at all! In fact, I constantly forgot to wear my watch in the gym.

What does this tell you, when someone who is obviously fascinated with health and technology can't be bothered? It shows I am human, and like a lot of people, am too busy, preoccupied, and stressed to take action on these constant intrusions and instructions on how to live my life.

Then everything changed for me when COVID-19 hit. Faced with lockdown for weeks, sitting in front of a laptop all day at home, and not being able to go to the gym, my whole routine had to change.

I had to take up running for a start (I hate running). And then started to use the ancient rowing machine in the cellar (bought second-hand when my sons started to row at school). And then doing yoga with Adriene on YouTube (first her easy 30-day program, and then more ambitious routines like Shakti Power Flow). Religiously. Every day for weeks on end.

Because I had a little more time, I finally worked out how to use my Apple Watch, and it quickly became a godsend to motivate myself to run (while offering an equally useful distraction technique with my newly compiled Spotify list).

It took the COVID-19 pandemic to hook me onto my smart watch.

The pandemic has certainly thrust into the spotlight this notion of health as our most precious asset. Long taken for granted by some, others are increasingly treasuring their health as a very positive side effect of this crisis. However, there are still many who could do more to nurture it, and some are still hell-bent on destroying it. Others are not aware of what they can do. But still the fact remains that too many people are trapped in environments causing them to be stressed, depressed, unable to act, or too pre-occupied with surviving day-to-day for their health to take priority. This is where systematic help is needed, and where government and other critical stakeholders need to act.

The COVID-19 situation has certainly stress-tested society in many respects; the data unfolding in the Western world shows that the deaths have been concentrated in older populations, especially those with underlying health problems, and in deprived communities.

The learnings from COVID-19 reinforce the fact that we must give priority to minimizing health inequalities and preventing ill health. We can achieve this through a focus on prevention, and by addressing the wider determinants of health.

A UK study[1] published in May 2020, the largest cohort study conducted by any country to date, quantified a range of clinical risk factors for death from COVID-19. The risk profile of people dying of COVID-19 was explored though a new approach to epidemiological research, the OpenSafely platform, leveraging very large datasets and timely data. This study found that people from Asian and black groups are at a markedly increased risk of in-hospital death from COVID-19, and contrary to previous assumptions, this is only partially attributable to pre-existing clinical risk factors or deprivation—further research into the drivers of this association is therefore urgently needed. Deprivation is also a major risk factor, again with little of the excess risk explained by co-morbidity or other risk factors.

Protecting our most vulnerable, guided by this research, has been at the forefront of the UK government's response to the crisis. However, there have been notable failings and criticisms, which have led to calls for a public enquiry on why the UK death toll is the worst in Europe.

Research has found that being obese increases the risk of needing hospital treatment for COVID-19[2]. About one in three British adults is clinically obese, classified as those with a **body mass index (BMI)** above 30. It is one of the highest rates in the Western world. Obesity is a risk factor for other health problems, such as diabetes and heart disease[3], which are also known to increase vulnerability to COVID-19.

Compelled to act by this data, the UK Prime Minister Boris Johnson, who came perilously close to death as a result of COVID-19 and with his BMI estimated to be 36 (putting him in the high risk group), declared a "War on Fat[4]." A signal for state interventionist policies to follow, the pandemic is providing an opportunity to encourage people to lead healthy lives, including eating less junk food and exercising more.

In the UK, a quarter of the population now has raised blood pressure, 4 million people have untreated hypertension, there will be 5.5 million people with type 2 diabetes in 10 years, and 70% of people aged 55+ have at least one obesity-related disease[5].

This is just the tip of the iceberg, and it's an unsustainable situation. All of us must take more responsibility as citizens, business leaders, think tank experts, politicians, and community champions to address the terrible burden of chronic diseases, most of which are preventable.

BC, "Before COVID-19", **noncommunicable diseases** (NCDs), including heart disease, strokes, cancer, diabetes, and chronic lung disease, were collectively responsible for almost 70% of all deaths worldwide according to WHO[6]. Almost three quarters of all NCD deaths, and 82% of the 16 million people who died prematurely, or before reaching 70 years of age, occur in low- and middle-income countries. The rise of NCDs has been driven by primarily four major risk factors: tobacco use, physical inactivity, the harmful use of alcohol, and unhealthy diets.

Like many other countries, the UK has been gripped in a healthcare crisis even before COVID-19 struck, with demand outstripping supply, made ever more crippling by a fast-growing aging population suffering from multi-morbidities. In the next 15 years, given our aging population, current estimates are that there will be some 16 million cases of dementia, arthritis, type 2 diabetes, and cancers in people aged 65 and over—twice as many as in 2015[7].

A holistic view of NCDs is needed. At the moment people are managed by a medical establishment with siloed notions of disease, but the latest science is showing how interconnected they are.

# Interconnected diseases

Our metabolism is comprised of biochemical reactions that keep us alive and work together in a coordinated manner that maintains good health. As metabolic coordination disintegrates, we start to age. Pair the disintegration with overnutrition and a sedentary lifestyle, and aging becomes the largest risk factor for most chronic NCDs.

The proportion of people suffering from more than one medical condition at the same time keeps slowly but steadily increasing. In high income countries like the UK or the USA, this multi-morbidity is mostly age-related, and slow demographic change has driven the steady increase in multi-morbidity. This trend will continue, and as multimorbidity has become more prevalent it's been studied more closely. There's been a shift in perception; multi-morbidity used to be thought of as a random collection of diseases and conditions accrued by a person over time. Now, it's starting to be recognized as a smaller set of largely predictable clusters of disease, all occurring in the same person. Of course, some multi-morbidities will occur entirely by chance; many, however, will be non-random, due to common genetic, behavioral, or environmental pathways to disease.

Type 2 diabetes is the gateway to multi-morbidity for many people; and, according to the Mayo Clinic, it's linked to Alzheimer's. Alzheimer's is the most common form of dementia, and it starts to develop in the brain up to two decades before symptoms of dementia begin to show. Researchers worldwide now agree that future treatments and preventions will have greatest benefit when given as early as possible in the disease. Some research studies have proposed that Alzheimer's disease should also be classified as a type of diabetes, called type 3 diabetes, with the hypothesis that it is triggered by a type of insulin resistance and insulin-like growth factor dysfunction that occurs specifically in the brain. Some people say that Alzheimer's is simply "diabetes in your brain."

"Metabesity" is a term coined by G. Alexander Fleming that refers to the constellation of cancer, cardiovascular and neurological diseases, diabetes, and the aging process itself, all of which share common metabolic root causes and potential preventive therapies. Targeting these metabolic underpinnings could be a productive approach to delaying, or even preventing, many or most of the chronic diseases of aging.

Premature and avoidable ill health degrades people's lives, local communities, and their economies. Up until COVID-19 struck, the developed world was largely ignoring this, and governments have failed to pursue the great gains that prevention, early detection, and mitigation can bring. Far more well-being and health can now be gained by preventing illnesses than by treating them; indeed, prevention will always be better than the best treatment. We now know better how to do so, but a change in public attitudes and cultural norms is critical to drive impact. Hopefully this will be one of the positive legacies of COVID-19 with the most impact.

## The move to prevention

For the UK's **National Health Service** (**NHS**) the pandemic has highlighted the urgency to promote prevention and early detection. BC the NHS faced massive increases in the number of people who will need treatment and care for preventable conditions—and great increases in demand for social care. The NHS spends many millions trying to keep people alive in hospitals for a few weeks at the end of their lives; yet it spends less than 5% of its budget[8] to prevent or arrest those diseases and impairments that degrade people's lives for many years.

Prevention is a central focus of the work I have co-led with Lord Geoffrey Filkin CBE for the **All Party Parliamentary Group for Longevity** (**APPGL**), and recently published in our report, *The Health of the Nation: A Strategy for Healthier Longer Lives.*

The NHS is one of the most efficient health systems in the world and delivers more activity per unit of funding than many other similar systems. However, it has never truly embraced prevention as a primary goal, and so its metrics and the preoccupation of its leadership focus on the delivery of care to sick patients, rather than the maintenance of health across the population, including the economically and socially disadvantaged.

The COVID-19 epidemic has made the case for prevention even more urgent and pressing. The APPGL National Strategy recommended increasing the budget the NHS spends on prevention from 5% to 15% by 2030, and shows how to achieve it, in terms of the focus of the health and social care system, the metrics by which we measure performance, and the nature of the leadership we need. Crucially, though, the general public needs to see itself as a key part of the change—doing what they can to keep healthy and well. Knowledge is key and digital health technologies can help nudge and incentivize people.

The lessons learned from the pandemic have led to innovative proposals to build "national health resilience" through a decentralized resilience model whereby we can strengthen the resilience of our personal health and community health and from there, build better national health. Employers could play a bigger role in helping individuals address their personal health risks and help with the related behavior change.

Inadequate data sharing, compromised by a lack of enabling data infrastructure, has increased calls for the science and innovation community to have better access to data from the public and private sectors to plug the data gaps and learn from data on healthy people—not just sick people—in the development of products and services to keep us healthy and well across the life course. Future fit models for data sharing to minimize our risk of future pandemics are explored in more detail in the next chapter.

My work with the **Academic Health Science Network (AHSN)** artificial intelligence (AI) program and the new **NHSX** team here in the UK for the past two years has focused on how best we can harness data-driven technologies to improve outcomes in health and healthcare.

This all started after meeting Melissa Ream, now the National AHSN AI lead for the national AHSN digital and AI group, at a health tech event in October 2017. I was chairing the session with Melissa and I distinctly remember having to manage a heckler who was asking many awkward questions about why we should ask people to be more involved in their health when it is the job of the NHS to do it.

I went up to the heckler afterwards to try and understand where he was coming from. It turned out that he'd had a key role setting up the NHS University (abolished in 2005) and he asked whether I had read the NHS Constitution. I knew I had at some point, so responded yes, but that I couldn't remember the exact details. He then went on a rant. He said that the principles of the NHS were that everyone should have access to NHS services free at the point of delivery. I agreed with him and voiced this whole-heartedly. So why was he so angry, I pondered?

What I realized pretty starkly was that no matter what I said, this person would not accept that it would be a good thing if people needed to use the NHS less and not more, because they were staying healthy. It was almost as if he was saying people have a right to live unhealthily, become chronically sick and use whatever NHS resources they can to be treated, rather than fix the problem at source. This cultural mindset trap is the single most important thing to change in the UK. We're a nation obsessed with the cherished institution that the NHS is (and I agree that it should be protected) but we don't realize that we need to become less dependent, even less addicted, to it.

Of course, we will always need great hospitals for medical treatments and emergencies, but I look forward to the day when the national headlines start announcing that due to reduced demand, hospitals are being shut down! Indeed, the Nordic countries have shown this can be done, and see closure of hospitals as an indicator of success with the nation's health.

All this made my chat afterwards with Melissa such a relief. She has been through the mill with many large scale "digital transformation" projects in her days with big management consulting firms and was now bringing her warm Texan charm and honed skills in diplomacy to the institution of the NHS.

Very soon after, Melissa invited me to help her start an AI ecosystem for the National AHSN Initiative. This lead to a big collaboration involving the Department of Health and NHS England, and resulted in the publication of "Accelerating Artificial Intelligence in Health and Social Care" in 2018, which then paved the way for a number of initiatives before the new NHSX division was launched in July 2019 to accelerate safe, ethical data-driven innovation in health.

Melissa and I have had the pleasure of working with exceptional individuals, including Indra Joshi, who is the Director of AI at NHSX and who has been heavily involved in the national COVID-19 response.

It has been fascinating to be involved right from the very beginning of developing the AI ecosystem, from identifying what companies and internal NHS teams are starting to use AI (and not just *saying* they are using AI) to working out how to overcome the barriers to successfully deploy data-driven technologies to benefit people. Key issues to address include data access and interoperability, commercial arrangements, ethical frameworks, workforce training, and public engagement to protect trust between citizen and state.

# How AI will change the focus of medicine

*"We're using AI and machine learning to look backwards and analyze significant amounts of retrospectively collected clinical data and prospectively collected clinical and digital data, to try and identify the relevant digitally collected endpoints that relate to clinical outcomes and disease progression. We're using AI because of the enormity of the data, to allow us to analyze the data critically, to identify patterns within the data, and enable us to build algorithmic models to detect neurodegenerative disease fingerprints in individuals at a much earlier stage than we do today."*

*– Carol Routledge, Alzheimer's Research UK*

The potential of AI is undeniable in health and healthcare, and AI has been driving many of the innovations to help individuals and communities cope with the COVID-19 pandemic—for example, there has been a rapid rise in technologies to enable remote consultations with doctors and tools to enable social interactions, especially for those vulnerable individuals in self-isolation.

Over the next few years, AI will transform business, home, health, wealth, and education. The technology is already improving people's lives, from intelligent personal assistants in our personal affairs (from predicting weather to selecting our partners on dating sites), to systems that protect our money from fraudsters. One day soon, AI could monitor and analyze the "health of the community," covering everything from environmental indicators through to levels of crime, engagement in public spaces, and discussions on web boards or social media—sort of what they are already doing in China!

There are many developments underway to harness this technology to predict risk of disease, diagnose, manage, and cure conditions, and build better environments to reduce stress, encourage physical activity, and nurture our health.

AI could change our relationship with our own health but also our interaction with the medical profession; it is interesting to note that people have adapted very quickly to remote consultations with their doctors during periods of the COVID-19 lockdown.

Treating unspecific symptoms requires experience, intuition, effective decision-making, and trust, which is a significant hurdle for machines[9]. After millions of years of evolution, humans have developed a capacity for contextual intuition that enables trained doctors to make sensible and timely decisions in uncertain, data-scarce environments. Even the most sophisticated AI systems that we have today would need to be improved significantly in order to mimic this ability.

Communicating with patients poses an even greater challenge for machines. Explaining the many nuances of a mysterious disease such as cancer requires emotional intelligence and the ability to build trust with patients, by delivering information effectively. Doctors need to be empathetic and understand cultural contexts too, so that they can consider a patient's social background when administering care.

For the foreseeable future, machines probably will not be able to match humans in helping chronically ill patients whose prognosis remains uncertain. Still, despite intelligent machines' limitations, they will become more and more widely used, to augment human's abilities even in intuitive medicine. Machines are already providing more data, upon which physicians base their diagnostic and treatment decisions. Machines are increasingly monitoring patients as well, helping to prevent human errors in hospitals and pharmacies. Increasingly, many more ancillary functions such as admissions, scheduling, and discharges will be automated.

Eric Topol, a leading cardiologist who has written several books including the acclaimed *Deep Medicine*, believes that the biggest problem in healthcare today is the erosion of the relationship between doctors and their patients, due to the lack of time doctors have to concentrate on care and compassion. Keyboards and screens have led to depersonalization of the doctor-patient connection. He believes that technology, therefore, should enhance humanity as the ultimate objective[10]. What this should mean for doctors is the ability to have all of the data about a person assimilated and analyzed, to have scans and slides read. That liberates doctors from keyboards so they can look patients in the eye and understand them as human beings, first and foremost.

It seems obvious that we can't pin our hopes on AI unless the workforce understands it and engages with it. This became obvious to me when I went to get a breast scan two years ago (in the NHS all women over age 50 are invited to get screened for breast cancer regularly). As my right breast was being clamped into the scanner, I asked the radiology nurse, a young New Zealander in her mid-twenties, a simple question about when she expected artificial intelligence to start affecting her job. She thought for a second, laughed, and replied with confidence "not in my lifetime."

That says it all.

Fortunately, **Health Education England** (HEE) and wider NHS arms length body partners are on the case to address this, not just for healthcare professionals but for citizens too. Alan Davies, HEE's Innovative Programs and Partnerships Director, says that, spurred by the need to increase the use of digital technology to cope with the pandemic, there has been a significant push on digital literacy.

For example, the planned NHS@Home programme leverages the NHS England Personalization team, NHSX, the **Empower the Person** (ETP) team, HEE's Digital Readiness team, and specialist third sector partners to target raising the level of citizen literacy via community digital champions—aiming ultimately to close the "digital divide" and reduce exclusion.

HEE's Library and Knowledge Management services are also simultaneously planning to progress a wider program of health literacy (for example, understanding what "vital signs" actually mean) via community libraries, prisons, and schools over the next 5 years as part of the forthcoming NHS People Plan.

# Diagnostics

Diagnostics is one of the best examples of an area where AI can help medicine. For example, we can use algorithms in radiology and imaging to help identify problems in x-rays and scans.

AI can be used more readily in diagnostics for two main reasons. Firstly, most radiology images are in a standardized digital format. That is, they provide structured input data for training purposes, compared to the unstructured and often non-digital data of health records, for example. This also means there are good datasets available for retrospective algorithm training and performance validation.

Secondly, image recognition machine learning techniques are more developed as a result than in other areas of medicine. The evidence so far shows that algorithms can, within constrained conditions, be used to identify the presence of malignant tumors in images of breasts, lungs, skin, and brain as well as pathologies of the eye, to name a few.

For example, AI is helping ophthalmologists to diagnose diabetic retinopathy—an underdiagnosed cause of blindness and a complication of diabetes—with an algorithm. In the consumer space, Apple's series 4 smart-watch app uses a deep learning algorithm to detect atrial fibrillation (AF). AF is asymptomatic for most and is a leading risk factor for stroke. This is the only app I seriously use in my Apple watch.

In dermatology, First Derm can screen 43 common skin diseases, from STDs to skin cancer using an AI algorithm-driven service that patients can use on their phones.

Over the last 5 years First Derm has collected a dataset of over 350,000 "amateur" smartphone dermatology images and adds another 15,000 images per month. The AI approach can give an anonymous quick screening of a skin concern that will let you know what next steps to take, and it also functions as a decision support tool for virtual care clinics.

AI is getting so good now that it could soon remove the need for a final human checking step in imaging protocols. At a recent AI Award event in the UK, work was presented by pioneering researchers who trained an AI algorithm on human biopsy slides to not only recognize the abnormalities inherent in successfully diagnosing a tumor in the material but also to recognize the lack of any abnormality—thereby removing the need for human checking (and freeing up valuable time and resources). The award judges were flummoxed, concerned that giving the award effectively endorsed the step towards replacing human checking—even though the AI model represented a superior system. This example signals the huge culture change challenge facing the wider adoption of AI in the coming decades in both the health and care profession as well as the wider public.

Along with the incredible advances we have seen in computer vision, and the sheer availability of data, it is perhaps not a surprise that AI has found its initial niche in diagnostics. However, AI is also fast emerging as a major tool to enhance operational efficiency in the complex, data-driven environments found in hospitals and other healthcare institutions.

# Clinical efficiency

In clinical settings, AI can help clinicians work more efficiently. More accurate diagnoses and predictions, powered by AI, improve both the productivity of healthcare workers and the health outcomes for patients.

One example is how AI is being used to identify patients at risk of unplanned hospital admissions in the Health Navigator program[11] at York teaching hospital in the UK. By highlighting these patients, nurses were deployed to help coach them over a six-month period on how to improve their health and reduce the risk of visiting A&E. The trial resulted in a 30% reduction in unplanned hospital admissions, and a 25% reduction in planned admissions.

Another interesting example, inspired by the use of AI in transport logistics, is an "AI-as-a-service" platform, Kortical, that can predict supply and demand for platelets for all the hospitals in England, taking into account diverse data such as weather and bank holidays. The AI predicts supply, which varies with who comes in, and which blood type and volume of platelets they donate, as well as demand, 1 to 7 days out, and finally the platform optimizes for logistics.

Finally, Streams is a mobile medical assistant app for clinicians. It was developed by the DeepMind Health team in collaboration with clinicians at the Royal Free London NHS Foundation Trust to help identify patients at risk of **acute kidney injury** (**AKI**). The app uses the existing national AKI algorithm to flag patient deterioration and supports the review of clinical information at the bedside. An independent evaluation showed that the app speeds up detection and treatment and prevents missed cases.

AI can yield efficiency gains to every part of the healthcare system— starting from medical research and drug development.

## AI-driven drug discovery and development

While AI can be used in personalized health prevention, to minimize our risk of disease, it can also be used to speed up the development of drugs we need when we fall ill. AI is disrupting the drug discovery and development processes, cutting costs and gaining much faster approvals while reducing errors.

Nearly $140 billion is spent globally on pharmaceutical R&D each year and yet results in only 30 to 40 new drug approvals. The R&D process, including how clinical trials are conducted, is inefficient but new tech companies are providing a smarter and quicker path for drug R&D, industry regulations, and new tools. There are many exciting ventures in this area.

BenevolentAI, for example, uses the predictive power of its AI algorithm to design new molecules, extracting a new hypothesis based on a knowledge graph composed of over a billion relationships between genes, targets, diseases, proteins, and drugs. Currently working with AstraZeneca and Novartis for example, BenevolentAI's machine learning capabilities systematically analyzes data to find connections between facts, and AI-based reasoning is used to extrapolate previously unknown connections at a rate and level of complexity that humans in the old pharmaceutical model can't do.

Insilico Medicine, as profiled in the Introduction, deploys a comprehensive drug discovery engine, which uses millions of samples and multiple data types to discover signatures of disease and identify the most promising targets for billions of molecules that already exist or can be generated de novo with the desired set of parameters. Generating novel molecular structures for diseases both with and without known targets, Insilico is now pursuing drug discovery in aging, cancer, fibrosis, Parkinson's disease, Alzheimer's disease, ALS, diabetes, and many others.

Insilico has been quick to respond to the COVID-19 crisis, and has been prioritizing target discovery, drug repurposing, and de novo drug design for the SARS-CoV-2 targets[12] in collaboration with a large number of groups and companies globally. It is clear that COVID-19 does not treat all age groups equally and is very different from many other infections. Many of the expected interventions such as vaccines and therapeutic and symptomatic treatments will not work as well in the elderly population.

Insilico are proposing to run clinical trials for low-dose rapamycin and RAD001 for prevention of COVID-19 and possibly even for treatment as single agents or in combination with Metformin, NAD+ boosters (commonly sold as supplements), and possibly other geroprotectors.

## AI and precision health

The ability for AI to develop precise drugs and other interventions to interact specifically with an individual's inherent propensity to disease and/or the disease itself is at the heart of personalized health.

This new approach in medicine that is predictive, preventive, personalized, and participatory is called "P4 medicine" and holds great promise to reduce the burden of chronic diseases by harnessing technology and an increasingly better understanding of environment-biology interactions, evidence-based interventions, and the underlying mechanisms of chronic diseases.

AI is the driving force behind precision medicine, using information about a person's environment, lifestyle, and biology, including in their DNA, to diagnose and treat diseases. By analyzing a patient's information, doctors can prescribe the treatments that are most likely to be effective, while minimizing drug reactions and unwanted side effects. The hope is that precision medicine will more accurately predict which treatment and prevention strategies will work best for a particular patient.

Until the scope of precision medicine surpasses that of intuitive medicine, healthcare professionals will continue to make medical decisions and interpret the data. The challenges we need to overcome before we "let the machines take over" are significant.

Not only will healthcare providers have to develop and adopt new technology, they will also have to collect, aggregate, and share the vast amounts of patient data. For AI to do its job it needs data, lots of it, to make intelligent diagnoses, advice, and predictions.

But it also needs the right data in a format that is machine-readable: data that is findable, accessible, interoperable, and re-usable (FAIR).

In theory, scientists and doctors should have access to a vast resource of genomic sequencing data and health records—helping them discover cures and treatments for every type of disease. But the reality is very different, with data locked in silos and often not even digitized; and only a small proportion of people have had their genomes sequenced.

AI can address some of this shortfall by leveraging deep learning approaches to overcome the obstacles inherent in large datasets and unstructured data.

The research community has started using AI-based tools within the Genomics England research environment (which currently contains over 100,000 genomes and over 2.5 billion clinical data points). For example, researchers are using machine learning methods to identify genetic mutation signatures associated with certain cancers, helping to identify and classify sub-types of the disease and to identify targets for new treatments. This has the potential to improve cancer diagnosis by making better predictions of disease progression, and to better stratify patients for more effective and efficient treatment. This could be key to delivering on the promises of the NHS Long-Term Plan to diagnose three-quarters of all cancers at stage 1 or 2 by 2028. Similar work is ongoing with rare disease, to identify driver mutations of particular conditions.

Developing models will be able to better predict the severity of outcomes based on genomic and clinical data. The 100,000 Genomes Project has recently been expanded to see 1 million whole genomes sequenced by the NHS and UK Biobank in five years, with the ambition to have 5 million people agreeing to have their genomes sequenced in the next 5 years to help UK citizens live longer better as a result of the insights gained from the data.

This data will be augmented by consumer DNA testing too as the cost of genetic testing comes down. However, there is the risk that private companies will be competing against each other and creating even more data silos, while deriving large profits from selling it to third parties, usually without sharing the earnings with the data donor. This could stifle research and innovation and prevent medicine and healthcare moving forward at the pace it should.

In response to the COVID-19 outbreak, the UK launched a whole genome sequence alliance in March 2020[13], backed by a £20 million investment, to map the spread of coronavirus. The venture will allow scientists and clinicians to unlock the secrets of the disease; uncovering the genetic code could arm public health agencies and clinicians with a unique, cutting-edge tool to combat COVID-19 and future pandemics.

# The ethics of data

> *"If we took every kind of search in the UK, we might be able to look at a lot of different factors for determinants of population health. However, this is delving into a different scope for secondary uses of data—something we need to have an open dialogue about as we might discover we have different views on sharing for wider benefit (for example to reduce health inequalities)....there is a lot of potential, but it needs to be done in an ethical way."*
>
> *– Indra Joshi, NHSX*

Ethical issues in AI are a big concern. Nowhere has this been highlighted with such force than the dilemmas posed by the COVID-19 pandemic. While the pandemic has thrown up the lack of data sharing infrastructure that could have predicted and avoided the pandemic in the first place, it has also raised the geopolitical tensions between citizen empowerment and state surveillance and the race for technological dominance between the USA and China.

As we have been seeing in countries like China, Singapore, and South Korea, intelligent sharing of smartphone location data has saved lives by tracing and testing the contacts of confirmed COVID-19 cases. But in the West, we have been woefully ill prepared—and many of the obstacles to data sharing are not just technological. To collect data at scale we need to have public trust and data sharing structures that empower citizens—and there is significant media attention on the issues of privacy and giving governments or Big Tech companies even greater control.

Ethical concerns abound in other areas of health data. There is big money in clinical trials using genomics data, but most data donors have not understood the value of their data, and have been commercially exploited, particularly in the developing world. However, new start-ups are trying to counter this. George Church, Harvard geneticist and co-founder of Nebula Genomics, for example, is aiming to sequence people's entire genomes and let them own it, allowing them to earn digital money by sharing it; this eliminates the middleman, so that people can sell their genomic data straight to drug companies and other data buyers. LunaDNA, another example, is aiming to "democratize genomics" through its community-owned platform.

Privacy concerns about data are ongoing, raised by high-profile cases such as Google's acquisition of DeepMind Health. In response to these and other ethical concerns with data, the UK has led the world in the development of the Code of Conduct for safe, responsibly applied AI for data-driven health technologies. This Code addresses transparency, accountability, liability, explicability, fairness, justice, and bias to minimize causing unintended harm, and ultimately, to ensure no-one gets left behind.

Many data-driven companies, small and large, that are in our homes right now have their sights on becoming our health coaches and healthcare providers, and since 2012 have invested most heavily in data management and analytics, wellness, and genomics.

According to CB Insights[14], the COVID-19 pandemic has generated a flurry of investment into areas like remote patient monitoring and telehealth but is also leading to a re-prioritization of health innovation to value-based care and the wider social determinants of health while tackling the very obvious inefficiencies in the US healthcare system, which relies on a transactional fee-for-service.

A greater focus on health prevention will be one of the positive legacies of the epidemic. Before COVID-19 the media were awash with announcements on innovations in AI that will make it easier to stay healthy. Recently, for example, researchers at the University of Warwick have shown how a non-invasive wearable sensor using AI can assess low glucose by tracking a patient's heart rate via ECG, meaning that diabetics may no longer need to use finger-prick tests.

The convergence of analytics technology, wearable and IoT devices, and machine learning has led to a new form of data for research, "digital biomarkers." A digital biomarker is a quantifiable indicator of a person's physiological and/or behavioral state captured via any number of connected devices, including wearable (that is, blood pressure monitors, actigraphy devices, or multi-sensor patches), implantable (that is, pacemakers, continuous glucose monitors), and IoT technologies (smart devices in the home, such as voice assistants, gait monitors, and pollution sensors).

The evolution of these devices, and the ability to remotely capture this data, is providing researchers with a windfall of novel real-time and near real-time insights. In combination with cognitive surveys and other validated instruments conducted via digital devices, this unbiased and ongoing flow of data will have profound implications for research in Alzheimer's disease, for example. Identifying digital biomarkers—or combinations of biomarkers (that is, sleep patterns, nocturnal blood pressure dipping, voice analysis)—that detect the early stages of Alzheimer's and other neurodegenerative diseases will help design possible interventions, whether lifestyle or drug, to delay or, one day, even cure the disease. This is the approach being taken by Alzheimer's Research UK's **early detection of neurodegenerative diseases** (**EDoN**) initiative, an initiative conceived and developed by Dr Carol Routledge (who is interviewed in this book).

This type of research could be accelerated through mass sharing of consumer data—where citizens donate their data for ethical research, also called "data philanthropy." Billions have been invested by pharmaceutical companies into potential treatments for dementia with no real cure yet in sight, yet digital biomarkers could help to identify interventions years before symptoms of cognitive decline begin.

One of the most interesting workshops I helped with in 2018 was looking at how consumer datasets could be harnessed for ethical aging research (working with Maxine Macintosh, a PhD student in neuro-informatics who founded One HealthTech). We invited companies like Mastercard, EDF Energy and retail groups holding vast datasets in the "non-sick" domain. I was wearing my hat working with UK Research & Innovation on the Healthy Ageing Industrial Challenge Fund, where my task was to excite companies on the opportunity to form collaborative ventures to help drive a marketplace for products and services to keep people healthy and well.

## Big Tech and our data

Apple, Amazon, and Google know the huge value there is in "non-sick" datasets, and they have the power, the customers, and the data to disrupt healthcare, betting on a future where they own consumer relationships and become the preferred one-stop shop for all "life services" in a new healthcare ecosystem that will feature medical-grade consumer applications in diagnostics (for example, Apple Watch, Amazon Echo) and therapeutics; a "clicks and bricks" delivery system for enhanced patient experience and convenience; and cloud computing and AI focused on personalized precision health.

Soon sensors on the outside of our bodies will start to migrate to our inner bodies. Alphabet's Verily branch is working on a miniaturized continuous blood glucose monitor, for example, that could assist diabetics in everyday treatment. Research on "smart dust," a dust-mote-sized system that can sense, store, and transmit data, has been progressing for years. Today, a "mote" is the size of an apple seed. Tomorrow, at the nanoscale, they'll float through our bloodstream, exploring one of the last great Terra Incognita—the interior of the human body.

How do we feel about these motes designed by Big Tech infiltrating our bodies? How will the law keep up with this invasion of body and privacy by the most powerful companies in the world, and how will we ensure this trawling of data is done in an ethical way?

## Data for the public good, not profit

Big Tech senses a big opportunity to take over our health. And has for some time, because data is the most precious asset on earth and, unlike oil, grows in value the more it is used. Governments need to understand this too.

We have already seen some nations moving fast, like China, which is collecting data on their citizens—who have no choice in the matter—to create the biggest citizen dataset in the world to fuel China's social credit program and their ambitions to lead the world in AI, as described in the Introduction. This data collection will extend to genomic data too—with sequencing becoming cheaper and more reliable and as research is advancing to the point where genetic findings can drive prevention and underpin treatments. According to Peter Diamandis, China has begun centralizing healthcare data, tackling a major roadblock to developing longevity and healthcare technologies (particularly AI systems): scattered, dispersed, and unlabeled patient data.

Backed by the Chinese government, China's largest tech companies—particularly Tencent—have made strong entrances into the healthcare market. Just recently, Tencent participated in a $154 million financing round for China-based healthcare AI unicorn iCarbonX. Hoping to develop a complete digital representation of your biological self, iCarbonX has acquired numerous U.S. personalized medicine start-ups. Considering Tencent's own Miying healthcare AI platform—aimed at assisting healthcare institutions in AI-driven cancer diagnostics—Tencent is quickly expanding into the drug discovery space, participating in two multimillion-dollar, U.S.-based AI drug discovery deals just this year.

Tencent's WeChat has entered healthtech too and is starting to do deals with other countries as part of its international ambitions; for example, Tencent recently partnered with the UK's Babylon Health, a virtual healthcare assistant start-up whose app now allows Chinese WeChat users to message their symptoms and receive immediate medical feedback.

Alibaba is another Chinese giant moving into healthtech, and released its cloud-based AI medical platform, ET Medical Brain, to augment healthcare processes through everything from diagnostics to intelligent scheduling.

In response to COVID-19, China has amalgamated COVID contact tracing into WeChat and AliPay, using augmented reality, data uploaded by individuals, and the ability to scan QR codes in order to manage flows of people.

As described earlier, other countries, like Estonia and Finland, are already harnessing their data safely and ethically to drive new capabilities, industries, jobs, and prosperity.

The UK has a once-in-a-lifetime chance, right now, to get into gear and leverage its national data assets to become the world leader in ethical AI in the post-COVID "new normal" period ahead.

The UK has rich and diverse datasets and these have the potential to bring significant societal and economic benefits by enhancing and maintaining the nation's health. While mining medical records for patterns to furnish key insights into health and care, as demonstrated by the OpenSafely study mentioned earlier in this chapter, is still in its early days, it is most advanced in Britain for two reasons[15]. The first is that the NHS has created a vast medical market dominated by large patient-record companies; the second is that primary care is the first point of call for healthcare and they hold the most unified datasets, "from cradle to grave," in the world. This contrasts the situation in China, where people go straight to hospital. In Scandinavian countries that do have joined-up records, their small, homogenous populations make them less interesting for research. The system in the USA is highly fragmented with many private providers.

To improve our health, we need to move beyond data in healthcare, and study data from healthy people. Presently, health data research is focused on "sick data" (that is, NHS data) when healthcare comprises only 10-15% of the overall determinants of health. We need to broaden the data view, to encompass the wider determinants of health (60% behavioral, social, and psychological, 30% biological/genomic), and leverage insights and solutions from data science across the life course to deliver improvements in health and increase healthspan.

But the public sector needs to be engaged and reassured on ethical issues before open data approaches and data philanthropy, where data can be donated for the public good, can become more widespread and create an ethical data alternative to data models driven purely by profit.

Big Tech sees commercial opportunities in the UK's rich "birth to death" dataset in the NHS, creating healthcare apps or medical devices that could be sold to health providers or exported across the world too. However, the public are increasingly uneasy about Big Tech getting ever more involved in our lives, including health. There have been many media stories about the NHS treasure trove of data being "raided and profiteered by profit-hungry data power grabbers." Also, that if the NHS hands multinational companies control over identifying citizens, curating and integrating their personal data integration and delivering care apps, the UK will lose sovereignty over data and digital innovation—particularly at a time when Britain is trying to secure a global leadership position in AI outside the EU.

In response, there are moves afoot to devise a clear strategy for realizing the value of NHS data that will influence the shape and terms of its data partnerships with Big Tech—with policy informed by a better understanding of what the public sees as fair regarding value sharing (not only data sharing) and evidence on the value of NHS data assets and potential value-sharing mechanisms.

But we need the right data infrastructure too, and the right mixture of national and regional approaches to create the best environment to leverage data for the benefit of its citizens.

## Moving from national to regional data models

Recent health data research and digital innovation investments have been concentrated in disease-specific, hospital-centered precision medicine, in national digital infrastructure, and in the best-funded biomedical research centers.

Regions not covered by these investments are some of the most deprived, with high disease burdens and grave inequalities, and they are potentially the UK's most valuable data-generating communities. The North of England did not receive substantial investment in the **Digital Innovation Hub** managed by Health Data Research UK (HDRUK) that aims to become a UK-wide life sciences ecosystem providing responsible and safe access to health data, technology, science and research, and innovation services.

The HDRUK system is based on a national hub-spoke model and its first priority has been in clinical trials and treatment. Regional data models might work better for communities and their citizens, especially in "left-behind areas" with the worst healthy life expectancies.

Professor Iain Buchan is behind one such regional model—the **Civic Data Cooperative (CDC)** model. I was introduced to Iain by Siddhartha Chaturvedi, who leads Health and Responsible AI for the AI for Society program at Microsoft. Iain is Executive Dean for Population Health and Chair in Public Health and Clinical Informatics at the University of Liverpool, and Director of Digital Strategy and Partnerships for Liverpool Health Partners. He previously founded and grew the UK's largest health informatics research team at Manchester, raising over £100m in funding and publishing over 250 papers, and has spawned new scientific, engineering, and social approaches to health data, including the impactful Connected Health Cities (referred to in the Introduction) and the #DataSavesLives movement.

So, given his background, I trust he knows his stuff. He is proposing a move away from the national hub-spoke model to a civic data model based on a network of CDC. He is setting one up in Liverpool, one of the poorest areas in the UK. The big idea behind it is that data is seen as a currency for inclusive economic growth and service improvement in the local area, with the local community more comfortable with the idea of sharing their data out of civic belonging and pride.

Any value that is created through local data can be fed back into the local community, much like electricity on the National Grid.

In this model, "Citizens' Juries" decide on new data sharing partnerships. Data governance activities are accountable to elected members and thus to the public to build and preserve trust. Trustworthy national infrastructure is used wherever possible to link data while preserving individual privacy. The CDC is constituted to be part of a national/international grid of regions that can borrow strength from larger numbers of data across the network (for example, for studying rare diseases).

The CDC model is interesting and begins to answer the "the future is here—just not evenly distributed" issue. It could be an interesting model to test out harnessing insights from both "sick" and "non-sick" datasets through an "Open Life" data framework described in the next section.

AI has the potential to level up access to good health and healthcare around the word—ensuring the future is evenly distributed. In many ways the least developed nations have an advantage over more developed countries—not burdened by legacy systems and old ways of thinking, and enabled by mass access to cheap but powerful new tools like smartphones, we will see more and more examples of poor countries "leapfrogging" richer ones using the latest technology.

The COVID-19 experience has highlighted the potential for "decentralized health resilience", and models like Iain Buchan's CDC model are emerging as powerful vehicles to encourage civic data sharing at local levels (where trust can be cultivated and nurtured) in the development of solutions that address local problems. Professor Iain Buchan has argued that if we had the national grid of civic data cooperatives in place alongside disciplined national management of shared algorithms, the UK would have been better placed to respond to COVID-19.

Even in the absence of local Public Health Services we have seen the power of public services and community groups that have self-organized well during the COVID crisis.

## Evolution of the doctor-patient relationship

Through the ages we have always viewed our doctors with reverence and respect, and many still see them as authority figures. There is something about this bond of trust we seek and hold dear with those who look after us; and something profound and reassuring about the Hippocratic Oath that stipulates, first, "do no harm." Some are saying that we need a new oath as we see technology changing the relationship between doctor and patient, with the emphasis changing from "What's the matter with you?" to "What matters to you?" Everywhere we're seeing the phrase "no decision about me without me," which shows how patients are really becoming far more involved in their healthcare, and this can only be a good thing. But there is still so much to do to change cultural norms, at least in the Western world, away from seeing health equating to "sick care" when it really should be regarded as our greatest personal and societal asset to protect.

There is a lot of wisdom in the practice of ancient Chinese medicine, where patients only paid their doctors when they stayed well!

## Conclusions

We have seen how technology has made our lives easier in many ways. On the other hand, we need to avoid the temptation of sitting on our sofas all day lulled by the sheer convenience of being able to do everything from the palm of our hands!

Rather than consume we need to contribute to and be active participants in our health.

Mass data sharing by citizens could fuel the largest research program ever contemplated in the UK—harnessing data as a public good in an ethical way that Westerners would find acceptable from a social and privacy perspective, and driving the development of desirable products and services to keep us healthy and well.

We may balk at the idea of Google nudging us into positive behaviors while profiting from our data, and we may be horrified at the idea of the State amassing all data on our lives to fuel a social credit policy like they do in China—but could we one day find it quite acceptable that the NHS provides rewards for walking or vouchers to eat healthier foods? Why not invest more taxpayers' money into prevention rather than yet more hospitals where none of us want to be?

AI could be harnessed in this future vision of health. With smart regulation and ethical practices the public can hopefully trust that AI is being used properly and safely. The following interviews will show you how—from potentially finding out how to stop or treat dementia, to ensuring we harness technologies in a way that leaves no one behind and we care for people in the most human way possible.

# Interviews

The following interviews are with experts at the cutting edge of science, technology, and the future of medicine. Carol Routledge is an expert in digital biomarkers that may one day help us find the cause and cure for dementia; Shafi Ahmed is probably the world's best known futurist and surgeon, having live beamed the first surgery in 360 virtual reality to the world in 2016; Indra Joshi is the head of AI at the new technology arm of the NHS, and a leader in the ethics of AI; Michelle Hawkins-Collins, formerly head of Futures at Virgin, is now a gerontologist and expert in end-of-life care; and Bertalan Mesko, also known as The Medical Futurist, gives us a glimpse of what the future of medicine might look like.

# Carol Routledge

*CMO/CSO, Small Pharma; Former Research Director, Alzheimer's Research UK and Managing Director, Early Detection of Neurodegenerative Diseases (EDoN) global initiative*

I first met Carol, who was Research Director at Alzheimer's Research UK, at a workshop on harnessing consumer datasets for ethical aging research in 2019 that I helped organize and chair with Maxine Mackintosh, who at the time was finishing off her PhD in neuro-informatics at UCL (and had the idea in the first place, being the trailblazer she is). At the time I was helping Innovate UK find companies for the Healthy Ageing Industrial Strategy Challenge Fund bids. Carol was one of the participants and there were about 100 other delegates, including from some big companies like MasterCard, IBM, and AXA, who we mixed and matched into groups to see how best we could leverage "non-sick" consumer datasets to identify aging biomarkers for ethical research purposes. It was early days, and companies were just cottoning on to the potential value of their consumer data being linked to other datasets to drive developments in aging research, including predicting risks and identifying interventions in early stage cognitive decline.

Since then I have gotten to know Carol better through her involvement on the strategic advisory board for the All-Party Parliamentary Group for Longevity behind the development of The Health of the Nation: A Strategy for Healthier Longer Lives. In the science, genomics, and technology advisory discussions (expertly guided by Lord James O'Shaughnessy), a lot of discussion was had on the role of aging biomarkers to detect signs of Alzheimer's disease earlier and accelerate the identification of interventions (whether lifestyle or drugs) to minimize risks, delay progression, or even cure the disease.

A day before the launch of the APPG's National Strategy on 12<sup>th</sup> February, Alzheimer's Research UK announced it was launching a global initiative, **Early Detection of Neurodegenerative diseases (EDoN)**, to harness and analyze a wealth of digital data to develop signatures of disease—or "fingerprints"—that can be detected using wearable technologies. Developing digital fingerprints that can be detected using phone apps and/or wearable technologies like smart watches would provide a low-cost approach to identifying those most at risk of disease, and research shows that 85% of UK adults would be willing to take a test that could tell them if they were in the early stages of a disease like Alzheimer's, even before symptoms show.

The collaboration aims to secure at least £67m over the first six years, with an ambition to attract up to £100m of total investment by 2030 to build and trial its diagnostic device on a large scale. Initial funds towards the initiative have already been secured from Bill Gates and Iceland Foods Charitable Foundation. With potential new treatments for early Alzheimer's on the horizon, Alzheimer's Research UK believes that now is a critical time to act to identify very early brain changes in diseases like Alzheimer's. EDoN, of which Carol Routledge is Managing Director, sees Alzheimer's Research UK join forces with leading organizations in data science, clinical, and neurodegenerative research to collect and analyze clinical and digital health data such as sleep, gait, and speech patterns, to develop early digital fingerprints of diseases like Alzheimer's.

**Tina Woods**: In your view, what are the key points or messages that people should understand about living longer with AI?

**Carol Routledge**: The first thing to understand is that AI facilitates what we are all doing. I don't think it's this huge new invention of something completely different to what we normally do, but it is something that facilitates and will facilitate a lot of what we do. AI is clearly beneficial, but I do realize it's quite difficult to understand exactly what AI does and doesn't do and what it is and isn't.

In terms of living longer, I work for Alzheimer's Research UK and focus very much on research into understanding, treating, preventing, and diagnosing the diseases that cause dementia. For me, rather than just living longer with AI, it's really about living longer healthily. I don't think we should be thinking that we all want to live till we're 120. I don't know whether it is good for world economics to live until you're 120!

What we really want to do is ensure that in those later years in life we are able to live incredibly healthily, and using AI and machine learning and all of the other computer-generated enhancements that we can create with AI have got to benefit us living longer healthily.

**Tina Woods:** What technology or use of AI do you think will have the biggest impact in helping people live longer, better lives now, and five and ten years from now?

**Carol Routledge:** AI and tech will have a huge role and already are having a huge role. Focusing on dementia and the causes of dementia, one of those roles is care. A number of researchers, as well as companies and organizations, are looking at how you help people live in their homes for longer.

There are all kinds of digital technology, and rapid analysis of the data from it, which can help people to stay in their homes more safely. Small sensors are able to monitor various different symptoms of a person; that can include monitors for movement, wearables that track when you go and turn on the kettle to make a cup of tea, how long it takes you to remember you turned it on and come back, how many times you turn it on before you actually make a cup of tea. It all starts to talk about your memory, your cognitive function and thought process, and how confused or not you are.

There's a lot of in-house technology that measures a number of different parameters regarding behavior and physiology from people.

That may help understand what stage of the disease you're at, and if the disease is progressing, but it also helps people to live more safely at home as well. On the care side, the amount of technology is increasing, and the use of technology is increasing, enormously.

**Tina Woods**: How many people are taking advantage of that? Are people actually using all this new technology?

**Carol Routledge**: In the dementia space they're mostly being used in a research setting, I believe. Lots of organizations are still at the stage where they're conducting the research to understand how useful this technology is, how it will facilitate somebody living safely in their homes for longer, and what one can and cannot measure. I think it's at the research stage rather than being rolled out widely.

Having said that, there are of course technologies like wearables and apps on your mobile phone. The use of wearables is widespread. I don't know how useful that is right now in terms of understanding if people are living healthier or living longer more healthily; I'm not sure we're there yet.

From an Alzheimer's Research UK point of view, we're going to use AI to try and develop early detection tools for a number of reasons: it helps us understand dementia diseases better; it provides people with the opportunity to make the right lifestyle choices earlier; and there is almost universal opinion that if we were able to give drugs at the early stages of these diseases, they may show significant benefits. We don't know that yet, because we can't detect the diseases at a sufficiently early stage yet but we do know that they start decades before symptoms are apparent.

We're using AI and machine learning to look backwards and analyze significant amounts of retrospectively collected clinical data and prospectively collected clinical and digital data, to try and identify the relevant digitally collected endpoints that relate to clinical outcomes and disease progression.

We're using AI because of the enormity of the data, to allow us to analyze the data critically, to identify patterns within the data and enable us to build algorithmic models to detect neurodegenerative diseases' fingerprints in individuals at a much earlier stage than we do today. Even from a research point of view, lots of researchers are utilizing AI for identification of novel drug targets for drugs that are already out there on the market, trying to assess whether any of those drug mechanisms would have utility in treating the root causes of dementia and other diseases. Google's DeepMind have made progress in early detection of acute kidney failure, and that's very similar to what Alzheimer's Research UK are doing in the dementia space with AI. It's all about detecting diseases early.

I can't even list the number of things that this will facilitate. Even at the level of measuring cognitive function, there's the example of Cambridge Cognition. They do a lot of cognitive testing of people for all kinds of reasons, not just in the dementia space, but also multiple sclerosis, ADHD, so many other disease areas. They're now using Alexa-like technology, that is, voice-activated technology to ask the appropriate questions and collate the data, the answers to the questions. They have developed a watch that enables them to do exactly the same thing, that is, to collect data remotely. I think more and more we're using technology to deliver the queries and assimilate the data from those tests.

In psychiatry as well, a lot of tablet-based apps are being used as initial triage before the subject moves on to see either a psychiatrist or a psychologist. For me, when I look at that I think "oh no, I'd much rather speak to a person than a tablet" but actually, a lot of people who have depression and other psychiatric disorders actually would rather speak to a tablet first. It is increasing clinical triage, significantly helping the resourcing issues around accessing appropriate medical care. It's being used for many, many different reasons, and again it's enhancing and facilitating many, many things that we do.

**Tina Woods**: You mentioned the data that you're collecting. Who are your research partners who've given you this data?

**Carol Routledge**: In the initial instance the data owners are researchers who have been running a longitudinal cohort for a significant period of time. Some of the cohorts have been running for the last seventy years. They've been collecting data on people who age normally and on people who age with the diseases that cause dementia, so we'll have data from people at all different stages of those diseases.

It's difficult to say whom that data really belongs to. Certainly, one has to get consent of the subjects in those longitudinal cohorts, and one has to access data through **Principle Investigators (PIs)** who are leading those cohorts. I think increasingly, and not only in the UK but also in other countries, there's much more motivation to share this type of data. The individuals to whom that data belongs are much, much more willing than in the past to share all of that information for research or to enhance research. There are a number of different hurdles to cross, and who the data actually belongs to it's difficult to say, but I think there's a huge push to start sharing.

**Tina Woods**: Are these researchers from hospitals, academic institutions, or pharmaceutical companies?

**Carol Routledge**: In terms of what I was just talking about, that's clinical research data, either from data gathered in clinical trials or data gathered in these longitudinal observational cohorts. We may end up looking at some of the data other people are looking at, like primary and secondary care records and clinical data from hospitals and GPs, and then of course all the clinical data, which includes clinical trial data, data that people can collect from wearables, from phones and from apps.

I know again a number of different groups of researchers are also using consumer data; ARUK are not using consumer data for their early detection initiative. Researchers are also utilizing social data from social sites like Facebook, which again we're not; I think it's more difficult to understand the signals from that. There are lots of different types of data, but if you decide to use them, they each bring their own problems to the table.

**Tina Woods**: Are you working with Amazon Alexa and voice data?

**Carol Routledge**: We're not working with Amazon Alexa, but we do want to use speech data and are working with organizations like Mindstrong, and with a lot of academic researchers. We've been speaking to Samsung, but a lot of the data that we want to utilize in the first instance is real clinical data rather the more social health data. We're working in partnership with a lot of organizations, but mostly on the clinical research side.

**Tina Woods**: In the future, do you think there'll be more of a focus in the consumer space? Do you plan to reach out to organizations with that kind of social data?

**Carol Routledge**: For early detection we'll focus very heavily on clinical data and then digital data that is collected using phone apps and wearables. I think as we start to understand the signals, even in primary and secondary care data, I think we would be happy to enhance the data and the modeling that we have with primary and secondary care data, and if it's feasible and people started finding the appropriate signals in consumer data, then why not?

The next core step is to really understand how and what might deliver truly clinically relevant data, and what might just yield something that's interesting but not as relevant. If you consider the brain training apps and the cognitive gaming apps, I think we're still probably quite a long way from understanding exactly what they're delivering and what they're showing.

With AI, however, we will get there. We will understand what changes these kinds of interventions actually make; we'll be able to find signals in all types of data and then we will be able to strengthen and make more sensitive those signals through AI.

**Tina Woods**: Looking ahead 15 or 20 years, where do you predict you're going to get the most insight into all this?

**Carol Routledge**: I think in 15 to 20 years we will have a digital tool that will be able to measure and detect the diseases that cause dementia one to two decades earlier than we can now. Probably even earlier than that.

I think we will be in a place where in-house tech devices really are enhancing the lives of people living in their houses and alerting carers and families when there is a specific medical issue at a much earlier stage. I think a lot of these assessments will be much more automated. It sounds quite cold, but more automation enables us to enhance the care of people and that includes emotional care.

**Tina Woods**: The pharmaceutical industry has failed to come up with any effective drugs to treat dementia so far. Where do you think the pharmaceutical industry is heading when it comes to dementia?

**Carol Routledge**: One of the hypotheses is that we start treatment dementia diseases too late. The data is now starting to provide evidence that we are treating the diseases that cause dementia too late, and so there are a number of ways that the pharmaceutical industry could benefit from early detection of dementia diseases. If we can start right at the beginning, if we're able to detect these diseases early, we will start to much better understand the early stages of these diseases, which mechanisms go wrong first, and that will give the pharmaceutical industry new drug targets to aim at.

We can hypothesize, but we still don't absolutely know what triggers neurodegenerative diseases. Are you born with them and something triggers them off? Or do they start to evolve 40, 50 years before you see symptoms? A if they do, what processes go wrong first? We don't know. If we understand that better, then we may be able to select much more relevant targets for drug development that may show efficacy.

If we're able to do that, we still have to find the right stage of the disease to treat with those mechanisms. At the moment we've had a number of anti-amyloid-beta therapies that have gone into late stage clinical trials in symptomatic subjects, and even though there have been trends—and some of the earlier stage clinical trial data have shown significant effects—overall, they've spectacularly failed to show significant efficacy. But these drugs are still sitting there "on the shelf," and a lot are associated with five or six years worth of subject safety data, but we just haven't been able to show they work. If we are able to detect these diseases at a much earlier stage, then why not evaluate those drugs at a much earlier stage? And you never know, based on how the disease progresses, they may actually show significant efficacy at an earlier stage of disease progression.

There are also other aspects to this, especially around making the right lifestyle choices to enhance your own health. I've just come back from the **Alzheimer's Association International Conference (AAIC)**, and a number of papers were presented there showing a significant association between making the right lifestyle choices, by trying to alleviate some of the risk factors that happen in mid-life, and lowering the risk of getting dementia even if you have genetic risk factors. The right lifestyle choices include things like exercise, no smoking, moderate alcohol intake, eating the right foods, just things like that which can significantly reduce the risk of dementia and/or significantly delay the onset.

If you can inform people at an earlier stage that they have the early stages of a disease and they are at risk of dementia, then you can also provide people with the opportunity to make the right lifestyle choices. Detecting disease early is hugely important. That's not just in the UK—I think across the world, if we can move from acute care to much more preventative care, it has got to be beneficial. I'm sure it will save a huge amount of money as well as improve the lives of people in a significant way.

**Tina Woods**: I understand there's a big genetic factor when it comes to the diseases that cause dementia, and recently the epigenetics aspect has started to be investigated, looking into genetic expression. What do you see happening in those research areas?

**Carol Routledge**: As you know, epigenetics and genetics are slightly different and we know a lot less about epigenetics, but you're right that they both play a significant role. We think some of the lifestyle choices and lifestyle changes that we can make that have a positive impact, we think they may work in part by influencing epigenetics. I'll touch on genetics first.

There exist genetic variants that affect the likelihood of you developing dementia, like ApoE4, TREM2, among a number of additional mutations. When you put these together, you can calculate a polygenic risk score. It measures the risk of a person progressing to dementia, as well as the duration or the time to onset of dementia (though the latter is not very accurate at the minute). Polygenic risk scores alone do not predict with certainty when or if in your lifetime you will progress to dementia. A paper was recently presented at AAIC, covering a blood test for the measurement of amyloid beta, suggested that this blood test could predict the increase in amyloid in the brain. The test measured the levels of amyloid beta 1-42 versus amyloid beta 1-40 to produce a ratio of those two forms of amyloid beta and this predicts to some extent the increased levels of amyloid accumulation in the brain.

The accuracy of those predictions was approximately 88%, but if the predictions also took into account additional risk factors, such as age, which is one of the largest risk factors for dementia, and the genetic variant ApoE4, the accuracy of that prediction increased to 94%. The aim was to utilize the blood test to increase the selection of individuals for amyloid drug clinical trials in that it increased the accuracy of screening the appropriate individuals using PET imaging to assess people with increased amyloid load. Given the costs of PET screening, a reduction in failure rate would incur significant cost savings.

On epigenetics, lifestyle changes look like they're linked to epigenetics, but we don't understand how. Equally we do not understand sufficiently how lifestyle choices can influence dementia risk. A lot of the data thus far has come from association studies, but there are new studies like the **Finnish Geriatric Intervention Study to Prevent Cognitive Impairment and Disability (FINGER)** study, which are prospectively studying the effects of lifestyle on dementia risk. This study was initiated in Finland, and the people enrolled in the study were put onto a strict exercise, diet, and lifestyle regimen to help understand whether changing lifestyle can modify the onset of dementia. The study has been progressing for at least two years and the data is starting to indicate a separation between the test group and the control group in terms of the onset of mild cognitive impairment. That difference may be due to epigenetic changes.

**Tina Woods**: Consumer DNA tests have already shown that even well-informed people can panic a little when they find they have genetic variants that are linked to diseases. When it comes to taking genetic information from people, what's the ethical way to share it with them? How much should be shared?

**Carol Routledge**: In ARUK's early detection project, we're looking long and hard at how to ethically handle all this data. Individuals often want to join these studies and join these cohorts because they want some information back, but one has to be cautious about the data that is provided to the individual.

For example, it is not really ethical or accurate to provide a risk factor for dementia to an individual. A risk factor can take into account many different aspects, but equally cannot predict whether "you will have Alzheimer's disease in your lifetime," or doesn't predict that you will progress to dementia in your lifetime. However, potentially a calculated risk factor could be used to promote a healthier lifestyle.

The medical device that the EDoN initiative is developing will be used within a medical infrastructure so that information can be fed back to the individual with the appropriate support.

One other aspect of using AI to mine significant amounts of data is the potential risk of unblinding.

Even though you're starting off with anonymized data, based on the number of questions being asked of the data, you run the risk of non-anonymizing the data and identifying individuals. There are some risks and there are some downsides, but I think as long as we pay attention and we're careful with what we do and why we do it, those negatives can be minimized.

**Tina Woods**: If we're going to make a big difference to our lives with data and AI to analyze it, how do we need to work better together to make that come about? What do you think are the responsibilities on all of us, as citizens, governments, and businesses?

**Carol Routledge**: I've worked in the pharmaceutical industry for significant periods of time. I am a great believer in the pharmaceutical industry and they play a key role in the development of therapeutic treatments.

At the moment, we still hope to accurately detect and diagnose Alzheimer's disease. While we know a great deal about the progression of Alzheimer's disease, we struggle to accurately diagnose mild cognitive impairment; the pharmaceutical industry and other researchers are looking to technology to facilitate the stratification of patients for clinical trials.

Stratification of patients at an earlier stage of disease should increase the success of interventional clinical trials biotech and industry are keen to collaborate in the early detection space. Technology companies such as Apple and Samsung are also keen to enter this space because they potentially have technologies that will enable early detection and diagnosis.

In terms of government, I think there's a huge ask to really support dementia research. This includes approaches for the early detection of disease as this supports the move away from acute care towards prevention. The government provides significant funding for dementia research but it is important to see some of this funding being put to ward research focused on the prevention of disease that cause dementia. Government could help unite sectors behind detecting diseases that cause dementia early. There are many sectors with a significant interest in this, such as the NHS, patients, carers, patient groups, GPs, memory clinics; obtaining buy-ins from all key stakeholders is important to move an initiative like this forward.

What such initiatives cannot do is increase the burden on the NHS and so we need to be able to much more accurately, efficiently, and effectively triage the appropriate people into a clinical diagnostic infrastructure.

**Tina Woods**: What should be the next steps we take to improve that infrastructure?

**Carol Routledge**: At the moment the referral rate into memory clinics is poor. That's nobody's fault, there are few accurate tools for detecting these diseases early and so the referral rate is inaccurate. The ideal would be to identify individuals with signs of early stage disease potentially through an annual health basis. The UK are really keen to use health checks as a means to understand onset and progression of disease.

ARUK's early detection tool could be rolled out for use on an annual health check basis with the sensitivity of the assessment partly coming from the longitudinal aspect of the measurements. This may allow us to much more accurately triage individuals into clinical diagnosis either through brain health clinics or memory clinics.

**Tina Woods**: We've had a massive dementia campaign running in the last couple weeks in the Daily Mail. Do you think people aware enough of the warning signs, of what dementia actually is and how it's caused?

**Carol Routledge**: No, we're not doing OK on that point. ARUK are providing appropriate information on this, and that is clearly beneficial, but awareness in the general population is still very low. People do not have awareness about what dementia is, about what the diseases that cause dementia are, that Alzheimer's is one of those diseases that causes dementia, that you can actually make the right lifestyle choices to delay the onset of dementia.

The awareness has to come with understanding. I think if people realize that diseases cause dementia then this should provide optimism, and hope that we can slow or stop these diseases. Once we understand those diseases, then it should be possible to develop treatments that slow down or stop the progression of the disease.

We've done that with HIV, we've done this with some cancers. We can cure some cancers now; we have great screening programs in place for a number of other cancers. Why can't we do the same for the diseases that cause dementia?

**Tina Woods**: Can you have a good life with dementia? How can technology help make life better even when you have dementia?

**Carol Routledge**: That's an incredibly interesting but difficult question. There are a number of conferences I've been to that have used phrases like "live well with dementia," and it causes all kinds of reactions from family members and carers, including incredibly aggressive responses.

People say "you stand there and glibly say 'living well with dementia' but nobody lives well with dementia. The diseases that cause dementia are truly devastating."

The question we have to ask is: devastating for whom? I think, certainly for Alzheimer's disease, most of the devastation is to the family of the person living with dementia and not necessarily the person themselves.

Potentially, cognitive impairment and the memory loss are not quite as devastating as some of the other symptoms of dementia. Psychiatric symptoms are possibly the most devastating symptoms and they are often the symptoms that put a person in hospital or into care.

A good life with dementia really does depend on what your symptoms are. It depends how the disease progresses and it depends on how effective your medication is. A great-aunt of mine died of Alzheimer's disease a couple of years ago, maybe little bit longer than that now. She was on Donepezil for ten years, and for her, it really did benefit her. But for lots of people who take Donepezil, it gives them very little benefit and even there is benefit, it's for a really transient period of time.

**Tina Woods**: What technologies have you come across that help people reckon with these very difficult symptoms of memory loss, disconnection, and things like that?

**Carol Routledge**: In terms of technology, that's difficult, however, looking at preventative approaches is extremely important. Cognitive reserve, and the level of cognitive reserve as one progresses down the stages of disease, makes a big difference. Data suggests that higher cognitive reserve may be linked to a slower onset of dementia or a reduced risk of dementia but we are at a very early stage of understanding this.

It is worth noting that living with disease is not the problem, but living with dementia is devastating. Regarding technology, perhaps the use of brain training apps, and methods to increase your cognitive reserve may be helpful but this has yet to be shown. I think the phrase healthy body, healthy brain is perhaps the best way to look at reduction of dementia risk right now.

**Tina Woods**: I've read that if you have a high cognitive reserve, you may not show any symptoms for a very long time, if ever. Does anyone know how people get to this high cognitive reserve? What is that, and how can you protect that?

**Carol Routledge**: One thing we must be really clear about is to say that just having a high cognitive reserve does not necessarily mean you will never get dementia if you have Alzheimer's disease or another neurodegenerative disease. That said, there is certainly a significant association between cognitive reserve and either not progressing to the stage where dementia symptoms become apparent or delaying the onset of dementia. I think it may relate back to the plasticity within your brain.

One of the reasons we believe that you don't see symptoms of dementia for a significant period of time is that the brain is incredibly resilient. Even as your neurons die, remaining brain cells can make many more synaptic connections, and it's the synaptic connections that really dictate your cognitive reserve. Even if neurons die, if you can increase synaptic connections in the ones that remain, then they can kind of bypass the function of neurons that have died. If you have an incredibly resilient brain, then it will take you significantly longer to reach the stage of dementia if you have Alzheimer's disease. At least, that's how the theory goes, and it makes perfect sense to me. Your cognitive reserve is really associated with just how many connections the synapses in your brain make, and there are millions.

I think we need to understand fully what research is telling us about the underlying risks of dementia, cognitive reserve likely to be one of them. A recent study studied the association between marital status and dementia. The study compared single or divorced individuals versus married people, looking at both men and women, and trying to understand if the risk of dementia differed based on whether the individual was single or married.

The study that the risk of dementia in women who were single or divorced was significantly higher than if women were married, but actually there was only a difference when you looked at women who were in an older age range. The conclusions from these findings suggested that if you were a divorced or single woman 70 years ago, then your social network would be very limited because single women did not tend to socialize as much as married women. Today, single women socialize as much as married women.

This really is akin to the comparison of social isolation versus social connectivity. Social isolation is suggested to decrease cognitive reserve. I think cognitive reserve is an enormously important piece of the puzzle because it keeps those synapses really active.

**Tina Woods**: What is the recipe to keep your cognitive reserve going?

**Carol Routledge**: It could potentially start out as simply as keeping socially connected. So, loneliness and not speaking to people is suggested to decrease cognitive reserve. It's one of the potential reasons that hearing impairment in middle age is a risk factor for dementia; interestingly, it's actually midlife hearing impairment rather than elderly hearing impairment that's the risk.

Perhaps it's different now because the hearing aids are much smaller and much more discrete, but if you had to wear a much larger hearing aid in midlife, you possibly would not have worn it. Not wearing a hearing aid if the individual needs to, probably increases social isolation.

So possibly it starts from things as simple as staying socially connected, but there are also "brain training" apps available online. This technology potentially increases use of the higher decision-making centers of the brain, this in turn increases the synaptic connectivity of your brain. Even Sudoku and crosswords likely help; anything that keeps your mind quite active.

**Tina Woods**: You mentioned hearing aids as a tool to keep socially connected, and I've read that they're also helpful just to keep a flow of sensory information to the brain to keep it active. Is there a lot of research around sensory stimulation?

**Carol Routledge**: I think there definitely is. At Alzheimer's Research UK, we co-fund research with Action Against Hearing Loss to really try and understand what loss of hearing does to onset of dementia and progression of disease, and then how one can prevent that.

**Tina Woods**: What do you think is the secret to a long, happy life?

**Carol Routledge**: Some would say to be married forever to a loving partner, but really, it's just being healthy. I'm not going to say "never" to anything, you have to do all the things you want to do, but you should absolutely do exercise, eat well and try to stay healthy. Stay socially active, have friends, build a network and stay very engaged. Stay healthy and connected.

The other thing that we've discussed in the All-Party Parliamentary Group is poverty. You don't have to be rich, but in this day and age to still have people living in the poverty is fairly horrendous. It brings on many risk factors including an increase in the risk of dementia.

The social determinants of health are significantly important, they really are. Other than age, they are the highest risk factors. They are hugely important, but again, it's not easy to solve, even for the UK's poverty, never mind the world.

**Tina Woods**: Will we ever have a pill to cure aging, that stops all the diseases of aging?

**Carol Routledge**: There's currently a lot of controversy around this; people have different opinions about whether or not it is right to prevent aging. In my opinion, it is not. Our cells are programmed to die, and perhaps this is what they should do.

Disease isn't an acceleration of aging. Disease is disease, and it causes the abnormal cell death of certain cells. For dementia, it's patterns of neuronal cell death in the brain but this is not the same as healthy aging. Do we want to slow down aging? I personally do not think we do. However, we do want slow down or prevent the death of specific groups of cells which cause disease and cause us to live with disease as we age.

My concern about anti-senescent drugs, and I think that concern at the moment is unfounded, is that certain cells are meant to turn over in your body. They are programmed to die. What would happen if they don't? I think we have to be really, really careful what we do in terms of anti-aging drugs and anti-senescent drugs. It's the cells that cause disease that we really want to do something about rather than aging.

**Tina Woods**: When it comes to the anti-aging debate, what ethical concerns do you have? Is there anything that hasn't been properly considered as AI and technology keep expanding the possibilities?

**Carol Routledge**: Some people, and I'm not one of them, really do want to live for much longer. There are all kinds of issues associated with that, mostly because our cells aren't really programmed to live beyond a certain period of time. If we start to develop anti-aging treatments that prevent the aging of all cells my first question would be "why?" Why would one want to do that? I'd also ask how will our planet cope with that?

One of the key reasons that dementia, the prevalence of dementia and the incidence of dementia, has increased to the level that it has is because we are living longer and more people will live to an age where they will get dementia.

On the other hand, we are treating many conditions which increase the risk of dementia such as heart disease, diabetes and so on. But one outweighs the other, and in addition, we have no treatments that stop or slow down dementia disease, and so dementia rate is still increasing.

I think the ideal is to age healthily, not necessarily to live longer, but to live healthily as you age.

**Tina Woods**: What have you learned from the COVID-19 pandemic?

**Carol Routledge**: Personally, life has definitely changed for me, but not as drastically as one might think. I'm still engaging with family and friends, but via technology rather than in person (other than my younger son, who is back from university and socially isolating with me). I still take my dog for a long walk, twice a day, and so I'm getting plenty of outdoor exercise; but I'm definitely missing social contact. I'm very much missing my older son, and missing other family and friends. I also worry about the long-term impact this will have on children, on the elderly, and on the mental health of many individuals. I'm concerned that there will be an ever-widening of the gap between the outcomes for the wealthy and the poor.

From a work perspective, I'm still incredibly busy, but with the key difference that I'm attached to a laptop for at least 12 hours a day. Meeting technology has been incredibly impressive, but there is a much stronger feeling of being "tied to the desk" literally all day, every day. Researchers have been very inventive in their pursuit of maintaining progress in their research work, which is incredibly useful for the field of dementia research. It is very noticeable that clinical researchers have been pulled back to the "front line," but they still persevere to meet their research objectives, which is admirable.

I miss working in the office—home working has been relatively straightforward, just very socially isolating. I worry about the impact COVID-19 will have on dementia research funding, particularly for charities that receive an income through donations; but mostly I worry about the medical impact COVID-19 is having on people living with neurodegenerative diseases. I appreciate how rapidly many researchers have incorporated evaluation of COVID-19 impact into their research, often utilizing digital technology and remote monitoring to do this, but for families, carers, and front-line clinicians this impact must be devastating.

## Shafi Ahmed

*Professor, Futurist, Surgeon, Innovator. Entrepreneur. Teacher. Transforming Healthcare Globally*

There are so many superlatives to describe Shafi—pioneer, innovator, humanist, philanthropist, futurist, but also dear friend and kindred spirit. I feel privileged to have been able to work with him and know him.

I first met Shafi when I invited him to join the editorial board for the GIANT Health event in 2016, which I helped set up and launch. The GIANT experience was completely exhausting but exciting too and a lot of its success was down to having Shafi involved, for his knowledge but also his black book. The launch took every ounce of energy and drive I could muster for months and two days later, after it was over, he texted me to see whether I was ok, knowing how much it had taken out of me.

He didn't know that I had just discovered my father died—but Shafi has this 6th sense and it was his humanity that sent that text to see how I was. To this day I am forever grateful that I was able to see my father before he died—and say the things that I needed to say to him—and not let my obsession with work take that precious moment away from me.

So, where do I even begin to describe Shafi's multiple talents and achievements? I had first heard of him when he was in the news around the world on 14 April 2016, when he performed the world's first virtual reality operation recorded and streamed live in 360 degrees. This was viewed by 55,000 people in 140 countries and 4,000 cities and reached 4.6 million people on Twitter.

Shafi is a multi-award-winning cancer surgeon working at The Royal London Hospital and is on a mission to democratize access to high quality medical education globally. His online videos have been watched hundreds of thousands of times, earning him the accolade of most-watched surgeon in human history. He has set up surgical education programs in over 20 countries, including conflict zones.

He is a member of the NHS assembly advising the government on the NHS Long-Term Plan and was awarded the Future NHS Award by members of Parliament in 2018. He was also the Asian Star in UK Tech in 2018. He won the Silver Scalpel as best national trainer in surgery in 2015 and has been given the accolade of the worlds most watched surgeon as has streamed live operations using Google Glass, virtual reality, social media, and on national television on Operation Live, which was shortlisted for a BAFTA award in 2019.

He was the Associate Dean of Bart's Medical School and an elected member of council of the Royal College of Surgeons of England where he led the international and global health program. He has been recently appointed as an advisor to the Abu Dhabi government for digital transformation of health and innovation.

He is faculty at Imperial College, Bart's Medical School, Queen Mary University, Bradford University, Harvard Medical School, and Singularity University, where he teaches on innovation and digital transformation.

His most recent endeavors are setting up a digital health academy in Abu Dhabi and working with Vodafone as the UK connected health ambassador.

**Tina Woods**: What are the key messages that people should understand about living longer with AI?

**Shafi Ahmed**: We need to look at human resistance and what age we can live to. Currently, the oldest living people in the world are around 115. That hasn't changed for a long time. Some would argue that biologically, we can't actually survive more than that period of time unless things fundamentally change within our genotype, or the epigenetics (gene expression modification).

A better question would be, how we can live better with AI? This would include a better quality of life due to less chronic diseases and illnesses. Our life cycle is that we are born, we generally go to college, and then we start working. We work for the most active part of our lives until we reach around 60-65 years of age allowing us the option to retire. We are more active, physically we are fitter, and mentally we are more agile in the first few decades of our lives. We go through a curve of exponential growth in everything we do, but then it plateaus with the natural deterioration of biological processes. The average life expectancy is around 70 to 84, depending on where you live in the world. At the age of 50 or 60, we have to accept that we roughly have 20 years left of life.

If AI is used correctly, it will help doctors and healthcare workers to offer a better service. AI will also make healthcare around the world more affordable, more accessible, and more equitable on the whole. Will AI replace people? Not yet. I think the key message for our patients and for the public is that AI is augmenting our practice. It will help doctors to perform their jobs and tasks more efficiently.

I've traveled to many countries, probably about 35 in the last three years, working with governments, working with universities, and working with healthcare organizations. The one thing that remains true for all countries is that there is little or no more extra money for healthcare. We simply cannot afford healthcare any longer, as things stand.

If the premise is that there's no more money in the world, what can we do collectively? We have got to recreate healthcare in different ways. We have to be smart. We have to reimagine healthcare to make our resources go further. That's the reality of the economics of the world we're living in. We're facing an increase in population, more chronic diseases, and more burden on healthcare services. That's only going to get worse.

"Globalization 4.0" is a term that's been coined recently. The Fourth Industrial Revolution, which includes AI, will actually help mankind and will globalize healthcare. AI will be the main disruptor of healthcare in the next 10-20 years; it will be our silent partner.

A fundamental change to delivering healthcare will be driven by data. We have a wealth of data, but at the moment we're limited because the data is often of poor quality and isn't connected around the world. Healthcare systems struggle to get the correct data. In the next few years, there will be an explosion of data for all of us. As an example, data could come from wearing sensors that look at basic physiological parameters like blood pressure, pulse, respiratory rate, or temperature. There are already companies recording this information. We have seen that during the pandemic that indeed as there has been less face to face contact we are seeing much more utilization of digital remote monitoring devices particularly for chronic disease like diabetes and Asthma/COPD.

If we imagine the future, we could swallow pills and then analyze the data from our gut. There might be sensors on our skin that can tell us our oxidation levels and look at our electrolytes without having to have blood tests taken. We might have corneal implants to measure the blood glucose.

We have already seen watches like the Apple Watch used for **electrocardiogram (ECG)** monitoring for atrial fibrillation. The key to the success however of all these ideas is whether they will be accepted and achieve mass adoption.

We should also talk about genetics. When I was studying for my PhD, back in the year 2000, the Human Genome Project was just producing its first genome. This received amazing coverage because it was the first time that we'd been able to isolate all the genes and sequence them. The total cost for this project was thought to be around $2.7 billion and involved many countries worked together to sequence that first genome.

Fast forward 20 years and in 2019, the amount charged for entire genome profiling is about $600. Within two years, the cost will probably be $100. In four or five years, it will be less than $10. Within five years, every person on the planet could have their human genome profiled, providing lots of data.

We would then have to think about how to manage all this data. The human brain can't cope with too much data. We would need sophisticated and powerful machines to do analysis and perhaps quantum computing may help analyze personal and population data. This would also help us to recognize trends for individuals and for the population as a whole. AI will help us to assemble data, extract it, and analyze it. This would give us an overview that would ultimately improve outcomes for every patient with data driven care that is both personalized and more precise.

AI is just one technology. People tend to forget that many technologies will combine in this new world. I always say that this is the most exciting time to be alive in medicine. This is the first time in history that we have such an incredible amount of rich technologies coming together at the same point of human existence. It is an inflexion point for humanity. The question is, how do we build these technologies to coexist and support one another?

I'm not sure that everyone wants to live forever. I'm not sure that we need to live forever. If we can promise that people will live for about 70 or 80 years, how can we make that time effective? Think of the advantages of being able to maintain your health right through those 80 years.

Today, you could be riddled with a chronic disease that is debilitating. You might have a stroke, develop dementia, or have a mental health disorder. In the future, doctors might say, "Actually, we can prevent some of these problems, but your existence is going to be uniform. You will be well in yourself for that period of time only."

I think most people would take that offer straight away. Is life worth living if you're severely debilitated? That's a philosophical question. If you have a stroke and you can't move for many years from the age of 40 or 50, is that life? It is conceptually, but wouldn't you prefer to have a different kind of outcome?

At the moment, life is very much governed by cycles. Wouldn't it be great if we could have a second, third, or fourth life in that same framework? We could work for 10 years at one company and then say, "I'm still fit enough. I'm going to do something else with my life." I think that will improve our quality of life because people need challenges and also, they have a desire for change.

Maybe we could apply for a job at 50 as if we're applying for a job at 20, with the same energy and enthusiasm. We can then have a society made up of people who contribute more over the course of their lifetimes.

**Tina Woods**: Do you see health as being an asset in the same way that you might describe wealth as an asset? Many people take their health for granted.

**Shafi Ahmed**: We do take our health for granted. We're born with health and we all assume we're going to be healthy when we're younger but less healthy when we're older. Wealth, of course, is different because we have no wealth at the beginning, but we have wealth at the end of our lives, hopefully, because we've worked for all those years.

What we might prefer in life is to have our wealth at the beginning when we're fit enough to spend it and then perhaps to have no wealth at the end when we've got diseases and other things to worry about. I think health is an asset, but it's not a suitable asset because we're just born with it, whereas wealth is something that we derive through hard work. We could argue, by the same token, that we don't maintain our health as well as we should.

**Tina Woods**: How do you think that AI and data-driven technology can be used to protect our health?

**Shafi Ahmed**: Data is not just about your bodily functions: it's about your finances and your profiles on social media, etc. All that data matters and becomes part of you. Having mined all of that data, can we give you a better understanding of where you are in terms of your current health, or what the future might hold for you? Can we predict your risk of illness?

This analysis would not just be about chronic diseases but about your whole well-being. Often, mental health gets forgotten about in this whole context because it's a bit more difficult to understand, difficult to treat, and we're not quite sure where the parameters lie. AI may help us to figure out what's happening in society as a whole with mental health.

As a cancer specialist, when people come to see me, they often mention that there are clinical trials somewhere and ask my opinion. I have no idea at that point in time about all of the clinical trials being carried out across the world, but those people are clinging to life. By the time they've got to stage 4 of the disease, every day counts; they want the opportunity to live longer. People will be desperate to look for any information when they're in that situation.

Often, what we're missing is a sophisticated system to be able to analyze all that data that comes through, including all the clinical trials, to offer our patient the right treatment choices.

At the moment, decisions on treatment come from oncologists, surgeons, and pathologists all just discussing a case together and using conventional wisdom about what's the right approach. AI would look at all of the data and evidence for us because we can't possibly keep abreast of every clinical trial in the world, even perhaps results from phase 2 or unpublished trials.

We are only able to see a limited number of patients during our clinical practice over a number of years. Every week I see four or five new patients for example with a new diagnosis of cancer. AI would be able to assimilate the information from millions of patients around the world and give me the ability to offer advice and treatment that's far more personalized and precise.

**Tina Woods**: In the NHS in the UK, there is starting to be more focus on preventative health. Where do you think that's going to take us in the next 10 years? How can we help people to understand what the risk factors are for poor health?

**Shafi Ahmed**: We're driven by what's currently around us, which is our jobs, but actually, very few people sit back and ask, "What motivates me? What makes me work? What is driving me forward and how is my health being managed?" It's only when you don't have your health or you reach the end of your life that we tend to decide on the need to figure these things out.

We are a number of things, including emotions and biological parameters. We have data from our body, but we also have the way we think and behavioral issues to consider. We can look at factors such as whether we're smoking or drinking, or what kinds of food we're eating. Social media can also record our emotions and who we're connecting with. One idea would be to capture all of that data. We could then go to Google or into an electronic health record and see how all that data is connected. We could also examine data from other people who have health issues.

In medicine, we talk about diseases being caused by environmental factors all the time. Can we define those factors better? Hopefully, we'll be able to improve healthcare by understanding what drives a lot of the problems we see. We could put illness into context; we've never had that ability before.

If we're talking about simple prevention, we currently use screening for things like breast cancer. Screening takes place for those considered to be higher risk, but wouldn't it be great to take that much further and screen everybody? We shouldn't select people for screening based on their age group alone. Yes, there's more incidence, perhaps, but what about the rest of humanity? Do they not deserve to be screened? Why are we rationalizing healthcare? Everybody deserves the opportunity to prevent illness at the outset. Everybody should have the knowledge and the data to make choices for themselves about preventing illness.

**Tina Woods**: In your view, what will have the biggest impact on helping people to live longer and better lives?

**Shafi Ahmed**: We're moving to an era of data-driven healthcare, as I mentioned. We're still trying to figure what that might mean. The next important topic will be looking at how to keep people out of a hospital or both primary and secondary care. Once you have someone in the system, it's a huge resource issue. We need to change the emphasis from sick care to "well" care.

How do we predict the onset of disease? Can we prevent it? If we can't prevent it, can we prolong the period that it doesn't arise for? If it does arise, can we then minimize the outcome of that particular illness so that it's bearable and it doesn't cause a huge problem.

Another crucial element is access to healthcare. We're more connected; Almost everyone has a smartphone and internet access around the world. We need to consider access to information, transparency of data, access to our own health records, and access to specialists around the world.

We're going through this exponential phase where so much information is available. This means that we should be more sophisticated and flexible. It used to take time for data from clinical trials to come through, for example, but now we're seeing data arrive almost immediately.

**Tina Woods**: With all these changes, what role will the individual have to play?

**Shafi Ahmed**: One of the main problems with healthcare is that it's very paternalistic in the way that it functions. Doctors and healthcare professionals often tell patients what to do and how to manage things. Doctors design treatments and decide on pathways. What I will say is that we underestimate patients. We should form potential partnerships with them as agents for change.

Patients have the desire to be involved in conversations to drive healthcare forward. We just assume they're not tech-savvy and won't understand what we do. If we think about the use of the internet, the biggest rise of internet use in America is currently coming from people over the age of 60. In China, WeChat, as a platform, is so powerful that people use it for transferring money or booking tickets, looking at health records, booking appointments, and so on.

We don't include patients in the conversation often, but they need to be empowered with the fact that they are going to be responsible, with us, in driving healthcare forward as stakeholders. Ultimately, the patients are the end users. They are the people who are going to benefit the most from what we do, whether it is good or bad. We need to understand that and let them be an intimate part of the discussion.

I talk about ethics all the time. You can't introduce a new treatment or a new technology without including patients as part of that journey. If you just throw the technology at somebody, they're going to resist it immediately because people are resistant to change. Healthcare is also stuck with dogma and tradition.

The question is, how do we empower people with the knowledge and skills to be able to function in this new world that we're creating for ourselves?

We need to say to people that "healthcare is changing and we can't afford it as things stand. Your first point of contact in the next five years will not be a doctor; it may be an avatar, a hologram, or an AI chatbot."

There are many questions to answer. Is face-to-face contact more important? Would patients be happier if their data was given straight to them? How would patients cope with that data? Would we need to support them? Would bad results make them worried or scared? What would be the fallout from that? There are ethical issues around this whole new system we're working on.

**Tina Woods**: Could you elaborate on the ethical issues?

**Shafi Ahmed**: We've had issues already with AI machine systems and people questioning the ethics around their implementation, access to personal data, and what the uses of that data are. The conversation about data is relevant to this whole discussion.

I personally would be very apprehensive about sharing data or people accessing my data without knowing what they are using it for. But last year, we carried out an experiment around the idea of having a data donor card, rather like a donor card that you have for organ transplantation consent. This experiment asked, "Would you like to donate your data to benefit other people and to benefit healthcare?'

**Tina Woods**: Would this donation of data be after death?

**Shafi Ahmed**: No, just generally. Using data after death is another topic entirely. This experiment was asking people if they would let their health data be used now. The question was asked at a conference with an audience of 400 participants. Apart from one person in the audience, the remaining 399 people said yes—they would be happy to share the data.

The public wants to give data. They trust us with their data for the greater good. However, when asked whether the data should be monetized the audience overwhelmingly said no. This is an important area that we desperately need to have clarity on the value of the data and how we share and possibly reimburse patients.

**Tina Woods**: Who would "us" be?

**Shafi Ahmed**: Whoever is trying to use that data in a way that's constructive in healthcare. The other part of that equation is that people are scared of their data being given away because of issues we've seen with cybersecurity and data being a commodity in the current world we live in.

Where's that compromise? Do we end up anonymizing data donation to make it secure? We have to have that conversation. I think as we go forward, the situation will eventually be resolved, but it will never be perfect.

**Tina Woods**: Should governments have a role in that conversation?

**Shafi Ahmed**: Yes, absolutely. They should be helping us, along with those at the forefront of delivering healthcare, and ethics committees, to make these decisions. It's a difficult conversation. We know that data is precious to a lot of people and evokes strong emotions. We need to decide how to use data in a way that's measurable, controllable, and safe for our patients.

**Tina Woods**: In medical school, you have the ethics training and "do no harm" and all those sorts of principles. Do you think we need a new form of ethics training in this age of AI?

**Shafi Ahmed**: Yes, we do. Ethics must evolve. If you go back to medical school, the curriculum needs to be redesigned. One of my big complaints is that the whole medical school curriculum hasn't evolved for 50 years; it's much the same. The curriculum is still about five or six years long, for example. It's still based around the fundamental basic sciences and the clinical sciences.

Why is medicine still a five- or six-year program? Why can't we teach doctors in three years or four years? The curriculum has become more and more crammed with more subject matter coming in. Curriculums should include the healthcare that we will be able to deliver in five or 10 years. Are we training these new doctors to understand new systems or this new world that we're going to be living in?

There will be fundamental problems and challenges that we've not faced before. Do we have the right people to teach the skills needed? Are students ready when they qualify? We need to change the curriculum to introduce technology, innovation, entrepreneurship, and the ethics behind all of these things so that we produce a new cohort of doctors that are relevant to today, not relevant to 20 years ago. We also need to make sure that the doctors of the future understand and will contribute to the innovation of healthcare. Their minds will be able to help us to make healthcare better.

**Tina Woods**: I know you are hugely involved in medical training. Could you explain how you are working to democratize access to medical training and also your plans for the hospital of the future that you are building in South America?

**Shafi Ahmed**: First of all, medical schools need to change, so I introduced a program into Bart's Medical School that is the first medical school in the world to embed innovation, technology, and entrepreneurship into the curriculum for all students. It teaches them how to innovate and how to be the new leaders of tomorrow.

In typical medical training, the students start in the first year and are very diverse with different skill sets but when they qualify, they are very similar. We are almost creating one-dimensional doctors. But human beings are much more complex and need challenges every few years, they have many other facets. Some doctors have the skills to code or perhaps run a business, for example. We don't tend to support or nurture those other faculties and skills in medicine.

Fundamentally, doctors aren't happy at the moment. We're losing lots of doctors because of the healthcare system. New generations want a better quality of life and two or three careers within their lifetime. There is a new breed of doctors called portfolio doctors. Unless you design a curriculum for those people and modern working practices, you shouldn't be surprised when they leave medicine.

Much of the work I've been doing has been around how we educate people and scale-up education. I want to give access to world-class training and learning to people all over the world. At the moment, your education is defined by two parameters only: your location and your access to finance or resources. It doesn't matter what you say about life; education isn't free for everybody. It depends on where you're born.

**Tina Woods**: Would you agree that location is also a huge factor in healthcare?

**Shafi Ahmed**: Yes, it's about not having access to medical care. How do you overcome that? We're now putting satellites in the air and we've got cables under the sea. The world is much smaller and the internet's going to help with healthcare.

For me, my existence as a doctor for 26 years has meant that I've gained a considerable amount of knowledge. I've made mistakes of course and I've learned how to operate. I've learned how to deal with complications and complex diagnosis. I have that knowledge and that's the only asset that I really truly have.

Patients pick doctors because of their experience. If you need a second opinion, you go to someone who's got more experience. Ultimately, when you leave the earth you don't leave that knowledge behind, but how do you share it with more than one or two people? How do you leave it as a legacy for millions of people around the world?

Teaching people, by using virtual reality or other technologies, can make that possible. How do you improve the lives of many? That has to be our mission. I always tell people not to think about one-to-one but about one-to-many. How can we impact many people?

I'm now going off to South America, to Bolivia, and taking a sabbatical from my hospital work to open a new hospital. The idea is to build a modern healthcare system or at least attempt to. No one knows what the perfect system is. Everyone talks about this model of reimagining healthcare and the hospital of the future.

We've got an opportunity in Bolivia in a place called Santa Cruz de la Sierra, which is the second city in Bolivia but the largest city in terms of population. We're going to figure out what a digital hospital looks like. What technology will it require? How do you educate the patients? Will they come on the journey with you? What's the social reengineering required to help support these patients on this new journey? Can we create something in a poor country?

I've got all the right people in the team; they're all futurists. We want to create a vehicle that will allow society to access healthcare in a different way. We're hoping it's better than what we have currently, of course. We don't know the answer to that right now. We will, I'm sure, make many mistakes trying to figure this one out.

We've got the perfect opportunity to recreate training for medical students to allow them to become future doctors. In Bolivia, we've got a population and government that are receptive. The hard bit will be creating a safe and effective hospital with good governance that can then be augmented by technology. It's always got to be that way around; you can't throw technology at the thing. We need a functioning hospital and then we can add technology where we think it will make a difference.

**Tina Woods**: How will the technology be different in the hospital?

**Shafi Ahmed**: We will be using data-driven technology, with as much data available as possible from the outset. The new hospital, for example, will try to have everyone's genomic profiling done. All that data will be on a central system, which will be open access. We want patients to have access to their data, so we'll produce an app for that. We will add in **application programming interfaces (APIs)** with all the connections.

The hospital will focus initially on the diagnostics, such as scanning. Next, the data will bring AI into the system. Ultimately, we will use AI chatbots as the first point of contact to create a triage system. This will prevent people from coming to the hospital unnecessarily. There will also be a platform to allow people to have remote consultations if necessary.

On the wards, there will be quite sophisticated systems of digital assistants. The first point of contact in the hospital itself will be a digital assistant that gives advice about the hospital and how to navigate the hospital pathway.

In the rooms, we will have advanced beds and perhaps infrared cameras. We'll also be doing 3D printing where we think it would be useful in A&E.

We're introducing facial recognition and voice recognition. Facial recognition will be initially for the staff to access parts of the hospital and then, if that works, we might run it out to patients going forward. I think voice technology is a really powerful thing that we haven't really explored enough. We want to be able to use it to support people.

We will try to access a surgical robot in Bolivia and will hopefully train people on using robots, which will be a new concept for them. We want everyone to be able to access training in these areas.

Most importantly, the culture of the workforce has to evolve and change, which is part of our mission. It's change management both for the staff who can drive the change and also the patients who will be accessing that healthcare system.

**Tina Woods**: Will the use of technology allow caregivers and nurses to spend more time with patients?

**Shafi Ahmed**: Yes, definitely. People often say that with all this technology, there will be less time actually spent with patients. In fact, if you look at the statistics, 10 or 20 years ago we spent our entire conversation with a patient with a paper record in front of us. Now, of course, that's changed.

I carried out a study in my own clinic. I actually only spend about 15% of my time talking to the patient and the rest of the time I'm looking at the computer. I'm accessing results, booking results, booking scans, etc. No one has said, "Don't look at the computer; look at me." Patients accept doctors entering information onto computers. The next step is just normalizing the progression of this.

There are always going to be people who will complain. You just have to be empathetic to what's required for any group of patients or individuals.

**Tina Woods**: You use robotics at the moment; would you trust a robot to do surgery on you?

**Shafi Ahmed**: I'd say that we're not ready to be completely replaced by robots just yet. People worry about this, but it won't happen for a period of time; it could be 30 or 40 years away. Initially, robots will augment our practice.

People will accept that robots could help surgeons to make pre-operative decisions about operations. Robots might soon offer assistance during the operation. In the past, operations have always been navigated by our brains. What if AI, during the operation, could navigate for us? That would make outcomes better.

I've seen robots that can join together to do intricate things that we never thought could be done by robots. The autonomy of robots is the next step in their evolution. We're not ready for that, so there's no point in discussing it.

We can talk about how to automate, assist, and augment, giving us more time to do other things that patients need us to do. Diagnostics is an example. If you have diagnostics that are quickly, easily, and more accurately reproducible by AI machines and robots, why would you want to do that yourself?

I think that, as we go forward, advancements will make the conversation about being replaced by robots much easier. As surgeons, we're not there yet, but I don't dispute that one day, robots, in certain areas, will be able to do our jobs as well as we can.

**Tina Woods**: Humanity is at the center of all this. How will you ensure that that will be protected?

**Shafi Ahmed**: That is very difficult with technology and we have to be very careful. There's always going to be the early adopters, then mass adopters, and then there will still be some people who still don't want to change. As I said before, ultimately, we're trying to create a safe and effective hospital. We should always support those most vulnerable in society.

You don't have to cater to everyone at the beginning. Those who want to access the data and technology can do so. Something like 3D printing splints, for example, will be accepted by everyone. The other parts I think we have to be very careful about. We need a gentle approach to change. We don't want to forget the human side of things where it's relevant.

There are certain parts of medicine that we have assumed that we can't really change at the moment. I'm a cancer specialist. I break bad news every Tuesday to four or five new patients when giving a cancer diagnosis. Before the pandemic we thought that this could only be done via face to face as we have to have some humanity with eye contact, empathy, and closeness. The pandemic has changed this and now we are breaking bad news via the telephone or video. We need to understand the changing relationship between our patients and clinicians.

Interactions have to be based on what's best for the patient at that time. It is vital to remember that technology is only an enabler and has to be used sensibly. In my opinion, AI overall has the ability to make us more human by allowing more patient-centric care.

# Indra Joshi

*Doctor, Director of AI, NHSX*

I first met Indra in 2016 at an event run by One Healthtech, a network which campaigns for the need and importance of better inclusion of all backgrounds, skillsets, and disciplines in health technology. Indra is a founding member of this network (together with Maxine Mackintosh who introduced me to her) and at the time Indra was looking for her next big move.

Fast forward to 2020 and Indra is one of the leading AI and ethics expert in the world. She is the Director of AI for NHSX (that brings teams from the Department of Health and Social Care, NHS England and NHS Improvement together into one unit to drive digital transformation and lead policy, implementation, and change). She leads on the creation of the £250 million NHS AI Lab. Her other responsibilities include overseeing digital health standards, evidence, and AI policy.

The NHSX team aims to deliver on the vision for technology set out by the Secretary of State for Health and Care, which is guided by four principles, drawing on emerging thinking on designing technology safely, ethically, and effectively for the values and interests of civil society: 1) user need; 2) privacy and security; 3) interoperability and openness; and 4) inclusion.

I first started working officially with Indra in 2018 when NHS England joined forces with the **Academic Health Science Network (AHSN)** AI Initiative directed by Guy Boersma to jointly develop the report *Accelerating Intelligence in Health and Care* that Melissa Ream and I were immersed in.

It eventually became a collaboration between the AHSN, NHS England, and the Department of Health and Care. Melissa, Indra, and I were the co-authors of the report that launched at NHS Expo in September 2018, including the first baseline analysis of how and where AI and data-driven technologies would impact the NHS, and what support would be needed to unblock its potential.

Since then Indra has been the driving force behind the world's first Code of Conduct for socially responsible and ethically applied AI (with Jess Morley, another trailblazer).

The Code of Conduct is a core resource for anyone involved in developing, deploying and using data-driven technologies in the NHS. It provides practical "how to" guidance on all the issues surrounding regulation and access to data. The Code has been recognized around the world as a leading source of guidance to ensure that AI is responsibly and safely used, and addresses the need for more agile regulation—that is safe, effective and proportionate—in an environment where the pace of innovation is always going to be quicker than the ability of regulatory authorities to keep up.

Most recently I worked with Indra as a contributor to *Artificial Intelligence: How To get it Right. Putting policy into practice for safe data-driven innovation in health and care.*

Indra is a straight-talking, no nonsense, get-things-done sort of person—no surprise why we get along!

**Tina Woods**: How is the NHS leading the world in AI-driven health technology, and how does your role fit into that?

**Indra Joshi**: In the UK, we've actively made a decision to focus on this. If we take a wider lens view, we as a government have set up an Office of AI that sets the strategic direction for AI across the sectors, which includes a focus on training and upskilling.

We've also put investment and resource behind our infrastructure from the early Test Beds program to the Centre of Excellence in digital pathology and radiology to help the development of data-driven technologies and the advancement of digitization. These are all building blocks and enablers.

We've built some early tools, such as the Code of Conduct, which helps lay out some of the principles to follow when developing data-driven technologies, we've recently published a buyer's guide to AI health technologies. In this current climate, the health service has been approached with numerous offers of help, some of those from AI-based technology companies. We drafted a buyer's guide to help commissioners make informed decisions. It's about creating an ecosystem for safe development and deployment of AI-based technologies, that's what the AI Lab is set out to do.

**Tina Woods**: Is the NHS leading the world in AI?

**Indra Joshi**: That's a difficult question. We have a world-leading health system, we are incredibly lucky that no-one goes bankrupt because of bill incurred from an NHS hospital treatment. This is based on the NHS Constitution that at its heart offers excellent healthcare with access to all.

We've got a world-renowned research environment and have heavily invested in the digitization of health records and the data infrastructure. These are all building blocks for making it a world-leading healthcare system utilizing AI.

**Tina Woods**: Why is it so important to have a code of conduct?

**Indra Joshi**: We're quite lucky in health that we already have quite a robust ethical framework. When you're doing medical research, you have to get ethical approval, and that is through the Health Research Authority. Regardless of AI, we already have quite good, robust ethics.

Now, with the advent of technology and Big Tech firms and smaller companies coming in, it's not always clear what approvals you do need and when you don't need them. What we wanted to do was lay out the basic principles you need to follow when developing data-driven technologies.

They also cover more advanced concepts: Have you thought about the ethical frameworks? Have you thought about bias and proportionality? Have you thought about the evidence base around what you're doing? Does your product classify as a medical device and therefore need regulatory approval? What's the commercial aspect? Have you considered security, and the often overlooked aspect—have you considered how accessible your product is?

Pulling it all into one place makes it quite simple and easy to access. We've got a lot of work to do to make this much more usable in a practical toolkit, which we're working on currently, and I hope we have something more usable in the foreseeable future.

**Tina Woods:** You mentioned the Hippocratic Oath; do you think need a new oath to take into account the new roles of technology? Do you see the code of conduct sort of providing the solution for the time being?

**Indra Joshi:** It's always difficult, when you create something new. You sometimes have the start-up mentality that this could be the next big thing, but it very quickly becomes yesterday's news! The Hippocratic Oath works brilliantly, but it works in a very patriarchal way. You go to your doctor or you go to your clinician; your clinician holds the knowledge.

With the advent of technology allowing a democratization of health and care, we're moving away from that; so, how do we not only educate people towards successful democratization, but also let go of that patriarchy? Maybe we do need a new wave of Hippocratic Oath.

**Tina Woods:** So, you've mentioned a few risks around transparency, accountability, explicability, fairness, justice, and bias. Where do you think the main risk is?

**Indra Joshi**: That's a really difficult question to answer. Personally, I think there will be a risk of bias. If you look back at clinical trials, they've not always included the right type of people. My biggest personal fear is that the inbuilt society biases we have will be built into technology, and then it's very hard to change that.

For example, in an emergency setting, quite often you get people who have no fixed abode or don't have any personal details on them. In that case, you often write down generic information on them. This is a bias we have. We could do much better at trying to find out more information about them, but due to time pressures and other factors we tend to skim over it. We just input that data, and then that data is there in the system. There's no changing it, and it becomes inbuilt into the system, and it's not real data; it's our own prejudices.

As another example, when somebody comes in and says, "I've got a cough and a cold", sometimes we write down "flu-like symptoms"; that's actually quite different. Flu is a strong diagnosis. It's something that's quite bad. Now, if somebody comes in with a cough that doesn't necessarily mean they have flu, but it's our inbuilt laziness. We just brush that inaccuracy off as fine.

Whether chest pain is cardiac or not is another example. There's a huge amount of information behind that, but often it's just a best guess that's written down at the triage stages. Any diagnosis machine will only do what it's programmed to do, with what it's seen in the captured data. Some of our inbuilt laziness can seriously affect the reliability of anything that machine produces.

There's a huge amount of education that needs to happen with us, in terms of inputting good data and having good data capture, and also in not allowing our inherent biases, that we have as humans, into the system.

**Tina Woods**: The Health Secretary's quoted as saying the NHS aims to become "a truly predictive, preventive, and personalized health and care service." What do you think the NHS will look like in 2030?

**Indra Joshi**: A wise person once told me that you can't predict what will happen in 20 years, because 20 years ago we would never have predicted today. I can talk about what we're building right now: we're building an app. It's called the NHS app, which is a front-door portal in your pocket for anybody living here in England to access their own personal health record, book appointments—those types of things. There's so much scope we have to build on that to make it a lot more personalized.

I think by 2030, if we carry on the trajectory we are, there's huge scope for us to boom with these things that we're already building today. There's no reason why we couldn't start plugging and playing things like wearable data. For example, I could input my steps into my **Personal Health Record (PHR)**; that has the potential to make it maybe not predictive, but certainly a bit more personalized.

At the same time, we're seeing a huge amount of investment, and the advent of much more personalized clinical trials. With access to real-world data, real-world evidence, we could understand many more things, like identifying a cohort that we think a particular chemotherapy will work on. If we continue the trajectory, we're on, we could maybe see some of the early stages of those results coming into health and care. Whether they're in the NHS or not, who knows?

From a much more digital perspective it's just about getting the basics. Wouldn't it be great if we had a more robust infrastructure; equipment that communicates effectively with other parts of the system and the right standards?

If we can get those basic fundamentals right over the next 10 years, I think we can say we've done something useful.

**Tina Woods**: Do you think that being able to see their medical information's going to change the whole way in which people see their health? Do you think people want that?

**Indra Joshi**: From experience, there are people who care about that kind of thing; and then, there are people who think "This isn't my responsibility. That's why I go to the NHS". For those people who care about their health and who want to take ownership of it, they will see this as a huge asset. They'll think it's brilliant to have all this information. I believe those people will be people who have long-term conditions, or who are carers who care for somebody.

For somebody even like myself—I'm a mother of two—I have no real need to look at my medical record. I luckily don't have a long-term condition; so, for me, it's just not particularly important.

There'll probably be a cohort like me who think it's nice that that information is there, but may think they don't really need it. It's a bit like Deliveroo. When I need it and when I access it, great. Otherwise, why do I need it? I can make my own dinner.

**Tina Woods**: Do you think we'll ever reach a time when new technology is doing such a good job of keeping us healthy and well that the NHS will start to shrink? Is that a scenario that's been contemplated at any stage?

**Indra Joshi**: There's a huge drive at the moment on wellness versus illness. If that drive continues, I think there'll be much more of an awareness, like we have now about climate control and energy use, where we're developing reflexes not to use plastic and use paper instead. Hopefully, that drive will build reflexes in the same way within health.

People will be more aware; and I think you can see signs of that already especially with the recent pandemic. The need for information and the focus on health and wellness has changed perceptively over the last few months.

As we see an increasing democratization of information and importantly an effective utilization of that information—we will hopefully see more people feeling enabled to manage a condition or an acute episode.

Whether the NHS will shrink or not, I don't know. I'd love to think it might become more focused, but I have friends who are GPs, and I think of all the 90 other things that they do out of 100 that have got nothing to do with healthcare, but to do with social care or well-being, or administrative tasks, it might be a while before those are reduced.

**Tina Woods**: The NHS is measured very much by activities. Do you think there'll ever be a time when the metric starts to shift towards prevention, and that the NHS will be measured on that? As part of that, do you think the citizen should be taking more responsibility?

**Indra Joshi**: We need to move from saying we're going to prevent something to an outcome space. We're slowly driving towards outcome-based healthcare, but I would say especially with the advent of digital technology we need to be clear about the outcome we're trying to achieve. It's not necessarily the number of apps that you download. If the goal is a meaningful reduction in blood sugar levels, what proportion of your population has achieved that? Should we then pay you based on that reduction—it is an interesting debate.

**Tina Woods**: How do we shift the focus away from acute healthcare and towards the other factors that are at the root of keeping people in ill health? How do you think AI will help there?

**Indra Joshi**: Maybe it won't. We need to weave the social concept back into our society that allows us to say these social determinants are proving more and more to cause ill health. Loneliness, anxiety, depression can be driven by technology. We are seeing a rise in young teenage depression. There are many factors to this, but one relating to technology could be seen by the rise of online bullying and the feelings of inadequacies felt by social media use.

How can we, then, create that community atmosphere? We're humans. At the end of the day, we're people who like communities. We like stories. We like talking to and being with people; a lot of that has been lost with technologies, but also with the current flow of life that we live in. That has been hugely evident with lockdown measures and the rise of depression during this time.

We need to focus on well-being and keeping healthy.

**Tina Woods**: Do you think we need a new social contract between society, government, citizen, and business?

**Indra Joshi**: I just wonder whether we need to inject a bit more humanity and care into it all. So many of us are willing to just throw money—or, if we don't have money, expect the state to throw money—at a problem, and we're quite unwilling to sort out that problem ourselves. I wonder whether there's something about redefining coping mechanisms and redefining life, to get back something we've possibly lost along the way.

**Tina Woods**: A £250 million AI fund was just announced for the NHS. Where do you think that fund will be focusing its efforts?

**Indra Joshi**: It will be a mix of getting technology into the health and care system through the recently announced AI in Health and Care award and as I mentioned before, creating an ecosystem for the safe deployment of these technologies.

**Tina Woods**: The healthy lifespan gap between the poorest and richest citizens is now 18 years, which is pretty shocking. How do you think AI will help to solve this?

**Indra Joshi**: From a purist, academic viewpoint, the great thing about AI is that it sees things that the human eye might not see or the human brain might not conceive. For example, take retinopathy; diagnosis of illness via examining pictures of the retina. An AI can determine age, sex, or other diseases by looking at retinal images. We can't as humans because we literally can't see it.

AI can get even more powerful when we crowdsource that information. We have to understand that the machine has the power to look at things that we, the humans, don't always look at. It can help us find new truths. With the advent of deep machine learning, that's just a drop in the ocean. I think those are areas with massive potential for AI, but I think we've got a long way to go before we actually see it.

**Tina Woods**: AI is having a huge impact in drug discovery. Do you think we'll ever have a pill to cure aging?

**Indra Joshi**: I think what we'll find is that aging is always going to happen. I don't know enough about cell regeneration, but I don't think you can reverse it or stall it. From a practical perspective, I don't think there'll ever be a single intervention to *cure* aging.

**Tina Woods**: Are lifestyle, nutrition, genomics, and other omics a big focus of your work?

**Indra Joshi**: We have another unit, called the Office of Life Sciences, who work very much around the research and life sciences agendas.

This is something that's on their radar and that they want to focus on. They're working with polygenic risk scores and accelerating the detection of disease; understanding what the genome holds; understanding the social environment around it.

**Tina Woods**: How do you think we can find out what information about ourselves we really want to know? What is the ethical thing to do with that information?

**Indra Joshi**: There is a lot of products and devices that can help us already find out information about ourselves, but a lot of these come at a cost. For example, fitness trackers, remote heart rate monitoring devices, blood pressure monitors, mood trackers, period trackers, I could go on. The list is long of things you can find out about yourself if you want to.

However, there is a big divide between those who can find out that information because they can afford to and those who'd like to know that information, but can't afford it or those products and devices are designed to enable them to have access to it.

The ethical questions arise when there is third-party use of that data without you knowing or consenting, with the implementation of GDPR here, we have some frameworks to avoid that—however we have quite some way to go before this is universal.

**Tina Woods**: How do you see this data ecosystem kind of unfolding in terms of connecting up all these different datasets?

**Indra Joshi**: We need to have a consistent language and have consistent input, as I mentioned earlier, and that's still going to take some time. But there is work underway with programs such as the Exemplars to getting there.

We've launched the digital innovation hubs, from HDRUK, growing pockets of data for research and for understanding things that we don't know yet but might discover.

**Tina Woods**: Taking everything that we've talked about into account, what do you think is the secret to a long, healthy, happy life?

**Indra Joshi**: A simple and stress-free lifestyle with someone who loves you.

My grandma died in her sleep. She was perfectly healthy; just said "that's it" one day and then didn't wake up the next day. They had a stress-free lifestyle, with none of the refinements that we have in the way we live, and none of the unnecessary stress we put ourselves through. Don't get me wrong; maybe that's the magic pill!

**Tina Woods**: So, I guess—because linked to that question is, you know, it seems that there's that sort of wisdom—that comes from exactly those sorts of stories. And do you think AI will ever beat that wisdom, those sorts of secrets to a long, healthy, happy life?

**Indra Joshi**: What AI could do is disseminate that wisdom like the wildfire of fake news. Imagine if you could do good fake news.

**Tina Woods**: OK. What do you personally do to keep healthy and happy?

**Indra Joshi**: I think I take life with a pinch of salt. From a personal perspective, I've seen a lot of people die. It can get to you. After a while I just said to myself that shit happens, then life happens. Take it with a pinch of salt. You never know what's going to happen tomorrow. I definitely don't live each day as if it's my last, but I try not to take things too seriously, and to have fun. It's the biggest thing I do to keep healthy is to keep happy. I try and see my friends regularly, have a boogie in living room with my kids and good giggle with my partner.

**Tina Woods**: I imagine you've seen a lot of deaths in the emergency room which are not of the person's choosing. Do you think it's desirable that maybe AI will help us to program our own death?

**Indra Joshi**: Program our own death—how depressing. I don't think we'll ever use AI to program our own death. What I think it could be is like a friend that you trust, but a virtual friend.

We don't like them much yet, but we have some chatbots. Thinking really futuristically, maybe in 30 or 40 years' time, you could have an AI agent in the emergency room call out things that you might not consider, or have access to that person's notes. Quite often, when people come in you don't know who they are. They're in extremis, so you just plug away at your normal thing. If you knew this person had programmed into their medical record that if this accident or illness happens to them, they definitely don't want a particular treatment, and they have done that in a conscious state of mind, we could potentially see that. Or to call somebody for you, or even to say I definitely don't ever want to be tubed, no matter the reason, because X, Y, and Z. We could potentially see that.

**Tina Woods**: How do you think AI could help us live longer?

**Indra Joshi**: I'm not sure they will help you live longer but they might help you live easier. At the moment, you can clap your hands and the lights turn off, and that's fine. If somebody, or some AI, could manage my life—and I think AI has huge potential there because it can go across multiple diaries—it can suddenly free up time. By freeing up that 30 minutes of diary management that I have to do with my husband every week, maybe I could do something like go for a run. Maybe that could help me live longer. I think while AI in its direct sense probably won't help, it could help on the wider things.

**Tina Woods**: What do you think of the idea of a life dashboard? If you could set how you want your life to be, and AI could help you make certain decisions?

**Indra Joshi**: Wouldn't that be brilliant? In our house, we have strategy and operations, and if AI could be the operations then we could all just have time to strategize, and that would be great. We know it would be delivered because that's the thing, isn't it? Where do you find the time to fix the light bulb or the roof? Then, you have to scroll through the internet and find the tools or the craftsperson. If you could just say "OK. Here are my life problems for the next month. Go off and do it" it'd be brilliant, wouldn't it? But we're definitely nowhere near that.

# Michelle Hawkins-Collins

*Aging-well activist, researcher and Gerontologist*

Michelle was Head of Futures at Virgin Care when I first met her about 5 years ago. Looking at her LinkedIn profile before our meeting I remember being struck that she was Head of Happiness at the Flying Dodo before joining Virgin. The Flying Dodo promotes better ways of doing business—one that focuses first on the happiness of its customers and employees, and that measures success on the triple bottom line of people, planet, and profit.

Not surprisingly I was intrigued, especially as I had been researching the B-Corp movement at the time—which focuses on balancing purpose and profit for a more inclusive economy—wondering why it was struggling to take off in the UK when it was the guiding principle behind so many major US corporations such as Ben & Jerry's and Patagonia.

I was instantly stuck by Michelle's charm, a wonderful combination of warmth, humor and intelligence, and we had a great conversation about health tech and how Virgin Care was going to drive system change in the NHS by its customer centricity.

Over the years since then we have had various exchanges, including when I was on the hunt for "unusual suspects" to participate in the Healthy Ageing Industrial Strategy Challenge Fund bids; the brief was to find exciting businesses who may not otherwise think about grant funding but who could be ideal corporate candidates to get involved. Innovate UK has a slick machine for smaller scale bids, but this time it was different and they wanted imaginative clusters of big companies coming together to work with academia, third sector, and the SME sector for large-scale projects to drive transformational change and see the creation of a "healthy aging marketplace" of products and services that could rival the world in post-Brexit Britain, and capture a nice slice of the many trillions up for grabs in the export market.

Michelle was on my "unusual suspect" hitlist, and when I spoke with her in 2018, she was just about to have her first child so the timing was off. But when I picked up with her afterwards, she had decided to take a career break and study gerontology with baby in tow. She wanted to really understand the human needs as people get older, including at the end of their lives, right before they die, which is a topic so many people feel is so hard to talk about.

But she put me in touch with her previous boss at Virgin to see if she might like to join the All-Party Parliamentary Group for Longevity and introduced me to many others, including the Hoxby Collective and CentricLab. She is a great connector!

Michelle's boss at Virgin Care gives her glorious reviews while she was there: "During her time at Virgin Care, Michelle built up an excellent understanding of the health and social care system and was instrumental to the organization in coming up with new models of care, pioneering innovation, setting up the Transformation function, and challenging us to think differently." I am not at all surprised that Michelle had such an impact and was delighted when she agreed to be interviewed for the book!

**Tina Woods**: What are the key points and messages that people should understand about living longer with AI?

**Michelle Hawkins-Collins**: There are three key points that come to mind. Firstly, people need to understand that they're already living longer with AI. This isn't something that will happen or may happen in the future, it's happening now.

Computer systems in particular are already simulating human intelligence capable of learning, reasoning, and self-correction. I've spent the majority of my career in healthcare, looking at examples of this like Moorfields Eye Hospital in London where AI technology is being used to read retinal scans, or Barts Health NHS Trust and University College London, where AI is analyzing heart scans to understand what is happening with heart flows in a non-invasive way. I think people have a fear of AI without understanding it and knowing that it's already happening today safely and with great benefits.

Similarly, AI is transforming our ability to predict, and therefore prevent and diagnose, disease early. AI could be the answer in really starting to see a shift in focus back on prevention and away from just treatment and sickness data. This would be an enormous benefit for the NHS by reducing demand—not just looking by changing the way we supply healthcare, but by changing the demand for healthcare through prevention and early diagnoses.

Secondly, good governance is needed to reduce some of the fear around AI technology. Many breakthroughs can be brilliant or terrible depending on what you're looking at. Take nuclear science as an example; nuclear science can both wipe out and sustain life. It can be used destructively as a weapon and wipe out an entire population but it can equally be a solution for clean energy to meet human needs, although clean energy is very different still from green energy, but that's a whole other topic.

One of the most important design features for AI is that machines need to know that their objectives can change. The purpose they were originally created for does not have to be their sole purpose. Stuart Russell, a computer science professor at Berkley in California, called it "humility in machines." This needs to be a mandatory feature for all AI development so that AI doesn't stay on a fixed path when the world changes. This will help protect against unintended consequences and allow us to retain more control.

If a machine understands that what they're looking at may need to change then we can't specify entirely in advance where we want the future to go. Equally, machines cannot predict everything, particularly when unpredictable humans are involved in the real world. This is something self-driving cars with AI must overcome. A self-driving car has to take into account that humans are unpredictable and be able to change its course and route because it doesn't know everyone and can't predict everything. This is very different to the scenario of AI playing chess in a controlled environment against one person with a defined set of options for every move.

Thirdly, people need reassurance that AI won't replace roles and de-value their professions. When we think about healthcare, my prediction is that AI will automate and streamline what are currently time-consuming tasks for people, things like checking scan images, or data crunching and analysis.

If you take data analysis, AI is better placed to do this given the infinite memory of machines vs. the limited short-term memory of humans. Rather than taking away from health professional's roles, this will instead allow doctors, nurses, and other healthcare professionals to have better information and more time for person-centered care. That means getting to know patients as people with unique life histories and circumstances that affect their health and well-being and seeing them as part of a system not purely as a condition. That's where the unique human expertise lies.

Or take the COVID-19 outbreak. A Canadian AI company called Blue Dot was one of the first to identify the threat of COVID-19, and many AI systems are trying to predict and understand the virus in a vast ocean of unstructured big data. However, such early warnings and insights generated by AI are useless if they aren't interpreted by those responsible for formulating and implementing a response plan, that is, humans.

**Tina Woods**: In your view what will have the biggest impact in helping people to live longer, better lives: now, in five years, in ten years, and beyond?

**Michelle Hawkins-Collins**: I think the biggest thing is going to be individuals (and not just health and care professionals) having joined-up health and well-being knowledge which is readily accessible and understandable. At the moment, knowledge is fragmented, challenging to access, and hard to understand. The COVID-19 pandemic has been a good example of why system data alone is not enough with the track and trace app dependent on 60% of the population downloading and using it. Moreover, it illustrates the need to join up with private sector corporations like Apple and Google early on since they own the mobile platforms on which a Track and Trace app would run. So perhaps no wonder this project has stalled... COVID-19 has also highlighted the dangers of only having access to and reporting on data from one part of the system (in this case hospital data) since this created a misleading picture of the reality on the ground and skewed international comparisons.

However, knowledge alone doesn't change behavior, and behavior change is challenging because it requires in-depth understanding of individuals, including their motivations, fears, and unique life courses and circumstances. AI is well positioned to compute such complexity, to help build a more complete picture of individuals. This would in support personalized care by identifying which levers would most likely lead to behavior change and what support a particular individual needs to achieve this.

This is a world away from our current tendency to look at one condition from a medical perspective. Take a doctor's surgery, for example, where I've often seen notices announcing "the doctor only has time for you to bring one thing to discuss in your 10-minute appointment." But we're never just one symptom or condition and 10 minutes is never enough to fully understand an individual's true needs.

**Tina Woods**: How can we use technology and AI to really tackle the social determinants of health in a way that we're not doing yet?

**Michelle Hawkins-Collins**: Firstly, I think the reason we haven't tackled the social determinants of health is because they're so much harder to understand. They're not easy to reduce down and it's hard to identify individual drivers because the determinants are inter-related. Because of this complexity, a universal program for supporting people to live longer and healthier lives will only go so far because everyone has totally different life courses with different amounts and types of accumulated advantage and disadvantage.

If we use the power of AI to piece together patterns, recognize them, and learn over time, I think we'll be able to understand the way in which social determinants play a role in determining health and well-being outcomes. AI may even identify new determinants not currently considered. For example, I've just completed a research project into feeling valued which shows the profound impact on a broad range of health and well-being indicators in later life including biomarkers of inflammation, health behaviors, disability, and even mortality.

If AI can show how social determinants play a role in determining lifespan and healthspan, then many so-called diseases become something that don't just happen to you. They instead become something that's created by you and your environment. That creates a very different paradigm, empowering people to take responsibility for their health and making the reduction in social inequalities an absolute priority for our society and systems therein.

**Tina Woods**: What will be the role of technology, and in particular AI, in moving forward the democratization of knowledge, and behavioral change?

**Michelle Hawkins-Collins**: AI will soon be able to aggregate and analyze data in a way that humans never could. This will have huge benefits in being better able to understand the drivers of disease. Take integrating datasets in healthcare. Information Governance makes this almost impossible task where humans are involved in the process. But a machine can match the two sets of data without the need for any human input. In so doing, we then have access to a huge wealth of joined-up knowledge and information to create a complete view of service users whenever and wherever a professional needs access.

Imagine joining data from health apps into more formal healthcare records. For example, apps that look at their sleep patterns and show users the percentage of time they've been asleep, what time they went to sleep, what their screen usage was. In piecing all these little snippets, AI could create a vibrant picture of a person that enables personalized care as well as identifying new insights that will change the way that our society and systems are designed. It's crazy that health and social care is still so divided with different commissioners, budget priorities, two sets of policy documents....

**Tina Woods**: When you talk about the enormous power of linking data, what data are you referring to? Older, existing data?

**Michelle Hawkins-Collins**: There are many different data sources. For example, I have my consumer-driven data like the Apple Health app. There's my social data, like how much time I spend on a social site and who I know on my social networks. My geolocation data showing where I go and when. And then there's my data within organizations and government. Imagine the power of joining all of this together.

In comparison, look at the very limited data that my doctor will look at when I go in for an appointment. If that's all we're going to look at, we're going to miss things that could indicate unmet needs and avoidable illness and suffering and we're never going to have a preventative healthcare system. Informed consent will be critical though to enable the joining up of data, and explaining to people the benefits of sharing their data and any risks in a clear way. That means not using legal waffle, technical jargon, or marketing fluffiness.

**Tina Woods**: Data and tech often reinforce common-sense wisdom like getting your fresh air or plenty of exercise. How do you think AI can help augment this wisdom in our daily lives?

**Michelle Hawkins-Collins**: I think in a very practical way AI will shine a light on how we live and how we spend our time, and whether we're spending it wisely. I always find it really interesting that my iPhone tells me how much screen time I have. I'm trying to reduce my screen time and suddenly it pops up and it shocks me! I think "I need to reduce that" and I do start to turn it down. I don't have time to look into all the different apps I have for analyzing my sleeping, steps, eating, screen usage, and even air quality so using AI to will help filter through the clutter and the current infobesity we're all suffering from. I'd to think like AI could support a time bank for the future, telling us how we're investing our time today and how we could invest better to get a greater payback on our health and happiness. After all, time is the ultimate currency, not money.

**Tina Woods**: This idea of a joined-up health app, it seems that we've got all the technology to be able to do that. What's stopping us?

**Michelle Hawkins-Collins**: The market is too fragmented in terms of who owns and controls the data and there's a lack of oversight to create any sense of coherence. We need a single interface but competition is precluding the collaboration we need. Apple is trying to collate information through one user interface, Google is competing with another, and then individual apps compete with their own niches. People might have all the information on their phones but it's in 15 different places. Who will lead this joined-up health app? I really don't know. But if you want to get health professionals on board, any interface will also need to appear within their existing systems and not with a separate login.

**Tina Woods**: How else might AI and tech help with the behavioral change aspect of better health?

**Michelle Hawkins-Collins**: As I mentioned before, AI could help identify what will be the most effective behavioral change approach for a particular individual and how much support an individual will need through computing big data. Everyone has different motivations and barriers to change. It may be that AI has a role in health coaching to enable behavior change—something which seems to be booming in the US. I recall a solution called SimSensei Kiosk where a virtual human simulates being a therapist or a nurse and is able to detect potential stress indicators. The interesting thing about this is that it moves machines closer to empathy with the avatar, for example, being able to mimic body language and show active listening behaviors like smiles and nods. And some emerging evidence suggests that people may be more honest and comfortable sharing information when they were talking to a machine versus a human because they aren't being judged.

This could have big benefits for conditions or situations which people may find embarrassing or may not feel comfortable talking about like sexual health or mental health.

**Tina Woods**: We've talked about democratization of data and knowledge, and we've talked about behavioral change; what do you think is the role of the citizen in all this? How do citizens need to adapt or change?

**Michelle Hawkins-Collins**: Our current model of health and well-being is one of dependency but the democratization of data and knowledge creates an opportunity for citizens to lead the change. Firstly, by having a complete view of their health and well-being for the first time and secondly through this being delivered in a format that is easy to understand. I still think you'll need health coaches or similar to support people through behavior change as having the knowledge is not the same as acting on it.

Empowering people to be responsible for their health and well-being needs to start as early as possible—from conception onwards—to create health and build resilience. You only have to look at the way in which COVID-19 spread to see why resilience is so important, with severity of symptoms linked to chronic illnesses such as diabetes and respiratory disease, which are in turn often linked to diet and lifestyle.

This will require good governance because empowering people means less control for the system. But this may emerge from society rather than government. Extinction Rebellion provides an interesting example of how a social movement has co-created their own set of values. If you look at the London protests, they were, by and large, well-behaved and elected people acted as intermediaries between officials and the protesters to maintain a peaceful protest. There is an interesting shift in culture and society now, enabled by social media and technology connecting people. It's really interesting to see where it will go.

**Tina Woods**: Absolutely. Do you think the same sort of shift will happen in the AI space?

**Michelle Hawkins-Collins**: I do. I don't think you can stop it happening.

**Tina Woods**: What about the role of government in either stopping or enabling the role of the citizen in all this?

**Michelle Hawkins-Collins**: As I mentioned earlier, at the moment, there is insufficient regulation and oversight of AI to provide assurances and safe boundaries to innovate within. That's not just at a national level. Governments should look at the international level and come together around how they create oversight around AI to make sure that the potential is optimized, and the ability to be destructive with it is minimalized. AI is a global citizen—it doesn't have to adhere to border controls or customs.

That feels a bit uncertain with the UK leaving the European Union as this would have been a key platform for coordinating large-scale regulation.

Government's role is also investing in the future, so if AI is something that is an important part of the future—which we believe it is—how are you going to train and educate people, particularly the younger generation? On top of that, AI is developing so quickly that we can't just look at education for younger people, it has to be throughout people's lives. So how do we train and empower people to use it better?

Finally, government will play a key role in creating the conditions for AI development and diffusion.

For example, suitable mobile connectivity across the country. For technology to be connected, it needs to connect to something, and yet there are still areas in the UK where you've got poor signal and no 4G coverage. This created a real barrier for me when making some of the simplest improvements to healthcare delivery such as providing clinicians with a mobile working device. Government needs to take responsibility to put that type of infrastructure in place. But at the same time, they must not be pressured into putting infrastructure into place that presents uncertain health risks. This means having a government that is able to stand up to pressure from companies and other governments to balance progress with public health safety.

**Tina Woods**: Poverty and lack of education both massively affect health and well-being. Do you think the individual citizen can be empowered with information to create pressures about this on government and society?

**Michelle Hawkins-Collins**: They can but I don't think information is enough in itself. We already know a lot right now, but not enough is being done to address inequalities—just look at the *Marmot Review 10 Years On* report. The original Marmot report came out with stacks and stacks of evidence around the lifetime consequences of poverty and lack of education, and while some progress has been made, it's been woefully limited. People can now expect to spend more of their lives in poor health than before and the health gap has grown between wealthy and deprived areas. This is unacceptable.

While each of us can take our own actions without waiting for the government, we do need political leaders to step up and drive structural transformation at the highest level. Take for example the five-year cycles of government, let alone how government departments are structured and the peerage system. How can long-term investment be made across the lifespan to ensure healthspan aligns with lifespan when every 5 years there could be a different government with a different manifesto, budgets, priorities, and personalities? Social determinants of health are not quick 5-year fixes but more like 50-year investments. My experience of healthcare is that services work on an even smaller 12-month timeframe with omnipresent pressures of "we can invest if will it save money this year and help us meet the budget cuts? If not, we'll have to delay it."

**Tina Woods**: Where do you think business should and could have a role in knowledge democratization and behavioral change?

**Michelle Hawkins-Collins**: Firstly, competition needs to be replaced with constructive collaboration, putting the long-term interests of society before the short-term interests of shareholders.

Deregulating intellectual property, including patents, copyrights, and trademarks will be a big part of democratization. While many argue this would disincentivize innovation, I think the collaborative commons example would prove otherwise with innovators coming together to co-create and open-source software. Businesses could support the next generation by teaching social entrepreneurship and why business should be a force for good in schools and universities. This would include businesses proactively reporting on and being accountable for their impact on profit, people, and the planet—that is the triple bottom line. Being accountable for people and planet would naturally incentivize knowledge democratization and behavior change. B-Corps companies are a great example of this.

However, if businesses are taking decisions on sharing knowledge, they will need to have watertight ethics. What is the risk of harm? Should all information be shared and to everyone? For example, let's say you're sharing information on mortality. Imagine a business that has the ability to predict when you will die—and you can see various algorithms right now which are very accurate in predicting whether you will die within the next 12 months. Now imagine a consumer buys this information. Maybe that person is very positive and if they find out they're likely to die within the next 12 months, they make sure they maximize their next 12 months and they plan for a good death. Maybe, though, that person is actually in a very vulnerable state. They find that information out and panic, triggering a breakdown. How can a business predict the impact of sharing that kind of information for an individual?

**Tina Woods**: How can we ensure that we don't create tragedies and unintended consequences for people?

**Michelle Hawkins-Collins**: Businesses must first see their role as being a force for good in the world and not just for making profit. In so doing, they must take responsibility for the health and well-being of people who buy their products.

This is very different from the current practice of shifting responsibility to the consumer the minute they buy a product and tick a consent box disclaiming all responsibility for harm. However, businesses also need to be held in a safe space through regulatory frameworks.

My worry is that policy and decisions makers within government do not have sufficient understanding of AI to be able to create such regulatory frameworks—how can you regulate something you don't fully understand? We shouldn't take these things lightly either. People are talking about the development of AI being as significant as the Industrial Revolution, reshaping the way society is run.

**Tina Woods**: How do you think technology is going to shape these societal structures? We hear about social capitalism, or purpose-driven businesses—where do you see the future in terms of business?

**Michelle Hawkins-Collins**: I think one of the benefits within AI and technology is in visualizing the full impact of decisions and therefore having the potential to create a more sustainable and equitable society. Businesses don't yet have to report on the full impact of their business operations. Wouldn't it be great if the Financial Standards Authority made triple bottom line accounting a mandatory requirement of the financial profession, and not an optional one to aspire to?

**Tina Woods**: We know China's galloping ahead with AI and its social policy, and of course Europe is a much more regulation-heavy sort of culture. Why do you think there are the differences that we're seeing around the world in all this?

**Michelle Hawkins-Collins**: There is an appetite for long-term planning in the Chinese perspective, because they do plan for the future, and I wonder how long ago were they thinking about investing in AI versus our government? I don't know the answer to that, but I suspect it was part of their strategy many years ago.

AI isn't going to wait for bureaucracy and politics, it will go ahead regardless. So, I think our government needs to balance regulation with pace and speed, and if it doesn't then we will be left behind. Whether that's a good thing or a bad thing, nobody knows at this point in time. That's why I think we need an international perspective on this versus countries doing their own thing.

**Tina Woods**: Moving that discussion from a high-level one back down to the level of the individual, what do you think is the secret to a long, happy life?

**Michelle Hawkins-Collins**: I want to challenge the question there, around what people's perception of "long" is. I see people looking at "long" in terms of number of years lived and chronology of age, and through the study of aging, one of the key conclusions is that chronological age is of little benefit or value other than looking at the time of year in which you were born and the cultural influences around that cohort.

What is much more important is people's psychological age and biological age. When you're looking at psychological age, there really is something in the saying "you're as old as you feel." "Long" is also subjective. Somebody may lead a long life in their eyes and die peacefully at 40 having packed so much in, and somebody may lead a long life and live to 100, but actually not feel it is long enough and have regrets. I think there's something around the secret of a long life being very much in accepting death and subsequently embracing what really matters in life.

It's no secret that the foundations for a long, healthy, happy life are set very early on. As Frederick Douglass said, "it is easier to build strong children than it is to repair broken adults."

The other thing that I have seen, alongside the very common-sense things like exercise, eating well, drinking water, sleeping well, is being able to cope with change and loss. There is not enough support or thought given to how we help people to cope with change and loss in life, and that is absolutely related to successful aging.

Every human is aging and, as a result, they experience loss. This could be in the form of bereavement, but also loss of youth, loss of identity after retirement or becoming a mum, loss when our children leave the home. And yet I never really hear people talking about loss? Those who are seen as successfully aging are often people with the ability to adapt to change. How are we helping people to adapt to change? What support do we give them at key life transitions? I think that is an under-acknowledged and under-invested area in the pursuit of leading a long, healthy, and happy life.

**Tina Woods**: When it comes to successfully dealing with these transitions, these losses, is there any way that technology and AI can help with that?

**Michelle Hawkins-Collins**: I think there is. I led an insight project in my role as Head of Futures at Virgin Care and developed a new model for understanding older service users based around the different stages of aging. The model went through 5 phases of aging: Active, Adaptive, Assisted, Dependent, and, finally, Departing. With the right information inputs, AI could predict when people are transitioning so that they can either be supported through the transition to the next stage or be supported back to the previous stage. This challenges the view of many that loss of independence is inevitable through a linear aging process. It isn't and the opportunity to create health is possible at every age.

I see a huge opportunity for AI in particular in identifying and supporting the adaptive stage of living. Let's say you're an active person and you like cooking, but you're finding it really hard to grip and use a knife. Maybe you have arthritis, or your joints have seized up a little bit. AI could notice that you are spending less time cooking and that you're buying more ready meals and automatically suggest pre-chopped vegetables in your online shopping basket, which would be more nourishing than a ready meal and would support you in maintaining dexterity. Or, it could suggest a chopping machine in your Amazon basket with a YouTube video showing how to use it.

That could be a really powerful way of supporting people to remain as active, and independent, and healthy as possible for as long as possible with AI nudging you into better behavior.

**Tina Woods**: You're a former Director of Transformation and Head of Futures at Virgin Care—are there any other examples or opportunities you can think of where the business community could work with researchers and academics to explore opportunities for products and services that could help with these transitions?

**Michelle Hawkins-Collins**: I think the role of academia is one to bring up. A lot of businesses are put off from working with academia because academics have their own set of rather onerous objectives that often compete with commercial priorities. In market research you move quickly to stay ahead of the competition. When you involve academics for independent assessment, things can go much slower as they pursue academic rigor and style over getting something quickly implemented.

There's huge value in academia though and there's a risk that valuable knowledge and insight is being wasted. I'll give you one example of a really good AI study by Stephen Weng in 2019, which could have profound implications for housing, town planning, and the car industry. If all such stakeholders came together, they could dramatically improve the health of the nation.

Weng looked at how well AI could predict premature all-cause mortality when looking at chronic disease in the UK in a middle-aged population. He looked at two different types of AI learning to contrast against our standard algorithm model, the Cox model. The Cox Model was 44% accurate in predicting mortality. However, when Weng looked at the random forest and deep learning AI models, the random forest model was something like 64% accurate and deep learning was 76%.

Moreover, when Weng compared the three different types models, they showed differences in which variables predict premature mortality.

Deep learning was the most efficient predictor and, in contrast to the Cox model, it identified air pollution as a key predictor of mortality, along with alcohol and certain medicines. Now, I don't know what's been done with that, but I look at that study and think, my goodness, we're chasing things that our common predictor model looks at, like age or gender, but actually the most important predictor could be air pollution. Only last year, the UK was referred to Europe's highest court for failing to tackle illegal levels of air pollution.

How can people like Weng be funded to keep doing this valuable research and designing studies in such a way that they become immediately translatable and usable so that businesses with the funding and government with its policy leaders are able to be aware of such work and to shape it for greater impact?

**Tina Woods**: From your research, what do you think people need to know about death and dying?

**Michelle Hawkins-Collins**: The first thing is the importance of trying to move to from a fear of death to a place of acceptance. A dear friend of mine, Sue Brayne (author of *The D-Word: Talking About Dying*) said to me recently: "The denial of death makes us believe we are immortal and invincible. It turns us into maniacal consumers to prove we are immortal; it makes us fight each other for more and it makes us believe we are separate and above the laws of nature." This is bad for us as individuals and for the planet. Yet, when we accept our mortality, death becomes a great teacher. Through all our pain and suffering, it shows us the true nature of love and connection to people and the planet.

In our Western societies, we have become distanced from death and dying. People are living to an older age and they often die outside of the home so many people do not experience the loss associated with the death of a friend or family member until they are into mid-life, let alone see a dead body. As a society we're much less exposed and build less resilience to this kind of loss.

We need to start trying to have a conversation around death being a normal part of life from the earliest age and that's why I'm working with pre-school settings.

Fear of death or lack of acceptance may also have some unintended consequences. It may drive behavior like avoiding people who are ill or dying leading to them feeling isolated, or people who are ill or dying not having their wishes expressed in the way that they want. In the UK the majority of people (about 1 in 2) die in a hospital and yet most actually want to die at home.

AI could play a valuable role in this by helping us to plan ahead and crystalize the finality of life and what really matters. If we're able to predict how much longer we have or even to know our risk of developing diseases, then we have time to plan and to support people in coming to terms with this—both the individual in question but also those around them who will experience loss. Clearly this is a contentious area and not everyone will want to know their life prediction, but I think it's interesting to reflect on the questions: what if you someone told you today how long you were going to live—would you change anything?

Another simple thing people which would help people to experience a good death is to make an Advanced Care Directive or living will. This is a written statement setting out your wishes and preferences for care, including the treatment you would want to refuse if you become too unwell to make or to communicate your decisions.

**Tina Woods**: You mentioned that we already have the tools that can predict your likelihood of dying within a year. Do you think there will be a day when everyone is using these tools?

**Michelle Hawkins-Collins**: At a professional level, yes. At an individual level, no. Many people will find this too hard a concept to come to terms with and it could be harmful, so it would need to be assessed on a case by case basis. However, normalization of death and dying in our society from early years onwards would make this a possibility for future generations.

However, I do worry about the impact of the COVID-19 pandemic. Think about all the fear-fueled headlines and commentary in the media around dying from COVID-19 and the government's single-minded focus on saving lives rather than focusing on maintaining or enhancing quality of lives. I've been deeply affected by thinking of the many people who have died alone in hospital and of loved ones who have not had the opportunity to fully grieve. This will have repercussions for generations.

An algorithm to predict susceptibility to disease rather than death may be a more palatable alternative, however, for sharing with individuals. You can see from COVID-19 that those most affected had underlying health conditions, which increased their risk of catching and dying from the virus. Having this kind of information could change behavior and create a more resilient society. I can see this kind of a tool being used every day.

**Tina Woods**: How can you have a good death? What are the key principles that one has to consider to have a good death?

**Michelle Hawkins-Collins**: Being able to plan ahead for what a good death means to you, and your family and loved ones understanding this, is key. Friends and family members unfortunately can bring additional stress as well as comfort to someone who is dying, so we know that a good death isn't just about the individual dying, it's about the people around them and how they're processing and coming to terms with it. In this way a good death is beyond the person dying and includes supporting loved ones in coping with that loss.

I was chatting to a palliative care nurse with 30-40 years of experience a couple of weeks ago and her reflection was that there were four aspects of life which link to a good death. There's the physical aspect of life, like how you look or what you own; the intellectual aspect, your intellectual achievements; the emotional aspect of life, how you're feeling and relating to those around you; and finally the spiritual aspect, which is around what life means to you.

Through the course of our lives, a lot of people look at the physical and intellectual aspects of their achievements, like their career, professional status, and titles; where they live; how they dress; and what they look like. When it comes to end of life, things change—what really matters is your emotional connections and your spiritual meaning of life. A good death is about cultivating those aspects throughout your life and not waiting to the end. I've been writing my own life review recently rather than waiting until my last days of life so that I can reflect on all the different passages of my life to understand who I am, what brings my life meaning, and how I can be the author of my own life story for the remaining chapters. If this was normal for everyone to do, imagine the change that would make to individuals as well as society as a whole. I certainly believe it would create a better world to live in.

The hospice staff that I have spoken to have done some brilliant projects to help people have a good death by thinking about legacies. Whether that is made concrete by creating a memory book or recording videos for children and family members at key stages doesn't matter—it gives us a sense of continuing and being part of life.

**Tina Woods**: In this book we talk to a lot of people who believe in immortality and look at some of the extraordinary things that are happening in aging research. If we were able to be immortal, do you think we would be losing something about being mortal?

**Michelle Hawkins-Collins**: I do. If we didn't have the end in sight, we would act very differently. I've actually reflected on this in the context of machines not knowing that they're going to die and the impact of this with AI. The very fact you know you're going to die forces you to take different decisions and to consider the legacy you want to leave.

If you're immortal, well, then you can do what you want. There's no consequence. I think very different behavior would be generated by knowing you can live forever—I would question why people want to live forever.

Most people who are chasing immortality probably need therapeutic help to understand why they're chasing that. What is it that they haven't accepted about their own death and about dying?

The pursuit of a longer healthspan is absolutely the right thing to do, but I personally disagree with the pursuit of longevity alone or immortality.

Think of the planet—how are you going to sustain the growing population? Think of the resource implications. Would we stop people procreating?

If machines start doing a lot of the roles traditionally performed by people to support a population moving towards immortality, what does that do to an individual's sense of value? One of the fundamental things of human nature is the need to be valued and feel that we've got a role. One of the great roles you can have is in the legacy of having children, or in bringing them up, in teaching, educating, and sharing knowledge. What happens to us as human beings if that disappears?

**Tina Woods**: How do you think that concept of value ties in with the ethics of the technology and the AI that we create around longevity? Could there be unintended consequences to that?

**Michelle Hawkins-Collins**: There are going to be huge amounts of unintended consequences from AI in general as it's venturing into unchartered territory. This comes back to the comment I made earlier about Stuart Russell's "humility of machines" and the importance of AI not having a fixed objective. What we have to do is expect there to be unintended consequences and to design mechanisms to pull things back when these are encountered. To be honest, this probably goes for people as well as machines! Many people aren't humble enough to admit that they may not have the right answer or that circumstances have changed, and this can be equally dangerous.

So, in terms of how AI might affect an individual's sense of value, we just don't know. Like anything, it can be positive or negative depending on how we use it.

But one thing we must do at every level to ensure it is used to its most positive potential is to involve people in those discussions—at every stage of the life course—and not exclude people because they are hard to reach.

Before I became a mum, I was working within innovation and change projects within children's healthcare services. My ideas for innovation and the future of children's services are very different now that I'm a mum. I had a whole different lens on the world before. How can you possibly comprehend the impact of longevity and aging for a 90-year-old, or somebody that feels like they're 90, when you're not there yourself?

# Bertalan Meskó

*Doctor, Director of The Medical Futurist Institute*

I first heard of Bertalan Meskó in 2013, when I was working with pharmaceutical companies on "patient centricity" strategies, at a time when patients were the least important customer segment to target in this industry. Pharmaceutical companies only needed to worry about doctors and payors—and for good reason, as they had the power over drug prescription and budgets. Big data and AI were just starting to enter the pharmaceutical lexicon while Google, IBM, and Apple quietly started plotting their strategies to capitalize on consumer data to make their billions from the enormous healthcare industry.

Things have changed dramatically of course since then, and the pharmaceutical industry is having to wrestle with disrupters discovering and developing drugs far more quickly than they can, the data scientists and AI experts they desperately need being lured by much better salaries and job prospects by tech companies (big and small), and a push for prevention and fewer pills being demanded by struggling healthcare systems, doctors, and consumers alike.

Meanwhile, Bertalan has been an ongoing, steady presence, updating all the powers-that-be and slumbering pharmaceutical giants of the threats ahead, reminding them how doctors' professions would change, how the pharmaceutical industry needs to think about a world demanding prevention, and how patients don't want to be patients at all—by staying healthy and well for as long as possible!

Bertalan calls himself The Medical Futurist and is the Director of The Medical Futurist Institute, analyzing how science fiction technologies can become a reality in medicine and healthcare. As a geek physician with a PhD in genomics, he is also an Amazon Top 100 author, and has been featured by dozens of top publications, including CNN, the World Health Organization, National Geographic, Forbes, TIME magazine, the BBC, and the New York Times.

The mission of The Medical Futurist Institute is to initiate public discussions about how the old paradigm of the paternalistic model of medicine is transforming into equal partnership between patients and professionals and how it is aided and augmented by disruptive technologies.

When I spoke with Bertalan, he struck me as genuinely sincere and incredibly serious while still being very young! I'm not sure how old he is today but he must have been very young when he started Webicina, a website curating medical resources of social media either for medical professionals and patients, which is how I first came across him.

What struck me about our conversation is the importance he placed on the cultural components of a paradigm shift being so much more important than the technology—this is the biggest challenge.

**Tina Woods**: In your opinion, what is the secret to a long life?

**Bertalan Meskó**: Well, it's a big package. It's a package that contains a bit of luck, a good healthcare system that takes care of some things, and self-consciousness. By that I mean that everyone should know what perspective they have towards their health—what they could have, and what they want to have.

I'm really talking about what the secret to long life could be. Right now, for most people, they would think that it's just having a good healthcare system and a lot of money, and that's true right now. We know that the 1% of the wealthiest Americans and UK citizens live 10 years longer than the bottom 1%—just looking at pure income. That's because of the access to care. These financial differences lead to biological ones and that's where digital health technologies come into the picture.

If I'm self-conscious and I know exactly what I want to achieve in my health—in my case, I want to live. I see myself being 100, boarding the spaceship to Mars on my own legs. I have this vision about the future of my health in itself and having some kind of healthcare system takes care of the rest.

That's what digital health does; it makes you the point of care, and then you just need a little bit of luck. Right now, in my estimation, it's 80% luck, 20% decisions. We're working hard to actually reverse that, to make it 20% luck and 80% decisions.

**Tina Woods**: What do you mean by decisions in this case? How do you think we can raise that self-consciousness?

**Bertalan Meskó**: The biggest change in the history of medicine altogether is the notion that digital health brings into the picture. It's that there's no ivory tower of medicine anymore.

As a patient, you are no longer just an element in a huge system of things that take care of you; you should take care of yourself with the help of amazing medical professionals and advanced technologies.

So, when I say self-consciousness, I mean that we must become empowered, engaged experts about our own health or disease management. I simply cannot expect my medical professionals to make every decision over my head, without contributing to the responsibility, putting every weight on their shoulders.

That's what we have been doing for decades, and now we know that burning out in medicine is now a medical condition—that's based on the World Health Organization regulation, which is an amazing step forward. The reason why physicians burn out is that they have to take all the weight. They have to make all the decisions. They have to know everything, but it's physically impossible to know everything with 31 million medical papers out there, and every patient is different. It's never going to be the exact same medical condition.

It's impossible for a physician to know everything. So, we have to contribute. To do that I need to know exactly what I want to get out of my health and to know I can bring value to the table regarding this discussion. That's what I mean when I say being self-conscious about your health.

**Tina Woods**: How are we going to tackle that problem of getting people to become more and more proactive? And what is the role of technology there?

**Bertalan Meskó**: I think this paradigm shift has been going for about 15 years ago, using the devices of social media and the internet. Now, it's common sense that if you want to access information about your disease, or your symptoms, or your treatment you can easily do it even if you don't want to post information online.

You still might want to turn to your medical professional for guidance about finding the right information in this jungle of digital information.

Acceptance of technology has also changed. My favorite example for that is what happened with diabetes patients in the US who knew that, technologically, they could have an artificial pancreas system. There was a working one five years ago, but the Food and Drug Administration only approved the first device about one and a half or two years ago. In between, patients started creating their do-it-yourself artificial pancreas, because they knew how to do it.

This movement, the OpenAPS movement, they could access all the elements and even the necessary algorithms. And they didn't want to die from having low blood glucose levels while sleeping, without anyone in their medical team making a mistake about their treatment. They have to be proactive because it's about insulin management, and they know what kind of health issues they might face if they don't take care of themselves.

Other people have no health issues for now, or do have health issues, but they feel like they're being taken care of. So, I don't think that we must transform every patient to be digital, but I hope that we can let every patient make a decision about whether they want it or not. Right now, there is no freedom of choice in healthcare. Where you live, how much money you've got, what language you speak—especially if you don't speak English; these will have a huge impact on the quality of care you receive and the length of life that you have.

If we can improve access despite these factors, when we look at how healthcare is becoming globalized, we could have a chance to let people decide. If I have real freedom of choice and I do want to use these advanced technologies, and I'm willing to give up some of my privacy, share my health data through these channels for the chance for a longer and healthier life; if I choose that, I'm the patient of the future.

I'm fine if someone says that they are more than fine with what they have right now and they will go to the healthcare system when they need it, and they will be taken care of and that's what they need. That should also be fine. The problem right now is that the people who would love to use technologies to at least have a chance to live longer and healthier lives, they don't get that chance. I just don't think that's fair, and that's what digital health is fighting for.

**Tina Woods**: How do you think that choice is going to evolve in the future: this trade-off between privacy, freedom of choice, and healthcare? How do you think that's going to pan out, and where do you think we'll see most of the interesting shifts take place?

**Bertalan Meskó**: I finished an analysis about this recently and I spoke at GLOBSEC, a policymaker cybersecurity event. They've identified four major themes or four major models for digital health, and all of them are based on the freedom of choice patients have in this technological world.

The first was China, where patients don't have much freedom of choice because the system, including the AI-based social credit system, builds in whether or not you have the right to use these advanced technologies.

The second model was where patients didn't have freedom of choice, not because they were pushed to use technology but because otherwise, they wouldn't have any kind of care at all. An example is Rwanda, in Africa. After the genocide, they didn't have the resources to build a normal healthcare system. So, they took a leap in provisioning help, and medical drones delivered packages there. Today, they have AI-based electronic medical record systems and about 60% of the country has access to telemedicine, which is quite exceptional for a country like that. But they don't have freedom of choice, because otherwise they wouldn't have care at all.

A third model is where a healthcare system works. I could use many countries as an example, but consider the US, where patients have freedom of choice and they have these technologies and the need, the urge, for using more data in development and in management into the practice—but physicians are often without good incentives. You need incentives and good policies. So, the freedom of choice is there, but the technology cannot break into the system easily.

The fourth model is the best practice model. It's Estonia, where policymakers decided to implement the technologies right now. They wanted to give people a freedom of choice whether they want it or not. If they do, they get access to it. If they don't, they still get the same healthcare system they used to get. That's the paradise scenario.

Even your grandfather there would have just received his genetic test reports. A lot of that cohort were really surprised that the government spent money on them at the age of 80 to get a DNA report to prevent diseases from happening, that this prevention approach was being applied to them even at the age of 80, but I think that was a really important part of the program.

It's not a major model that we see regarding the freedom of choice and the chance that digital health can provide us with. I'm not good at social sciences, but I know that when people have faith in how the government runs certain processes, then it becomes much easier to implement new things. In places like Estonia there's excellent security—they've even used blockchain—and transparency when it comes to how the government deals with the data.

**Tina Woods**: There's always the common-sense advice about health: fresh air; get plenty of exercise; eat well; get your eight hours of sleep. Can AI or any technology ever beat the accumulated wisdom of history, the common sense of the ages?

**Bertalan Meskó:** For at least 30, but probably closer to 40 years, we have known the secret ingredients for a long and healthy life. We know these: don't smoke; don't drink alcohol so much; exercise; sleep well; eat well. Still, if you go out on the streets and ask 100 people how many of them do at least half of these things, I think that number would be astonishingly low.

While we know exactly what steps we would need to take to live longer and healthier lives, I think we have been educated and cultured about healthcare into considering ourselves as passive components of this. When that's how I think, how can I come to the table with a need or a question? I just go there when I need help, and they take care of me without my contribution.

That's why compliance with treatments is only 50%. I mean, show me an industry where the efficiency is 50% globally—it's almost physically impossible, but healthcare works like that. We've known these things for decades now and still not much has changed, although millennials live in a much healthier way than their parents. I've seen some good McKinsey reports about that. It's OK, but it's still not enough.

I think only technology can change this, can really lead to a paradigm shift. When I see the transparent and objective data about how I perform every day, whether I exercise enough or not, how I can shape my diet, what kind of genetic predispositions I have for various conditions, I can prepare. When I see my life in numbers, all gamified and visualized and brightly colored, that becomes a new scenario where I find a new kind of motivation in life. I'm trying to live like that.

I know it's obsessive, what I do, but I have to do it to show people that with some simple technologies and some data, even just in an Excel spreadsheet, you can contribute a lot to improving your lifestyle. Only technology can change this, in my point of view.

**Tina Woods**: Is there anything we can learn from the Big Tech companies, which may know more about us than we do, to make it easier for us to behave better or to make better decisions?

**Bertalan Meskó**: They definitely know more about our online habits than we think they do. That's what I agree with. I'm not sure if they know more about us than ourselves. The one thing they are amazing at is how to mine that huge amount of information and make real-life outcomes of it, like advertising solutions.

I wish medicine worked in a similar way, but medicine isn't that linear. The same medical conditions might appear in different people with different first symptoms. Even if they appear with the same exact symptoms and biomarkers and everything else, different patients might express their feelings and their symptoms in a different way. Real-life healthcare is such a diverse topic, such a diverse industry that it will never be a case of just inputting data into an algorithm and getting the perfect cure or treatment as the output.

That's why I think it's always going to be a combination of human creativity and judgment, and computing power. These learning algorithms are contributing to this. What we can learn from these Big Tech companies is that healthcare is becoming so technology-based and globalized that just healthcare, medical technology, and pharmaceutical companies cannot bring to patients the solutions that those patients need—and app companies can.

I published an analysis about how Tencent or Microsoft, and after that, Google, Apple, and Amazon, are marching into healthcare. They have almost zero knowledge about how healthcare works. Many of them don't seem to realize how important medicine is, and how we can't use some things if there is no evidence behind it. But still, what they do, the technologies they create are amazing apps. Healthcare companies will be far, far behind for decades.

It seems that for patients, the in-between line would be the ideal way forward; using technologies from mostly tech companies for medical healthcare purposes and using the expertise, the knowledge, the background of hundreds of years that caregivers and healthcare companies have to make those work. That's necessary to get clinically meaningful outcomes from using those technologies. That's one thing we can learn from those companies.

Another thing is what I call patient design, which is sometimes treated as an evil expression by pharmaceutical and healthcare companies because it's different from patient centricity. Patient centricity means sending out a few questionnaires to patients about the treatment or the technology they are doing. That's not enough.

Patient design means that you involve patients not just from the first step, before designing any treatment process technology for them, and you involve them at the highest level of decision-making in the company, at the CEO level of the company. You see this happening in some pharmaceutical companies, and even the FDA now has a patient engagement advisory board. That's the biggest thing that healthcare and pharmaceutical companies can learn from tech companies because tech companies are very much involved with the end users.

The way healthcare works and has been working for hundreds of years is that they decide to develop a treatment for patients with diabetes, they design it without them. When the treatment is designed, they would like to test it, but they don't ask diabetic patients what they think. They ask anybody else—from peer medical professionals, to researchers, and developers and policymakers: not patients. Then you make the patients use it. It's ridiculous. They haven't been involving patients from step number one and that's the biggest thing we can learn from tech companies.

**Tina Woods**: Do you see the Chinese social credit policy as exciting or concerning?

**Bertalan Meskó**: I might be the worst person to answer this question! I believe so much in the freedom of my own choice that I don't like even thinking about the notion of living in a country where they push me to use something, they push me to reveal privacy, they push me to share data which I don't even want to and I have no choice in that. They just make me share it.

Even if I lived a healthy life, I contributed to society and I contributed socially to society, so that I would get the advantages in that system, I wouldn't like that. I wouldn't want to live in such a system.

**Tina Woods**: What do you think are some of the other ethical issues in AI?

**Bertalan Meskó**: There's a really huge range of issues that come to my mind, from bio-terrorism to freedom of choice about using technologies, to diversity issues. For example, women's health issues are being neglected by companies. Companies that try to address women's health issues, they usually don't have any female leaders or even female developers in the company, by their own estimation.

AI is being developed in countries with a lot of supercomputer power. Those countries have a far better chance to make artificial general intelligence happen. From there, they would have an exponentially larger chance to do, actually, anything they want. Simply through having access to data—to data we pay for.

Either through private insurance or health insurance, your healthcare data belongs to you and it should be a human right to be able to access your own healthcare data. It's ridiculous how hard it is for people to access it. The way the technology is accessed even now creates biological differences; it creates differences in the job market.

Then there's the way AI replaces certain jobs. The Moravec paradox in AI research shows that it's much easier to code high intellectual-level tests than sensory motor skills. So, it's much easier to replace a CEO with an algorithm than to code an algorithm to mimic a three-year-old climbing the stairs. What happens when CEOs are getting replaced by AI but miners are almost impossible to replace? When AI changes the job market, what are we going to do with medical professionals? They have to change or modify their jobs because of how algorithms can contribute to what they do.

These are the major issues that come to my mind, but I'm sure I missed many important ones because there are so many. The black market using advanced technologies from 3D bioprinting; the tissues and organs for transplantation; or from black market 3D printers to print out medications on demand at home, without any pharmaceutical companies' input. All these mean that digital health right now poses a huge threat to humanity, even though digital health is the only way forward for healthcare to make us a point of care.

If policymakers, decision-makers, and governments don't act wisely and in time, we might find ourselves alone with health problems that we know we can solve with technologies which are not regulated and not safe. When it's about your health, when it's about your family's health, you will reach out to those technologies and find a way. I would do the same. That's one nightmare scenario we don't want to reach and we can only avoid reaching that with revised policies and incentives right now.

**Tina Woods**: In your view, what will have the biggest impact in helping people to live longer, better lives, now, in 5 years and in 10 years?

**Bertalan Meskó**: I think what will have the biggest impact in those three time points is pure data. Now, it's pure data. In 5 years, it's the potential projections of the pure data; and in 10 years, it's AI doing anything it wants with our data.

Right now, we just have the pure data. I can look at my Excel spreadsheet, I can look at my Fitbit watch, I can look at my smartphone's data sheets about different gadgets I'm using, and I can make more informed decisions about my life. My primary care physician knows that I want to bring these to the table because I want to live a long and healthy life. Right now, I'm accessing data, but without her help I would be doomed in this jungle of data and digital and healthcare information.

So, right now the biggest impact is usually accessing data. Data that's been around for decades, but we've not been able to obtain it and collect it and look at it and visualize it. Now, we can, through the technologies that we're using every day.

In 5 years, it could be the projection of that data. If you go to the doctor in 5 years and the doctor tells you—after we've measured your lifestyle parameters, lifestyle choices, your biomarkers and everything else we should measure about you—based on the 1 million similar profiles of other patients in the last 5 years, you have an 80% risk of glaucoma.

It would also show you how your vision would change. You could look at a smartphone scanner, perhaps, to show what having glaucoma feels like, how your vision changes looking through the camera. It changes your vision for your future health. It's quite the picture that if you keep on living the same way—this is going to happen to you. 1 million patients have suffered the same after having the same lifestyle for 5 more years. It's powerful.

Then in 10 years, by artificial narrow intelligence, or maybe by then we'd be very close to artificial general intelligence, we might be able to project this retrospectively.

To go back and try to come up with reasons why you've got this issue, or this or that symptom; to explain why you need a certain treatment right now; to create personalized treatments based on your genetic molecular makeup.

My lifestyle choices could be affected by a checkboard on my smartphone that can tell me the right words I need to hear when I'm making a lifestyle decision. All these things could surround our lives in an invisible, seamless way, affecting every decision that we make, and every decision our caregiver makes for us or with us. These are the three things that can have the largest impact on the future of our health.

**Tina Woods**: From your perspective in medicine, what's life going to be like as a doctor, and what will it feel like in a hospital over the next decade?

**Bertalan Meskó**: I might be too romantic here—my vision is around the care. Every trend that we are looking at, including projecting the possible directions it could take, shows that patients will have a lot more choices because of data. Many of them will realize that they can bring value to the table. They can be an expert of their health and disease management, they just need guidance.

Right now, patients need the key to the gate of the ivory tower of medicine. Let them in, tell them what to do when they get out and how they can comply with the therapy they have been prescribed. Maybe in a few years' time, these patients realize that there is no ivory tower, there is no gate, there is no key; they just need guidance in the jungle that they're living in right now.

Even myself, being a physician and a researcher, I have a really hard time getting meaningful outcomes of my data collections and the data sheets that I'm using. Maybe that will be the biggest change for us. For physicians, I really hope that in a few years' time, we realize how important it is to replace the repetitive parts of their job because of advanced algorithms.

We would only let healthcare professionals do really creative types of work that require a human judgment, that require their expertise, their experience, their background. Everything else, from administration to a radiologist checking 40 images could be checked by an algorithm. Some parts of medicine really require human expertise and we could make it happen with less burnout, less stress, and physicians could enjoy what they do more.

Right now, if you show a medical student what a physician does every day and ask them whether they want to remain in medical school, many of them would leave right away. You do administration 60% of your time and doing administration 60% of your time doesn't sound so exciting for your future profession. We are doing it wrong. These AI algorithms could change that.

I hope that policymakers could look at healthcare as though they were in a cockpit in a flight: looking at all the data, predictive analytics, and seamless, constant iteration of how the processes in healthcare work, and improving them together. It doesn't sound so futuristic. In Dubai, I've seen a hospital where they do exactly that. They have about 20 monitors looking at everything that's in the digital hospital. No paperwork, obviously. And this way, it could be objectively analyzed and quantified, and then informed decisions could be made about how to improve the healthcare process itself.

In research, I hope that they could use the deep learning algorithms that they're using now in many clinical trials, some of which are in silico. Then we wouldn't have to test drugs on real patients. I hope I can tell my children in 10 years' time that when I became a doctor in 2009, they used to test drugs on patients, and that was the barbaric era of modern medicine. It can only change with the use of advanced algorithms.

While there are many technologies from VR to robotics which are amazing and important, the biggest thing here still is the cultural transformation that's going on.

I like the metaphor of a recent study, where they showed that if they just gave VR devices to patients when they stay at hospital for a long time, hoping that it would help them reduce stress and pain, nothing happened. But when the physicians asked their coaches to explain what to expect on the VR device and how to use it, and they remained partners in that, the study showed they could quantifiably measure a reduction in pain scores for patients.

That's an example for what digital health means. There's a whole area in medicine that's turning into an equal partnership. Technologies are unique elements, but how we look at them is what matters.

**Tina Woods**: We know that 90% of the social determinants of health isn't linked to sickness data at all. It's actually genomics, behavioral, social data. How do you think we can shift that, and what will the role of technology play?

**Bertalan Meskó**: We know your zip code affects the length of your life more than your DNA. I agree that these numbers are correct, but we must also address the issue of personalization. For example, for a black person who lives in a rural part of Washington DC I think social determinants will take up more than 90% of, you know, how long and how healthy a life you can have.

I think the issue is not how to reverse this, but how to make sure that everyone gets a personalized assessment about what kind of chances they can have, so they could then decide what they would like to have.

There are many people who don't want healthcare as long as they have no symptoms, but with a prevention plan you will have a higher chance to get the most out of your health in the long term.

Even though we know social determinants make up such a big aspect of this, that they have such an impact on longevity, no medical professional, no researcher, no healthcare system, can do anything with it. It's such a high-level kind of analysis that without AI, we are literally just guessing.

I had a whole genome sequencing service. I know what conditions I have a risk for. For example, I know from those insights that I have an 8 times higher risk for a particular condition than the average population. This is huge, and it's important to me to know about that. But what if there's a cultural determinant like an environmental effect around my location, or in the air quality, that has a bigger impact? I want to know about that, but I can't. There's risk on both counts, but we can't even measure this part of the risk. Using these advanced analytics, maybe we could have a better chance to make this assessment.

**Tina Woods**: There's a lot of data out there that is far more important for us to be aware of in terms of impact on health than even our healthcare data itself. What is it going to look like in 5-10 years in terms of technology raising our awareness of all these other threats to our health?

**Bertalan Meskó**: We don't even have to go 5 or 10 years from now. There is an application in asthma and there's one in managing migraines, both with similar features. They give out notifications to their users tailored to the user's personalized features, the options they've selected, and what they need in their health management, that will let them know if that the area they are traveling in has, for example, high pollen levels.

This data is available publicly. Patients have smartphones, so they have the technology for that. They just have to merge these two together. It sounds simple to merge these datasets with the personal smartphones that we have. I think that's a possibility already. I have a camera at home—a security camera—that analyzes air quality all the time and it gives you notifications when dust concentration is so high that it affects the carbon dioxide concentration too. If we have high levels of that, we can't think that clearly.

I think the technology is already there, but it isn't as widespread as it could be. That could change—the way patients are becoming empowered, a patient with migraines has quite a motivation to change how they live and improve their condition.

They'll look at everything, every option that they have. The way that digital health is breaking into people's homes and into their smartphones, I think will be the driving force behind bringing these technologies to the masses.

**Tina Woods**: Of all the predictions about medical technology you've ever made, which one did you get most wrong?

**Bertalan Meskó**: Whenever I focused on a prediction on a certain technology, I was wrong. It's a good lesson for me too, because what I preach is that the cultural components of a paradigm shift are more important than the technology that they're using.

With Google Glass, I made a big mistake when I expected it to break it through the wall, and it's far, far away from that. It reminded me that the real lesson is that technology should not be the focus. Telemedicine, AR—that should not be the focus. The real needs of patients should be the focus.

In the eastern part of Hungary, telemedicine will play a major role; in Budapest, in the capital city, VR devices or AI-based medical record systems could be important in hospitals. But what matters is how these people look at technology, and how we adopt or reject them: not which microchip comes out next year.

**Tina Woods**: Do you think we're ever going to be immortal? Is the technology heading in that direction?

**Bertalan Meskó**: I love this question. I was in a Wired panel in London two weeks ago and they wanted to talk about digital health. And the first question they asked was about nanotechnology. I told them that this is by far not the most important issue in healthcare now. Right now, my patients can't even access their medical records, but they're already thinking about nanotechnology.

Philosophically I think at some point we might be able to reach some forms of immortality—certainly not the kind that we see in movies and science fiction books.

It would be absolutely enough for me to just giving a chance for 90% of the population to live more than 100 years in quite a healthy way. I would sign anything and everything right now for that.

Thinking about the chance for immortality is certainly fun. I think by the time we understand at a level of 80% how our brain works, then we could maybe find a way to upload our information. I used to be much more optimistic about that, but since I've spent the last few years in researching AI and feedback on medicine and healthcare, the more I see, the more I read, the more I know about that, the further and further away I put that line.

Consider the technology for singularity. How could we get there? I've been playing chess professionally for six months to understand the algorithms better because I thought that by learning that, I could learn how algorithms face challenges, and it's really hard to mimic anything that we have in the brain. Philosophically, I think it's going to be possible at some point. I don't think that our generation will see any of it.

**Tina Woods**: If immortality seems a little far-fetched, let's consider a more feasible target. What do you think would happen if we could all live beyond 130?

**Bertalan Meskó**: If we stick to 130, that's an easier figure to imagine. The oldest person ever to live I think reached 122. It is technically a little bit more within our grasp to hit that 130 mark. The reason I chose 130 is that there was a nature study concluding that the biological limitation that people have is around 125 - 130. It would give us the chance to live to that biological milestone; we could really fulfil our biological potential.

The question we have to ask is if this is something that we want. Assuming that we can live relatively healthy and happy lives up to that golden age, is this something that we want? Discussing that question means that we also have to discuss the social implications and the ethical challenges.

Just one of the hundreds of ethical issues of most of us living to 130 is that it would mean that most of us would live in healthcare already, so we would be quite involved in healthcare. We'd need some kind of carer—robotic ones or real-life ones—that would be heavily involved in healthcare systems. Nowadays, you only go to healthcare when you are sick. In this future, healthcare becomes by far the biggest industry in the world because everyone is affected by it. That means major shifts would happen in how healthcare is organized, in how we would take care of the health of the people that we have, and what kind of chance we would give them to live a respectable life in the last decade of their life.

When I have discussions with people about this now, I'm 34, so I assume I should last for at least another 70 years. I think that's reliable. People who are 45 or 50, and they talk to me about this as though they have 20 or 25 more years, and I tell them: no, you're shooting for at least 50. The first person who will live until 130 is certainly alive right now. Knowing how science and technology has become available, I can't imagine that that one person hasn't already been born. I'm sure they're already alive and that there are many people who will live to more than 130. The condition they'll be in is a different kind of question here, but they have a chance to shoot for more than 130.

Pensions, the way society is organized, the way healthcare impacts everyone's lives: all these things will contribute to a new kind of world that we are living in. And then, many people might start thinking about leaving for a planet—when we become multiplanetary species—like Mars. That raises different questions, but it's still not immortality. It's a rational question to ask, whether or not we'll reach immortality. But 130 is something we'll shoot for.

# Final thoughts

The COVID-19 pandemic has highlighted the importance of civic society in building resilience in the face of a crisis. Learning from this, we need to give power to people in their local communities and heal the fracture lines that have been exposed—especially by addressing the health and wealth inequalities that have put the most deprived and vulnerable at the highest risk of dying from COVID-19.

We can choose to protect our health and increase our wealth by empowering our citizens rather than relying on state control. While South Korea, Taiwan, and Singapore have used tracking applications to control the spread of the virus, they have benefitted far more through quick, extensive testing, accurate reporting, and the willingness of their populations to cooperate. But to achieve such a level of compliance, you need trust. People need to trust science, to trust public authorities, and to trust the media.

We also need shared values that bind us together as humans first and foremost. This requires all stakeholders in society to come together in a spirit of global solidarity. In order to defeat the virus and avoid future pandemics we need to nurture health as our greatest asset—individually, locally, and at community and national levels—and share information globally in a way that serves all of humankind. We explore this in the next chapter.

# References

1. *Factors associated with COVID-19-related hospital death in the linked electronic health records of 17 million adult NHS patients, OpenSAFELY collective*, May 2020 https://opensafely.org/outputs/2020/05/covid-risk-factors/

2. *Coronavirus: obesity doubles risk of hospital, The Times,* May 7 2020 https://www.thetimes.co.uk/article/coronavirus-obesity-doubles-risk-of-hospital-qnpl5p7cc

3. *NHS uses fitness app to pay patients to avoid diabetes, The Times,* February 23 2020 https://www.thetimes.co.uk/article/nhs-uses-fitness-app-to-pay-patients-to-avoid-diabetes-8svgdzs0f

4. *Boris Johnson to launch war on fat after coronavirus scare, The Times,* May 15 2020 https://www.thetimes.co.uk/article/boris-johnson-to-launch-war-on-fat-after-coronavirus-scare-flgswhmvx

5. *Projections of multi-morbidity in the older population in England to 2035: estimates from the Population Ageing and Care Simulation (PACSim) model, Oxford Academic,* May 2018 https://academic.oup.com/ageing/article/47/3/374/4815738

6. *Major NCDs and their risk factors, World Health Organization,* 2020 https://www.who.int/ncds/introduction/en/

7. *Projections of multi-morbidity in the older population in England to 2035: estimates from the Population Ageing and Care Simulation (PACSim) model, Oxford Academic,* May 2018 https://academic.oup.com/ageing/article/47/3/374/4815738

8. *The Health of the Nation, APPGL,* February 2020 https://indd.adobe.com/view/85a7129f-f900-41fa-9a9d-024d13f0aaf5

9. *Here's what AI means for the future of healthcare, World Economic Forum*, 11 January 2017 `https:// www.weforum.org/agenda/2017/01/heres-what-ai- means-for-the-future-of-healthcare`

10. *Cardiologist Eric Topol on How AI Can Bring Humanity Back to Medicine, Alice Park, Time*, 14 March 2019 `https://time.com/5551296/cardiologist-eric- topol-artificial-intelligence-interview/`

11. *NHS Vale of York rolls out predictive analytics to cut A&E admissions, Owen Hughes, Digital Health*, 4 October 2019 `https://www.digitalhealth. net/2019/10/nhs-vale-of-york-rolls-out- predictive-analytics-to-cut-ae-admissions/`

12. *Insilico Medicine COVID-19 news, Insilico medicine*, 2020, `https://insilico.com/ncov-sprint/`

13. *UK launches whole genome sequence alliance to map spread of coronavirus, UK government press release*, 23 March 2020 `https://www.gov.uk/government/news/ uk-launches-whole-genome-sequence-alliance- to-map-spread-of-coronavirus`

14. *State Of Healthcare Q1'20 Report: Investment & Sector Trends To Watch, CBInsights*, 2020 `https://www. cbinsights.com/research/report/healthcare- trends-q1-2020/`

15. *The pandemic has spawned a new way to study medical records, The Economist*, 14 May 2020, `https://www.economist.com/science-and- technology/2020/05/14/the-pandemic-has- spawned-a-new-way-to-study-medical-records`

# CHAPTER 5

# BUILDING UP ASSETS FOR THE 100-YEAR LIFE

*"A child born in a rich country today has a very plausible chance of living to 100; while this increase in life expectancy has been happening for decades, we continue to structure our lives the way our parents or even grandparents did. Unless deep seated social change occurs then a longer life is a gloomy prospect, making longevity a curse and not a gift."*

— *Andrew Scott, Co-Author, The 100 Year Life*

In 2018, Earth became home to more people aged 65 years and over than children under five, for the first time ever. The 50-plus population now represents four generations, including the Baby Boomers and Generation X. By 2031, the 50-plus population will include millions of Millennials; Generation Z will begin to join the cohort in 2047.

This growing aging demographic has long been generating concern that this will weaken economic growth as the number of people of working age declines and governments' fiscal burdens will worsen due to higher pension and healthcare costs[1]. The COVID-19 pandemic will only exacerbate the economic burden.

From an individual perspective, the biggest worry about old age is simply not having enough money. We know that income is associated with happiness[2], but debates persist[3] about the exact nature of this relationship. We don't need a huge amount to be "happy." According to a worldwide poll of 1.7 million people from 164 countries around the world published in Nature[4], the happiest people earn between £46,000 and £58,000 (in UK terms). After that, day-to-day happiness pretty much levels off. However, in order to be able to look back on your life and feel truly satisfied with what you've achieved, the poll found that you need to be earning around £74,000 per year (in UK terms).

It's clear that having more wealth means having better health. Wealthier people have access to better healthcare and access to a more controlled lifestyle; wealth brings stability to one's life. We can, however, clarify that further. Recent research[5] has now clarified the link between income and a longer life: a study at UCL found that having a net household worth of £488,000 by the age of 50 adds nine years to your life, compared to those with just £28,000 of assets. The study also found that those extra nine years will be lived in good health because more affluent people are more likely to remain fit, active, and independent in their later years. The only snag is that, according to a report from the BBC[6] in 2019, based on figures from the Resolution Foundation, the average 51-60 year-old only has a total net worth of around £275,000. That falls a long way short of that nine-year life bonus.

I am 56 and must admit that until the COVID-19 pandemic immediately slashed all my income through cancelled contracts, I hadn't spent nearly enough time thinking about the money I will need later in my life. My husband constantly nags me about putting more into my pension, yet it still doesn't take over my more immediate concerns like chasing the next contract or sponsorship deal. Perhaps subconsciously I have been lured into a false sense of security, knowing that as a Baby Boomer I can expect to receive in benefits and services over a fifth more than I paid in tax, at least according to the Resolution Foundation, a British think-tank. But today's workers, like my sons, may not have it so good, and the COVID-19 pandemic may make the long-simmering intergenerational battles go into overdrive.

This once-in-a-century pandemic is expected to create the worst recession in 300 years, eclipsing the Great Depression of the 1930s in the UK. The "new normal" is unleashing a tidal wave of social experiments, and is already creating changes in working practices in two months that would have taken years to happen and will likely persist. While the older generations will be hit hard, others are predicting the youngest will bear the full force of the long-term economic fallout.

## The multistage life

Andrew Scott, Professor of Economics at London Business School, co-wrote the acclaimed book *The One Hundred Year Life*[7], which sets out the challenges and opportunities that living longer brings. The book describes how as we are living longer we are moving from a three-stage life, split into education, work and retirement, to a multistage life, with periods of learning, building up both tangible assets (such as income, property, savings) and non-tangible assets (like social networks, building up skills in a process of "re-creation").

I read the book when I started my health innovation business at the age of 52, a little over three years ago. It resonated completely and helped me assuage the panic I initially felt as the newbie "oldie entrepreneur" about the time it would take for the contracts and revenue to start flowing (building up my "intangible assets," as they are described in the book). It also helped me manage my feelings of terror that I would fail spectacularly in a youth-obsessed male-dominated tech industry. I concentrated my energy on learning about artificial intelligence, industry disruption, and health technology and went to as many free meet-ups and conferences as possible to expand my networks (again, building up my intangible assets by learning and developing connections in these new areas).

Scott argues that in the UK we need to shift our economy to enable more people to work for longer, as other countries have done and are planning. As a professional "gigster," I have taken matters into my own hands, but companies need to become fit for the times and make it easier for people to live and work flexibly, especially those with caring responsibilities. Every increase in working age by one year is a permanent 1% boost to GDP[8]. ONS estimates[9] that if the employment rate of people aged 50 to 64 matched that of those aged 35 to 49, it would add more than 5% to UK GDP, or £88 billion. It would be interesting to see how every increase in working age in terms of the extra GDP gained could translate into greater capacity for the government to fund care.

Andrew and his co-author Lynda Gratton published the follow-up book[10], *The New Long Life – A Framework for Flourishing in a Changing World* in May 2020, during the COVID-19 pandemic just when the lockdown was in the process of being partially lifted. Scott argues that our experience of the pandemic has served a far deeper purpose—it has been a dramatic stress test of our individual resilience and collective arrangements, revealing the insecurity of our lifestyles in the face of a sudden drop in earnings, and the importance of our social networks and contact with partners, family, friends, and neighbors, that many of us took for granted.

The pandemic is calling for a complete overhaul of the social contract, which was being hotly debated and discussed before the virus unleashed its havoc.

# New map of life and extra time

MIT Sloan School of Management predicts[11] that given the average level of savings in advanced economies, many people currently in their mid-40s are likely to need to work into their early to mid-70s; many currently in their 20s (many of whom could live to be over 100) will be working into their late 70s, and even into their 80s. Yet, while many people know they will have to restructure their lives and careers, corporations are unprepared, compounded by governments and institutions slow to respond with policies to facilitate the societal shifts underway. This problem has only been made more urgent to address given the pandemic.

Julia Randell-Khan is a consulting fellow on the *New Map of Life* initiative at Stanford University's Center on Longevity[12], led by Professor Laura Carstensen. It aims to change narratives about growing old to conversations about long lives and to identify and implement the changes needed so that people can live well for a century of more. Longevity demands rethinking all stages of life, not just old age—recognizing that as we have been living longer, the years added to our lives have been in the middle, and not at the end. Indeed, this "extra time" is the focus of Camilla Cavendish's excellent book of the same name. This extra time requires a fundamental rethink of how we live our lives and may be defined more by extending our vitality than by preventing disease.

A future more focused on maintaining health and well-being could extend that time further, especially as technologies harnessing interoperable data on health and lifestyle will lead to the creation of products and services to keep us healthy and well, as we describe later in this chapter.

Consumers will increasingly realize that aging is malleable and this will motivate them to keep healthy too. The wider determinants of health, including education, environment, nutrition, and income, all influence the rate at which we age. Across a variety of measures, such as cognitive function, physical strength, mortality rates, and incidence of diseases, people are in effect aging more slowly. This highlights how we need to distinguish between how many years since you were born—your chronological age—and how fit and healthy you are compared to other people, in terms of your biological age.

Policymakers should recognize that while chronological age is a useful predictor of health outcomes, it is not the best predictor of people's needs and abilities. There is an increasing need for policies more aligned around biological age and people's individual circumstances. By focusing on biological age, our policymakers and business leaders may respond differently to emerging needs and trends. Certainly COVID-19 has stimulated real ingenuity in and zeal for more work on biological age in the scientific community, with a dizzying array of studies looking at how to build up resilience to future pandemic threats by targeting the mechanisms of aging. A particular area of interest is immunosenescence—recognizing that the immune system becomes impaired with age—and another is interrupting the underlying mechanisms linked to "metabesity," causing the chronic diseases of aging, as explored in earlier chapters of this book.

Beyond the science, there is also the whole debate around how people will work, retire, and pay for their later years. How will lifelong learning evolve? How will people live in their homes and in what types of communities? How can people build up their assets for a longer life? These are all the questions that the Stanford Center on Longevity's[13] New Map of Life is exploring.

In my interview with Julia Randell-Khan, she highlighted the mismatch between policies that focus on a much shorter life with the reality on the ground for those of us who are living much longer. Big areas such as education and work need to be completely redesigned and remapped around the need for lifelong learning, for example. She argues for the sort of programs being offered at the National University of Singapore, for example, that encourage older people to keep developing their skills, so they can keep being effective learners with the mindset to keep reinventing themselves.

She says that it is about being curious and open to new things and new experiences, which includes trying out technology to see how it could help us have better lives.

Most important, though, is connecting this to having a sense of belonging, purpose, and worth at every stage of life. It links to the human spirit and looking after your fellow humans, moving beyond the individual to embrace community and new social compacts to support long lives. She cites research on social engagement that shows how people with very little from a socioeconomic point of view can derive a huge amount of value and sense of worth from contributing and being part of their local community.

In Japan, "living with purpose" is called "ikigai," and in Costa Rica, it's a "plan de vida." The words literally translate to "reason to live" and "life plan," respectively. A 2014 study found that having a purpose was associated with a lower risk of mortality[14]. According to John Day, MD[15], author of The Longevity Plan[16], whether your goal is to beat cardiovascular disease or cancer, or even to live a long and healthy life, study after study has found an association of purpose in life with all kinds of better health outcomes—an effect that stands regardless of age, sex, education or race.

Expecting good things to happen[17] may be key to a long life too. People who were optimistic had greater odds of achieving "exceptional longevity," or living to 85 and beyond, according to a study published in the Proceedings of the National Academy of Sciences[18].

Optimistic people are more likely to have goals and the confidence to reach them, so optimism may help people cultivate and maintain healthier habits. Previous studies[19] have found people who are highly optimistic have a lower chance of dying prematurely from stroke, heart disease, and even cancer.

## Technology and longer lives

On the point of technology, I caught up with my good friend Bradley Schurman, formerly Director of Global Partnerships with AARP, founder and CEO of Demogera, and an expert on social policy and innovation in aging, to get his views. I spoke with him before the COVID-19 pandemic struck and then again afterwards (where he is keeping busy writing his own book on the Super Age at his home in Washington DC). He highlights two trends running in parallel. AI is becoming more and more embedded in our everyday lives, and we're also developing a collective interest in living independently for longer. They coincide where you have AI embedded not only in the home, through devices like Amazon Echo or Google Home or other devices like Nest, but also into everyday monitoring devices like Fitbit or Apple Watch.

He explained that these devices will help not only measure our overall health long-term in a more effective way and give our physicians better real-time longitudinal data about our health, but they'll also enable us to live independently for longer: "that's everything from the light-touch stuff, like tech that monitors sleeping patterns, or motion sensors that light a path the bathroom in the middle of the night, to the hidden device, the hidden innovations that are embedded in devices like the Apple Watch."

He adds that within the home, AI can learn behaviors, and we're starting to see outcomes from that with fall prevention, for example. But for all the good that there is with AI, there are some challenges as well, which come mainly from the speed at which this transition is happening.

While it will be and already is a job killer for some industries, it also presents new opportunities for new industries to develop. I agreed with Bradley that the hiccup with all of this is that, essentially, our entire education system is built on a medieval model. How do we get all people, and older people in particular, to understand the value of upskilling throughout the course of a lifetime?

Bradley asks the important question: "What's going to happen when AI really takes over or helps in a way that benefits significant numbers of people? We're looking at urban areas first; rural areas are still really lagging behind as it relates to not only cellular but also broadband technologies. I think what's often forgotten in that conversation is that those countries didn't really have legacy networks that they had to keep up too. It's super easy for a country like China that literally had nothing, or a country like Kenya introducing their mobile banking model. They literally had no infrastructure to leapfrog, so they could build the infrastructure from scratch. The reality is that it's a hell of a lot cheaper to put up mobile towers and manage a mobile infrastructure than it is to manage an analog one."

We had an interesting conversation about social credit, and what we could take from the Chinese social credit policy to Western democracies. He observed, "In addition to social credits, we should also be thinking about health credits. If people want to live an unhealthy life, good on them, but I shouldn't have to pay for it. It's not quite fair for me to be the burden, the financial burden, on the rest of society when I knowingly engage in unhealthy behaviors. I think we have to take a look at why social credits came into play in China. For the Chinese, historically, everything was built on reputation. Deals were built on reputation, not systems. This is actually not at all dissimilar to what happened in the West during the industrial revolutions. When everyone was moved to the cities, all of a sudden that social credit, which was something that naturally developed in small communities, didn't exist anymore in the big cities.

It was easier to take advantage of people because you didn't know if they were good or bad. So, in my understanding of social credit, that's part of the reason why it developed."

Bradley pointed out that there are already many institutions that take care of social credit for us, but they are dispersed. There are groups like the Better Business Bureau. There are review aggregators like Yelp and TripAdvisor. There are private sector tools, both analog and digital, that have impacted businesses and life. China is just taking a very different and centralized approach to this.

He makes the good point that our economies are in a period of dramatic transformation, with Western economies based around consumption and measuring their success by GDP. So, everything that we do is based on producing and consuming, and that's how we say we're successful. When our populations start to shrink, it's very likely our GDP will shrink too.

He asks, "does that mean a country is any less successful, because they don't have a high GDP? The United States has the highest GDP in the world, and there are terrible social problems here right now. Incredible numbers of people live in poverty. Incredible numbers of people are undereducated. Is that the best way to approach things? Jacinda Ardern, the Prime Minister from New Zealand, implemented the well-being index recently, and I think that might be the direction we will eventually take."

New Zealand's well-being index is cited widely as a model for the future, and Jacinda Ardern has been widely praised for her response to the COVID-19 pandemic, which has exposed social fracture lines with such terrifying force. We now have a looming problem emerging when the economic fallout leads to redundancies that are expected to hit the older workforce hardest.

The fallout will be worse due in part to the agism that pervades many societies. As we emerge from the pandemic it is incumbent for leaders in business, government and wider civil society to reframe and reset how we see aging. We need a different narrative that speaks to the opportunity—not the burden—of living longer and address the whole life course including education, employment and retirement. Critically, governments need policies that provide support for those who are unable to continue working while providing incentives to work for those who can.

Yvonne Sonsino, Global Co-Leader of *Next Stage*[20] at Mercer said, "in order to harness the benefits of living longer, a new social contract is needed to encourage employers to help people remain in productive and engaging work beyond their 50s, by adopting age-friendly practices such as flexible working and carers' leave, helping people acquire new skills, and providing in-work support such as health screening and financial planning advice. Our research shows that people potentially run out of pension savings some 8-20 years before they die on current estimates of life expectancy. Enabling the funding of longevity through meaningful work is already a necessity."

Post-COVID, she argues, "it will be even more important that diversity and inclusion is addressed, with age diversity the last bastion to tackle. Agism is still rife, and the high unemployment caused by the pandemic will make it even harder for older workers to get their fair share, and their financial wellness taking a huge hit. More creative employment models that offer more flexibility will be needed more than ever. A number of Mercer's global clients are trialing new hybrid contracts that offer flexibility and more security than a gig worker, but less restriction than a full-time worker, while also providing training and reskilling opportunities too."

# The future of retirement and insurance

I interviewed Mike Mansfield, Director of the Longevity and Retirement Centre at Aegon, a life insurance, pension, and asset management company, and he says it is important to maintain good health as part of your retirement planning. Lifelong learning is important too. The job market is changing and this will accelerate as we emerge from the pandemic. People starting in a career, when they leave college or leave school, may well find that their career is going to evolve over time. They will have to change and keep their skills up to date, and this will continue as you get older.

Mike adds that preparing for retirement is very multidimensional but overall, saving earlier for retirement is a key need. People should have a written plan for their retirement and a backup plan in case things go wrong, or when things go wrong.

Chris Madsen, Head of Global Underwriting at Aegon, who works with Mike, adds: "we know from the retirement survey that it's tough for people to plan for the long-term. This is where the role of companies as well as government comes into play. We need to make sure that people start saving early, that they understand these trade-offs, and that there are societal fail-safes in play if for whatever reason people aren't able to save for their retirement."

Companies are recognizing how intense an impact financial stress can have on a person's health, and there are increasing examples of US-based corporations rolling out programs in the workplace to help their employees and customers improve their overall financial health. One example is Citibank that has partnered with major wellness brand Well + Good to offer financial wellness tips via a specially branded Wellness and Finance portal. Their goal is for employees to learn how to reduce day-to-day financial anxiety and take meaningful steps towards personal long-term financial goals.

The aim of the project is to help employees feel confident that their finances are in good shape, and so reduce their financial stress; ultimately, removing that stress will improve their employees' overall health.

Start-ups are also getting in on the act. Chris adds, "We're seeing some start-ups that have quite interesting solutions. This could be something as simple as an app that every time you buy anything, asks, "Do you want to save something for yourself as well?" There's an old saying that you shouldn't forget to pay yourself. In other words, every time I buy a cup of coffee that's a couple of euros, I put 50 cents away for myself and that adds up over time. You can set up the same prompt if you go to a restaurant, or even buy groceries; you can always pay yourself, and you probably won't really feel the difference, but over time that money will accumulate—as long as it's in an account that's truly segregated."

Mike agrees that technology can help people save by making it easier, citing the Revolut bank account as a good example: it rounds up purchases to the nearest pound or euro, takes the difference and puts it into a savings account. It's a painless way to save money over the course of a year or a lifetime.

These ideas are all beginning to gain traction and hold significant promise, because it's really easy. More and more of us pay on our mobile phones. Making it really easy is part of the answer, but again the money needs to be put into a segregated account. It's potentially something that employers can support and incentivize wider society too.

Mike points out that behavioral economics can also nudge people to save more for their retirement. A good workplace example is when people are coming up to a crown birthday or getting a pay rise, and the employer can give them a nudge to put a little bit more into their retirement savings account.

Mike added that there are quite a few insurance companies and financial institutions that are encouraging people, whether through a lower premium or other means, to adopt a healthier lifestyle; and also offering people options to make it easier for them to adopt a healthy lifestyle. He cautions that this is an evolving area, and we need to make sure that we don't lose the principles of solidarity that are so important with insurance. This includes ensuring that people aren't excluded from joining these programs because of a disability or some other factor that categorizes them as high risk.

Government also has a key role to play in encouraging healthy behaviors in the first place, perhaps through tax policies to incentivize people to save and to make healthy choices. This was the case with the sugar tax in the UK, which has helped to cut down the amounts of sugar and unhealthy snacks that people eat. More recently, the UK government has initiated a range of measures to tackle the obesity crisis including a change in advertising rules so that junk food adverts cannot be seen on television before the 9 PM watershed[21], as well as a ban on chocolates, crisps, and sweets at the checkout and displaying calories on menus in restaurants and pubs.

Workplaces are changing and so too have employers' responsibilities to encourage healthy living. The pandemic is throwing up the differences between "workplace" and "workspace," and raising questions about an employer's responsibility to encourage healthy habits for those working from home. More people have chosen to be self-employed or freelance and working on different types of contracts, and this is likely to increase with companies having to shed staff. The insurance industry will need to rise to the challenge and help people access some of those products and schemes that help them save for retirement and maintain a healthy lifestyle, whether in the workplace or workspace at home.

The other growing trend is people needing to take time out of work at different points in their life for caregiving responsibilities, or perhaps for a mid-life sabbatical. The insurance industry will need to provide flexibility within the products and services that they are offering to allow people to make those choices.

## The new social contract

Mike has identified 9 essential design features for the "new social contract" including sustainable social security benefits, opportunities to save, lifelong learning, and a positive view of aging in an age-friendly world. Crucially, he argues, "it is very important to celebrate the value of older individuals—of individuals at all ages— and the contribution that people make at every age to society. We need to make sure that people of all ages have the opportunity to continue to stay economically active as long as they want to, until a point in time when they feel they want to retire. Agism is present in the workforce. It can be a barrier to people getting a job or feeling fully included when they are working. It is something we really need to check ourselves for."

Feeling valued and having a sense of purpose keeps people motivated. Chris cites recent research that shows having a purpose in life and the ability to plan is a good indicator of all-cause mortality. He says, "some of these characteristics can probably be taught or structured, at least to a point. In other words, if I'm healthy and I can work longer and it's something I enjoy, then I also have a purpose which then, in and of itself, helps me have a healthier life. There's a bit of circularity here, but I think those are the type of dynamics that we need to tap into. At the same time, if you're happier and still working and you're healthier, not only do your health costs decrease but you can actually get away with a lower amount of savings to fund your longer life."

I asked Chris how people could add 5 more years of healthy years to their life, and he said that—in addition to regular moderate physical activity—food and diet are incredibly important: "looking at the variation of food in particular, when you talk about health inequalities then you have to consider the general deterioration of food combined with the reduced means that a significant proportion of society has to purchase food with. Combining these two elements results in quite poor health consequences for a significant proportion of society. It is known that ultra-processed foods are really bad for mortality."

He added, "an interesting thing about that is that we're not just talking about cardiovascular disease or cancers; we're talking about those, of course, but poor diet affects all other causes of mortality too. We know that there's a significant link between poor diet and the chance of dying from anything. These things are all interrelated, but from where I sit food is a key ingredient in any plan to achieve an increased healthspan."

When asked how AI would help increase healthspan, he felt that over the next decade and a half to two decades, advances in genetics—with the proper guardrails—will become key. He said, 'I see AI making significant inroads in the area of genetics. It's not that long ago, only in 2003, that the genome was finally mapped. Five years ago, we were beginning to understand the basic levers, but on a very rudimentary basis; a gene would be turned on or off and a researcher would study the consequence of that. What we're seeing now is polygenic scoring. What you now get from 23andMe and several other similar companies is essentially, "This combination of genetic markers is producing this type of outcome with this probability." That's just the beginning; if we look at it in another five years, I think AI will provide a much better understanding of all of these interrelations. AI will also begin to take into account things like our bacterial profile and our microbiome—that's where the link to food and diet comes in again, because we all process food slightly differently. That's based on our genetic profile, but also encompasses our epigenetics as well as our microbiome.'

Some insurers are starting to reward people for healthy behaviors by sharing the savings from reduced healthcare costs as a result. It is a win-win for all stakeholders: there is a clear financial interest for the insurer to subsidize good behavior, individuals stay healthier and there is less demand on the healthcare system. Who could argue with this?

Chris feels a market will keep growing around products that reward healthy behavior. He added that we are seeing this in car insurance already, where a lot of people get their driving behavior evaluated, either directly through their mobile phone or through a GPS device in the car, that shares all of your driving information and scores you every time you drive. That score is then translated into some sort of premium incentive.

Given that insurance is the business of assessing risks and pricing policies to match, it is no surprise that AI will potentially disrupt the insurance[22] industry by being able to quantify risk[23] in a way that traditional insurance cannot. With big data and algorithms, the practice of underwriting and pricing can be much more precise and specific to the unique considerations of each individual, which challenges the entire business model of traditional insurance.

Reza Khorshidi, Chief Scientist at AIG and Principal Investigator at Deep Medicine Program at University of Oxford, explains: "Insurance is the business of transferring the risk to its optimal owner. Historically, this optimal ownership was through insurers' financial strength; with the developments in science and technology related to risks, however, this notion of optimal ownership in the next few decades is to be redefined. For instance, who is the optimal owner of your health risk? Someone who can delay the onset of some diseases for you? Someone who can give you better lifespan and/or healthspan? Someone who can protect your health and wealth? And you see the point. Of course, the ideal answer is a mix of all of the above plus some more probably.

But if you look today, many of these characteristics of the ideal ownership of risk are distributed in the public sector and various industries in the private sector; many of them, such as longevity, we can argue are yet to be defined by some emerging entities. This is what makes insurance an extremely exciting area to watch in the next decade."

An entirely new industry called Insurtech is emerging, and many interesting start-ups have entered the race, like Yu-Life[24], Lemonade, and Dacadoo[25]. Yu Life incentivizes life insurance through a reward scheme—with customers able to earn "yucoins" by walking or completing mindfulness challenges—and these can be exchanged for airline miles or discounts with major retailers like Amazon. Dacadoo partners with insurers and reinsurers to provide health risk quantification.

Lemonade[26] is a new type of insurer well known for its speed, issuing policies and paying claims in a matter of minutes using AI. Lemonade's business model is based on a transparent fee model, fast claim settlement, and social good. It discourages dishonest claims by donating excess money (over a fixed fee, expenses, and claims) to a charity of the customers' choosing. Lemonade's vision is to disrupt traditional insurance's misalignment of incentives between the insurer and the insured and apply behavioral economics with transparent transactions to benefit consumers while promoting social good.

Roughly three-quarters[27] of health insurance executives (72%) say investing in AI will be one of their top three strategic priorities for the coming year, according to a recent survey by Accenture. Instead of calculating insurance premiums using historical data collected by actuaries, AI allows insurers to interpret complex real-time data from their customers and provide solutions tailored for the individual.

In this way insurers, like Vitality, can reward their policyholders showing healthy behaviors with lower premiums[28]. Policyholders are incentivized with Fitbits and smart watches to encourage them into a preventative health regime; data collected is analyzed by the insurer who sends positive feedback on their fitness activity, sleep or nutrition, for example. A participant's health insurance premium can be repriced over time based on their behavior. Over time, health insurers can receive direct insight into the effectiveness of their wellness programs on various disease groupings, highlight claims expense savings, and improve efforts for disease interventions.

Among the largest investments in AI tech in the insurance industry has been in fraud detection, with more than 75%[29] of insurers reporting the use of machine-learning algorithms to flag fraud cases in 2016, according to the Coalition Against Insurance Fraud.

In the healthcare claims process[30], AI has the potential to dramatically speed up claims' approval. For instance, when claims are being processed, automatic checks are performed to establish whether authorization is required, whether it has been granted, and whether the claim is within the defined limits. How fast? A pilot program spearheaded by Prudential in Singapore credits AI with reducing the time to process hospital claims by 75%; a claim that once took nine days to process can now be settled in a mere 2.3 seconds.

## Pensions

With pensions, it's much less clear. Chris Madsen from Aegon explains: "As an insurer we're liable for the payout of the annuity, and whether it starts at age 65 or 67 or 68, it doesn't really matter. It starts at some point in time, and then the longer that the person lives, the higher the liability of the insurer. Clearly, the financial interests there are not fully aligned.

Structurally, we're already beginning to see changes to this; for decades there's been a shift from defined benefit plans to defined contribution plans. Increasingly, the choice, in terms of funding pensions or funding your retirement, is left up to individuals."

Before the pandemic, a little more than 10% of UK pensioners had total assets of £1,000,000 or more, according to the Office for National Statistics Wealth and Assets Survey—that means there are more than a million "millionaire pensioners" in the UK. Time will tell how the pandemic will erode these pension pots in the long term, but it is clear that government and workplace retirement systems are under strain.

The UK recently introduced "pension freedoms" that allow consumers to cash in their lifetime savings and spend the money as they wish. This has generated a plethora of different financial products taking advantage of this greater flexibility but there is a still a need for better retirement income products, such as drawdown and non-workplace pensions, and more tailored advice.

For example, as home ownership has increased this has created more opportunities to lend affordably to older borrowers; in one such new structure, the borrower commits only to paying the monthly interest on the loan, and the balance is eventually repaid by the sale of the borrower's property. These sorts of equity release products provide greater flexibility at a time when there is much more uncertainty around the extent of your working life and your longevity. However, this flexibility also means that you are being asked to take responsibility for increasingly complex financial decisions in later life, including comprehensive planning for your retirement, and with serious thought given to periods of ill health.

There are groups that recognize this. For example, **The Pension Advisory Service** (**TPAS**) and insurer Aviva are experimenting with programs[31] to help middle-aged people evaluate their jobs, finances and health, as well as their plans for later in life. In 2018, TPAS targeted a small group of self-employed workers, aged 35 to 50, with one-to-one phone conversations. There are now plans to make this midlife check-up an online program.

Another trend creating both opportunities and challenges is the switch to digital and data-driven products and services. Better design will address some of the challenges of older people feeling nervous about using new technologies.

However, regulation is needed to minimize the risk of unscrupulous firms using data and information to identify and exploit customers. In the UK, 5 million older people are targeted by fraudsters each year. The increased levels of cognitive impairment and social isolation in older populations compared to society at large increase the likelihood of successful fraud, and so this group is relentlessly targeted by scams. Despite the fact that over 3 million caregivers in the UK provide financial management support, it's hard to deliver that support effectively.

Fortunately, there are a number of start-ups that have developed technological solutions to these problems. Kalgera[32] is one example; a personal finance platform that helps safeguard the financial lives of vulnerable people. It uses AI and neuroscience to detect vulnerability in financial transactions, and provides a secure way to share this information with a user's trusted family and friends, alerting them too to the possibility of fraud. The Toucan[33] app works in a similar way, letting users share their bank balance status with a trusted friend or carer, and using a simple traffic light system to keep their trusted partner up to date on their financial status.

Morgan Ash[34] has produced a model of assessing vulnerable customers, similar to the techniques used to assess consumers for credit scores, and the **Society of Later Life Advisers** (**SOLLA**) is creating a computer-based training program that assists financial advisers in identifying vulnerability. As systems like this become more commonplace, the financial services market can start to really understand the impact of financial vulnerability, and change the recommendations they provide to suit each individual client.

# The longevity marketplace

Older adults are an increasingly powerful force as workers, consumers, entrepreneurs, and active participants in their communities says Paul Irving[35], chairman of the Milken Institute Center for the Future of Aging. In contrast to the post-war generation, they are more demanding, aspirational, and discerning— and do not want to be seen as passive victims resigned to take anything on offer.

They are also increasingly socially conscious. Consumers and employees alike want to deal with businesses which are socially responsible, and more and more investors are considering **Environmental, Social, and Governance (ESG)** factors in portfolio selection. According to the Global Sustainable Investment Alliance[36], topics of particular interest include climate change, the effects of emerging technology, and the diversity and general composition of a company's board of directors. Demographic issues, including the impact of aging, are now joining this list of concerns. Moreover, ESG investors increasingly seek alignment with the UN's Sustainable Development Goals, which include population health imperatives.

At a series of Round Tables held in London to look at how the lessons from COVID-19 could inform the APPG for Longevity's Health of the Nation strategy, the idea of a risk management framework for health, akin to that already in place for climate change, was mooted by John Godfrey, Corporate Affairs Director for Legal & General, a multinational financial services company specializing in investment management, lifetime mortgages, pensions, annuities, and life assurance.

He argues that health is 10 years behind the climate change agenda but this could be a neat way to incentivize business: "10 years ago in business the concerns about warming and climate were the preserve, really, of a minority group regarded as somewhat eccentric. People thought there was a trade-off between doing the right thing for the environment or the climate and making money.

Today, that has turned right around. It's now mainstream for all businesses to be thinking about their climate impact. How exposed are they to climate risks? And are they aware of opportunities to mitigate global warming and to play their part fixing the climate crisis? Now firms are held to account for what they're doing in that space. I would like to think that, in time, we will have the same risk management framework for health or well-being."

To any logical investor, this makes sense, especially when business has so much to gain if they get it right. Apart from the social imperative, the commercial opportunity is staggering: according to AARP, the impact of the 50-plus cohort on GDP is equivalent to the third largest economy in the world (and this is probably still true, irrespective of COVID-19). In 2018, 56 cents of every dollar were spent by the 50-plus population in the U.S. and this figure is set to rise to 61 cents by 2050.

While the pandemic will affect projections, the Longevity Economic Outlook[37] published by the AARP on the first day of 2020 originally predicted that the economic contribution of the 50-plus population will triple by 2050 and argued for private and public initiatives to improve the quality of work into the retirement years[38], provide better lifetime learning[39], training and support for late-life entrepreneurship[40].

Crucially, business needs to adapt and evolve with the times, and show far more imagination and creativity to invent products and services that will attract older adults. Ageist attitudes and old stereotypes persist and many products and services available to an aging population do not resonate with older consumers.

There are many myths to be busted, including older consumers' affinity for technology. In 2018, the 50-plus age demographic in the U.S. spent a very substantial $140 billion on technology (compared with $136 billion among the under-50s). Tech demand among the 50-plus population is expected to surge in the coming decades (reaching expenditure of $645 billion in 2050). Yet tech firms seem largely unaware of this high-performing and fast-growing market.

Today, 91% of people aged 50 and older report using a computer, with 94% of them reporting that technology keeps them connected to friends and family. This goes beyond smartphones and apps and is starting to reach homes too in this new "age tech" industry, helping older consumers enjoy their lives. The COVID-19 pandemic will have pushed many older people outside their comfort zone to get to grips with more new technology too. It was basically a sink or swim moment of disruption.

An emerging issue related to the use of AI in digital applications is the need to ensure that algorithms are being trained on the data from older age groups for products serving the older population, otherwise we run the risk that we are already seeing with gender and racial biases seeping in through a reliance on white male datasets, for example.

## Age tech

According to Dominic Endicott, Founder of 4Gen, "age tech" is where fintech was in 2007 and can be categorized in 4 groups: 1) services purchased by older people; 2) services purchased on behalf of older people; 3) services traded between older and younger people; and 4) services delivered to future older people.

In the category of services purchased by older people, a great example is what GreatCall and Lyft are doing via a partnership called GreatCall Rides[41] in which GreatCall customers can access the Lyft car network without requiring them to master a smartphone or an app. Another great example is Pill-Pack, a company recently acquired by Amazon for $1 billion that assembles all your medication and delivers it in a package designed to avoid errors.

Most businesses improve if they become more in tune with their customers. Think about something like Meals-on-Wheels. Then think about online food delivery services, either cooked or pre-prepared.

What if we could harness the digital infrastructure that already exists to deliver a more nutritionally balanced and interesting set of choices to our oldest citizens? Or home care, which is often still managed in a very old-fashioned way, but can be improved by remote sessions, use of home sensors, and improved scheduling algorithms.

Services traded between older and younger people is also an exciting category. This could include mechanisms by which older citizens could transfer assets to younger citizens while providing them enough control and insurance against the future, and the right incentives to the younger citizens to reach certain milestones. Or ways in which different generations could barter and even bank services—for example, someone could "bank" care hours, to be "spent" for their spouse's own care needs.

This is the idea behind Give & Take Care[42], an organization pioneered by the late legendary scientist, engineer, and inventor Heinz Wolff[43], aiming to provide care for the elderly and a secure future for the young by allowing fit adults to "bank" an hour of care for their old age by delivering an hour of care to an over-60 today. Couldn't this type of time bank idea evolve into a digitally-enabled solution using "care coins"?

## Wealth tech

Before the pandemic, AARP[44] estimated that spending among people aged 50 and older on financial services and insurance would more than triple by 2050. In the U.S. almost two-thirds of expenditure in the financial services and insurance industry—or 65 cents of every dollar—is attributable to the 50-plus age.

The "wealth tech[45]" industry refers to a new generation of financial technology companies, products, and services that will enhance retirement, investment, and financial planning to generate more wealth. New companies are arriving on the scene offering advice based on AI and big data.

These include:

- Robo-advisors—automated services that use machine-learning algorithms to provide users with advice based on the most profitable investment options, yield targets, user's risk aversion profile and other variables.

- Robo-retirement—another version of robo-advisors that is especially popular in the United States. Companies in this category specialize in managing retirement savings.

- Digital brokers—online platforms and software tools that put stock market information and the possibility of investing within anyone's reach.

- Financial products designed for investors expecting to live 100 years and beyond.

- Banking services for people over 60, or "longevity banks," resembling a traditional fintech banks but dedicated to older clients.

New digital financial services are challenging traditional banks[46] by targeting niche groups of customers. The theory is that they stand a better chance of getting people to switch banks if they tailor-make services at groups[47] who feel they are being under-served.

Like we are seeing with insurance, as everyday experiences become digitized and connected, customers are demanding—and smart businesses are providing—a technology experience centered on the unique preferences and profiles of individuals. Open Banking pioneered in the UK has created a model to open up competition and innovation in banking around the needs of the consumer, by putting people in control of their data and making it easier to move, manage, and make more of their finances.

It is a collaborative model in which banking data is shared between unaffiliated parties to deliver enhanced capabilities to the marketplace, and was set up in the UK in response to the **General Data Protection Regulation (GDPR)** and the **Payment Services Directive 2 (PSD2)** to push control over data to citizens.

The Open Banking Standard is spurring innovation and disrupting the big banks, while giving citizens' rights and creating an open, free market. Open Banking has stimulated the fintech ecosystem and is now moving into the realm of Open Finance and Open Insurance, potentially disrupting huge swathes of other businesses in the finance sector, including insurance and pensions.

There is no reason why this model can't be taken elsewhere in our lives. We are seeing moves to Open Finance and Open Insurance. Why not Open Health and, ultimately, Open Life?

Healthtech is more complex than fintech but is still amenable to open innovation and the significant opportunities to harness "non-sick" and "sick" datasets across the life course to develop new products and services. An open data approach will maximize federated open market innovation, competition, and efficiency. Taking a user-centric design approach and ensuring common interoperability will drive up rates of adoption and inclusion while reducing friction and confusion for the end customer.

## Personal data: our greatest asset?

Data is often called the "new oil" but this is not an accurate description—oil is depleted the more you consume it. With data, the more you share it, the more valuable it gets.

As consumers and citizens we don't often consider how we can exploit our data, but enabling the sharing of our personal data in a manner controlled by us is at the heart of concepts like a Personal Data Store[48] to better visualize and market personal data.

This is what is driving entrepreneurs to create secure data marketplaces like **Hub of All Things** (**HAT**)[49], Meeco.me[50], and Mydex[51] to put data in the control of the citizen/consumer and provide a mechanism to monetize this data.

Monetizing data is also at the heart of the **Data Dividend Project** (**DDP**)[52] conceived by Democratic presidential candidate and entrepreneur Andrew Yang, and described on its website as "a movement dedicated to taking back control of our personal data." Yang is most well-known for his support of a universal basic income[53] of $1,000 a month for every American, forming the basis of a human-centered economy[54], which entails a form of capitalism that measures economic success by peoples' well-being rather than by corporate profits or GDP. Yang's project is driven by the desire to dismantle Big Tech's control of data making them billions while the rest of the population lives paycheck to paycheck. Yang's ultimate goal is for Americans to be able to claim their data as a property right and get paid for it if they choose to share it.

However, there are a few problems. First, our individual data is not that valuable from a financial perspective. Estimates on what user data is worth vary widely[55]. They include evaluations of less than a dollar for an average person's data to a slightly more generous US$100 for a Facebook user. One user sold his data for $2,733 on Kickstarter[56].

Second, Yang's model does not calculate the value that emerges from high-level patterns that emerge out of aggregate data that can provide incredible social utility, especially in health. The collective value of aggregate data is at the heart of SITRA's human centered data economy (described earlier in this book) being pioneered in Finland.

Yang has a point that we're freely giving away all kinds of data to companies that analyze, sell, and profit from it. Most of citizen data is unknowingly "captured" by modern devices. Going about our daily lives can generate hundreds of data points, from where we travel, to how much time we spent in different locations, to what we bought, ate, or drank.

Sensors, for example, can discreetly collect usage and behavioral data, often in previously unobserved private settings (such as in the home or when we are asleep) in order to anticipate and respond to our needs (adjusting temperature or lighting, for example) using machine learning and AI. Data from fitness trackers, internet browsing, mobile phones (geolocation), and countless other devices are also captured without us being necessarily aware.

The extent and potential value of the data collected remains unclear to users and undermine the aims of GDPR according to a paper by Nature[57]. Digital services and distributed devices now increasingly operate on a linked-up basis, in which information is shared between networks of devices and service providers, making use of unique user identifiers to provide seamless data sharing and personalized experiences using machine learning and AI. Such seamless experiences are rooted in identification technologies used to manage authentication, data access and transfer, and link together disparate sources of user data for inferential analytics. Clearly, these hubs leveraging multimodal AI can be of significant commercial value.

As citizens become more savvy following data breaches and scandals like Cambridge Analytica, there are concerns over an emerging "surveillance capitalism," a concept coined by Shoshana Zuboff, Harvard Professor and author of *The Age of Surveillance Capitalism: The Fight for a Human Future at the New Frontier of Power*[58].

Zuboff argues that surveillance capitalism was created by Big Tech more than a decade ago when it realized that collecting "data exhaust" could be combined with analytics to produce predictions of user behavior. Fast forward to today and this data is being used by Google to extend its business from simple search to email to mapping to trying to build data models of entire cities. It's why Amazon invested millions to develop the Echo and Alexa. It's why there's a proliferation of products that begin with the word *smart*, virtually all of which are simply interfaces to enable the unobstructed flow of behavioral data that previously wasn't available, harvested from your kitchen to your bedroom.

The new GDPR regulation was a useful tool to signal to citizens and consumers who was in control of their data. In response, in 2017 a consortium of some of the biggest tech firms including Microsoft, Apple, Google, and Facebook, announced the **Data Transfer Project (DTP)**[59], an initiative designed to facilitate the exercising of users' right to data portability under the GDPR via common data interoperability standards and data transfer mechanisms. Data portability and interoperability are central to encouraging data sharing on a mass scale, but will it solve ongoing citizen concerns over "surveillance capitalism"?

Regulation is key here. Even the Big Tech giants are coming on side for appropriate regulation in the presently under-regulated environment. Sundar Pichai, chief executive of Google parent Alphabet, said recently[60], "there is no question in my mind that AI needs to be regulated. It is too important not to. The only question is how to approach it."

Azeem Azhar, tech futurist and commentator, argues for greater regulation of large, AI-driven, platform-network companies. This is a simple point of power and scale and what he calls "the AI lock-in loop"[105]: data begets AI, begets better products, begets more data, begets better AI, begets better products. Raising regulatory costs deters competitors and AI's lock-in loop benefits incumbents, so regulation could risk driving their monopolistic power even more if not done in the right way.

The EU is leading the way on devising regulation to rein in the monopolistic power of the tech giants. Margrethe Vestager, the EU's competition commissioner, is on a mission[61] to rein in the dominance of the world's biggest technology firms. The pandemic has made this mission even more urgent as the world moves to doing everything digitally. Vestager has succeeded in giving huge fines to Google and Apple for anti-competitive behavior, but they were limited to the common European market—and are minor annoyances for the world's most powerful corporations. So, the pandemic provides an opportunity for Vestager to convince other countries to follow her lead.

# Data assets on a global scale

The EU is also leading the way with efforts to harness the social value of data. This is especially clear in the area of scientific research, which depends on the exchange of ideas, knowledge, and information and serves a valuable function in a democratic society. The digitization of data has transformed researched but the boundary between private sector research and traditional academic research is blurrier than ever and is subject to GDPR. Corporate secrecy, particularly in the tech sector, is a major barrier to social science research; companies controlling the most valuable data are using the excuse of data protection obligations to escape transparency and accountability.

The **European Data Protection Supervisor (EDPS)** issued[62] a preliminary report that recommends more dialogue between data protection authorities and ethical review boards to facilitate access by researchers to data held by private companies in the interest of wider societal benefit with data seen as a public good. Hopefully, this will make it easier to share data across national borders for health and medical research.

This will support the EU's aim to develop a framework[63] for trustworthy AI, based on excellence and trust. In partnership with the private and the public sector, the aim is to mobilize resources along the entire value chain and to create the right incentives to accelerate deployment of AI, including by smaller and medium-sized enterprises. This includes working with Member States and the research community to attract and keep talent. As AI systems can be complex and bear significant risks in certain contexts, building trust is essential.

The COVID-19 pandemic has highlighted more than ever the need for effective data sharing, and a global call to action[64] is underway by a number of groups, including The GovLab[65], The World Economic Forum[66], Open Data Institute[67], the Global Partnership for Sustainable Development Data[68], and others to facilitate re-using data between the public and private sectors[69] in vehicles called "data collaboratives."

Data collaboratives can harness aggregated and anonymized data—including from telecommunications, social media, and satellite feeds—and track disease propagation better than traditional models. Such data gathering has been crucial in response to Ebola[70] in Africa (Orange) and swine flu[71] in Mexico (Telefónica). But generally, the data needed in these situations have been widely dispersed across government, the private sector, and civil society and not used in a systematic and sustainable way during and post crisis.

The European Commission's Expert Group[72] on Business-to-Government Data Sharing recently stated that "much of the potential for data and its insights to be used for the benefit of society remains untapped. Due to organizational, technical and legal obstacles (as well as an overall lack of a data-sharing culture) business-to-government (B2G) data-sharing partnerships are still largely isolated, short-term collaborations."

Despite the data obstacles, however, the COVID-19 pandemic has shown the eagerness and enthusiasm of the scientific community to collaborate. Indeed, scientists were able to sequence the genome of the virus and develop several promising vaccine candidates in a matter of days[73], and the Coalition for Epidemic Preparedness Innovations is already preparing promising vaccine candidates for clinical trials.

Scientists have also been quick to search for COVID-19 treatments by drawing on libraries of compounds that have already been tested for safety and by applying new screening techniques, including machine learning, to identify antivirals that could be ready for large-scale clinical trials within weeks. Companies like Insilico Medicine are leading the way here.

This sort of scientific collaboration and use of AI is also needed in the global search for new effective antibiotics, with antimicrobial resistance an urgent global problem. A recent study in Cell[74] showed how MIT researchers trained a deep neural network to screen more than a hundred million chemical compounds in a matter of days, designed to pick out potential antibiotics that kill bacteria using different mechanisms than those of existing drugs. Using their algorithm to perform predictions on multiple chemical libraries they discovered a molecule called "halicin" that successfully wiped out dozens of bacterial strains, including some of the most dangerous drug-resistant bacteria on the World Health Organization's most wanted list.

The team did additional predictions from over 107 million molecules curated from the ZINC15 database, and identified another eight antibacterial compounds that are structurally distant from known antibiotics. This work highlights how AI can be used to expand the antibiotic arsenal desperately needed to address antimicrobial resistance. These new compounds will be further studied in clinical trials.

# Healthy Longevity Globally

Turning to diseases of aging, how can we utilize global data sharing to fast-track research and achieve healthy longevity all over the world? The **Global Future Council (GFC)** on Human Enhancement and Longevity considers global data sharing as 1 of 4 critical workstreams. One model of best practice exists already[75]: the **Alzheimer's Disease Neuroimaging Initiative (ADNI)**[76] project, which has strict rules designed to encourage sharing of collected data among its members including both public and private research institutions. To address GDPR challenges new approaches to consent management[77] or dynamic consent[78] are being trialed in the UK and EU and by global organizations including **Global Alliance for Genomics and Health (GA4GH)**.

Recently, the US **National Academy for Medicine** (**NAM**) announced the Global Roadmap for Healthy Longevity Grand Challenge[79], backed with $35 million in funding. It is an international, independent, and multidisciplinary initiative that will be informed by workstreams in three domains: 1) social, behavioral, and environmental enablers; 2) health care systems and public health and 3) science and technology. It is convening thought leaders from biological and behavioral sciences, medicine, healthcare, public health, engineering, technology, economics, and policy to identify the necessary priorities and directions for improving health, productivity, and quality of life for older adults worldwide. Its recommendations are due out in late 2020, and will be focused on making later life happy, healthy, and meaningful[80].

I was invited to Singapore by NAM in February 2020 to speak about the work I have been doing with the **All Party Parliamentary Group for Longevity** (**APPGL**); this was 10 days before the launch of the Health of the Nation on 12 February. I had a fascinating 3 days and took away a number of insights about what living and growing older in Singapore might be like. My first conversation in Singapore was with the taxi driver I found through the Grab app (Singapore's version of Uber)—he used to be an airline attendant but decided to change jobs when he wanted to be close to home to care for his aging father. The sense of family and community is very high in Singapore, he explained. But so is government control. He was annoyed that he could not use his pension the way he would like and was envious of our pension freedoms in the UK.

Bearing in mind I arrived just as the world was waking up to the coronavirus threat, I was greeted at the hotel with a welcome bag containing hand sanitizer, facemask, and government guidelines. The hotel reception assistant had been instructed by the government to take temperature readings of all guests as they arrived. Throughout the next 3 days hand sanitizers were stationed at every single entry point in buildings and major meeting places.

This shows how closely involved the government gets to protect their citizens' health. No wonder Singapore is doing so well in the worldwide longevity rankings.

In Singapore the average life expectancy is 85—among the highest in the world—and about 24% of the labor force is 55 or older, up from 14% in 2008. But, being a progressive country, it isn't focusing on building nursing homes. Instead, the island city-nation is investing $3 billion to support lifelong learning and employability, health and wellness, financial literacy, and multi-generational housing, among other initiatives[81].

Singapore embraced a "multistage stage life" including a 70-item initiative to make the country a nation for all ages. Singapore recently unveiled a national development plan in longevity[82], including a preventive and active aging program that starts for citizens at the early age of 40. Companies like Prudential Singapore are also leading the way here, allowing its employees over the retirement age of 62 to continue to work[83].

To sustain economic growth, Singapore over the next decade is raising its retirement age from 62 to 65 and requiring employers to re-employ men and women who want to work until at least 70. The government there also gives businesses a 3% credit to offset wages of employees over 50 and makes grants to companies so they can modify jobs for older workers.

In addition, wellness programs in all communities include regular screenings for chronic diseases, and activities such as Tai Chi and dance lessons. National Silver Academy, a network of colleges and community-based organizations, offers post-secondary education to older people, who can take courses in technology, business, literature, and other subjects, and who often share classrooms with youth. A SkillsFuture program teaches Singaporeans of all ages necessary skills for future jobs, and a MoneySense program teaches young and old alike how to manage money and invest.

Singapore's small size (population: just 5.8 million) and a lack of U.S.-style partisan politics battles make it easier to implement a nationwide longevity plan. Instead of focusing on frail old age, Singapore is trying to support people all the way through their long lives and demonstrating how to change the narrative from "aging is a burden" to "longevity is an opportunity."

Japan is another highly progressive country with respect to longevity, and is considered a super-aged society[84]. It has a population that is expected to decline, from 128 million in 2004 to 109 million by 2050 and already has more than 8% of its population aged over 80. By the 2040s, only 35% of the population will be under 50.

A number of government initiatives have helped Japan prepare for this dramatically aging population shift, including Japan's Plan for Dynamic Engagement of All Citizens[85] and the Council for Designing a 100 Year Life Society[86].

At the recent International Longevity Policy & Governance Summit Kenji Shibuya, Director of the new Institute of Population Health at King's College London, and Senior Advisor to WHO's Director-General and involved in the Japan's Future Innovations Working Group, said the experience from Japan highlights the importance of empowering individuals, promoting inclusiveness, and developing social ecosystems to seize the opportunities of living longer. Mr. Otani Soshi, deputy director for healthcare industry policy at Japan's Ministry of Economy, Trade, and Industry, added that long term solutions will require business innovation and collaboration involving a diverse mix of industry expertise to come up with novel solutions for healthy aging at mass scale.

In my interview with Mike Hodin, CEO of the **Global Coalition on Aging (GCOA)**[87], he agreed there are lessons to learn from how Singapore and Japan have tackled their aging demographic in a positive manner. He takes the view that creating an environment with the right tax incentives to enable innovation is key, as is an education system that promotes lifelong learning, which, through enabling active aging, will itself enable a healthier aging.

Engagement across the life-course, whether in our 20s, 80s, or 90s is an essential part of 21$^{st}$-century healthy aging. With reference to Singapore he says: "it has been a great model that connects healthy aging to economic growth. Singapore's low tax rates are a model for innovation that is an often unrecognized engine for healthy aging, especially valued as we launch the WHO/UN Decade of Healthy Aging and the OECD advances its Aging Societies' Strategy. Moreover, Singapore's leadership in the Age-Friendly Cities Program is exemplary and a pathway through which they're crafting public policies around reframing and reimagining the very notion of work and retirement, skill development, and training across the life course."

Mike and GCOA are focused on supporting companies to grow the longevity marketplace or the Global Silver Economy, highlighted at the first-ever global forum July 2019 in Helsinki in partnership with the Finnish government as they assumed their EU Presidency where aging was the theme. GCOA is also working with companies and governments to tackle the underlying but profound cultural challenge of agism—a critical barrier to progress worldwide. He said, "even within healthcare itself, the culture, the subliminal culture of agism, is probably one of the biggest barriers to continued progress. For example, an 84-year old may have age-related macular degeneration and not the often presumed normal condition of aging that assumes deterioration of vision—agism! Or, early signs of heart failure—growing tired, weak, or feeling poorly—may not, as the agist view holds, be a normal part of aging but early signs of heart failure. Nor should we assume that osteoporosis is an acceptable condition of aging, which cannot be treated effectively to avoid first fractures or certainly the second fractures. Across the healthcare system, not to speak of overall society, we too often still associate health deterioration as normal parts of aging."

A positive narrative on aging, talking about it as an opportunity rather than burden, is essential to ignite a marketplace for healthy aging, which is the focus of Mike and GCOA's work globally, especially prompted by the Decade of Healthy Aging, the G20 Aging leadership, and the OECD Economic strategies for work and retirement shifts. But it is also the goal of the Aging Society Grand Challenge launched in 2017 by the UK Government.

Since the pandemic began, the **Global Coalition on Aging (GCOA)** has been helping businesses respond to the tragic impact of COVID-19, navigate its disruptions, and work towards innovations to save and improve lives. This includes the launch of the COVID-19 Insights Series, which sparks dialogue to develop industry-led solutions, like telehealth and vaccines, reimagine the future of work, improve healthcare delivery, expand elder caregiving as essential work, and combat agism. GCOA has also worked with its members to advance thought leadership platforms on the key shifts brought by the pandemic, from the exploding need for remote care to the impact on personal finances. Looking ahead, GCOA will continue to serve as the global business voice on aging—helping to define how the private sector can respond to and recover from COVID-19 in our aging world.

# The UK approach

Tackling ageism has been a running theme in the work of the APPGL in the UK and The Health of the Nation Strategy for Healthier Longer Lives[88] launched in February 2020 to fulfil the government's goal "for everyone to have five extra years of healthy, independent life by 2035 and to narrow the gap between the richest and poorest."

This strategy argues much of the impact will come through actions to address the four key unhealthy behaviors, through policy and legislation. For example, building on what works to stop smoking, minimizing alcohol consumption, making it easier to exercise, delivering on the Childhood Obesity plan, and more recent anti-obesity campaigns being implemented following the pandemic. A big part of this is steering the NHS to take prevention seriously by changing its reward metrics to ones that focus on reducing these four big risks. The NHS spends less than 5% of its budget on this—it must do much more to control its own demand growth. Far more attention on local communities and place-based approaches is critical too.

The strategy argues that business needs to be the solution, not the problem, and must maximize their vital contribution to improve the health of the nation and promote a socially responsible healthy longevity marketplace.

At the height of the pandemic the All Party Parliamentary Group ran a series of online round tables to explore the role of business in the new social contact and set in train one of the core recommendations of the strategy: a Business Coalition for a Healthier Nation to incentivize socially responsible business practices for health, including the development of a possible index to measure contribution to the nation's health.

The round tables achieved consensus in a number of areas.

First, business has to step up to the plate and play a bigger role in the health of the nation. Social return on investment needs to be more widely promoted in the business agenda in the new normal. Good social impact will in time lead to good commercial shareholder impact. The Business Coalition could commission an index to measure business contribution to health, and a positive index could provide a source of competitive advantage.

Business has a real role to play in designing the new world of work, with a responsibility to sign up to an age-integrated workforce and ensure digital literacy and inclusion. The business community could come together to work on a sensible model to restructure employment—how jobs are constructed. A positive outcome could be greater flexibility and better employment for older workers, especially those with caring responsibilities.

There was clear endorsement of the view that health equals wealth— but wealth also equals health, particularly in regard to well-being and social care. COVID-19 has impacted those in the poorest health and in deprived communities, and it is more important than ever to keep people healthy for longer and managing underlying long-term health conditions better. The primacy of health over GDP is being recognized, and New Zealand's well-being index has been cited several times.

COVID-19 has shown we need to strengthen the resilience of our population, and that includes better use of technology in care, better housing for older people, and having a robust public health strategy. The UK will be more resistant in future through better health of the population. We need to prioritize the health of our communities and our local areas and build from there for decentralized national health resilience.

The round tables were clear in the need to tackle nutrition and the obesity crisis. Data so far shows that diabetes and obesity significantly increase the risk of dying from COVID-19. There is inadequate regulation in the food industry, as well as limited knowledge and skills in the general public. Employers could play a critical role in communicating and addressing the risks that diabetes and obesity pose to health, for example, and could play a much greater role in encouraging personal health management. Personal risks like mental ill health and diabetes that are common in the workplace are very similar to the risks of the vulnerability that we've seen in the population to COVID-19.

More agility in innovation is needed. We need more flexible and adaptive regulatory frameworks to support business and academic collaboration. And we need to consider regulatory frameworks to encourage business to step up to the plate and provide products and services that enable individuals to take decisions. While business is focused on survival in the period, this means we have to make health a part of—indeed, essential to—that survival and not an add-on.

Finally, the round tables were clear that there is a need for better access to data from the public and private sectors, requiring the appropriate legislation and governance structure to identify gaps where biology, behavior, and environment interact with personal health management and population health management. The Health of the Nation Strategy outlined the need for an Open Life Data Framework, and this could take the form of a Data Collaborative to which participants from different sectors exchange their data (both sick and healthy data) to create public value and ultimately help deliver on the APPG goal of 5 extra years of healthy life expectancy while minimizing health inequalities. This is responding to what GovLab and other global initiatives are calling for.

The Business Coalition for a Healthier Nation is now being set up, with the support of central government. Matt Hancock, UK's Secretary of State for Health and Care, supports the Coalition, saying that "as employers, investors, and innovators, business will make vital contributions to reduce future pandemic risks through prevention, improve healthy life expectancy, and build economic resilience in communities across our nation. If this pandemic has taught us anything it's that our health and prosperity are completely interlinked."

## The "new normal" is here to say

As we emerge from the pandemic, it is clear that our lives will not go back to normal. For me personally, the crisis has certainly introduced some financial pain and much uncertainty about my livelihood and those of my immediate family. It has made me appreciate many things I used to take for granted. For example, my initial reaction to not being able to book home food deliveries was initially that of extreme annoyance, until I received an email from the CEO of Sainsbury's explaining that this was due to ensuring those most vulnerable could be served first. Then my reaction turned to humiliation at my selfishness, and then very quickly to relief that this action was in place. For three weeks it became a daily quest to search for food before the shelves were empty. My sons and I took it in turns and our strategies got more and more exacting as we became better informed with local intelligence (the halal shop down the road was a particularly reliable find, with rice, flour, and toilet roll always available!). When we were granted food deliveries again, we would be delighted with any substitutions provided for out of stock items.

I have never felt better connected with friends and family. Before COVID, "BC", weeks often turned to months before I would speak to my sister in Vancouver or best friend in San Francisco, but not anymore with our weekly zoom-ins.

Aside from the financial woes, I have never been so productive with my work. I am quite savvy on the technical front anyway, and manage my own websites and databases, I can use InDesign, set up mail merges and manage my own accounting—I can pretty much do anything a small office needs to be able to do from my home, all virtual. But not having to travel to meetings has made a huge difference to the amount of time available to focus and get things done.

Using technology to move from physical to virtual meetings has provided some space to experiment too. Running four round tables virtually to inform the Business Coalition for a Healthier Nation allowed us to involve a much wider group in an open process. Seeing the sea of 200 faces and names on a zoom call, being able to go in and out of break-out groups, and using the chat function to spark off ideas and conversations from such a rich diverse group was an interesting social experiment in itself! Hierarchies were flattened, everyone was less formal and more candid, and the insights richer as a result.

What has struck me most about the pandemic is how important digital skills and literacy will be for everyone—young and old—in the "new normal" ahead. Education and work will be forever transformed, and we need to ensure that everyone has access to these tools, otherwise we run the risk of creating huge digital divides, which would be a most unwelcome legacy from COVID-19.

# Interviews

The interviews that follow represent an eclectic, visionary mix of people challenging orthodoxy and the status quo, utilizing the potential of technology in new areas of our lives across our lifecourse. A massive part of that is recognizing the colossal potential of "life data": from the development of aging biomarkers in geroscience, to innovations in preventative and predictive health, to the development of novel financial services products to bridge health and wealth.

Brian Kennedy, Director of the Centre for Healthy Aging at the National University of Singapore and Nishikawa Kazumi, from Ministry of Economy, Trade, and Industry of Japan, both share their perspectives from "super-aging" societies in Asia. Sergey Young, Founder of the Longevity Vision Fund, and Dmitry Kaminskiy, Managing Partner of Deep Knowledge Ventures, are both pioneers in longevity investment and predict significant opportunities ahead in the longevity crystal ball. Siddhartha Chaturvedi is a visionary at Microsoft, driven by his quest to use open data and AI ethically to address health inequalities and improve the health of people and communities around the world.

## Sergey Young

*Founder of Longevity Vision Fund, Development Sponsor of Age Reversal XPRIZE*

Sergey Young is a longevity investor and visionary with a mission to extend the healthy lifespans of one billion people. I first met Sergey Young at the Longevity Leaders conference in February 2019 when he launched his $100 million Longevity Vision Fund, one of the few longevity-focused funds in the world. It was a very quick introduction but I could see he meant business.

Sergey's interest in longevity came when he, like 70% of other people who start thinking about longevity, was faced with his own decline in health. A few years ago Sergey went to see a doctor who told him that his cholesterol was very high, which put him at a much greater risk of a heart attack. His doctor's first recommendation was to take statins (cholesterol-lowering medication) every single day for the rest of his life. Shocked, Sergey asked for another solution and the doctor said the only other alternative was to change his lifestyle, eat healthy food and exercise more... simple advice that sadly most people won't follow. This triggered the wake-up call and path that Sergey is now on. Sergey's goal is to live to 200 and help others do the same.

My first proper conversation with him was just after setting up the APPGL and I was hoping he would get involved and support us, which he did by joining the Finance and Business Advisory Board.

Sergey has been an investor and venture capitalist for over 20 years, which includes managing a $2 billion private equity fund. He is an Innovation Board Member at the XPRIZE Foundation, a nonprofit organization founded by his role model Peter Diamandis, and Development Sponsor of Age Reversal XPRIZE, a global initiative designed to cure aging and age-related diseases. He believes we are on the brink of a Longevity Revolution, with new scientific discoveries and exciting technological advances now making it possible to reverse aging and treat previously incurable diseases.

Sergey is in the process of setting up Longevity@Work, a free corporate health and life extension program designed to help employees adopt longevity-promoting lifestyles. Sergey is also writing *The Science and Technology of Growing Young*, a highly practical book on the 3 Horizons of Longevity, which maps life extension technologies available today and in the near future that could extend our healthy lifespans up to 200 years. And if that wasn't enough, Sergey is building an online longevity platform at `https://sergeyyoung.com/`, which already offers free access to an excellent selection of articles and practical tools such as Longevity Diet scoring tests.

Sergey is charming and is adept in mixing in any environment. He can switch from uber-tech Silicon Valley talk of living forever to the more down-to-earth and tempered view of healthspan in London. He is a family man and, in his own words, a "happy co-founder of a diversified portfolio of 4 kids."

When I interviewed him at a café in London, he spoke about how important family is in living a good life, as well as the simple pleasures like delicious food. We talked a little about what it takes to write a book, and I shared my experience of writing for Forbes. com.

He has been a great colleague and supporter, providing important perspectives from the Silicon Valley view of the world to what we are doing with the APPG, while also being involved in the many events and activities throughout the year.

**Tina Woods**: In your view, what are the key points or messages that people should understand about living longer with AI?

**Sergey Young**: Human beings have been striving towards longevity evolution for the entire life of our civilization; and it's only with the arrival of AI and associated technologies that a longevity revolution can actually happen. The first and most important thing to consider about AI is to understand how disruptive it is, in positive terms, and how it can revolutionize the overall healthcare space.

Look at the ability of AI to perform highly precise diagnostics. AI can diagnose certain types of cancer better than doctors alone. At Longevity Vision Fund, we have invested in Exo Imaging, a company that develops hand-held AI-assisted ultrasound imaging devices. After the device performs the scan, it sends the image to the cloud, which is then analyzed by AI. The doctor then reviews the scan and the AI-driven recommendation.

The second thing is that with the use of AI technology, we could make longevity affordable and accessible for everyone. For me, that's one of the most important components of AI—potentially making the incremental cost of applying longevity treatments to a million or even a billion of the population close to zero. That changes people's perspective, so our work at Longevity Vision Fund is recognized as part of the common goal of making longevity more accessible and affordable, which is important. On the other hand, we've seen cases where technologies start to divide societies. We see that division with Brexit, with the protests in the US. But AI could be a unifying and positive theme for us as a nation—and as human beings in general.

The third point is that from both a personal and business perspective, we need to understand that AI is going to play a massive role in the next 5 to 10 years. It's a big theme, another big shift, which is happening. The market will grow and companies which use AI will have a disproportionate competitive advantage against their competitors and peers. We need to be aware that it is important for us as businesses and as human beings; we need to take it into account.

**Tina Woods**: What do you think is going to be the impact of AI when it comes to increasing our healthy lifespan, like we're starting to see now; and what will that impact be in 5 or 10 years?

**Sergey Young**: The first big impact will be that AI will help to make medicine more personalized. In today's world, the cost of customization is massive. Personalization right now requires substantial human time and labor, which brings immediate cost implications. In the near future, we'll be looking at a very different concept of medicine and healthcare—one which is personalized via AI. The healthcare you'll receive would fit you better and do a more effective job in extending your happy and healthy lifespan. This way, AI will empower individuals, and even whole populations, to take control of—and responsibility for—their own health.

Combine all the personal health data we can collect on ourselves with the ability of AI to process that data and, in 5 to 10 years from now, at least half of the treatments, interventions, and recommendations that we'll receive will be personalized to each one of us instead of the generic mass-adapted advice we now get. This way, we can not only give people back control of their health but actively involve them in the longevity discussion.

I also think that we could finally win the war against cancer with the help of AI and big data. If you get diagnosed early enough, the recovery rate for some types of cancer can be as high as 93-100%.

That's the big "if" here: if you do early diagnostics using AI, you can make use of its ability to potentially provide you with a more accurate and precise analysis than doctors without it. And if you use AI to support and inform doctors' decisions, the outcome is incredible. In 5 to 10 years' time, we're going to be right in the middle of our victory against cancer, and that will be in substantial part driven by users of AI.

The second big impact in increasing our healthy lifespan will be a paradigm shift for many of us—the opportunity to take a more active role in our own health. I have a very simple example. I'm wearing an Apple Watch right now, which monitors how much time I spend in deep sleep each night. Every time I do something, when I meditate, drink coffee, or enjoy a glass of wine in the evening, it has the effect of either shortening or extending my deep sleep. I can measure that with my watch. This gives me the opportunity to track the impact of my daily activities on my sleep, adapt my behavior accordingly, and then see the effect that new behavior has. I'm doing a feedback loop to improve—in an experimental way—the amount of time I spend in deep sleep each night.

**Tina Woods**: Sometimes cancer is spoken about as a chronic disease, as something to manage, but there are cancer vaccines for some strains as well. How do you think cancer treatments are going to develop and change over the next 10 years?

**Sergey Young**: You can see the change coming in your own networks of friends and family and colleagues. 10 or 20 years ago, if you found out someone had cancer it was like the kiss of death. It's not anymore. There are still a lot of dramatic cases and, very sadly, people still die, but I see a lot of new cases when people survive and they would not have even a decade ago.

40% of the Big Pharma R&D budget globally goes to cancer. 10 years ago, 1 out of the top 10 drugs in the US by revenue was anti-cancer therapy. The rest was Viagra, statins, and so on. Last year, 6 out of those 10 drugs were anti-cancer.

They are very expensive: it's a $150,000 to $1,000,000 treatment. But I think with the help of AI and other technologies, and the overall capital influencing the cancer sector, we'll see these prices drop down significantly and become more affordable to the general public. I believe the UK authorities just made a deal with one of the Big Pharma companies on a heavily discounted price for the purchase of one of these expensive treatments as well.

**Tina Woods**: If we ever did create a cure for cancer, that would make a whole host of cancer treatments unnecessary. That starts to introduce some real tensions in our current healthcare as business paradigm. Where do you think government and business sit and how do they need to respond to the healthcare opportunities that are coming?

**Sergey Young**: When we think about healthcare from a US perspective, we tend to think about insurance companies, healthcare providers, Big Pharma. But in 10 years' time, the biggest healthcare companies are going to be Apple, Google, IBM, and Microsoft.

We'll win the war on cancer, but not because we'll follow the current approaches more efficiently. We'll win this war because we're going to be doing very different things with very different players. Will Big Pharma be an important part of the solution? Obviously, yes. Big Pharma is still going to have a very big place in healthcare of the future. But human health and our fight with cancer is such a complex problem, it requires big data. It requires the use of AI on statistical data about the overall population, and that will be provided by the Apples and Googles of the world.

I don't think that it's going to be necessary for the government to substantially change the regulatory system, in this case, because I think the current balance will work. The way it's regulated at the moment is that you have intellectual property protection periods, and then these drugs go into the generic space. In just 10 years' time, we're going to see a massive inflow of anti-cancer treatments, combined with an opportunity to use AI and big data—citizens' data. That's what will create a disruptive force to help us win this war.

**Tina Woods**: I've heard of examples like the Melloddy consortium where Big Pharma companies are looking at a collaborative, open-source approach. Where do you see that trend going and how is that going to change business?

**Sergey Young**: Longevity Vision Fund invested in Insilico Medicine, an AI in drug discovery company, and they have an amazing investors' table. Qiming Venture Partners, Sinovation Ventures, Baidu Ventures, just a lot of different and very interesting players. They do collaborate a lot with Big Pharma, specifically for the first part of drug development. I see the use of AI as very complementary, even for the current pharmaceutical business model, specifically outsourcing the earlier stages of drug development like design and validation of drug candidates to the companies which use AI.

The only obstacle here is that we thought we would live in a global world. We don't anymore, because of the very protective stance that was taken by some governments on citizen data and on investments across the country, specifically against a perceived or real Chinese threat. I think the current trends on separation of economies, regulatory regimes, and then sometimes prohibition of cross-border investment can damage the collaborative approach.

**Tina Woods**: From where I'm sitting, it seems that there are three broad pools of access. There's the US; Europe, which has GDPR and other similar legislation; then the whole Asia-Pacific region, and China in particular, leading the way in AI. Do you think that kind of separation is going to continue?

**Sergey Young**: Well, it's said that technology has no borders. Whether we want it or not the world is becoming global because of a lack of technological barriers; technology works everywhere. So, we're going to see conversion. We're going to see the arrival of new leaders. I spent a week in China in October 2019 and went to the Beijing Genomic Institute and Shenzhen. They do such amazing things there, and they're going to work for the whole world.

**Tina Woods**: Could you give us some examples?

**Sergey Young**: When I was in Shenzhen, at a conference for around 300 people, there was a presentation by, I think, the Beijing Genomic Institute. I stepped away for two minutes and when I returned, there was a chart on the screen that said, "We're considering cloning human beings to populate Mars." It was up there after literally my two-minute break, and everyone was talking about it, saying, "Well, that's an interesting idea."

For better or worse, the different regulatory and ethical norms in China will be able to stimulate certain breakthroughs at some time in the future, for example genetically engineered humans.

**Tina Woods**: There's incredible innovation going on in China because it's less regulated. You mentioned earlier the division of society and that technology could help close the social gap but could also make it much worse. Do you see China playing a role in closing or widening the gap, in terms of who gets access to all this new technology?

**Sergey Young**: I think that as soon as you can afford wearables or a mobile phone, you have access to 80% of the necessary tools to prolong your healthy lifespan. The Apple Watch has already saved quite a few lives in the US; it can already diagnose atrial fibrillation. It can detect when you fall down suddenly. It can call emergency services for you; and it's all for the price of £300. I think there's a huge affordability component in technology integration. And in a way, it's agnostic—be it Samsung, Huawei, or Apple.

I think the technological component is more important than the focus on particular countries. I think where China and India are particularly important is in their massive population numbers, which obviously means that they have bigger platforms to scale and implement their technologies in comparison to the US or to Europe. WeChat, for example, is far more sophisticated than any other messaging platform.

I spent a couple of days with Tencent last September and it's just amazing how they've integrated WeChat into the Chinese way of life. They have a much more integrated view on the human life, from citizen score to healthcare data and the usage of this data for drug development and personalized medicine integration when their doctor receives their health data. I used WeChat for one week, and it's just the biggest ambassadorial feature for this integration. It's incomparable, in terms of functionality, to WhatsApp, Telegram, and the other similar apps.

**Tina Woods**: As an investor, how do you choose your investments? Obviously commercial opportunity plays a part, but is there tension between that and wider social opportunity?

**Sergey Young**: First of all, we're obviously focusing on affordability potential. For example, take Exo Imaging, which makes highly portable ultrasound imaging devices. The ultrasound-imaging device in the hospital next door is likely to cost more than $100,000 and needs to be used by someone who's had at least two years of specialized training. Exo Imaging's device costs 20-40 less than that, which provides a much more affordable way to get early diagnoses of two killer monsters—heart disease and cancer. Affordability potential is very much the first thing we look at.

Secondly, we look at the very delicate balance between monopoly and a low barrier to entry. We need to reach an optimum because if there's a monopoly this is not necessarily good. Companies have a vested interest in protecting their own franchise and there's a great desire to kind of monopolize markets.

On the other hand, when you talk about such a fragmented sector as supplements: you know, I'm a great believer in them. They seem to work for 30% receptive to the placebo effect. But everyone can go into the supplement business these days because it's all herbal or generic. It's just very difficult to imagine a sustainable business model for supplements.

**Tina Woods**: Are you worried that tech giants are going to be taking over our health? How does that influence your approach?

**Sergey Young**: I had an amazing discussion with the team at Vitality recently. The biggest partnership they have is with Apple. I mentioned a Morgan Stanley investment banking report to them that was published in April 2019 about Apple and healthcare and I literally told them: "watch out for Apple. They might just do their own in-house solution in this area."

Frankly speaking, my goal is to improve people's lives, rather than make money out of it, so I'm somewhat indifferent whether it's going to be done by Apple or any of our portfolio companies. I just want to make sure we have enough participants in the system, and then the statistics will work in our favor. I think we, as human beings, tend to think very black-or-white. We think in an "either-or" way. But I think life is much more complex and very complementary, so I see a combination of Apple and a lot of other different solutions as the outcome.

Thinking like that might be helpful in terms of solving this fundamental problem. At Longevity Vision Fund, one of the things we assess in companies we are looking to invest in, is whether Apple—or other Big Tech players—could do the same thing. If this is the case, we're very careful with proceeding with that particular company, but otherwise we're fine. The beauty of working in longevity is that even if you lose financially, the whole world might still win—in different ways. I'm happy with that, and so are my investors.

At Longevity Vision Fund we have a high degree of diversification and invest in different fields: early diagnostics, medical devices, AI-assisted drug discovery, therapeutic and drug delivery platforms. We invested in Juvenescence, co-founded by British billionaire and philanthropist Jim Mellon, and Life Biosciences, co-founded by Harvard Medical School professor David Sinclair. We're OK with this portfolio approach.

We just can't build a pure drug development portfolio ourselves because of the relatively small size of the fund for the capital intensive therapeutics field. Having said that, we do invest in therapeutic and drug delivery platforms, including gene and cell therapies, as with one of our latest portfolio additions Sigilon Therapeutics, co-founded by MIT professor Robert Langer.

We also support visionary innovations. We dedicate 5-10% of our capital to technologies such as human avatars, replaceable body parts, and human brain/AI integration. I'm not entirely sure the economic model is there yet, but we do want to follow this with our capital and access to associated entrepreneurs and start-ups. We need to understand how this wave of development will influence the definition of human beings, as well as our longevity potential.

**Tina Woods**: You mentioned the Longevity Vision Fund, the LVF. What has it been like to be part of that?

**Sergey Young**: Longevity Vision Fund is probably one of the most rewarding parts of my life. I have an opportunity to meet people like you, participate in associations such as the UK Parliamentary Group on Longevity, meet different entrepreneurs, government representatives, and organizations.

In the early stages of LVF, we told to our investors that if they only want to make money in longevity, then this isn't the right place for them. You'll probably make an OK return (because I can't imagine how you could lose money in such a grateful and growing area) but you'll need to have a different paradigm in mind—making the world a better place and improving the general affordability of longevity technology.

But if you want to help make the world more united rather than divided, then LVF is the right place for you. I'm really happy to have like-minded investors, which makes my job as founder of LVF so rewarding. I'm very grateful.

**Tina Woods**: Silicon Valley has a little bit of an image issue in terms of being seen as very focused on extending their own lives. Do you think that helps or hurts the drive for longer, healthier lives?

**Sergey Young**: When you think about Silicon Valley's super successful entrepreneurs, their wealth base is anywhere between $10 billion and $100 billion. We can sometimes become critical of other people's success and the ways they use their wealth—especially previous generations: purchasing yachts, castles, real estate, expensive cars.

That's not what these guys are buying, even though these are the alternatives available to them. I'm actually pretty cool with them investing in longevity and life extension rather than luxury items. I'm very supportive about anyone's choice to fund longevity research instead.

For every breakthrough technology, it always starts with crazy people and crazy money available to a very select group in the world, and then it starts to become more and more democratic and affordable. We're just in the beginning of this whole cycle. I'm very supportive of what they are doing.

**Tina Woods**: How do you understand and communicate the difference between life extension and healthy life extension, which is often called healthspan?

**Sergey Young**: The difference between a healthspan and a lifespan is a tricky one. In every audience, if you ask who wants to live to 150, you'll probably find that between one-quarter and one-third of the audience responds positively. The rest think of longevity as something depressing.

I think we're all trying to find the balance in communicating our aim to the public. We are all dream-driven. We want people to live a healthy and happy life.

So, what language should we use to communicate this? There are a lot of assumptions, and we've all seen people in the final part of their life who were in a very unhealthy and fragile state. And when we talk about longevity, people project it's that part of life we're offering to extend.

I think it's a matter of getting our positioning and communication issues right, because in reality, our lifespans will get progressively longer. It's happening already. Over the last century, our lifespan has doubled, and that's going to continue. Now, in the next 10 to 20 years, we'll obviously see some cases where it didn't work out all that well for someone, but that's part of evolution. It's going to be done anyway. I think we will look at life extension as a positive thing, that we're making people healthier and happier as a result.

**Tina Woods**: Tell me a little bit about the XPRIZE. What are you trying to achieve, and what is the Age Reversal XPRIZE trying to achieve?

**Sergey Young**: XPRIZE is a very Californian thing. To make something like XPRIZE, you go to Elon Musk, Mark Zuckerberg, Eric Schmidt, and you say, "Do you want to solve this global problem?" It could be plastic in the ocean, carbon dioxide in the air, and so on. They say "Yes." You take $20 or 25 million of the sponsors' money, go out into the world and say, for example, "The first team to create a device which will transform carbon dioxide into an economically viable product will win this cash prize."

As a result, without massive funding, you usually have around 200 to 400 teams all over the world competing to solve the problem. There are 50 to 80 countries who participate in coming up with a solution, and you pay the winner. It's a very effective impact platform. It's all pro bono, and it's amazing that you can leverage big names to attract a lot of very young—and very brave, in a way—aggressively creative talents. It's very unifying. There are teams from Africa, Latin America, the US, Europe, Russia, India, China, you name it.

It's my favorite impact platform because for a relatively small amount of money you can solve big global problems. The outcome of the first XPRIZE was the first private spaceship, which is now known as Virgin Galactic after Richard Branson bought the rights for it. That's an amazing thing. I've always dreamed about an XPRIZE for longevity—a competition where the winning team achieves the maximum age reversal effect on statistical samples.

It's obviously difficult to define the challenge because we're talking about human health and human lives. I still don't know exactly what the exact definition of "age reversal" will be, but I think we're getting very close to defining it.

We're probably going to launch the competition later in 2020. I still need $19.5 out of $20 million for the prize fund, as I'm putting my own money into it. But this is just the beginning. I'm pretty sure there will be no lack of interest in running this XPRIZE.

**Tina Woods**: What trouble are you having defining the goal of Age Reversal XPRIZE?

**Sergey Young**: The current thinking is to take a set of biomarkers, have the teams try to reverse aging, and assess their success from measuring the desired change in biomarkers. I appreciate that it needs more definition because the general public might not be so comfortable with the whole concept, and that there are also different interventions that could be viable—this is just our current thinking, as we have a lot of radical ideas on that front. It would be premature to set out right now exactly what the definition of the competition and the winning team's results should be.

I have this great opportunity to work with Steve Horvath, the inventor of epigenetic clocks; Aubrey de Grey, the "grandfather" of gerontology, as well as other Longevity Pioneers and life extension enthusiasts all over the world. It's been very rewarding. It's great that my financial support can make such a huge difference in terms of our ability to facilitate this process.

It's a privilege to look at how amazing minds and great hearts compete and collaborate with each other to try to solve the world's biggest and most common problem—aging.

**Tina Woods**: Let's talk about the whole concept of longevity escape velocity—that we're all going to reach the point at which life expectancy starts to be extended faster than time is passing. Some people are saying that escape velocity could be reached by 2030, that by 2045, we're going to be immortal. What's your take on that?

**Sergey Young**: I'm actually against immortality. I think if you take out death from the human life equation, from the human life cycle, we lose something very important about being human. Think about this: if we were immortal, we'd still be exposed to death, but only in very rare cases. That would mean that we would all become very fragile. We'd be pretty much unable to handle the stress of someone ceasing to exist.

I also think immortality is just not feasible in the next 100 years. I think we can continue extending the human lifespan—I like Aubrey de Grey's "medical" metaphor about the car and the extension of its longevity. Look at old cars. Some of them were created 100 years ago, but they're pretty rare exceptions. I think immortality is a very controversial concept, so I avoid it. I try not to raise it because it's just impractical to think that we can reach it, and I actually don't want to reach it.

We're talking about life extension. We're talking different numbers here. Before we'll ever have the choice to become immortal or not, we're going to achieve additional 50 or even 100 years of healthy life. It's really not about immortality for now.

**Tina Woods**: Even if we're not going to be immortal, what do you think the impact of us all living much longer is going to be on society?

**Sergey Young**: Our life expectancy is probably around 75 years, depending on country and gender. By living to 100, we can add an extra 25 years to the life between work and retirement.

It's amazing. You could do a lot of things, get a new profession, make your dreams come true. That's all with the assumption that these extra years are broadly healthy years.

As far as any problems go, I think human beings will sort them out. About 100 years ago the average life expectancy was 45 to 50 years, and if you asked someone then: "What's going to be the impact on society when life expectancy reaches 75 years?", they'd think you are crazy. You'll find a lot of academics 100 years ago who said the world cannot handle it, that society cannot handle it. But since it will be such a gradual change, and because there are over 7 billion people on the planet, I think it will evolve without us actually understanding what the discontinuities and fundamental changes are. There are a lot of funny things. I've just calculated that for my 200th birthday, even if I only invite my immediate family, it would be about a 5,000-person party. If I include my friends and colleagues, it would be approximately a 15,000-person party. There are not many real estate properties that could accommodate that. That's the funny way of hoping we'll sort it out.

**Tina Woods**: How do you see a balance forming between medical interventions and lifestyle elements when it comes to increasing your healthy lifespan?

**Sergey Young**: I think that human health or healthspan is such a complex issue. If one solution existed then evolution would have found it long ago. I think the answer will be a combination of things: lifestyle changes, what Big Pharma does, the things hi-tech does; and, of course, data analysis with AI is important. I see a place for a lot of factors, and I appreciate the complexity of decisions and actions a person would need to take to extend their healthspan and lifespan. Everything from early diagnostics and access to treatments, to lifestyle changes, like controlling diet, water, environment, and peace of mind using sleep and meditation to decrease cortisol levels.

**Tina Woods**: Do you think there'll ever be a pill to cure aging?

**Sergey Young**: I think we'll have a combination of treatments and lifestyle changes that would extend someone's life quite significantly. Is there one solution? Probably not. I actually like the concept of "longevity in a pill," that we developed here in the XPRIZE Longevity Lab in California in April 2019, when people creatively looked at the appeal of exercising, the appeal of meditation and so on.

It's a very interesting concept, for the lazy human beings that we are, to be able to just take a pill. But in fact, what we need to do is to try to stimulate lifestyle changes. We can't rely on the much easier choice of taking or not taking a pill.

**Tina Woods**: How could AI be mobilized to help us through our inherent laziness? Do you think we understand ourselves and why we don't take up these healthy habits well enough?

**Sergey Young**: If you want to make a change in longevity, you have three levels you could work on: the government, business and corporations, and on an individual level. So far, your lifestyle choice has been mostly driven by your own discipline, and your awareness of the lifespan implications of your lifestyle choices.

I actually think that corporations are going to play a huge role in making workplaces more longevity-driven. I think it's a combination of changing the corporate culture and availability of very positive, longevity-friendly choices that's instilled within an organization. Add that to individual choices on a personal level and that should work. I'm not sure about the government role here.

When it comes to mobilizing AI, there's real power in closing the feedback loop. Reminders are a very helpful way of reinforcing and stimulating adherence and self-discipline. Look at the Vitality app, and what Vitality does: it rewards you with a cup of coffee from Starbucks every week, just to motivate you to do your 10,000 steps a day. That's amazing.

**Tina Woods**: It's said that your health outcomes are 10% medical, 30% genomics, and 60% social and behavioral factors. What's the role of AI and government in making significant changes in that social area?

**Sergey Young**: Are you implying that the government has an active role in terms of managing us?

**Tina Woods**: Who do you think is responsible?

**Sergey Young**: If this is going to happen, it's not going to be because of government interventions. I think the UK especially has a positive history of understanding where regulations are required but also accepting they are primarily a tool to stimulate other players—individuals or corporations—to play an important role. Governments should be active in regulatory aspects. Regulating Big Pharma, lifestyle choices in terms of things such as sugary drinks, maintaining the quality of meat, quality of food and so on; and then letting other players and market forces make this change.

I think we often imply that current players will make this change. I am arguing that the arrival of technology is actually going to be more disruptive and helpful in terms of giving access to education and technology to different parts of population and society. It'll be a leveler. That means the government's role in regulation is very important.

One of the biggest problems is that it's so new for all of us, including governments. We don't even know what the right choices and balances in terms of regulation are yet. Take health data, for example. We discuss in parliamentary group meetings if data can give the UK a competitive advantage in creating longevity-enabling societal breakthroughs. I think that yes, it can. We just need to be careful and thoughtful as to how we implement this, but I think it can be a huge driver on that front.

**Tina Woods**: Taking together everything that we've talked about, what's the secret to a long, healthy life?

**Sergey Young**: Whenever I only have 30 seconds to talk to someone about longevity, I say one thing. Having your annual check-up, which I think should be as extensive as possible, is really important. There are so many diseases that can be cured at an early stage, so understanding and having early diagnostics is very important. That's my "30-second longevity speech" I give whenever I have the chance.

I had this conversation at border control one morning at London Heathrow airport. I was having my passport checked by an officer who asked "what brings you to the UK?" I told him that I'm writing a book on longevity, I'm participating in this parliamentary group, and I'm probably going to be on Sky News. He asked, "Longevity? So, what do we need to do?" So when I have my 30 seconds, I try to get people to focus on that one point because they already know the rest.

**Tina Woods**: So, you listen to your grandma, who tells you to eat your greens and to get fresh air?

**Sergey Young**: I'm a great believer in that! I also like the framework that was put together by Ray Kurzweil. It's called *Bridges to Immortality*. He wrote the article back in 2010, and it is my number 1. Just stay on the bridge of healthy living. Just be healthy for another 10 or 15 years, so when you get the chance, your body and your mind is actually worth extending.

If we damage our body and our mental capacity, then we might face the problem where our bodies will no longer be worth the effort in terms of extension. Using Aubrey de Grey's metaphor, your car would be too old to try and repair. So take the best possible care of yourselves—both physically and mentally—to make sure your car can go as long as possible in the 100-year race (and maybe even beyond).

But most importantly, make sure you enjoy the ride and have lots of fun along the way!

**Tina Woods**: What have you learned from the COVID-19 pandemic?

**Sergey Young**: From these challenging times, here are my top five lessons learned in short. I wrote a full thought piece about this, which is available on sergeyyoung.com[89]:

1.  **Our civilization is more fragile than we think**

    Among rapid technological breakthroughs, global economies that were centuries in the making, and the comfort of our daily routines, it's surprising how fragile our civilization really is. The service industry came to a halt. Travel plans got cancelled. Major events were suspended until further notice. And it all happened practically overnight.

    **Takeaway**: treat the crisis as an opportunity to help you build your tolerance to uncertainty. Some of life's best moments—such as going after a dream job or choosing to become a parent—often start with going through doubt and indecision and coming out on the other side.

2.  **Prepare for the unknowns**

    With past recessions typically caused by stock market crashes, high-interest rates, and falling house prices, it was completely unexpected that a novel viral threat would hit the global economy as hard[90] (if not harder) as the Global Financial Crisis in 2008.

    **Takeaway**: create a practical risk map for your business or personal finances that would survive not only threats that are foreseeable—but also the "known unknowns."

3. **We are learning what matters the most**

   In the light of devastating deaths[91] due to COVID-19, we are reminded that health is our true wealth. As the virus threatens layoffs and bankruptcies, we are gaining renewed appreciation for our jobs as important sources of happiness and fulfillment, not just income.

   **Takeaway**: appreciate all the people and things in your life, even those you may be taking for granted.

4. **We are rediscovering ourselves**

   We are born with 24 hours in the day—but how much time do we spend doing what we truly want? How do we deal with more time to ourselves, given our limited 8-second attention spans[92] (less than a goldfish)? This is the first global experiment of its kind, which will reinvent the way we work, socialize, and spend free time.

   **Takeaway**: use this once-in-a-life time opportunity for personal growth to emerge into the real world with a better understanding of who you are.

5. **Mother Nature is speaking to us**

   For decades, we've abused the environment. Plastic pollution, resource depletion, and water contamination are all embarrassing examples of how we treat Mother Nature. It's about time she fought back and shut us down.

   **Takeaway**: if Greta Thunberg wasn't enough of a wake-up call, this epidemic certainly is. Treat Mother Nature with kindness, and it will do the same for us.

### Final thoughts: we are climbing our personal Everest

Did you know that chances of dying while climbing Mount Everest[93] and from coronavirus in Wuhan[94] are about the same? The lessons learned are similar, too. Safety needs to be a top priority. Preparation is key to survival.

How well we learn these lessons, and what we do with them thereafter, is up to us. So, don't give up and use these challenging times to become stronger, better, and tougher!

## Dmitry Kaminskiy

*Founder and Managing Partner, Deep Knowledge Group, Longevity Capital, Longevity Bank, Co-Founder, Longevity International*

I was introduced to Dmitry through a mutual investor contact in June 2018. At the time I as immersed in finding "unusual suspects" for the Healthy Aging Industrial Challenge Fund, working with Eric Kihlstrom, who was the Interim Challenge Director, as well as co-writing the report Accelerating AI in Health and Care for the AHSN Network with Melissa Ream.

I was interested and intrigued by Dmitry's background in longevity (which at the time was in its very early stages of being even considered an industry, seen instead more like snake-oil territory). We met at an empty members-only café in central London and discovered we had shared interests in how technology could be harnessed for wider societal good, and were also very competitive and motivated by being first at the cutting edge.

Dmitry achieved success in the fintech industry before expanding his activities in both business and the non-profit sector to advance exponential and disruptive technologies to accelerate positive paradigm shifts in finance, healthcare, and AI.

I helped him initially with some of the reports on AI and health being published by his group, Deep Knowledge Group. He then invited me to a number of events held by the **All Party Parliamentary Group for Artificial Intelligence (APPGAI)**; at one of the dinners held at the House of Lords he graciously introduced me as a leading longevity expert (which of course I was not at the time!).

Dmitry suggested setting up a social enterprise to do something similar to what the APPGAI was doing and try to develop a national plan for healthy longevity. Dmitry had just finished doing a big report on the longevity landscape for Israel and took inspiration from what they were doing. I had long thought that with the work I was doing for the Healthy Aging Industrial Strategy Challenge Fund, while there was significant government money being invested to seed the "healthy longevity marketplace," there was no plan in place to focus this investment on achieving the goal that the former Prime Minister Theresa May had set, to deliver 5 extra years of healthy life expectancy by 2030 while minimizing health inequalities.

With the help of Eric, we set about warming up people to the idea of creating the APPGL and then it was born, which then got to work to design The Health of the Nation: A Strategy for Healthier Longer Lives that was launched less than a year later in February 2020.

Throughout 2019 Dmitry and I worked together to launch the first International Longevity Policy & Governance Summit. This was linked to the launch of the Longevity AI Consortium at King's College London.

Since then Dmitry has been immersed in developing advanced AI solutions for longevity including novel applications of life data for insurance companies, pension funds, healthcare companies, and government bodies. He has set up Longevity.Capital and is now creating the Longevity Bank. Dmitry is betting that in the near future there will be increasing demand for new age-friendly financial institutions that make banking easier and safer for the aging population. His Longevity Bank aims to capitalize on the $15 trillion market opportunity of the underserved 50+ age group, with the intention to collaborate rather than compete with mainstream banks like HSBC, UBS, and Barclays, who are all making their first data-driven approaches to combine health and wealth in one offering.

Ultimately, the Longevity Bank will differentiate itself in two main ways: first, by preventing financial exploitation of its customers and second, by offering tangible rewards for keeping healthy using health tech and age tech. It aims to make the online and mobile banking experience easy, safe, and trustworthy for the older generation, taking advantage of the latest AI.

**Tina Woods**: In your view, what are the key points and messages that people should understand about living longer and better with AI?

**Dmitry Kaminskiy**: We should be CEOs of our own health. AI is able to support us in this very significantly. In the form of data and data science, AI can be a very powerful force in our lives. For example, Google Maps helps us to find the most efficient pathway through a town. In the next five to 10 years, AI assistance will not only help us to optimize our lifestyles, but delay and prevent different issues with our health. AI will provide a second opinion, or maybe even a third opinion, that might correspond or not correspond with the thinking of human doctors. The strength of AI systems will increase so significantly that they may become managers of our health instead of us. The problem is that it's not easy to predict exactly how the landscape will look 15 or 20 years from now. It's easier to look at the next 10 years.

**Tina Woods**: Of course, technology is also part of the wider context of other developments that are happening. What do you think will have the biggest impact on helping people to live longer, better lives? Are there any things happening that technology can potentially support?

**Dmitry Kaminskiy**: In the next few years, we'll have enough data to start analyzing what the exact factors are that negatively and positively impact health and longevity. There are a number of questions surrounding pollution, the environment, fitness, and lifestyle. I'm a little bit skeptical about whether these factors actually have significant negative impacts on longevity.

I'm not saying that they don't play a part; I'm just saying that I haven't seen clinical trials that confirm this. In the future, we will be able to use mathematical tools to assess what's healthy and unhealthy.

**Tina Woods**: It sounds like you're saying that the huge amount of data that we're accumulating isn't currently of sufficient rigor and it's not evidence-based enough to really be able to provide meaningful information to help us to live our lives better. Can you talk about the biological markers of aging? They are tools that we can use to assess the impact of all these data inputs.

**Dmitry Kaminskiy**: "Biomarkers" is a term that is applied to biomedicine and biotechnology. They are applied to measure the efficiency of drugs and how well they are providing positive/ negative inputs. Mostly, they are tied to one particular disease or one particular case; they are not typically analyzed in combination.

A combination of hundreds, or maybe even thousands, of biomarkers are associated with aging and longevity. 10 years ago, there was no such term and it's only in the last five years that the concept has started to become something real. We have been able to propagate a lot of data, including life data. Currently, there's data that could be analyzed in association with diseases, but also in association with a healthy state of life.

In the next few years, the quantity of data that we can gather about people will increase exponentially. At the same time, the efficiency of AI algorithms will also increase exponentially. These two trends will create a synergetic partnership. In just a few years, there will be more and more systems that are capable, at least partially, of analyzing combinations of biomarkers of aging and longevity. We'll have longevity predictions in real time, and we'll be able to provide recommendations based on this.

**Tina Woods**: These biological markers of aging could be physical, genetic, digital, and others. Can you give an example and explain how AI could be used to identify patterns?

**Dmitry Kaminskiy:** Let's imagine that you had some wearable device and you could take a blood test very frequently with it, say once a week. This would mean that you could analyze micro-portions of blood and the testing would be portable. From these tests, you could get a nice set of biomarkers and parameters.

Another example is that currently, the most powerful AI tools being applied to humans are actually to do with face recognition. Imagine that just from taking a selfie, you could extract a lot of data.

**Tina Woods:** Would wrinkles around your eyes be an example of something you could measure?

**Dmitry Kaminskiy:** Yes, and the point is that in the next few years, these kinds of tests will actually be quite efficient.

**Tina Woods:** It's basically being able to measure your progress over time against your own personal baseline, isn't it? There could be any number of different data points that you could input to provide this personal baseline, and these would be biomarkers. I've heard that gait speed at the age of 45 is a very significant indicator of how long you might live. These sorts of inputs will give us predictive risk in terms of someone's life course. Is that accurate?

**Dmitry Kaminskiy:** Yes. The most successful systems will be those that are able to use absolutely diversified sources of data.

**Tina Woods:** What we're talking about is the vast amount of data about us that can hold clues as to what our risks are. This is the whole concept of the social determinants of health. There still seems to be a preoccupation with the 10% of data gathered when someone is ill, instead of a focus on genomics and also the behavioral side. Why is there still so much interest in that 10% of data when this vast universe of the remaining 90% could hold much more information on our ability to live longer?

**Dmitry Kaminskiy:** I think it's as simple as the data about sick people being very well associated with actual death cases, whereas data about healthy people isn't associated with longevity as easily.

Only now are live systems starting to be developed to study biomarkers of healthy states. Even in scientific circles, only biomarkers of aging associated with decline have been looked at, whereas we should be identifying biomarkers that can be, in a very tangible way, associated with longevity and a continuous state of health. These biomarkers should be diverse and they should also be simple and actionable. At the same time, they should be as precise as possible and as personal as possible.

Developing these biomarkers is the priority of my investment fund, Longevity.Capital. These biomarkers will be capable, in a mathematical way that is scientifically backed, of providing feedback on longevity. I actually consider this area to be one of the biggest business opportunities, but I also want to give something very precious to people: better health.

Longevity.Capital is taking part in a longevity consortium at King's College London. We've already created a partnership agreement between King's College London and Zurich University, and we have plans for developing this in Singapore, Japan, Israel, and so on. The idea is to develop panels of biomarkers of longevity and the associated states of health with multiple parameters. We want to be able to make predictions from data in a significant way.

**Tina Woods**: Presumably, part of this work will be about understanding what the most important biomarkers are, either in terms of population health or individual level. Is that part of your philosophy as well?

**Dmitry Kaminskiy**: Yes. Some recommendations could be positive for very few people, or they could be positive for multiple people.

**Tina Woods**: One thing that keeps on coming up as an important area is sleep. This can be associated with a high risk of dementia. Do you think that sleep is a key biomarker for aging? What about something like exercise?

**Dmitry Kaminskiy**: Sleep was actually scientifically validated as having a very straightforward correlation with longevity. Sleep is a very efficient tool for improving nerve behavior, but it also supports the processes of the entire body.

When it comes to playing sports, the issue is that, most likely, fitness doesn't technically extend life. Someone who plays sports is living a more active and fruitful life, but there isn't yet evidence that this supports longevity.

**Tina Woods**: I came across some research recently on the relationship between fitness and sarcopenia, or muscle wasting, which is a big issue as we get older. Do you have a view on this?

**Dmitry Kaminskiy**: Again, I think there's not enough data that neutralizing sarcopenia with sport has an impact on actual life expectancy.

**Tina Woods**: We could say that exercise has an impact on our quality of life. What is your position on quality of life versus longevity?

**Dmitry Kaminskiy**: I would say that the ethical way of treating people is not just to focus on extending their lives but extending the period of their lives in which they are healthy. We should also be thinking about how people manage their money, because if they are going to live longer with a high quality of life, they have to have longevity of their finances too.

**Tina Woods**: Exactly. Being financially secure is also important for our own peace of mind, stress levels, and so on. It's all interconnected, isn't it?

**Dmitry Kaminskiy**: Yes, absolutely. If we consider what a recommendation system should look like, it should be about a healthy lifestyle and also a healthy mind. To enjoy life, you also need to have some basic income or basic savings. All this should be considered as a blend of components connected to longevity.

**Tina Woods**: Would you say that what you're describing is wrapping health, wealth, psychological wellness, and social wellness into almost like our own personalized life dashboard?

**Dmitry Kaminskiy**: Exactly. We need an efficient AI system that will be capable of analyzing data and providing personalized feedback and recommendations. Over time, there'll be increasing numbers of these virtual solutions.

**Tina Woods**: I can see the beauty of this for an individual who wants to be, as you say, the CEO of their own life. On a broader level, the datasets and the data that you'd get if you pulled together all these individual dashboards at a population level are similar to what Google, Amazon, and Facebook are collecting. Is this their big plan?

**Dmitry Kaminskiy**: Most likely, along with Chinese corporations like Baidu or Alibaba. I think that 10 years from now, we will have longevity corporations that provide access to AI systems that give us a full scope of life goals related to health, wealth, and psychological wellness.

**Tina Woods**: How will they compete with the Big Tech companies? Google just acquired Fitbit, and there's been a lot of controversy over the sheer access Google has to the world's datasets. You've got the parallel example of China amassing all this data on its citizens to fuel its social credit policy. Who's going to win? What is the role of the citizen in all this?

**Dmitry Kaminskiy**: There will be no losers; everybody will win, including corporations that are capable of developing such systems. Citizens will be winners because they will be the users and CEOs of their own health. In terms of who will own the data, I think it'll continue to be an issue. The trend will go in the direction of there being very well-developed systems on which people will keep their life data, including health data. They will disclose the data to different corporations.

**Tina Woods**: You're talking about a decentralized, distributed sort of economy emerging, then?

**Dmitry Kaminskiy**: Yes, exactly. It will be different from country to country, in the sense that some countries will be liberal in providing citizens with safe storage for their data, whereas some countries, like China, may force people to keep their data in collective storage, and the government will have access to it. *The truth is that* nobody knows what we'll see 10 years from now. Technically, big stores of data will give some additional power to IT corporations who are developing more powerful AI systems. If there is trust created, people will share more data.

**Tina Woods**: I'm assuming that this feeds into your philosophy at Longevity.Capital. Is this what you're looking at?

**Dmitry Kaminskiy**: Yes. We see a very significant gap and not enough solutions for practical applications of, as you called it, a full dashboard. If we have more radical solutions for life extension, there should be a lot of other harmonized solutions for people, and this is impossible without efficient plans for normalizing the full scope of healthy longevity in real time.

**Tina Woods**: Taking everything that we've discussed into account, what do you think is the secret to a long, healthy life?

**Dmitry Kaminskiy**: The secret is knowledge; the more knowledge you have, the better you can understand what's going on and what's actually applicable. I'd say that the most crucial factor for actually being healthy and living longer is aggregating knowledge. Knowledge transcends power.

**Tina Woods**: What have you learned from the COVID-19 pandemic?

**Dmitry Kaminskiy**: The Deep Knowledge Group[95] is a consortium dedicated to technology-driven humanitarian action, across both its commercial and non-profit divisions. We support the development and deployment of DeepTech and Frontier Technologies, to improve quality of life for all of global society.

Early on in the overall COVID-19 pandemic timeline, when it became clear that it represented an unprecedented worldwide challenge, we made the explicit decision to repurpose many of our technologies; we took our quantitative and multidimensional analytical frameworks[96], benchmarking methodologies, big data analytics, and the sophisticated data visualization platforms[97] that have become a hallmark of our unique approach over the past several years, and we've applied them to the overwhelmingly complex pandemic that the world is currently facing.

Notable recent projects from this repurposing include:

- A 250-page COVID-19 Regional Safety Assessment: Big Data Analysis of 200 Countries and Regions COVID-19 Safety Ranking and Risk Assessment[98], which uses big data analysis to rank the economic, societal, and health stability of 200 regions globally. This assessment received significant coverage in the media[99] and widespread acknowledgement[100] by many official government representatives and agencies since its official release. This special case study in particular adapted and retuned the analytical methodologies first developed as part of a project conducted by Deep Knowledge Group's Longevity-focused analytical subsidiary, Aging Analytics Agency: Big Data Comparison Analysis of the National Healthcare Systems Progressiveness of 50 Countries[101], (which used 200 parameters and 10,000 Data Points).

- The COVID-19 MedTech Analytics IT-Platform[102], which was designed to serve as a comprehensive database of the most relevant entities and developments in the COVID-19 MedTech ecosystem. It covers all the major sectors and relevant activities from science to technology, R&D, treatment, diagnostic and vaccine development, and practical applications occurring globally, and provides data on particular scientific and technological sectors and geographical regions.

- The UK COVID-19 MedTech Analytics IT-Platform[103], which showcases, profiles, and visualizes connections and collaborations between entities active across the entire UK COVID-19 MedTech ecosystem. That includes companies, labs, R&D hubs, investors, funding, and the support bodies leading the fight against COVID-19. The platform was developed in an open-access manner, to provide proactive government representatives, companies, labs and scientists with the full scope of information required to accelerate the neutralization of negative COVID-19 outcomes within the UK.

Our ultimate motivation in conducting these analytics is to create an ideal set of tools and resources to assist governments, responsible bodies, and departments to optimize outcomes in the wake of the global COVID-19 pandemic. We want to help these groups identify best practices for restabilizing economic and social activity, in a way that does not compromise public health and safety.

This scope of projects is in a continual state of enhancement and expansion, and some of our specific upcoming releases include a dedicated "post-first-wave" analysis of risks and potentials for a second wave of coronavirus, a study of optimal methods of relaxing quarantine measures and normalizing economic and social activity in a way that does not compromise risk to the public, and a benchmarking of best practices for protection against new waves of COVID-19 and similar potential pandemics and critical biodefense risks.

## Brian Kennedy

*Director, Centre for Healthy Aging; Professor, Biochemistry and Physiology, National University of Singapore*

I first met Brian at the launch of Andrew Scott and Jim Mellon's Longevity Forum in November 2018. He had just moved to Singapore to take up his post leading the Center for Healthy Longevity at the **National University of Singapore** (**NUS**) and we chatted a bit about that over champagne and canapes at the evening reception.

From 2010 to 2016, Brian was the President and CEO of the renowned Buck Institute[104], where he remains as a professor and is internationally recognized for his research into the biology of aging and mission to translate research discoveries into new ways of delaying, detecting, and preventing human aging and its associated diseases. He is doing a lot of work with aging biomarkers but instead of picking just one biomarker, he tries to see how these different biomarkers interact with each other. He measures aging using inflammatory markers, using metabolomics, and incorporating measures of aging and things like facial pattern analysis, and various components of activity that can be recorded.

At NUS, Kennedy's broader goals are to develop new interventions to target human aging and to validate whether they work or not. We talked a lot about that in the interview, and how the whole supplements industry could be transformed; billions are wasted on anti-aging supplements, and biomarkers could be used to test whether they are working (or more likely not, and save people a lot of money!).

I caught up again with Brian after the interview in Singapore in February 2020, just as Asia was entering the grip of the COVID-19 epidemic. I had been invited by the **National Academy of Medicine (NAM)** Global Healthy Longevity Grand Challenge to speak about the work we were doing with the APPGL. It was the week before the launch of the Health of the Nation Strategy for Healthier Longer Lives.

I sat next to Brian at the dinner they held and he gave me the expat view of living in Singapore. He also introduced me to Victor Dzau, the President of NAM. A few minutes into our chat we realized we had lived on the same street in Montreal when he was a student at McGill University and I was 10 years old! The things you stumble on when abroad!

**Tina Woods**: In your view, what are the key points or messages that people should understand about living longer and better with AI?

**Brian Kennedy**: We have to think about what's causing all of these diseases. We need to move away from the attitude that we should just wait until we get sick and then do something about it; it's not working. This approach costs a lot of money and leads to a low quality of life. We should intervene earlier.

For at least 30 years now, we've been studying genetics and trying to identify mutations and extend our life spans. More recently, we've been trying to identify small molecules that could play a part. AI strategies are augmenting these biological approaches. I'm very confident that we're going to be at a point where we can intervene and keep people healthy for longer in the very near future.

**Tina Woods**: When you look at all the forces at work in society at the moment, what do you think will have the biggest impact on helping people to live longer, better lives?

**Brian Kennedy**: Awareness is the biggest challenge. Someone can change their lifestyle right now to live a longer and healthier life. I think that emerging technologies may have a much bigger impact further down the road, but we need a holistic strategy. Pills aren't going to work wonderfully if someone is living a terrible lifestyle. We need a society that encourages people to do the things that are good for them.

A huge problem in developed Asian countries is that children in high schools are under a huge amount of stress. These students are sleeping for four or five hours a night. It's not because they're out partying; they're studying and stressed. That's a behavioral pattern that, if continued, and it usually is, will lead to health problems much earlier in life. There needs to be increased awareness around this.

**Tina Woods**: You have an appreciation of the US situation versus the Singapore situation, where you're doing much of your work. There are some pretty shocking figures out there: life expectancy is actually falling in the US and there's growing health inequality. How do the situations compare when you look at both countries?

**Brian Kennedy**: In Singapore, the government is the same party that's been in power for a long time. One of the reasons why that party gets re-elected is that it has really improved the living conditions of the population. People in Singapore now enjoy a longer life span and a reasonably long healthspan. I think the government has realized, though, that there's going to be one retired person for every two people working in 10 years. Therefore, the Government is thinking progressively and looking for long-term strategies that can mitigate this problem.

In Singapore, the government pays a significant portion of healthcare costs. In the US, the healthcare system is broken. Of course, if you're wealthy in the US and you can afford the best care, then it's fine, but most people are increasingly finding it very difficult to survive on the money they have.

When I was the CEO at the Buck Institute for Research on Aging, I had the CEO of a hospital system in California come in. The hospital was thinking about philanthropy. I explained more about increasing people's healthspan and the hospital declined to give any money because success in this area was going to reduce its procedures by 60%. Hospitals in the US are paid based on procedures and not on healthy people. I think the US has a big problem in this regard. People are getting very wealthy off the back of the current system. The physicians want to help but are hemmed in by the system.

**Tina Woods**: Would you say that it's vested business interests and the short-termism of government that are the big issues here?

**Brian Kennedy**: I think that they are factors, yes. We had healthcare changes under Obama and now we have a president who has come in after him and tried to roll all of that back. It's really hard to imagine, beyond selfish reasons, why you would do that. People deserve to have effective health insurance.

**Tina Woods**: What have you learned from the Singapore experience that you think the US should take on board?

**Brian Kennedy**: Singapore's got a mixed public/private health system. Many people have private insurance, but there's a baseline of public healthcare that everyone has access to. Those systems tend to work the best, I think, because everybody gets reasonable healthcare. They might not get a private hospital room, but they will get care. At the same time, if they want to pay more to get better care, then they have that option. No system's perfect, but this one works fairly well.

The problem with Singapore is that, as I mentioned, as the proportion of older people increases, the healthcare system's going to be taxed to the limit. The polyclinics where people go to get their primary care, along with the hospitals, are going to be overwhelmed. The government could either build more hospitals, which would be difficult on a small island or do something about aging. There are currently exercise programs and the government is trying to get people out a bit more and get them to eat better. There's also support for new technologies.

I joke that Singapore's like Switzerland on steroids because everything runs efficiently. The government's very responsive to challenges that emerge. However, if you look under the hood, Singapore doesn't do preventative medicine as well as it should right now. When someone goes to a polyclinic for an appointment, the doctor usually has six minutes with them. How is the doctor going to impart any sort of health behavioral advice in that time?

My concern with Singapore is that it's easy for the government to rest on its laurels. Sometimes, if you want high-impact solutions, you need to take some risks. I see some risk-averse behavior in Singapore. But generally speaking, I'm pretty encouraged by the trajectory.

One of the things we're trying to do is look at biomarker metrics. If you get people to take an extra 2,000 steps each day, what will that do to their biological age? I think all of us believe that exercise is good for slowing aging and keeping us healthy for longer. What we don't know is how much exercise we need, so hopefully, we can start to tease that information out.

**Tina Woods**: I gather that Singapore also has quite an advanced lifelong education program. Does this help to keep people motivated to live a longer life?

**Brian Kennedy**: There's a lot of emphasis on learning, which is a good thing. We're still trying to encourage healthy behavior with studying, as I mentioned earlier. In contrast, I would argue that there's too little pressure on children in the US; we need to find a balance.

**Tina Woods**: Are businesses considered to be key custodians of the health of the nation? That's something that we're looking at really closely here in the UK.

**Brian Kennedy**: What we're trying to do is talk to businesses about the fact that the retirement age is going up. It was just raised to 67 and it may go higher. What we need to do is work with companies to try to keep people healthier for longer. There is a responsiveness to this; it's just a matter of getting the information out there.

There's a growing biotech sector in Singapore. Singapore's a great place for a small biotech company that is starting up because there are big tax incentives and a high-quality workforce that's available for high-quality research. Universities are very open to partnerships too. If we can create a biotech industry around aging, that'll provide an economic boost for the country as well.

Globally, there was almost no private sector money going into aging 10 years ago. Now there are companies, big and small, trying all different kinds of strategies. I'm involved with some of them and talk to most of them. Some of the strategies are crazy and some of them are risky. Some of them seem smart to me, but I don't think anybody really knows where the major breakthroughs are going to come from. That's a fun place to be in because it feels like things are just about to happen.

**Tina Woods**: There seems to be a lot of attention on sickness in most of the developed world. If we're talking about living healthily, we need to consider the social determinants of health. Why do you think there's so much focus on the sick space and so little on the wider aspects of health?

**Brian Kennedy**: All the research is on sick care too. I think that the reason for this comes from history; we didn't understand what we could do to stay healthy for longer 50 years ago. People had some vague ideas, but they didn't know what we know now. There were arguments about whether smoking was really bad for people, and so on.

Traditionally, nobody in healthcare has thought much about looking closely at healthy people. When they start becoming ill or feeling pain, that's when healthcare is used. Today, we understand that aging is the risk factor for many diseases. It seems obvious in retrospect, but sometimes it takes a while for these things to sink in. Now we know for sure from animal models that if we slow aging, it prevents the onset of most of these diseases.

We need to change how people think because everyone has been told that they can't do anything about aging, but they can do something when they get sick. It's funny because 30% of people get cancer and we try to do something about that. 100% of people age, but we see that as something natural. Fundamentally, I don't understand the difference there, but awareness is coming, and that's a big step forward.

If we can get people that are 50, 60, and 70 to really start to believe that they're going to have 20 or 30 more years of health, that may change how they think about their future. I had this debate a while back sponsored by *Intelligence Squared* (`intelligencesquared. com.`) The question was: should people live longer or not? Aubrey de Grey and I were arguing for yes. A philosopher and an ethicist were arguing for no. One of the arguments was that old people lose their creativity and they don't look to the future. The point was that old people don't innovate as much, so if we have more and more old people, we're going to suppress innovation. I don't agree with that. If we slow aging, who's to say that people aren't going to maintain a youthful way of thinking for longer?

**Tina Woods**: Is aging as big an issue for the world as climate change? Should it be seen that way? How are some of the issues and potential solutions linked to the climate change agenda?

**Brian Kennedy**: Aging is the same level of magnitude as an issue, mainly because of the demographics; 25% of the population is over the age of 65. We can sit here and try to treat one disease at a time, but others will follow.

In the same way, all of a sudden, we decided that plastic straws were the enemy. I'm not against getting rid of plastics; I just think focusing on straws is addressing a minor issue.

Another example is thinking that eating less meat is going to change the climate because it's going to alleviate the need for so many cows. We don't think about the fact that it's really the fossil fuels that are driving most of the changes to the climate. In both cases, there are people doing very well from the current system, and they're happy to point out things that motivate people to stay in it. We're seeing the same thing with disease: plenty of people make money from sick people.

**Tina Woods**: We're now starting to see climate change being talked about on TV, and we have Greta Thunberg in the news. What do you think is going to be the equivalent with aging?

**Brian Kennedy**: We need clear evidence that is easily accessible to the public. Modifications to aging may ultimately be available to wealthy people first, but they have the potential to be applicable to the whole population. What we have to do as scientists is be cognizant of inequality and do our best to develop strategies that are accessible. If you look at HIV drugs, they were available first to people near research centers, and then to the wealthy, and then to those in developed countries, but it's taken 30 years to get them into parts of Africa and other places.

People can pay a million dollars now and start doing gene therapy in an effort to live longer. I don't really want to advocate that strategy. From a research perspective, it's way too high risk and high cost. I need something in Singapore that will enable me to measure aging for the cost of $200 per person. I want to be able to go to the government and explain how I can save it money. That's the way to get things into widespread use; it's not about billionaires spending a million dollars on gene therapy. I'm not against people doing whatever they want; I'm not a socialist. At the same time, we're trying to focus our efforts on things that can help everybody.

**Tina Woods**: Could you talk a little about the work that you're currently doing?

**Brian Kennedy**: Almost everything I do is in Singapore now. My research trajectory has changed over the years. I started off working with yeast cells and now I'm doing human aging studies. It's been an interesting ride.

My main focus is trying to validate interventional strategies in humans. What we're doing in Singapore with the Center for Healthy Aging is tilting the balance toward clinical studies. We're thinking about what we have to do with interventions to show that they're having an effect on aging. Some people say that yoga's good for aging, some people say that exercise is important, and some people advise taking drugs. Until we have a biomarker that effectively measures biological aging and tests these different things against each other, we're not going to know what works the best and what's going to be the most cost effective.

**Tina Woods**: I'm asking this slightly facetiously, but do you think we'll ever have a pill to cure aging?

**Brian Kennedy**: The crux of your question is around the word "cure." Let's take slowing aging first, then we can talk about curing aging. When it comes to slowing aging, we may already have that ability. There's a company I work with that produces a supplement to target aging, and its products are available on the market in pill form. There's evidence in animal models that they extend healthspan.

In terms of what we're studying, we can compress morbidity in mice. The animals live a little bit longer, but what's really important is that their frailty is reduced dramatically. All of those strategies are safe and they're available today.

You could argue that people have been taking metformin for 30 years, and some people take rapamycin. Those could be pills that are slowing aging already.

I'm not sure we have complete validation for anything yet, but there's stuff on the market in the form of supplements that you can go and buy.

If we're talking about curing aging, that's a different question, and I think that that's where basic research still has to come into play.

**Tina Woods**: Some people believe that we will reach a point at which we will be immortal. Do you think that's going to be possible?

**Brian Kennedy**: The truth is that nobody knows right now. If you look at the invertebrate models of worms and yeast, you can see dramatic impacts on aging. If you look at humans, we've started living longer over the last 100 years, but our maximum life span is not going up as fast; there's an argument about whether it's going up at all.

Right now, I don't know if any of the interventions are going to have a big impact on the maximum life span of 120 or so years that we have now. We may need to talk about different strategies if we're going to attempt to increase that. However, we will have a hugely positive impact if we can reduce the period of morbidity and reduce frailty. We don't need to extend the maximum life span for this field to be successful; let me make that clear. The benefit of using animal models right now, in terms of basic science, is that we can try some of the more exotic strategies and see if we can change the equation in a more dramatic way.

**Tina Woods**: Would you say that what we're aiming for is living well and healthily until we just fall down dead?

**Brian Kennedy**: That's what happened to my grandmother at 101; her heart valves gave out. She got diagnosed at 98. Had she had surgery, she might have been a supercentenarian. The doctor didn't want to perform surgery on someone her age, but she was as clear as a bell up until the day she died.

**Tina Woods**: That's amazing. Science is really starting to shed light on the role of lifestyle, stress, nutrition, pollution, fitness, and keeping active in longevity. It seems to me that it's fairly obvious that nutrition and lifestyle are really important. They will get you to a certain point of healthspan. Where do you think the research is going to take us in the next phase of all this?

**Brian Kennedy**: There have been two great recent breakthroughs in aging research: one is finding potential interventions, and the other is the ability to measure biological aging. Otherwise, how are we going to test our interventions?

We have a range of different potential biomarkers, but we still have some key questions. Do all of these different biomarkers measure the same thing? Very few studies have been done looking at multiple biomarkers in the same people, and that's one of the things we're doing in Singapore. Another question is: how responsive are these biomarkers? Can you really reverse them or can you slow them down?

**Tina Woods**: Dementia is the disease that people dread the most. With all the work that you've just described, when do you think we will start to understand what the root of dementia is?

**Brian Kennedy**: What is it about aging that makes people get cancer or Alzheimer's? One thing we can do is start to focus in on that question a little bit more. We think about cancer, for instance, as an accumulation of mutations in cells. That doesn't just happen; it seems to happen later in life. Does that mean that protective mechanisms are declining and allowing mutations to occur, or that the responses to these mutations are not as good as they used to be?

Those kinds of questions have been asked in relation to cancer, but we really don't understand why age is an aspect of Alzheimer's. Is the disease based on an increase in inflammation? Is it based on aggregated proteins? We don't understand those things yet.

The question more specifically with Alzheimer's is whether making plaques go away is going to be an effective strategy. The field's been trying to do that for decades, and it's been relatively unsuccessful in humans so far, although there's always a new thing right around the corner. Maybe something will happen at some point.

I don't want to wait until I'm diagnosed. I don't want to start to have cognitive impairment and then take some pills to slow that down. I still think the strategy is to target aging. If we can get earlier diagnostics, that'll be helpful as well, and people are working very hard at that, but there's a lot of evidence that lifestyle modifications can reduce the rate of Alzheimer's.

**Tina Woods**: We know the tech giants are very active in the health field and there's all this data. Looking ahead, what do you think we're going to see in terms of collecting data to feed back into research?

**Brian Kennedy**: Whether collecting massive amounts of data is going to have a huge impact or not is up in the air. You can't throw things at a computer and expect it to come up with all the answers. Big data's going to be helpful, but how we think about it is still going to be important.

**Tina Woods**: What do you do personally to live longer?

**Brian Kennedy**: People asked me what pills I was taking for a long time. I decided that I wasn't going to do anything until I was 50 because I felt that the research was too immature and I was comfortable waiting until then. Then, I hit 50. My life is a bit complicated with all the travel, but I try to have a healthy lifestyle to the extent I can, including some form of exercise and a reasonable diet. I do eat red meat, but I try to limit the amount. I dramatically limit dairy. I also follow intermittent fasting strategies or time-restrictive feeding, and I think those are things that people can do without too much disruption. I'm currently involved with a company that's marketing supplements. I feel that I should try them too.

**Tina Woods**: Of course, the supplements market is not regulated and it's growing very quickly. Will your research be a good way of measuring whether these things work or not?

**Brian Kennedy**: Yes. The supplement market is already huge, as you say, especially if you look at anti-aging supplements. We're not doing something new; what we're doing is trying to inject science into the equation and validate what works and what doesn't.

I think many academics have decided that this market is so unregulated and there's so little science connected to it that they're just going to stay away from it. It's a myth to say that just because something is natural, taking a huge dose of it is going to be safe. But in general, these products are safer than using new chemicals that have never been in the human body before. If we can validate which supplements work, we will have a relatively low-cost strategy that could have a big impact.

The supplement company that I work with doesn't have a billion dollars and 10 years to test a compound. That's not how that industry works; it's not like the pharmaceutical industry. It does have great animal data and some anecdotal human data. The company has spent time in my lab and others trying to do research on compounds, and now it's paying for a clinical study in humans using biomarkers.

Everything is a little bit of an act of faith right now. I can't walk into a store and tell you which things are going to work and which things aren't.

**Tina Woods**: We're going to respond differently, aren't we, to many of these products?

**Brian Kennedy**: Yes, and that's another component. With the exception of maybe exercise, it's unlikely that every intervention is going to work for every person. The next phase is how we personalize strategies to target aging. One thing we're doing in animals is using AI to optimize the dose of a drug or a supplement in each animal as it gets older, as opposed to just giving every animal the same dose.

It's early days right now. We're doing experiments with rapamycin in mice. The AI is telling us that the optimal dose for 10 animals with the same genotype and of the same age is very different. That's in a genetically identical population of mice, so you can imagine what that might mean for humans.

I'm really interested in natural products. Everybody tells you to take vitamins. There are obviously important micronutrients, but when you look at the meta-analysis, they don't do anything for people. Generally speaking, there's little positive data on that. This doesn't stop everybody from taking their multivitamin daily. The question is: if we could optimize the levels of all these different vitamins, what kind of impact would that have? If we did it right, we could have a huge impact on people's health just with the micronutrients in the natural products that are already out there.

**Tina Woods**: Do you have any closing comments?

**Brian Kennedy**: Can we use AI to develop hypotheses about why we age? Can we go back to the basic questions using big data? Some of the work that I've seen on biomarkers is beginning to suggest that we can. The interface between crunching big numbers and coming up with theories of biology is really cool.

**Tina Woods**: What have you learned from the COVID-19 pandemic?

**Brian Kennedy**: Nothing in my lifetime has emphasized the importance of medical research as much as the COVID-19 pandemic. Molecular biology, virology, epidemiology, and acute medical care have all played an important role in helping us understand and develop strategies to mitigate its effects.

Certainly, as we all wait for a possible vaccine, this is an opportunity for science to come to the rescue and get the world back rotating on its axis. What has also become abundantly clear is that the anti-intellectual movement, which has gained steam in the US and spilled over to other countries, can do real harm. Instead of listening to the best forecasts of qualified medical experts, many political leaders have chosen strategies that have accelerated mortality rates and viral spread. Given the current state of affairs, with second waves occurring in many areas and the threat of second waves seemingly ever present, these "economy-first" approaches may ultimately backfire, leaving the virus with us for the near future.

The pandemic has also made me rethink the importance of aging research. For years, I have emphasized that aging is the biggest risk factor for a wide range of chronic diseases and that by slowing aging, it will be possible to prevent disease onset and dramatically improve life quality in later years. Chronic diseases are of course still with us and will continue to be the biggest driver or healthcare costs over the long-term. However, aging is also the biggest risk factor for complications from COVID-19 leading to mortality—and this is true for influenza and many other acute infections, too. Therefore, the pandemic has re-emphasized the importance of interventions that delay or reverse biological aging, allowing our bodies to respond to infections in a more youthful manner.

We need aging research and human interventions more than ever.

Personally, I'm having airplane withdrawal! I'm grounded in one place, Singapore, for longer than I can remember; at least a decade. This has allowed me to catch up on a backlog of papers to be published, and to get serious about my fitness program. However, I'm away from family and friends, and I look forward to seeing people again.

I will say that Singapore is a good place to weather the COVID storm. The government here has taken rational and generally effective approaches to deal with waves of viral spread. Hopefully, we'll see the end of this soon and life can return to normal. People are not made for isolation. We are social creatures, and one thing that has become clear for me is that living in a virtual reality world may be our long-term fate after all.

## Nishikawa Kazumi

*Director Healthcare Industries Division, Ministry of Economy, Trade and Industry, GOJ, WEF Global Future Council on Longevity*

I was introduced to Nishikawa Kazumi by my good friend Bradley Schurman.

"Nishikawa-san" was how Bradley referred to him in the initial email and I realized then there was a lot to I had to learn about Japanese culture and convention (it reminded me of the days only a year before when I had to acquaint myself with the rituals and protocols of referring to Lords, Sirs, Baronesses, Dames, and Right Honorables when I first started interfacing with the British government. My initial fear and panic about using the right terms eventually lessened when I realized most were very forgiving about the occasional slip-up—we are all only human after all!).

Nishikawa Kazumi is a Director, Healthcare Industries Division, of **Ministry of Economy Trade and Industry (METI)** of Japan. He is also a member of Global Future Council for Human Enhancement and Longevity, WEF. Before assuming current position, Kazumi held various positions in METI over a period of 23 years, including Director for Trade Strategy to cover trade strategy and global growth strategy of Japan.

I interviewed Kazumi while I was technically on holiday in Devon with my husband in September 2019. I was struck by how advanced Japan is in its thinking on many levels, including the government's focus on working with the business community in imaginative ways to harness innovation, and also the strong role that business has as an employer to keep people healthy and well across their lives.

Six years ago, the Japanese government instituted a program, H&PM, that stands for Health and Productivity Management. Six years on and more than 1,800 Japanese large companies and 35,000 Japanese SMEs have already started engaging with this program, completely voluntarily. What's more, they are seeing a return on investment, with H&PM companies outperforming other companies by 30%.

In an article Kazumi wrote recently for the World Economic Forum he explained that while direct evidence is lacking, H&PM should have positive effects on the rest of society and the economy, since healthier employees become healthier citizens and active consumers. He raised the point that **Sustainability Development Goals (SDGs)**, ESG mandates, and new concepts like stakeholder capitalism are making companies more focused on these wider effects than purely on financial returns alone. Some institutional investors such as AXA Insurance have started considering H&PM as one element of ESG.

The UK needs to learn from this, including the APPG's work and the new Business Coalition for a Healthier Nation being set up, which is exploring how best to engage and incentivize business to positively contribute to the nation's health in a new social contract.

I met Kazumi personally in Singapore, at the National Academy of Medicine's Global Healthy Longevity Challenge in February 2020.

**Tina Woods:** In your view, what are the key messages or key points that people should understand about living longer with AI?

**Nishikawa Kazumi:** Before we consider AI, people have to realize that in 21$^{st}$ century our lifestyles, workstyles, and mindsets should be changed to fit 21$^{st}$-century demography. As you may imagine, in the 19th century, elderly people were rare. In the 21$^{st}$ century, elderly people are the largest component of society.

Japan has already become a super-aging society, but by 2050 Japan will become an ultra-super-aged society, where roughly 40% of the people will be 65 or older. In such a 21$^{st}$-century demography model—or a 100-years'-life model—people have to realize that their health can and should be maintained until the very end of their life, to make them happier and keep their capacity to smile.

In the 70-years'-life model, where people die in their 60s or 70s, sometimes while they're still working, health is not as big an issue.

Younger people can enjoy their life without taking care of their health. However, in the 100-years'-life model, early indicators of health issues can affect your health after retirement, when you're elderly. Therefore, you have to maintain a **high quality of life (QoL)** throughout your life. This is a very important thing.

That's where AI, or big data, or the **Internet of Things (IoT)** will come into play. You have control there; to understand your vital data, your lifestyle and everything, you have to be very curious about your lifestyle data from a young age. Then, AI and the IoT and big data analysis can help you to understand your health more accurately and easily and keep it cost-effective to maintain. This is my big message for living longer with AI.

**Tina Woods:** Over the next decade, what will have the biggest impact in helping people to live longer, better lives?

**Nishikawa Kazumi:** The thing with the biggest impact in helping people live longer, better lives is health literacy. We need a health literacy mindset, way of living, and workstyle, so that people can be smarter and cleverer in understanding what is needed to maintain a high QoL for 100 years of life.

First, and fast, we need health literacy. Then, with the right mindset and good health literacy, that's when AI, data, and technology will help people to check their health status.

**Tina Woods**: Should government have a role in making sure that citizens have that level of health literacy?

**Nishikawa Kazumi**: We have the responsibility to take care of people who aren't health geeks. In other words, in every society, including the UK and Japan—all over the world—20% or 30% of people seem to be health geeks. Regardless of the government intervention, they will improve their health literacy by themselves. They will be able to find the solutions by themselves. Those people are fine. The other 70% or 80% of people who aren't healthy geeks or aren't interested in healthcare or their health status; these people are the main target of government intervention or government policies.

We would like to utilize not only traditional approaches to individual health but also new approaches to individual health. The traditional way is very easy. Medical doctors, hospitals, health checks—the NHS in the UK. In Japan, the national insurance system has an obligation to give each individual a health check every year; companies and businesses also have an obligation to provide health checks for their employees. This is a traditional one.

If you think about hospitals, they are very good at advising people who come to hospital; but they cannot approach someone who will not come to hospital. An approach to people outside the hospital, that's more community-based or business-based, is very important. Lifestyle-related industries and the community as a whole should have more of a role in sharing necessary health literacy with individuals. Therefore, the government is helping them to do that.

The government healthcare policy targets are not only about medical doctors, but also about lifestyle-related industry, businesses, and local companies. That's one part. The second one is an obligation for ordinary businesses or individuals to take care of health.

Especially in the UK or in Japan, where the national health system is somewhat perfected, government enforces these various obligations on individuals and businesses. But obligation is not enough. We try to provide incentives now, as well, both for individuals and business.

From a business point of view, occupational health has just been an obligation, a cost, for every CEO. 6 years ago, the Japanese government started—it was my ministry, together with the Ministry of Health—started health and productivity management. We pushed to management the idea that companies needed to invest in their employees' health status, to improve it. The return on that investment is improved credibility, improved productivity, and improved creativity, all of which improves the bottom line, the profit of the company. We call it H&PM, health and productivity management.

So, for example, Johnson & Johnson has done this for last 75 years, and they said that $1 investment generates $3 return.

More than 1,800 Japanese large companies and 35,000 Japanese SMEs have already started engaging with H&PM. This is an initiative, not a legal obligation, an investment, not a cost. This is a voluntary decision. I'd say there's a trend to see health as an asset that you need to invest in. Healthy companies have healthy employees, and that's a healthy asset.

**Tina Woods**: Have you seen any evidence that this program started 6 years ago has already started to show a positive impact?

**Nishikawa Kazumi**: The Nikkei newspaper—a Japanese newspaper—analyzed this, and their analysis of the last 5 years' data shows that H&PM works very well with regard to **Return on Assets (ROA)** improvement. Their full analysis says other very positive things. In our analysis, we have data that showed H&PM companies outperform other companies by 30%.

The US Chamber of Commerce approached the same issue from another direction. They made an individual analysis about costs of poor health to business, and they found that poor health decreases the Japanese GDP by 7%, the US GDP by 8%, and the Chinese GDP by 5.4%. We can find this kind of analysis repeated all over the world. Therefore, I am very optimistic about the possible impact of H&PM.

In Japan's case, our unique factor is that Japan is already a super-aging society. We lack younger individuals as human resources, which is very important in the current Japanese economic situation. That seems to be a strength for some countries, where jobs are fewer. However, in Japan, we have a lot of jobs but human resources are scarce. That makes recruitment, hiring good people, a very important business issue; a linked issue is retaining trained staff and convincing them not to resign. Retaining people is very important. Our analysis says that H&PM works very well for recruitment and works very well to retain important employees in their companies. The labor market has already given us a lot of evidence about H&PM outcomes.

**Tina Woods**: Going back to the role of AI and technology in general, where can you see AI having the biggest impact at the moment?

**Nishikawa Kazumi**: I would say lifestyle-related data is the key for success in healthcare. For example, let's think about dementia. Dementia is the big headache for aging societies. In Japan, we have 4.6 million people living with dementia already. This number will go up to 7 million by 2025, 9 million by 2035. There are no good drugs discovered for dementia yet. That takes time. We have to tackle dementia without relying heavily on the discovery of new and effective drugs.

We know that a healthier lifestyle for the brain is very important to cut the risk of dementia. However, one caveat there is that we have to be very careful when we try to get quality data about what makes a healthy lifestyle for the brain; when it comes to dementia, anything is good for the brain if we compare it to doing nothing. For example, sitting in your room doing nothing, with no interaction with friends and no stimulus to your brain; we know that's bad. That makes anything that bothers you not to be alone, or to make your brain work, seem like a viable risk reduction solution.

When we look at actual risk reduction strategies for dementia, some solutions are very cost-effective; some solutions are a good fit for specific people. Other solutions fit other people better—and finding a combination of solutions is more important than focusing on one specific solution. For example, the brain training games, quizzes, or the crossword are fine, but too tight a focus on crosswords prevents you from being social with your friends. That's counterproductive against dementia.

We need to create together accurate data for every individual, so businesses or academia can use that data to provide an adequately dementia-friendly lifestyle. Because of this, we started a new initiative, a Japanese version of the **Finnish Geriatric Intervention Study to Prevent Cognitive Impairment and Disability** (**FINGER**) study. The FINGER study was started in Finland by Dr Kivipelto of Karolinksa. It was a multi-intervention study to try and slow the speed of cognitive decline in older Finnish people. Together with Dr Kivipelto we started a Japanese version of the FINGER study to find good data or to identify good lifestyles for your older years.

We started our version last summer. The **Agency of Medical Research and Development** (**AMED**) was jointly founded by my ministry, the Ministry of Health, and the Ministry of Education. The AMED has a strong network across businesses, medical doctors, and academia.

They started this Japanese version of FINGER study led by Dr Arai, who is one of the heads of the Japanese gerontology institutions.

**Tina Woods**: Do you think digital biomarkers or genomics could be put to better use in this area of neuro-degenerative disorders?

**Nishikawa Kazumi**: Genomics is a big area; however, we should be very careful on the consultant team about using genomics data for diagnosis or the prescription of certain prevention solutions. We are very keen to advance it, of course; but in reality, we have to consider that direct-to-consumer (DTC) businesses are using genomics analysis, genome analysis, to tell people their risks regarding certain diseases. These DTC businesses are proliferating all over the world.

Despite that, any ordinary medical doctor will tell you that genome analysis alone cannot be considered good enough evidence for a medical doctor to say something about a disease you might have. In certain cases, biomarkers for genomics work really well to discover the best treatment option for a certain person. We have to invest more into genomics to make it really useful.

**Tina Woods**: How is Japan unique with respect to how it is managing its growth of the older population? How many opportunities open up in the 100-year-life society?

**Nishikawa Kazumi**: In every country, in the 21st-century demographics will change from a 19th-century model to a 21st-century model. In the 19th-century model, elderly people are only a few percent of the population. In the 21st-century model, elderly people are the largest component. 40% of the population will be elderly.

Japan is the first country—a full experiment—experiencing this transition from the 19th-century model to the 21st-century model. That makes Japan unique as a field in which to test new systems, new solutions, new ways of life, new mindsets.

I'm not sure exactly how many opportunities we have. The first one is that with regard to the labor market; in the last 10 years the absolute number of people in Japan is declining. Despite that, the number of working people is actually increasing, because the number of elderly people working late in life is increasing. On top of that, the health-age of elderly people is becoming younger and younger. Nowadays, the health of the average 70-year-old is equal to the health an average 65-year-old would have had 15 years ago. The Japanese have essentially become younger by 5 years, in the sense of walking speed and physical state.

That makes a dynamic change of working style, or a dynamic change in healthy lifestyle, very promising. We can change our future by doing something right now. If we do nothing, maybe our super-aging societies will become pessimistic. However, if we can provide a good model for a brighter super-aging society, it will provide goodness to the world.

From the government's point of view, there's the opportunity to test new policy; from the business or the academic point of view, there's the opportunity to test out new innovative solutions; and for investors or the economy, there's the opportunity to discover new markets.

**Tina Woods**: Can you tell us more about your work at the healthcare industry's division at the Ministry of Economy, Trade, and Industry? How are you involved in technological innovation?

**Nishikawa Kazumi**: Currently in Japan, Prime Minister Abe is very keen to realize a life-long active society, where people can be active, people can be happy, until the very end of their life. He directed every ministry to create one Cabinet Office strategy about healthcare, and the Cabinet Office is focusing on those healthcare strategies.

Under the healthcare strategies' Cabinet Office, we have similar secretariats for close ministerial issues. The healthcare industry division, that I'm part of, is assuming the secretariat role of creating new solutions, new industries and new innovations to help realize this active society. For example, as a secretariat of the Cabinet Office, we're hosting a next-generation healthcare industry committee with Japan Medical Association, Japan Hospital Association, and other health/social care-related groups as well as the Japanese Keidanren—the Japanese Business Federation—and also Japanese pharmaceutical companies, medical companies, IT companies and AI companies. That is our role and that's what we are starting right now.

We're trying to do two main things. One is to start new initiatives for people who aren't health geeks. Part of that is H&PM, which was designed, organized, and operated through the next-generation healthcare committee. Secondly, we're trying to create new healthcare solutions using innovative technology.

The most important thing is that we're trying to create new networks among different sectors and different peoples. Medical doctors have good relationships with the pharmaceutical companies, but less expertise with the younger start-ups. Caregivers for the elderly are engaged with the local volunteer groups, but they have less experience engaging with Indian AI companies. We're trying to provide a new networking opportunity, for academia, medical professions, and business, all over Japan and even outside of Japan. That is what we are doing.

**Tina Woods:** What are the some of the big things coming out of Japan that might be different or innovative compared to what we're seeing in the rest of the world?

**Nishikawa Kazumi:** I'll explain an example of the innovation we're seeing in start-ups. One is ExaWizards. ExaWizards is a Japanese AI company creating a communication tool to use with people with dementia. ExaWizards uses the traditional French methods of caring for the elderly.

A caregiver practices according to through the traditional way of the French, and they analyze how that caregiver does it by using camera, video, or other technologies. Then, they create new coaching with AI for every caregiver, so that caregivers can communicate more easily and more effectively with people with dementia.

Another one is more low-tech, but important, and unique: Triple W Japan. They created DFree—Divert Free. This is a gadget to predict your toilet time; that is, when you're going to need the toilet. The system is barely noticeable. It uses a sensor on your bladder that checks to see if your bladder is expanding, and then using the easy AI predicts if and when you'd like to use the toilet. This gadget was developed just 3 years ago, but in the last 2 years hundreds of Japanese elder care homes installed it. Other care homes bought it too, in the UK, France, China, the US: many care industries are interested in this one because toilet timing is a tiny thing for younger people but a very serious thing for an 80-year-old grandpa. I'd say this is a very need-oriented Japanese innovation, for super-aging societies.

**Tina Woods**: One Japanese technology we've heard a lot about are the carebots. Are there any other sorts of innovations like that that you can describe, to give some examples about where Japan is leading the world with these innovations?

**Nishikawa Kazumi**: We have a lot of robots—we have a lot of regenerative medicine and bio start-ups too—but maybe the most unique one is the Cyberdyne. It's a robot that attaches to your limbs, to assist you with moving, walking, or lifting something. They created the Cyberdyne assistance robot several years ago, and now they are trying to use it as a neuroscience treatment.

They started the development of the gadget as just an assistance robot. However, they found the robot can become part of treatment equipment for your neuro system. If you cannot, for example, move your leg, then when you try, the assistant—the gadget—will read the signal in your nerves and force your leg to move.

Then, and I don't know exactly why, your neural network will start to recover.

Cyberdyne is very famous, and a good example of the Japanese model. I want to get more focus on other technologies, like imaging data analysis. In Japan we have a lot of CT and MRI scans. That technology was spread all over Japan, and we have very good, professional doctors who analyze the images. That's created a large amount of data that includes not only images but also very high-level, qualified, professional analysis of the images. That can be used to generate a well-qualified AI system from that imaging data. AMED, together with the medical association, and medical academia have created this big imaging data AI system in Japan. Those millions of pictures are being labeled by many professional doctors, and it will become an excellent example of good AI.

**Tina Woods**: In what key areas do you think this kind of use of AI will help people live longer?

**Nishikawa Kazumi**: I don't know if it's the case in the UK or not, but in Japan, as I said, every individual has an obligation to take a health check every year. The Japanese national insurance system covers almost all Japanese: 120 million people. This data is stored by the Ministry of Health. They have bunch of big data about the health checks, and they view this data to draw up good health policy as well as good health insurance policy.

Next year, they will open this data up to individuals. They will return each person's data to them. That will generate an expansion of the Japanese Personal Health Record (PHR) business in Japan from next year forward, and that will help maintain healthy lifestyles for every individual.

Of course, just a yearly health check on its own cannot provide healthy solutions. However, a daily health check, daily vital signs measured using an Apple Watch or a Fitbit, plus yearly organized health check data; by combining these two we can provide more accurate, cost-effective PHR services to the Japanese.

Another example is the Tohoku Medical Megabank. All over the world, many universities are trying to create big cohorts of data. In the UK, I think that there's an attempt to gather 500,000 people's data with economics, or buying people's data; and in the US, there's an attempt going on to collect 1 million people's data.

In Tohoku, they've collected 100,000 people's worth of data, less than the UK and the US. However, they have a successful set of generational data, which means grandpas, grandmas, mothers and fathers and children. This three-generational cohort data is pretty difficult to create. Actually, the UK gave up creating one. However, the University of Tohoku succeeded in creating this big three-generational cohort of data. This will help scientific analysis on how the generational effects will affect one's health.

**Tina Woods**: How does Japan's data collection programs compare with something like China's, where they have access to a huge amount of data on their citizens?

**Nishikawa Kazumi**: In Japan, we say that we are the qualified data health system. Qualified means that our data is being gathered under our strict privacy laws as well as our strict ethical rules. Our gathered data is being analyzed by well-qualified Japanese medical professionals. The outcome of analysis relies heavily on the authority of the data, and the ethical rules or the privacy rules sometimes matter when people try to use the outcome of the results. For example, in the UK, ordinary UK people prefer to use drugs about which data is being gathered under ethical rules—and legally.

Japan has an equal level to the EU in security and privacy protections. Do you know the adequacy rule of the GDPR? There's mutual adequacy authorization between the EU and Japan, so GDPR is effectively embraced by the Japanese authorities.

**Tina Woods**: What will healthcare in Japan look like in 2030, or 2050?

**Nishikawa Kazumi**: As you know, the demographics are changing rapidly. In the 2040s, Tokyo or the big cities will have plenty of elderly people; really, too many elderly people. Our hospitals or elder care homes will be insufficient in number. On the other hand, in rural areas, the number of elderly people will decrease. That means the hospitals or elder care homes will have a lot of difficulty maintaining full service all over Japan. This is a reality.

We cannot transport the rural hospitals to city hospitals, and we cannot force people to relocate from a city to their rural prefecture. That means we have to rely heavily on technologies to fill the gaps: online medicine, autonomous vehicles; sophisticated health check systems with less professional medical involvement. These kinds of technologies are necessary. It's not desirable; it's necessary, for Japan to maintain a good healthcare system in 2030 or 2040. That's our incentive and opportunity that drives our policy to add innovation. Without innovation, we cannot maintain the good health system in Japan in the future.

**Tina Woods**: What do you think is the secret to a long, healthy life?

**Nishikawa Kazumi**: That question makes me smile! We have two types of approach to create healthy lives. One is, of course, the science-based, medicine-based approach to healthcare. The other approach is a more social-based approach to healthcare.

For example, if you are 90 years old and have a lot of diseases— you have diabetes, your bones are weak, and you have dementia; every doctor has some, you know, medical experience and medical knowledge when it comes to deciding what kind of food you can eat. Maybe if a patient has a lot of diseases and conditions, they can eat nothing. However, if you stick to that, people will die.

Rather than focusing too hard on the medical and scientific approach to food for the elderly, maybe the answer is that the patient would like some tasty food.

The medical, scientific approach is important, but the social, comprehensive approach to the health is also very important.

**Tina Woods**: What have you learned from the COVID-19 pandemic?

**Nishikawa Kazumi**: COVID-19 gave us three issues.

The first is a new issue; the importance of supply chain and logistics management of medical materials. Unlike food, energy, or industrial goods, the medical profession and governments have paid less attention to the sustainable procurement of medical supplies and materials in an emergency. China and other emerging economies produce and export facemasks, PPE, and surgical gloves to countries all over the world. The US, Europe, Japan, and other advanced economies produce and export ventilators, ECMO, and test kits. The global spread of COVID-19 created difficulties in maintaining the global inter-related supply chain. I have personally been busy procuring necessary materials globally, as well as increasing domestic production capacity.

Throughout this process, many non-medical industries, such as automotive electronics businesses, have played a big role in providing clean rooms, trained people, supply chain management, and so on. Also, while we observed many innovative ideas for **business continuity planning** (**BCP**) and Plan Bs emerge in response to the shortage of materials, this experience has highlighted the need for a new comprehensive supply chain management strategy.

The second issue is an acceleration issue, which relates to the application of digital technology to medicine. While digital health has been a hot topic all over the world, COVID-19 has accelerated the process drastically. Online medicine and consultation has flourished in Japan over the last several months, although it generates lots of challenges and issues to be solved.

The third issue is a reminder of the need for preventive medicine and life-support. COVID-19 provides more risk to less healthy people. We should invest more in being healthy before we get sick. Also, COVID-19 compels us to think about new models of elderly care. Current elderly care depends on human touch too much, and "online elderly care" is difficult. We need innovative solutions.

## Siddhartha Chaturvedi

*Global PMM Lead, Health Innovation and Responsible AI, Microsoft*

I met Sid through the work I have been doing with Melissa and the Academic Health Science Network AI and Digital team. He became involved as one of a few Microsoft members involved in the Core Advisory Group of external experts advising us on core initiatives.

Sid got whisked away to Microsoft headquarters in Seattle when he changed roles and took up a global position on health; we kept in contact and exchanged ideas regularly. He is a closet, or should I say corporate, serial entrepreneur, always coming up with ingenious ways of solving world problems. I always look forward to receiving his emails!

He is a loyal colleague too. I was very humbled when I realized he was up at the crack of dawn to join the round tables I was doing to inform the Business Coalition for a Healthier Nation as he was somewhere from a very different time zone (I never know where it may be—India, the USA?).

Sid belongs to the AI and Innovation team at Microsoft, with a specific focus on Health Innovation and Responsible AI. He is very involved in the "AI for Health" program, a new $60 million, five year program to empower researchers and organizations with AI to improve the health of people and communities around the world, recently expanded with a COVID-19 focus.

Sid spends a lot of time thinking about privacy, security, and ethics, is very devoted to reducing health inequities, and is a strong advocate for women's health, as a core lever to reduce inter-generational transfer of disadvantage.

I have to thank Sid for introducing me to one of his mentors, who is ex-Microsoft, Professor Iain Buchan, at the University of Liverpool. I have been fascinated with Iain's work with Civic Data Cooperatives, which engage local populations to harness data effectively in a trusted way to solve their own problems.

Sid, Iain, and I have exchanged lots of idea and thoughts on data, and the need for robust frameworks that govern the policies and practices to enable technology to play its role in improving health—going beyond the traditional health records to include lifestyle data as well. And for that to happen, interoperability and standards are crucial to enable the health decision makers—the large consortiums or governments, and any public partnership with private partners—to come together and solve big real-world problems.

Most of us are affected by our personal experiences, and Sid was very open in our interview about how his bronchial rhinitis and allergies have impacted his life and compelled him to imagine ways in which technology could help him and many others manage it better. We talked about all the different ways we could be harnessing data to help people minimize their exposure to pollution and pollens, and how environmental data and public data could enrich personal health information and nudge us to make better decisions unique to us.

Very prophetically given the pandemic now, in our interview we talked about Microsoft Premonition (their advanced forecasting system to predict the next epidemic similar to the way we forecast the weather) and the concept of "One Health"—that the health of the environment is intrinsically tied to the health of the humans that reside in it.

He pointed to me to the Centers for Disease Control definition of One Health: "One Health is defined as a collaborative, multisectoral, and transdisciplinary approach—working at the local, regional, national, and global levels—with the goal of achieving optimal health outcomes recognizing the interconnection between people, animals, plants, and their shared environment."

**Tina Woods**: What do you think are the key messages or points that are important for people to take on board about AI's potential in healthcare?

**Siddhartha Chaturvedi**: I think one of the key messages that we need to help get out for both the people affected by it and the professionals consuming/building solutions is to bridge the gap in understanding the hype and reality of AI—AI is a tool that amplifies other things you can do. AI (or any other similar technology) is like a wheel. A wheel is one of humankind's greatest inventions, but you have to put it on a car or an airplane for it to achieve something.

When we look at the overarching tech industry, we can map the moves over history from the abacus to the calculator, to Excel sheets, to mathematical modeling tools, to what we now call AI. What I want to reiterate is that AI is a tool which, when used correctly, can amplify what you want to do; and it can help you accelerate things that would take a longer period of time, uncover patterns that we might take ages to uncover. Those are the key takeaways that I want people to understand and know about AI.

It is as important as ever—probably even more so, now—that you have the right intentions and you ask the right questions, before you set up an AI model to just go ahead and do its stuff.

**Tina Woods**: Of course, AI has been around for a while. It's nothing new, but suddenly it's caught the attention of the public. Why is that?

**Siddhartha Chaturvedi**: The tools themselves existed for a long period of time, like you said, but in earlier eras, you needed a really powerful supercomputer to run all of these things.

In recent years, with computation advancements and the availability of cloud computation—basically large supercomputers that anybody can tap into—AI has seen a massive update. Researchers, developers, and small start-ups that could not train models on standalone systems can all of a sudden tap into these resources. That's accelerated the growth of what can be done with AI.

It's a set of tools that existed for the top 1% in the '80s or '90s and now exists for everybody. It's become much more accessible, both through technological advances and the access to infrastructure and learning. The environment and the ecosystem have helped to democratize it. I don't want to sound clichéd, but that is absolutely what it is.

**Tina Woods**: What do you think will have the biggest impact on helping people to live longer, better lives, now and in the next 5 to 10 years?

**Siddhartha Chaturvedi**: There are a few things that are coming together that I think will have a large impact. It's the sum of the parts that's the real thing, I suppose—but first, let's talk about the parts themselves.

The first is the idea of digitization at scale that has happened in the last few years, and has allowed us to have richer datasets. That's what's needed to power AI. I'll come back to privacy in a bit, I know that's a big issue, but we see an increasing availability of various tools and practices to address that.

The second is that we see an appetite for AI technology to permeate through industries. Now, for the first time, we're seeing a group of people who we can call citizen data scientists. Low Code / No Code platforms enable you to play around with datasets by yourself, in the industry of your expertise. AI's becoming much more accessible to domain experts, which wasn't the case earlier. You don't have to be a developer.

You don't have to be a coder. You can run machine learning models without having to build them from scratch and see what kind of insights you can glean from those models and datasets. Insights that only used to be available to people who were both proficient in machine learning and the industry domain, now find their way into the hands of single-domain experts, for many different ecosystems. Health is a big one of those.

The third thing that we see is the coming together of multiple disparate but connected datasets, and this is really good for certain topics such as diving deeper into social determinants of health as we try to understand the health of the population and the environment that they live in. We're seeing some really rich datasets coming together, personal health and allergies combined with weather data or construction data. You can overlay them with, let's say, mapping data exploring the routes that people take for their run. That's something that could be really helpful for long-term conditions such as asthma. So, if I have a high probabilistic chance of having an asthma attack, the maps could tell me not to go on a certain route or a certain path, and that could potentially improve my quality of life with dynamic interventions.

There are these small interventions that could happen in our daily lives or create habit engines that could prevent people from falling ill (due to known causes), or in certain cases just make them aware of what's around them. We're seeing these broad data ecosystems finally come together and give more meaningful insights that could lead to these micro-interventions.

There is something to be said about multi-year, multi-dimensional vision—and as humans, we sometimes struggle to switch from the low hanging fruit to the overarching vision—and that is where I think AI could have a significant impact: unearthing patterns and amplifying our decision-making capabilities on the precision health side, tailoring treatments and lifestyles to the individual by making sense of a longitudinal dataset of that person (as opposed to merely their healthcare data).

**Tina Woods**: Where do you see real promise in understanding and being able to address the social determinants of health? The non-sick aspects of health, the genomics and the environment, really need a space in healthcare. How do you think your work will progress on that front?

**Siddhartha Chaturvedi**: You know, you've put it really nicely in that question, where you say the non-sick need a space. The health of the population is dependent on your environment and your wellness, far more than it is dependent on the dataset of you being sick, as the sick-data is not a continuous set of data. I think this "non-sick" data space is essential.

For example, how do we measure epidemic outbreaks? The way we measure epidemic outbreaks is when people get unwell, they go to a doctor; and we get the idea that there are a certain number of people who have fallen ill in a particular area, so we know that there's been an outbreak. It's a lagging indicator.

One of the projects that Microsoft's invested in is Microsoft Premonition, which supports the aims of the One Health initiative of the Centers for Disease Control connecting human, animal, and environmental health.

Instead on relying on reported illness data, and then hoping for a seamless flow to decision makers, we asked ourselves: A fair few of the epidemics are mosquito-borne diseases. So, in those cases, why don't we capture the mosquitoes, and figure out what diseases are spreading by running a metagenomics test on the blood that the mosquitoes have captured? That doesn't allow us enough data to go down to the level of picking out who the affected person is, or where that person has fallen ill, so we can't do personal interventions. But what we can do is get those few days of a head start that might enable us to slow down the spread of certain epidemics before it is too late.

All this environmental data that comes in is in the category of "non-sick" data. In effect, you could have pre-emptive interventions from the environment.

Even from a personal well-being space, that's starting to appear. For example, I think kudos to Apple to build in the heart risk monitoring into the Apple watch. These new-gen devices which constitute the **Internet of Medical Things** (**IoMT**) could potentially understand what your baseline is; and for the first time, you can establish your personal baseline of what is normal for you, as opposed to being mapped to the "normal" as extracted from a large population set that, in certain cases, might not have significant representation of your physiological demographic.

For example, I have a high resting heart rate. Whenever I go to a doctor who does not know that, they think "oh, what's happening with your heart rate?". I explain to them that I have a high resting heart rate. They also have the context of the rest of the data they can access from me while I'm in the room. The doctors can feel my high heart rate, but then they can see the rest of me, and diagnose appropriately. And if they can't see something, they can ask questions.

What IoMT and connected lifestyle data enables us to do is to establish a baseline, and have that personal dataset move with you. I think this is going to get more and more important as we look at the global cosmopolitan; all these people living lives spanning multiple places or even countries.

I've been to four countries already, and I have disparate health datasets across all of them. Some of my data is in the UK; some of it in the US. Some of it will be in India; maybe a sliver in Singapore and France. Instead, the promise of me owning that data (and more) allows me to combine it with other information to give me meaningful insights about my personal health.

Coming back to your point, what's really important is that the health decision makers—the large consortiums or governments, and public partnerships with private partners—come together, and allow interoperability of data. They can only be allowed data providence in a way that enables dynamic consent, traceability, and transparency of use. We shouldn't allow that data to be monetized in a way that the citizen doesn't consent to.

**Tina Woods**: As citizens, but also as governments, third sector parties, and businesses, how do you think we all need to kind of rise to the challenge of AI; how can we really embrace the promise of this technology?

**Siddhartha Chaturvedi**: It opens up a new way of thinking about various business models and incentive alignments. For example, if we keep people from falling ill, certain drug sales will decline. But generic drugs don't always cater to rare diseases. And rare diseases aren't as rare as the name suggests. Drug development costs for precision medicine is high. I think by lowering the costs of drug discovery by leveraging AI and in-silico drug design, powered by richer personalized datasets, we could enable the pharmaceutical research to move into a new space of value creation for previously underserved disease areas, while bringing preventive interventions for common and, well, preventable diseases.

As a personal example, my dad was recently diagnosed with cancer. If I know that sharing my dad's dataset will allow somebody to find a potential cure, I would be more ready to share that data if I knew exactly what they were going to use that data for (to find a cure, and NOT increase my insurance premium). It requires trust. A lot of these companies have the responsibility and the burden of building trust with their other stakeholders. When you say that people don't want to share their data, it's usually because they don't know what you're doing with their data; that is because of a lack of trust, and rightfully so.

People might have been exploited previously, the fine print clouding the true understanding or intent of certain agreements. There hasn't been any structured education for them about what might happen with their data, or transparency on the use and impact.

That trust needs to be established before you can truly transform any part of health. But it could potentially be the biggest gamechanger— for example, if I were to be approached by a pharmaceutical company I trusted that said they needed my dad's data to use for his cancer research, I would say yes, of course. Then I'd say why don't you use mine too, and my sister's data too? That could really accelerate certain insights and learnings.

In the health ecosystem, we're still in the '60s era of the car industry, where we're building a prototype for almost every single thing. There are some very interesting companies pursuing in-silico drug prediction, like Ensemble MD based out of UCL, Schrodinger, Benevolent AI. As the Biomedical NLP space grows, we will see a significant impact on drug development, clinical trials, and treatment recommendations for edge cases. These are early days, but these people have really thought about the business model transformation that begets transformative change in health.

The other model to look at is the Spotify model. Spotify does not give me the ownership of a song. Spotify gives me access to a library of songs. Every time that we play a song through Spotify, Spotify pays a royalty to the artist. Flipping that model around, we could create a library of data where we own our own data; and if somebody wants access to our datasets, they pay a royalty. That, with dynamic consent, could be something.

**Tina Woods**: That idea of data sharing is a pretty fundamental disruption of the status quo, certainly in the developed, westernized sort of model. How do you think that's going to evolve, and do you think the developing nations will lead the way? Where do you think the tipping points are going to be that really drive that change?

**Siddhartha Chaturvedi**: Developing nations are resource constrained, which is why we see a lot of things happen slightly differently. I'll give an example of where I grew up: I come from a family of doctors, and my dad has never used a computer. But what he has is somebody called a medical assistant; probably somebody who wants to pursue a medical education, but needs an extra job. Think of paralegals in the legal profession. My dad never takes notes on a computer, in the sense of actively taking notes while talking to a patient. What would happen is his assistant would sit on the side and take notes, while my dad has a conversation with the patient. He looks over these notes, writes the final prescription, transcribing it himself. That is what ambient clinical intelligence aims to solve in some of the developed, technology-rich environments.

You also see telemedicine (in the broadest sense) sort of pick up over here in all these countries, because guess what? They don't have any other access to healthcare, so telemedicine is not a convenience sometimes. It's literally the first (and in some cases, only) point of access. I've worked in villages in rural Uttar Pradesh where people haven't seen a doctor for years, and it's harrowing for me to see that because less than 100 kilometers away, you have a fair few doctors in a place called Agra. For someone there, a phone call with a doctor would be transformational.

In developed nations, what you see right now is the notion of this versus that. Either I see a doctor in person, or I see a doctor over the phone. Which one would I prefer? In a developing nation, unfortunately—at least, in some of the places I have worked in— telemedicine is the only option. There's no this versus that.

A lot of people question if it's right to test out innovations in a developing nation. From a regulatory and legal framework, it depends, and in most cases, it's hard for me to answer that question.

From a human perspective, I would say, if someone didn't have access to a doctor, or (validated) medical advice, and they are getting access, sans any kind of exploitation, it should be explored. Given the right impetus, intent, and execution, we might see some developing nations leapfrog developed nations in new models of health access. It would be similar to the progression that happened with mobile phones versus landline phones. But for that, there are a couple of things that need to be true.

The first one is that for telemedicine or teleconsultation apps, you need to have the right infrastructure in place. Telemedicine is dependent on that. There's a conversation that's happening right now where a working group has been formed within the Broadband Commission for Sustainable Development within the ITU.

The second, slightly more nuanced, is threading the needle between clinical/symptomatic diagnostics (with newer enriched datasets) versus traditional diagnostic tests. What can you allow over telemedicine in this new world of longitudinal data?

**Tina Woods**: Are there any other areas where you would predict big changes?

**Siddhartha Chaturvedi**: Personalized treatments / rare diseases are the next big thing that I think will be tackled. With richer datasets coming in, cheaper technology, and the increasingly better Biomedical Machine Reading models, I think that's an area of progress that looks very promising at this point in time.

**Tina Woods**: Many people, certainly in the UK, will have heard of *Genomics England*. There are other various groups around the world. Are they all generally moving towards this open sharing environment? Do you think that's just going to increase over time?

**Siddhartha Chaturvedi**: Well, that's a fun question! Yes and no. There's an appetite for more information to be shared. But think about it, there are certain companies whose business model is built on holding on to that information.

It's heartening to see various companies talk and sign up to ideas like an interoperability pledge, but at the same time, there are a lot of companies that are dependent on their data being proprietary.

This takes me back to the original principles of the NHS. The NHS wanted to deliver the best care possible, free at the point of care; and therein, the intent of the organization is not to monetize data but to improve the health outcomes of people and the population of the UK in general. A lot of people joke that if the NHS was a private insurance company, it would have been bankrupt about 30 years ago. But the very fact that it's still running is a testament that it's willing to do the right thing for the people. Now, is that sustainable? Maybe, maybe not. I don't know. Can it be sustainable? Yes.

With all the new business models that are coming out, where you can anonymize data and share it without really sacrificing individual data, or use privacy preserving technologies like differential privacy, Genomics England's 100,000 genome sequence will be one of the richest data sources. What if you could create a new revenue stream to offset financial burden that the NHS is facing, without affecting the individual? When you see countries that have a single insurance pool system, there is an appetite to share data; to understand, to assess, and to deliver better health outcomes to the people.

But when you see people using machine learning to target and increase premiums, that's where a little bit of tension comes into the market. Why would those companies want to share data? Why would they want to give up on their competitive advantage over other companies? I think it's the assessment of business models that will help us understand where the ecosystem really wants to share; educating the public, increasing transparency and health literacy.

**Tina Woods**: Where do you think the data economy is heading? Who's going to win out?

**Siddhartha Chaturvedi**: I mean, idealistically, I think if everything goes right, then the people will win. Anybody else winning at the expense of the people would be a failure in my eyes, to be completely honest. If we are unable to use the data to deliver better value-based outcomes to the patients, to the citizens, to the people, then I think all we've done is widen the gap even further. I personally feel that government initiatives and regulations can be either an enabler or a restrictor, and I see regulation in healthcare as an enabler if done right.

A lot of companies, a lot of start-ups say it's because of regulation that they can't do certain things. But regulation allows you to build trust, in an ecosystem where it's really, really hard to do that.

Regulation allows you to say that you meet a certain set of guidelines and thresholds that are in turn trusted. This is the good thing about certain regulated countries around the world; the government takes the onus and the responsibility onto themselves to make sure that the new business models that enter the market actually deliver value for their citizens.

There's no healthcare business that can, or at least should, work at the expense of the people.

I see the potential for new business models, new start-ups, large and small. I can see the governments benefitting, as their primary objective is to the people.

Take my personal story of allergies. I would love it if Google Maps, or one of the other navigation apps, had a simple checkbox I could tick to have it show me where construction is going on, because I don't want to go into that area. Would I pay extra for that? Absolutely, because at the end of the day, I'm trying not to fall ill. The alternative is me wheezing through the day, being down with hay fever. I know that I will be safer, and I won't have an asthma attack.

I could say that I don't want the provider to know that I have a predisposition to allergies, but I do want these asymmetric data sharing processes, where I share my data with my device and the device does not share it with an insurance company. Instead, all the information I might need comes onto my device, and then my device runs machine learning on the edge that allows me to get insights that I need. Or I use computational techniques such as homomorphic encryption, but that I believe will need a separate call.

**Tina Woods**: There's been a lot of talk about the social credit policy in China, and of course, there are very different approaches to data in Europe versus the US. Where do you see some really interesting models of this new kind of social contract sort of emerging, with the various hats that you wear at Microsoft?

**Siddhartha Chaturvedi**: I see Finland and the UK right now as two of the places where I've explored slightly, but I also see private insurance companies in the US that are pivoting their models to enable personal ownership of data. In Europe, I think there's a focus on governments doing the right thing or at least trying to figure out how to do it. Intent and ownership is the balance that I think we need to strike in any social contract.

In the UK, I'm a big fan of this movement called Data Saves Lives. It's a very simple thing. They just tell you what data can be used for; that's a very powerful tool. That's what's needed across the world, data literacy in simple language. It's like terms and conditions. If you have 10,000 pages of text, most people won't read it. They end up legally liable for a lot of things that they don't understand; the terms and conditions don't educate them. Instead of those 10,000 words, we need 10 words, or 100 words, that really talk to them and help them understand in simple English: this is what we'll do with your data.

I see that as more important in the developed nations of the west. On the west of the Atlantic, I see a lot more appetite to explore new business models, limited trials that find out what can be done. Not just proof-of-concepts, but production pilots.

Sometimes we have to build new technological platforms to enable these pilots or models. One of the recent ones aims to build a platform that uses differential privacy to ensure data is kept private. This allows you to get to statistically significant results, without being able to decipher the individual's data. Such platforms will enable researchers across sectors including academia, government, and the private sector to gain new and novel insights. With the right architecture and governance, the resulting insights will open new avenues of research that will allow us to develop new solutions to some of the most pressing problems we face as a society while protecting the privacy of individuals.

All these technology evolutions are happening on top of datasets, and these are not happening just because of healthcare. These are happening because of finance and because of a whole bunch of other industries. That's another thing that has to happen— healthcare professionals need to sit down and explore technologies and business models that have worked in other industries and see if they can map to health in a responsible way.

**Tina Woods**: How do you think industries, and particularly the pharmaceutical industry, will change as a result of the developments we've seen in data? Will the fact that we've got more and more stakeholders really getting involved help people live longer and better lives?

**Siddhartha Chaturvedi**: I think there's a lot to be learned from the automation industry about keeping things running on time, and the aviation industry about making accurate predictions. Predictive analytics in those two areas has been leading the field. There's a good reason that the majority of the people who work on fluid dynamics are helping to set up the genomics workbenches.

I think with time there'll be a lot more cross-pollination of skills, where you will bring in people who have solved similar but different problems with teams that are deep domain experts on the problems that you're trying to solve.

I see a mix of two things happening. The first one is that you'll have cross-discipline experts coming together and trying to solve problems together, like somebody who's a subject matter expert on asthma working with somebody who is a city planner who has no idea about asthma, but who knows how cities are planned, and them working together not just have better health outcomes for an individual, but also to design cities in a much better way. I see this cross-pollination of problems happening sometime soon, because we see some of that already happening with the Smart Cities initiatives across the world. Connected Health Cities is one such example. [Connected Health Cities is a Department of Health funded program that operates across the North of England in four city-regions—North East and North Cumbria, Greater Manchester, the North West Coast, and Yorkshire]

The other thing that I expect is that health becomes an underlying part of architectural design, in the same as accessibility has now. Accessibility concerns arise from the first step when you're designing a new building or space: is this place accessible or not? How do I get somebody in a wheelchair in? These are questions that, now, you automatically ask yourself. I think health is going to become just as pervasive across other industries, and that means other industries are going to become more pervasive across health as well because we will need people from other domains to come in and help us understand how we can better predict with the new sensors that are available.

For example, if a smoke alarm goes off, is there a way we could report that firefighters should carry with them a couple of inhalers because there are two people in the house who are predisposed to asthma.

I'm just whiteboarding, but I think there are tangible examples that we can come up with that are better than that one.

**Tina Woods**: Is there anything you want to say a little bit more about some of the work that you've been doing at Microsoft?

**Siddhartha Chaturvedi**: We're doing a bit of work around the various topics, and really understanding how different factors play into healthy life. What can be proxies or sensors? We're trying to understand how weather change patterns or construction affect human health, and where in the value chain that sits.

It's primarily bringing all these multiple disciplines together and trying to explore the value we can get from them. In a more broader context, addressing the social determinants of health means bringing multiple disciplines together, to understand what the other factors are that affect health outcomes, and that will help us find out what can we do about it.

**Tina Woods**: Taking all this together and thinking about your own personal experience living with preconditions, what do you think is the secret to a long, healthy, happy life, and how can technology support that?

**Siddhartha Chaturvedi**: I think being able to leverage the goodness of the technology, with the peace of mind that I will not be penalized for it, is the biggest thing that helps me.

The privilege of having access to some of these tools and being a developer is that I can use ML models and bring simple things like public advisory for construction and my morning route together to make better informed decisions.

This peace of mind is the most important thing. Think of car insurance; if I drive on the road and if I get a dent in my car, first, I'm irritated that I've got a dent in my car. Then, I worry that because of that, my insurance is going to go up. That same thing happens with health insurance, and that means people are scared of falling ill.

Don't get me wrong, it is good to have preventive measures to not fall ill; nobody really wants to fall ill! But to be penalized for falling ill, and not being able to afford to fall ill again? That's almost a scary thought for me.

From a very personal level, I think if I can explore what technology can do to allow me to live a better, healthier life, without it adding to my worries, is going to be key in the future. I know I'm privileged in that sense, but if we really want to transform the way that machine learning and health AI work, that privilege needs to become the norm.

**Tina Woods**: What do you think are the key ethical issues that we need to get right?

**Siddhartha Chaturvedi**: Fairness, bias, and transparency. One important question to ask is if you're looking at machine learning models that only solve for part of the population. That might only work for a certain demographic because you only have data for that particular part of the population, but then you really have to work to get that missing data so that you can bring about parity, to bridge the gap, rather than expand it. There is no low-hanging fruit in healthcare in the long term. It *has* to be equitable.

Transparency is extremely important. For transparency at the AI level, we've built something called the **Explainable Boosting Machine** (**EBM**), which uses an open-source library called InterpretML, a new approach to explain the black box models of ML, and better understand why the AI is making certain decisions. Right now, with ordinary machine learning, you can see which factors are the ones that weigh on every outcome in general. But with InterpretML, you can see which factors weigh on a particular outcome. I can ask "Why did that model give that recommendation for me?" And I can get an answer to what factors led to that recommendation.

Transparency also needs to exist on the intent and approach level. I tell you what data I'm going to take, and what model I'm running that data through. I tell you the outcome I expect from that, and how I'll use that information. Transparency, in this sense, is going to be very important, especially going forward, because you need to lower the stress and the anxiety of the people that you're taking data from and give them some peace of mind.

Privacy and security are crucial to building trust.

On the population health side, the amalgamation of the massive datasets and methodologies like differential privacy are becoming more and more important. The onus lies with the technology companies, start-ups, and researchers to unlock those tools that will give us the broader ability to deliver on these ethical principles. These would in turn help us turn the principles into practices, whether they are guidelines, designing tools, or actual tools within models that you can use.

Another cool approach is homomorphic encryption. Homomorphic encryption enables a start-up to build a business model around a situation where my data resides on my phone, but the provider cannot see it. I can send my encrypted data to have an ML model run on top of it, but the provider will never be able to see my data or my result. The result is only visible to me, post-unencryption. These models would work in highly structured scenarios, where the AI has been extensively tested—for example, getting the insights for a route on my map, based on my preconditions, and my present state. These asymmetric machine learning models are really powerful because I get machine learning outcomes personalized for me, but none of my data is leaked out, ever.

**Tina Woods**: Do you think we'll ever get to immortality, and would you like to live forever?

**Siddhartha Chaturvedi**: Wow! I That is a tricky one because this is more of a philosophical question than anything else, and I think a lot of things might happen.

I don't know what the future holds on that front; we might find cures to the diseases of aging, but we might also discover new diseases which we haven't discovered yet because people haven't lived long enough.

I think there will be an evolution in longevity healthcare of some form, and I'm neither an optimist nor a pessimist around this; I'm more of a realist. Will that evolution help us live longer? Probably, and I hope so. What's more important is: will it help us live longer in a healthier way? It should really also increase the quality of life, instead of just prolonging life. Would I want to live for eternity if I was a preserved brain in a glass box? Probably not!

If advances in technology can help us live longer in a healthier way, that would be excellent. I'm hopeful of that. Will it increase our healthy years to the point where have become effectively immortal? I don't know. I don't want to contemplate that now, because I think the whole reason for working toward something is because you have some finite time that you spend on it. It would fundamentally change our whole notion of time.

**Tina Woods**: What have you learned from the COVID-19 pandemic?

**Siddhartha Chaturvedi**: I've been thinking a lot about mortality and morality.

As I watched the COVID-19 toll climb, I couldn't help but think about the various discussions I've had around mortality. My earliest one is a distant memory, from when I was 8 years old. We'd just moved back to Agra, and in a nutshell, my dad left his job as a doctor to take care of my grandfather, who had been given months to live.

He was 80; he stayed with us for another 8 years. And in those 8 years, he left an indelible mark on my formative years, molding my value system into what it is today.

Today a similar thought crosses my mind—as a global cosmopolitan Millennial, where is the line that I draw between building a robust career, and being away from the people I love?

Amid the anxiety and stress, COVID-19 gave me a moment to take a step back and take stock of my life so far. A continuous stream of water can carve a groove in a rock, but you can never really tell which day it appeared. I was trying to find that inflection point for myself and I realized it is a collection of the experiences that made me what I am today and a lot of it has to do with the guidance, mentorship, or even just chance conversations with people who have shared their lived experiences with me.

I have heard the story of a passionate vision transforming into a distant dream. When I asked some of the people the reason behind that, they said "life happened."

Our elders—and I use that term not with respect to age, but with relation to where someone is in life, someone with more lived experience than I—had dreams too. Perhaps ahead of their time. They might have lacked the opportunity, the time, or the means to execute their dreams, but that doesn't mean that they didn't dream.

More importantly, they often know exactly why, in hindsight, it didn't work out. That is a powerful lesson, waiting to be learned. They might not know AI, but they have life skills. A good student finds knowledge not only from their own experiences, but those of others; they, too, had dreams, but perhaps not the means. 30 years ago, my parents had to book a trunk call days in advance and wait in line for about an hour to have a 120-second conversation with their parents. Today, I can Skype my parents whenever I want, sometimes while having dinner with my family. The means have changed.

Which is why, with the means—and the possible cognitive overload—of a continuous stream of information today, it's imperative that we build a robust culture of care. Both to be cared for, as the Millennials face the prospect of burning out, and to care for the generations that have survived through transformations, and have knowledge to impart. The ageism pendulum has swung, and whereas once the ideas of the younger generations used to be dismissed, today the opposite might ring true for a lot of the disruptors.

We need to leverage people's lived experiences, to help find our own meaning and purpose. To move beyond the individual to embrace the community—and, as they say, it starts at home, which brings me to the morality of the innovations during this time. Regulation will take time to catch up, and the onus is on the individual and the community to do the right thing. I recently read a book called *Design Justice*, which talks about how people sometimes design solutions without really considering the people who will be the most affected by it. We saw inklings of it with the hoarders of PPE aiming to profit from market demand, versus the frontline workers having to make-do with cloth masks.

> *Everyone may have a different way of dealing with it as they find a path to make it through. It means you may try a lot of different modes depending on the day. One day is super productive and the next day is like trudging through mud. You can handle it five different ways in five different days. This is a true disaster. People's mothers, fathers, sons, daughters, and friends are not surviving. All this talk of data, data, data makes it easy to numb ourselves to the humanity of this. My only wish for each of you is to #1 be kind and patient with yourselves.*

*Have compassion for yourself and others. Compassion is actually different than putting yourself in someone else's shoes. That's empathy. Empathy is great, don't get me wrong. But this is a time for deep compassion. Compassion is about recognizing the differences in how others approach this disaster and not only accepting them wholly, but also staying fully connected to them. No one is in a different boat. Incredible levels of sustained stress only respond to huge amounts of self-compassion and compassion for others. What it doesn't respond to is judgment.*

*— Mitra Azizirad [CVP, AI and Innovation Marketing – Microsoft]*

To know that you are cared for, and to be able to care, brings a smile and in some cases becomes a reason for being. I hope that the pandemic motivates not just opportunities for optimization, but of true innovation at a societal level. Video conferencing enabled people to be closer while being far away—what else could we do to reduce the mental toll that COVID-19 might take on us? How could we work together to leverage lived experiences and innovative breakthroughs to not just build a profitable tomorrow, but a happier one? This is the time to care, if there was ever one, because neurologically we are breaking the habits we've taken literal ages to build. We need to create value, not just capture it—and it is an opportunity for us to really rethink frameworks in a whole new light. To respond, recover, and reimagine.

# Final thoughts

Technology and computing has advanced so that our lives can be understood and analyzed in minute detail, via the data captured not only from the many interactions we have with private and public organizations but also from the individual devices we use in our daily lives, like mobile phones. We could be using that data to develop highly personalized tools to guide and nudge us to make better decisions about how we plan and manage our lives.

If we were able to share that data on a global scale in a way we could trust, that protected our privacy and security, imagine how the world could benefit from the innovation that would be unleashed, whether it came up with that elusive cure for dementia, or predicted the next pandemic.

Data can understand lives. Data can improve lives. Data can save lives. So, what's stopping us?

# References

1. *The long, good life, Andrew Scott,* March 2020 https://www.imf.org/external/pubs/ft/fandd/2020/03/pdf/the-future-of-aging-guide-for-policymakers-scott.pdf

2. *The relation of economic status to subjective well-being in developing countries: A meta-analysis. Howell, R. T., & Howell, C. J.* (2008). Psychological Bulletin, 134(4), 536–560. https://doi.org/10.1037/0033-2909.134.4.536

3. *High income improves evaluation of life but not emotional well-being, Daniel Kahneman and Angus Deaton,* August 2010 https://www.pnas.org/content/107/38/16489

4. *Happiness, income satiation and turning points around the world, Andrew T. Jebb, Louis Tay, Ed Diener and Shigehiro Oishi,* January 2018 https://www.nature.com/articles/s41562-017-0277-0.epdf

5. *What your finances say about your health and longevity,* *Jack Rear, January 2020* https://www.telegraph.co.uk/health-fitness/body/finances-say-health-longevity/?WT.mc_id=tmg_share_em

6. *How wealthy are you? By George Bangham,* July 2019, https://www.bbc.com/news/uk-48759591

7. *The 100-Year Life, Lynda Gratton and Andrew Scott* http://www.100yearlife.com/

8. *Silver to Gold: The Business of Aging, Paul Irving,* *Rita Beamish, and Arielle Burstein* https://milkeninstitute.org/reports/silver-gold-business-aging

9. *Living longer: Fitting it all in – working, caring and* *health in later life,* https://www.ons.gov.uk/people-populationandcommunity/birthsdeathsandmar-riages/ageing/articles/livinglongerhowour-populationischangingandwhyitmatters/fittingi-tallinworkingcaringandhealthinlaterlife

10. *The New Long Life- A Framework for Flourishing in* *a Changing World, Andrew J Scott and Lynda Gratton* https://thenewlonglife.com/

11. *The Corporate Implications of Longer Lives, Lynda* *Gratton and Andrew Scott,* March 2017 https://sloanreview.mit.edu/article/the-corporate-implications-of-longer-lives/

12. *New Map of Life,* http://longevity.stanford.edu/

13. *Stanford Center on Longevity's,* http://longevity.stanford.edu/

14. *Purpose in life as a predictor of mortality across* *adulthood, Patrick L Hill, Nicholas A Turiano,* July 2014 https://pubmed.ncbi.nlm.nih.gov/24815612/

15. *The Longest-Living People in the World Have These 9 Things in Common, Emily Laurence,* October 2019 `https://www.wellandgood.com/blue-zone-power-9/`

16. *The Longevity Plan: Seven Life-Transforming Lessons from Ancient China, John D Day M.D., Jane Ann Day, Matthew LaPlante,* July 2018, `https://www.amazon.com/Longevity-Plan-Life-Transforming-Lessons-Ancient/dp/0062319825/ref=sr_1_1?ie=UTF8&tag=wellgoodauto-20&tag=wellgoodauto-20`

17. *A sunny outlook can help your body handle stress, Nina Elias,* November 2016 `https://www.today.com/health/sunny-outlook-can-help-your-body-handle-stress-t105032`

18. *Optimism is associated with exceptional longevity in 2 epidemiologic cohorts of men and women, Lewina O. Lee, Peter James, et.al.,* September 2019 `https://www.pnas.org/content/116/37/18357`

19. *Optimistic outlook on life may help you live longer, study finds, A. Pawlowski,* December 2016 `https://www.today.com/health/optimists-have-lower-chance-dying-prematurely-disease-t105663`

20. *People Are Living Longer, But Not Better—A New Social Contract Is Needed, Tina Woods,* `https://www.forbes.com/sites/tinawoods/2019/12/17/universal-access-to-the-longevity-dividend-calls-for-a-new-social-contract/#9b3d67d2b50c`

21. *Online junk food ads face total UK ban in drive to tackle obesity, The Financial Times,* `https://www.ft.com/content/d146ff14-d2f6-4aa9-8442-0594194a1eca`

22. *The Rise of the Autonomous Organization, Shai Wininger,* January 2018 `https://www.lemonade.com/blog/rise-autonomous-organization/`

23. *Precision Underwriting, Daniel Schreiber,* April 2018 https://www.lemonade.com/blog/precision-underwriting/

24. *Can Yulife breathe new life into life insurance?,* https://www.businessfast.co.uk/can-yulife-breathe-new-life-into-life-insurance/

25. *Dacadoo* https://www.dacadoo.com/

26. *Lemonade* https://www.lemonade.com/de/en

27. *Accenture Technology Vision for Insurance 2017, Andrew Starrs, Jim Bramblet,* April 2017 https://www.accenture.com/us-en/insights/insurance/technology-vision-insurance-2017

28. *Exploring AI and machine learning in health insurance, Srini Venkatasanthanam,* November 2019 https://www.dig-in.com/opinion/exploring-ai-and-machine-learning-in-health-insurance

29. *By the numbers: fraud statistics,* http://www.insurancefraud.org/statistics.htm

30. *Exploring AI and machine learning in health insurance, Srini Venkatasanthanam,* November 2019 https://www.dig-in.com/opinion/exploring-ai-and-machine-learning-in-health-insurance

31. *Governments And Employers Need To Get Real About Longevity, Carol Hymowitz,* December 2019 https://www.forbes.com/sites/nextavenue/2019/12/24/governments-and-employers-need-to-get-real-about-longevity/#725a203c115e

32. *Kalgera,* https://kalgera.com/

33. *Banking app among finalists for innovation award, Jennifer Turton,* January 2019 https://www.ftadviser.com/your-industry/2019/01/25/banking-app-among-finalists-for-innovation-award/

34. *Longevity—the biggest business opportunity of the 21st century, Lindsay Cook,* December 2018 `https://www.ft.com/content/c24cd8a8-e9b9-11e8-a34c-663b3f553b35`

35. *The Longevity Economy: Gigantic and Getting Bigger, Chris Farrell,* December 2019 `https://www.nextavenue.org/longevity-economy/`

36. *The Global Sustainable Investment Alliance,* `http://www.gsi-alliance.org/wp-content/uploads/2019/06/GSIR_Review2018F.pdf`

37. *The Longevity Economy Outlook,* `https://www.aarp.org/content/dam/aarp/research/surveys_statistics/econ/2019/longevity-economy-outlook.doi.10.26419-2Fint.00042.001.pdf`

38. *8 Policy Changes to Let Older Workers Work Longer, Chris Farrell,* March 2019 `https://www.nextavenue.org/policy-changes-older-workers-work-longer/`

39. *Learning New Things: No Audience Required, Elaine Soloway,* July 2019 `https://www.nextavenue.org/learning-new-things-no-audience-required/`

40. *5 Secrets of Success From Midlife Entrepreneurs, Kerry Hannon,* June 2019 `https://www.nextavenue.org/secrets-of-success-from-midlife-entrepreneurs/`

41. *GreatCall and Lyft Partner to Solve a Top Issue for Older Adults: Transportation,* November 2018 `https://www.greatcall.com/newsroom/press-releases/2018/greatcall-and-lyft-partner-to-solve-a-top-issue-for-older-adults-transportation`

42. *Give and Take Care, West Drayton,* `https://adoddle.org/app/projects/1324/give-and-take-care-west-drayton#overview`

43. *Heinz Wolff obituary, Tim Radford,* December 2017 `https://www.theguardian.com/science/2017/dec/17/heinz-wolff-obituary`

44. *The Longevity Economy Outlook,* `https://longevityeconomy.aarp.org/`

45. *AI Will Drive The Multi-Trillion Dollar Longevity Economy, Margaretta Colangelo,* December 2019 `https://www.forbes.com/sites/cognitiveworld/2019/12/07/ai-will-drive-the-multi-trillion-dollar-longevity-economy/#7edb9a834965`

46. *Fintech firms challenged to disrupt old order, Matthew Allen,* October 2018 `https://www.swissinfo.ch/eng/gauntlet-laid_fintech-firms-challenged-to-disrupt-old-order/44440870`

47. *How your personal banking can be tailored to fit your lifestyle, Matthew Allen,* December 2018 `https://www.swissinfo.ch/eng/challenger-banks_how-your-personal-banking-can-be-tailored-to-fit-your-lifestyle-/44629412`

48. *The API of Me, Chris Wood,* March 2017 `https://nordicapis.com/the-api-of-me/`

49. *Hub of all things,* `https://www.hubofallthings.com/`

50. *Meeco,* `https://www.meeco.me/`

51. *Mydex,* `https://mydex.org/`

52. *Data Dividend Project,* `https://www.datadividendproject.com/`

53. *Here Are the Results of the Biggest Universal Basic Income Trial Yet, Edd Gent,* May 2020 `https://singularityhub.com/2020/05/18/here-are-the-results-of-the-biggest-universal-basic-income-trial-yet/`

54. *Andrew Yang: We need a human-centered capitalism, Kevin Dickinson,* July 2019 `https://bigthink.com/politics-current-affairs/andrew-yang-2639022603`

55. *How much is your data worth to tech companies? Lawmakers want to tell you, but it's not that easy to calculate, Samuel Lengen,* July 2019 `https://theconversation.com/how-much-is-your-data-worth-to-tech-companies-lawmakers-want-to-tell-you-but-its-not-that-easy-to-calculate-119716`

56. *How much is your personal data worth? Billy Ehrenberg,* April 2014 `https://www.theguardian.com/news/datablog/2014/apr/22/how-much-is-personal-data-worth`

57. *Data protection in the age of big data, Sandra Wachter,* January 2019 `https://www.nature.com/articles/s41928-018-0193-y`

58. *The Age of Surveillance Capitalism, Shoshana Zuboff,* January 2019 `https://www.amazon.com/Age-Surveillance-Capitalism-Future-Frontier/dp/1610395697`

59. *Data Transfer Project,* `https://datatransferproject.dev/`

60. *Sundar Pichai supports calls for moratorium on facial recognition,* `https://www.ft.com/content/0e19e81c-3b98-11ea-a01a-bae547046735`

61. *Margrethe Vestager Is Still Coming for Big Tech, Ravi Agrawal,* July 2020 `https://foreignpolicy.com/2020/07/04/margrethe-vestager-is-still-coming-for-big-tech/`

62. *A Preliminary Opinion on data protection and scientific research,* January 2020 `https://edps.europa.eu/sites/edp/files/publication/20-01-06_opinion_research_en.pdf`

63. *White Paper on Artificial Intelligence: a European approach to excellence and trust,* February 2020 `https://ec.europa.eu/info/files/white-paper-artificial-intelligence-european-approach-excellence-and-trust_en`

64. *A Call for Action by The GovLab,* `https://medium.com/data-stewards-network/a-call-for-action-813669f32244`

65. *GovLab,* `https://datacollaboratives.org/`

66. *Data Collaboration for the Common Good: Enabling Trust and Innovation Through Public-Private Partnerships, World Economic Forum report,* May 2019 `https://www.weforum.org/reports/data-collaboration-for-the-common-good-enabling-trust-and-innovation-through-public-private-partnerships`

67. *The Open Data Institute,* `https://theodi.org/`

68. *The Global Partnership for Sustainable Development Data* `https://www.data4sdgs.org/`

69. *We can do better with Big Data for Social Good, and we should!, Richard Benjamins,* March 2020 `https://www.linkedin.com/pulse/we-can-do-better-big-data-social-good-should-richard-benjamins/?trackingId=QpjTyuvyge26S556cjPFYQ%3D%3D`

70. *Commentary: Containing the Ebola Outbreak - the Potential and Challenge of Mobile Network Data, Amy Wesolowski, Caroline O. Buckee, et.al.,* September 2014 `https://www.ncbi.nlm.nih.gov/pmc/articles/PMC4205120/`

71. *Combating global epidemics with big mobile data, Nuria Oliver,* September 2013 `https://www.theguardian.com/media-network/media-network-blog/2013/sep/05/combating-epidemics-big-mobile-data`

72. *Experts say privately held data available in the European Union should be used better and more,* February 2020 `https://ec.europa.eu/digital-single-market/en/news/experts-say-privately-held-data-available-european-union-should-be-used-better-and-more`

73. *How to respond to COVID-19, Bill Gates,* February 2020 `https://www.gatesnotes.com/Health/How-to-respond-to-COVID-19`

74. *A Deep Learning Approach to Antibiotic Discovery, Jonathan M. Stokes, Kevin Yang, Kyle Swanson, et.al.,* February 2020 `https://www.cell.com/cell/fulltext/S0092-8674(20)30102-1`

75. *Data linkage and sharing for healthy longevity: A global challenge,* September 2019 `https://www.openaccessgovernment.org/data-linkage/73750/`

76. *The Alzheimer's Disease Neuroimaging Initiative: A review of papers published since its inception, Michael W. Weiner, Dallas P. Veitch, et.al.,* November 2011 `https://www.ncbi.nlm.nih.gov/pmc/articles/PMC3329969/`

77. *Patient Perspectives on Sharing Anonymized Personal Health Data Using a Digital System for Dynamic Consent and Research Feedback: A Qualitative Study, Karen Spencer, Caroline Sanders, et.al.,* April 2016 `https://www.ncbi.nlm.nih.gov/pmc/articles/PMC4851723/`

78. *Dynamic Consent: A Possible Solution to Improve Patient Confidence and Trust in How Electronic Patient Records Are Used in Medical Research, Hawys Williams, Karen Spencer, et.al.,* January 2015 `https://www.ncbi.nlm.nih.gov/pmc/articles/PMC4319083/`

79. *The Global Roadmap for Healthy Longevity,* `https://nam.edu/initiatives/grand-challenge-healthy-longevity/global-roadmap-for-healthy-longevity/`

80. *How to make later life happy, healthy and meaningful, Victor Dzau and Celynne Balatbat,* January 2020 `https://europeansting.com/2020/01/21/how-to-make-later-life-happy-healthy-and-meaningful/`

81. *Governments And Employers Need To Get Real About Longevity, Carol Hymowitz,* December 2019 `https://www.forbes.com/sites/nextavenue/2019/12/24/governments-and-employers-need-to-get-real-about-longevity/#3ac2fd84115e`

82. *Longevity Industry in Singapore,* `https://www.aginganalytics.com/longevity-in-singapore`

83. *Prudential Singapore removes retirement age, Vallari Gupte,* October 2018 `https://www.peoplemattersglobal.com/news/employee-relations/prudential-singapore-removes-retirement-age-19647?media_type=news&subcat=global-perspective&title=prudential-singapore-removes-retirement-age&id=19647`

84. *Data linkage and sharing for healthy longevity: A global challenge,* September 2019 `https://www.openaccessgovernment.org/data-linkage/73750/`

85. *Japan's Plan for Dynamic Engagement of All Citizens,* `https://www.kantei.go.jp/jp/singi/ichiokusoukatsuyaku/pdf/plan2.pdf`

86. *The Prime Minister in Action,* November 2017, https://japan.kantei.go.jp/98_abe/actions/201711/30article2.html

87. *Shaping How The World Thinks About Aging,* https://globalcoalitiononaging.com/about/

88. *The Health of the Nation,* February 2020 https://indd.adobe.com/view/be47b228-f98d-416d-ba91-ae164307e5a3

89. *5 Essential Life Lessons Coronavirus That Can Teach Us, Sergey Young,* https://sergeyyoung.com/5-essential-life-lessons-coronavirus-can-teach-us

90. *US announces economic measures after markets plunge on virus fears – as it happened, Helen Sullivan, et.al.,* July 2020 https://www.theguardian.com/world/live/2020/mar/09/coronavirus-live-updates-outbreak-italy-lockdown-quarantine-uk-usa-america-australia-recession-fears-update-latest-news

91. *Cruise ship outbreak helps pin down how deadly the new coronavirus is, Tina Hesman Saey,* March 2020 https://www.sciencenews.org/article/coronavirus-outbreak-diamond-princess-cruise-ship-death-rate

92. *You Now Have a Shorter Attention Span Than a Goldfish, Kevin Mcspadden,* May 2015 https://time.com/3858309/attention-spans-goldfish/

93. *Surviving,* https://www.mounteverest.net/expguide/survivalrules.htm

94. *Coronavirus (COVID-19) Mortality Rate,* May 2020 https://www.worldometers.info/coronavirus/coronavirus-death-rate/

95. *Deep Knowledge Group,* `https://www.dkv.global/`

96. *Deep Knowledge Group—Analytics* `https://www.dkv.global/analytics`

97. *Interactive Mind Maps, Deep Knowledge Analytics,* `https://www.dka.global/interactive-mind-maps`

98. *COVID-19 Regional Safety Assessment (200 Regions),* `https://www.dkv.global/covid-safety-assessment-200-regions`

99. *Media Digest: Deep Knowledge Group's COVID-19 Assessments in press,* `https://www.dkv.global/media-news`

100. *Notable acknowledgments: Deep Knowledge Group's COVID-19 rankings,* `https://www.dkv.global/dkg/international-acknowledgements`

101. *Global Longevity Governance Landscape Overview 2019,* `https://www.aginganalytics.com/global-longevity-governance`

102. *COVID-19 MedTech,* `https://www.dkv.global/medtech-covid`

103. *COVID-19 MedTech UK,* `https://www.dkv.global/medtech-covid-uk`

104. *Kennedy Lab, Brian K. Kennedy,* `https://www.buckinstitute.org/lab/kennedy-lab/`

105. *The real reason tech companies want regulation, Azeem Azhar,* January 2020: `https://www.exponentialview.co/p/-the-real-reason-tech-companies-want`

# CHAPTER 6

# CONCLUSION

While many scientists and futurists believe we will be able to "stop aging"—and even achieve immortality—their conclusions have not addressed the more intractable aspects of the human condition. Religious leaders and philosophers have agonized through the centuries over what gives meaning to people. Every religion has a different approach to helping humans navigate this path.

It is obvious that "living longer better" will mean very different things for different people. I'm not sure anyone evangelizing about living to 200 would get the ear of a single mother, living on benefits, whose main worry is keeping the debt collectors away and putting food—any food—on the table for her kids.

Plato, the ancient Greek philosopher, explored the question "what is justice?" and proposed that it is not primarily a matter among individuals, but of society as a whole—which then leads to the vision of utopia, an "ideal society" founded on egalitarian principles of equality in economics, government, and justice.

Achieving utopia and curing the ills of society will not be fulfilled through technology and science alone. Certainly, technology can and should be harnessed for good uses, but in the end it is people who will decide the best course—at least until the machines take over.

# Health as our greatest asset for societal progress

The market economy remains one of our most impressive inventions. But the COVID-19 pandemic has exposed, in horrific detail, how our most vulnerable and those in poorest health have suffered the most; current structures are not fit for purpose to solve the challenges of now and tomorrow.

Many would argue that, certainly in the West, a new form of socially responsible, inclusive capitalism is needed, to harness technology for good uses in the "new normal" world ahead. The World Economic Forum is calling this "stakeholder capitalism" in its Global Reset initiative, to set the world on the right path.

Arguably, it is our young people who will suffer the most from the pandemic in the long term. Their mental health has suffered more than older populations, and I only have to look to my three sons to see that they see the future with less hope and optimism than I did at their age.

Heartening to see, however, is the incredible degree of compassion between young and old during the crisis—indeed, altruism and volunteering has been witnessed at full force in communities around the world. All this has increased the intensity with which we re-examine our societal structures and value systems, and our scrutiny of what a new social contract should look like.

The pandemic has made the world realize that health is our greatest asset and cornerstone of prosperity. Many of us have been asking this question: should success move away from pure wealth creation—calculated in terms of GDP—to something that looks at health and well-being, and a better quality of life for everyone? Should we follow Jacinda Ardern, and what seems to be working so well in New Zealand?

A greater focus by policymakers and government on health and well-being would certainly coax business into very different directions, and challenge assumptions and cultural norms on growing older and living longer.

# The fundamentals of living longer better

While technology will empower us in many ways, let's not forget that it is the simple things in life, whatever our age, that matter most. It is striking that in most of the interviews for this book, when asked about the secret of living longer well, and what they do personally to achieve this, it really boiled down to the fundamentals.

I often refer to Dan Buettner's work, where he coined the term "Blue Zones[1]"—the places around the world, like Okinawa in Japan and Sardinia in Italy, where people live some of the longest, healthiest, happiest lives. His research shows that people living in those zones all share five crucial ingredients: following a good diet, incorporating exercise, possessing a sense of purpose, having good social connections, and venerating age.

Diet is crucial. I have always eaten well myself, with lots of fresh fruit and vegetables; lately I have become obsessed with seeds! I take care to keep my weight in check and have to admit following intermittent fasting four days a week as a way to ward off the pounds during lockdown.

Tackling obesity at a population level, however, requires making the healthy choice the easy choice as well as the cheap choice. That's especially true in poor, deprived communities, affected by a range of other social and economic issues that create an unhealthy environment overall. Lack of green spaces, stress, and pollution are all contributory factors.

People living in Blue Zones don't need to go to the gym—they live in environments where being active is part of their way of doing daily things, like walking to the local shop, gardening, or doing work by hand.

Local communities can play a huge role in creating positive environments and strengthening social connections, and we have seen this during the pandemic in quite extraordinary ways. I now know which of my neighbors have cats, need help with shopping, are expert gardeners who can give advice on what will grow in the shade, or can lend a hand painting or putting up a shelf. In the process of finding out who these people are—living in such close proximity to me—what has unfolded is a rich microcosm of neighborliness that did not exist before the pandemic.

We should harness these lessons quickly to engage people locally in purposeful activities that promote health and social engagement. This sense of shared endeavor and purpose could form part of a rebuild of society, from the ground up, after the pandemic—but we need to act fast while the public mood is in this state of suspension.

Most importantly, in order to venerate age and value wisdom, we need to tackle ageism. Ashton Applewhite, a leader in the movement to dispel age discrimination and someone I admire, posits that policymakers, community leaders, and business pioneers should dismantle intergenerational divides and be guided by a commitment to bring the ages together[2].

What comes up over and over again in my work is the need for a shared language on aging (or maybe a lexicon for longevity!) to start binding us around what matters most throughout our lives. A shared language and a positive vision could spur multiple opportunities for innovation, employment, and economic growth for people of all ages, and shape the design of products and services and advertising strategies to grow markets of the future in a socially responsible way.

# Living greener and living longer

Living longer is linked to living greener. The solutions to achieve healthy longevity and address the climate change crisis are synergistic: active travel, less car use, more green spaces, better nutrition, and better air quality.

Investors and policymakers should recognize that the solutions fit well with the principles of sustainable investment, and should prioritize capital for large-scale, long-term social projects in preventative health, guided by **Environmental, Social and Governance** (**ESG**) mandates like we do for climate change.

There are many opportunities for businesses to contribute positively to health, in areas such as food (for example, supermarkets, supplements), leisure (for example, restaurants, hotels, gyms, and cruises) and retail (for example, well-designed, desirable products for the consumer). Businesses could be incentivized through ESG mandates, tax incentives, and policy initiatives to keep people well and out of the healthcare system—eating well, sleeping well, living better, dealing with poverty, and addressing loneliness.

Creative environments that enable more active travel and general physical activity is key[3]. Much of the world is afflicted with "sitting disease": born initially out of convenience culture, entrenched through increasing use of digital technology, and made worse recently during lockdown when we couldn't leave our houses and had to work from home.

I am fairly active—for example, I'm the sort of person who cannot stay still on an escalator. I have to climb up or walk down. I used to go to the gym every day until COVID-19 made me change my routine. I now run 3 km, row for 10 minutes on my rowing machine, and do 20 minutes of yoga on YouTube every day. I might even continue this as part of my "new normal"; my local gym re-opened recently, and I haven't thought twice about changing my new routine. Maybe when the weather starts to become wintry, I will change my mind. But maybe not.

The pandemic has shown how quickly we can make drastic changes to our lifestyles, abandoning long-held habits and practices. These shifts may not be short-lived, either; indeed, they may become permanent reminders of the dramatic behavioral and cultural shifts currently underway.

# The future we could live in

AI will have a huge role to play in the future of health. Personalized health and predictive prevention will accelerate via greater access to clinical, genomic, financial, behavioral, and environmental datasets in which AI can spot patterns and trends that humans can't. People will have better access to their own data, which will help them to engage more in their own health, and in all the decisions affecting their lives from birth to death.

The impact of AI is starting to be felt in most aspects of our lives, making us question who holds the power in society, and who will decide how to use technology to make our world better, or worse.

As the pandemic rages and shines a spotlight on the flaws of our current value system, the power of technology to help solve the world's greatest problems has emerged with startling clarity. AI has played a huge role in identifying more than 250 vaccine candidates for COVID-19 in less than six months. AI is helping researchers analyze gigantic datasets to forecast the spread of the virus, provide an early warning system for future pandemics, design new treatments, and identify vulnerable populations needing help.

But AI is just the tool—what has been most magical is the incredible degree of scientific collaboration, business partnerships, and civic cooperation we have been witnessing. This is the power of the people behind the technology.

Data is the richest renewable resource on earth, and only becomes more valuable the more it is used with AI. Our biology, and many other aspects of our lives, can now be understood and processed as zeros and ones. Could we take elements of the "bioeconomy" set out by Castilla-Rubio and the concept of altruism proposed by Zhavoronkov described earlier in this book? Could we move away from the vast concentration of wealth in a few companies that are now more powerful than most nations? Could we share our individual data in a way to maximize public health benefit and protect the planet?

The future is exciting, filled with opportunities that we can't yet imagine. But there is one thing the COVID-19 pandemic is teaching us, and that is how precious our health is. We need to cherish, nurture, and protect it. We can't take our health for granted.

Remember what world expert virologist Peter Piot, interviewed at the start of this book, said: prioritizing preventative health, to keep us all healthy and minimize the impact of future pandemics, is one of the top lessons we need to take away from COVID-19.

I will close with one final story.

My 83-year-old mother coped very well during lockdown in her flat. She had just moved in, and it was a great flat in a multigenerational neighborhood, with a lift so she could get in and out easily. She is someone who enjoys traveling around the world, visiting friends and family, and living life in a very bohemian, care-free sort of way, so I was more worried about her being isolated and lonely than about her health. She had always been "healthy as an ox," not having been in hospital or seen a doctor for 37 years, since her last child was born.

However, a week before I was due to send the final publication drafts for this book, I got a message that she was in hospital. It turns out she was in the early stages of heart failure, with sky-high blood pressure and atrial fibrillation. She was perilously close to having a major stroke and perilously close to dying.

She has recovered, thankfully (now taking medication), and is so grateful to be alive. But we—she, I, and the whole family—were terribly shaken that she was so close to succumbing to the silent killers of high blood pressure and atrial fibrillation, which can be measured so easily with a smart watch, which could have alerted her, very possibly years earlier, that she was at risk.

It is a salutary lesson for us all—our lives can be taken in an instant, COVID-19 or not. Enjoy it while it lasts and whatever you do, do what you can to keep healthy until the end. Technology can help you—and sharing your data for the common good can help everyone else too.

# References

1. *'Biologically younger' people who defy their real age often have 5 things in common, Hilary Brueck, Insider,* December 2019 `https://www.insider.com/blue-zone-residents-longevity-secrets-traits-2019-12`

2. *The future of aging, My prime time news,* June 2019 `http://www.myprimetimenews.com/the-future-of-aging/`

3. *Do stair climbing exercise "snacks" improve cardiorespiratory fitness? Jenkins, et al, Applied Physiology, Nutrition and Metabolism,* January 2019 `https://www.nrcresearchpress.com/doi/10.1139/apnm-2018-0675#.X2M2Gj-S1PZ`

# Index